INDIA POLICY FORUM 2019

VOLUME 16

EDITED BY
Shekhar Shah
Barry Bosworth
Karthik Muralidharan

NATIONAL COUNCIL OF APPLIED
ECONOMIC RESEARCH
New Delhi

Los Angeles | London | New Delhi
Singapore | Washington DC | Melbourne

Copyright © 2021
NATIONAL COUNCIL OF APPLIED ECONOMIC RESEARCH (NCAER)

First published in 2021 by

SAGE Publications India Pvt Ltd
B1/I-1 Mohan Cooperative Industrial Area
Mathura Road, New Delhi 110 044, India
www.sagepub.in

SAGE Publications Inc
2455 Teller Road
Thousand Oaks, California 91320, USA

SAGE Publications Ltd
1 Oliver's Yard, 55 City Road
London EC1Y 1SP, United Kingdom

SAGE Publications Asia-Pacific Pte Ltd
18 Cross Street #10-10/11/12
China Square Central
Singapore 048423

Library of Congress Serial Publication Data applied for

Disclaimer: The papers and the associated comments represent the views of the individual authors and do not imply agreement by the Governing Body, officers, or staff of NCAER or by members of the IPF panels.

ISSN: 0973-4805
ISBN: 978-93-91370-30-5 (PB)

All rights reserved. No part of this book may be reproduced or utilized in any form or by any means, electronic or mechanical, including photocopying, recording, or by any information storage or retrieval system, without permission in writing from the publisher.

Published by Vivek Mehra for SAGE Publications India Pvt Ltd and typeset in 10.5/13 pt Times by AG Infographics, Delhi.

INDIA POLICY FORUM
VOLUME 16 — 2019

Editors' Summary	ix

AEIMIT LAKDAWALA AND SANJAY R. SINGH
The Effect of Foreign Shocks on the Indian Economy — 1
Comments by Mihir Desai and Pami Dua   48
General Discussion   53

R. NAGARAJ, AMEY SAPRE, AND RAJESWARI SENGUPTA
Four Years After the Base-Year Revision: Taking Stock of the Debate Surrounding India's National Accounts Estimates — 55
Comments by Sudipto Mundle and N. R. Bhanumurthy   97
General Discussion   105

MAITREESH GHATAK AND KARTHIK MURALIDHARAN
An Inclusive Growth Dividend: Reframing the Role of Income Transfers in India's Anti-Poverty Strategy — 109
Comments by Abhijit Banerjee and Arvind Subramanian   161
General Discussion   167

RADHICKA KAPOOR
An Employment Data Strategy for India — 169
Comments by G. C. Manna and Rinku Murgai   208
General Discussion   213

SUDIPTA GHOSH, VIKTORIA HNATKOVSKA, AND AMARTYA LAHIRI
Rural–Urban Disparities in India in the Time of Growth — 219
Comments by Rohini Somanathan and Jeff Hammer   258
General Discussion   264

PURPOSE AND ORGANIZATION

This 16th *India Policy Forum 2019 Volume* comprises papers and highlights of the discussions at the India Policy Forum (IPF) held in New Delhi on July 8–10, 2019. The IPF is organized by the National Council of Applied Economic Research (NCAER), India's oldest and largest independent economic think tank.

The IPF promotes original economic policy and empirical research on India. The IPF commissions both empirical research and policy-focused expert reviews, the latter themselves based on robust, original research. It provides a unique combination of intense scholarship and policymaker engagement at the annual IPF Conference that reviews this research, leading to its eventual publication in this international journal.

An international research panel of India-based and overseas scholars with an abiding interest in India supports this initiative through advice, active participation at the IPF Conference, and the search for innovative papers that promise fresh insights. An international advisory panel provides overall guidance. Members of the two IPF panels are listed below.

Papers appear in the annual *IPF Volume* after revisions based on IPF discussants' comments, a lively floor discussion, and the editorial guidance provided by the editors of the *IPF Volume*. To allow readers to get a sense of the richness of the conversations that happen at the IPF, discussants' edited comments are included here, as is a summary of the floor discussion on each paper. The papers and the associated comments represent the views of the individual authors and do not imply agreement by the governing body, officers, or staff of NCAER or by members of the IPF panels.

The *Annual IPF Lecture* for 2019 was delivered on July 9 to a packed audience at NCAER by Professor Stanley Fischer, Former Vice Chairman, Board of Governors, US Federal Reserve. Professor Fischer spoke on "Modern Macroeconomic Policy."

In recent years, the IPF has also featured an IPF Policy Roundtable that allows a timely discussion of policy issues around topics of current policy relevance but where no papers are presented. The 2019 IPF Roundtable focused on "How Will the New Indian National Education Policy Deliver?" The names of the roundtable panelists and the moderator can be found at the end of the Editors' Summary.

ADVISORY PANEL*

Shankar N. Acharya *Indian Council for Research on International Economic Relations*
Viral V. Acharya *New York University Stern School of Business*
Isher J. Ahluwalia *Indian Council for Research on International Economic Relations*
Montek S. Ahluwalia *Former Planning Commission of India*
Pranab Bardhan *University of California, Berkeley*
Suman Bery *Bruegel*
Jagdish Bhagwati *Columbia University, Council for Foreign Relations, and NCAER*
Barry Bosworth *Brookings Institution*
Willem H. Buiter *Citigroup*
Stanley Fischer *Former Board of Governors of the US Federal Reserve System*
Vijay Kelkar *NIPFP and India Development Foundation*
Mohsin S. Khan *Atlantic Council*
Anne O. Krueger *SAIS, Johns Hopkins University*
Ashok Lahiri *15th Finance Commission*
Rakesh Mohan *Yale University*
Arvind Panagariya *Columbia University*
Raghuram Rajan *University of Chicago Booth School of Business*
Urjit R. Patel *Former Reserve Bank of India*
Shekhar Shah *NCAER*
Nicholas Stern *London School of Economics and Political Science*
Lawrence H. Summers *Harvard University*

RESEARCH PANEL*

Abhijit Banerjee *Massachusetts Institute of Technology*
Kaushik Basu *Cornell University* and *NCAER*
Surjit S. Bhalla *International Monetary Fund and NCAER*
Sajjid Z. Chinoy *J.P. Morgan*
Mihir Desai *Harvard Business School*
Shantayanan Devarajan *Georgetown University* and *NCAER*
Esther Duflo *Massachusetts Institute of Technology*
Maitreesh Ghatak *London School of Economics*
Jeffrey S. Hammer *Princeton University* and *NCAER*
Vijay Joshi *Merton College, Oxford*

Devesh Kapur   *SAIS, Johns Hopkins University*
Kenneth M. Kletzer   *University of California, Santa Cruz*
K. P. Krishnan   *Government of India*
Robert Z. Lawrence   *Harvard Kennedy School*
Rajnish Mehra   *Arizona State University*
Dilip Mookherjee   *Boston University*
Karthik Muralidharan   *University of California, San Diego* and *NCAER*
Ila Patnaik   *NIPFP*
Lant Pritchett   *Harvard Kennedy School*
Indira Rajaraman   *Former 13th Finance Commission*
Tarun Ramadorai   *Imperial College, London* and *NCAER*
M. Govinda Rao   *Former 14th Finance Commission*, *NIPFP*, and *NCAER*
Ajay Shah   *NIPFP*
Nirvikar Singh   *University of California, Santa Cruz*
Rohini Somanathan   *Delhi School of Economics*
Arvind Subramanian   *Harvard Kennedy School*
Arvind Virmani   *Chintan*

*All affiliations are as of April 2020.

PARTNERS

NCAER gratefully acknowledges the generous support for IPF 2019 from HDFC Ltd and Reliance Industries Ltd. Their support reflects the deep commitment of the enlightened leadership of these organizations to rigorous and independent economic policy research that helps promote more informed policy debates and evidence-based policymaking in India.

CORRESPONDENCE

Correspondence about papers in this *IPF Volume* should be addressed directly to the authors (each paper contains the email address(es) of the corresponding author(s)). All author affiliations in the papers are as of the IPF Conference. Unsolicited manuscripts are not accepted for review because the *IPF Volume* is devoted to invited contributions. Feedback on the *IPF Volume* itself may be sent to: The Editor, India Policy Forum, NCAER, 11 Indraprastha Estate, New Delhi 110002, or by email to ipf@ncaer.org. More information on the IPF is available on www.ncaer.org.

THE IPF TEAM

NCAER is responsible for development, planning, organization, and publication for the IPF. The editors and IPF panels are deeply grateful to the following NCAER staff for their dedication and hard work on the 2019 IPF:

Sudesh Bala	*Team Lead and overall coordination*
Namrata Ramachandran	*Special Assistant to the Director General*
Anupma Mehta	*Editing*
Jagbir Singh Punia	*Publication and production*
Ritwik Kinra	*Research assistance*
Sangita Chaudhary	*Team assistance*
Khushvinder Kaur	*Team assistance*
Praveen Sachdeva	*Conference production and graphics*
P. P. Joshi	*Hospitality and logistics*

Editors' Summary

The India Policy Forum (IPF) marked its 16th year with its conference in New Delhi on July 8–10, 2019. The primary goal of the IPF is to promote original policy and empirical research on India. The annual IPF Conference provides a unique combination of intense scholarship and commentary on the research, as well as a focus on its policy implications. The revised works are published in this journal and benefit from a wide international readership. Over the years, interest in India has grown to the point where there is now much more original research on India appearing in international economic journals. The IPF has also changed, making room for more policy-focused review articles that seek to define the best policy advice based on robust empirical research. It has also added more roundtable discussions on key issues dominating Indian economic policymaking. This annual journal of the IPF contains the five 2019 IPF Conference papers, the comments of the paper discussants, and a summary of the floor discussion of each paper.

The Effect of Foreign Shocks on the Indian Economy

In this paper, the authors, Aeimit Lakdawala and Sanjay R. Singh, document the impact of foreign shocks on India. India is becoming more intertwined with the world economy, exposing it to global economic spillovers. This has worked through channels such as greater reliance on trade, especially imported oil, exposure to financial markets and capital flows driven by global financial cycles, and fluctuations in the exchange rate. While there has been much work studying the transmission of foreign shocks to emerging economies, there has been surprisingly little research that specifically answers these questions for the Indian macroeconomy. The paper's contribution is twofold. First, the authors estimate the dynamic causal effects of international shocks by using the recently developed method of identification through external instruments. Second, they consider a comprehensive set of external shocks that are likely to have played an important role in driving economic fluctuations in India.

A key challenge in estimating dynamic causal relationships boils down to finding random variation in the treatment of interest. To tackle this issue, the authors rely on the recent progress made in the empirical macroeconomics literature of using identified exogenous shocks from the literature and then applying them using the innovation of external instruments.

The paper focuses on four shocks: US monetary policy, oil supply, uncertainty, and geopolitical risk. US monetary policy has been shown to be a driver of the global financial cycle, which is especially important for emerging economies like India. The authors use high-frequency futures market data to identify US monetary policy shocks. Given India's reliance on imported oil, an oil shock is a natural candidate. But since India accounts for a much larger share of total world oil consumption relative to production, they use an exogenous measure of oil supply shocks to identify the causal effect of disruptions in the global oil market.

The final two measures of foreign shocks in the paper involve uncertainty. Recently, both policymakers and academics have highlighted the importance of uncertainty shocks for emerging economies. The paper uses two different measures of uncertainty that are constructed from newspaper analyses. The first measure proxies for global economic policy uncertainty, and the second measure is a proxy for geopolitical risk.

The main empirical analysis in the paper uses both a vector autoregression and a local projection approach with a variety of Indian macroeconomic and financial variables. Reassuringly, the authors find similar results using both approaches. Their key findings suggest that US monetary, global economic policy uncertainty, and oil supply shocks have substantial disruptive effects on both economic activity and financial markets in India. But the geopolitical risk shock does not have a major discernible effect. Overall, US monetary policy and global economic policy uncertainty have effects similar to a domestic demand shock, while the oil shock has effects similar to a supply shock. From a stabilization policy perspective, this means that there is a trade-off involved in responding to oil shocks but not to US monetary policy or global economic policy uncertainty shocks.

In response to a contractionary monetary policy shock based on US policy rates, the Indian rupee depreciates, and the domestic stock market index and total foreign reserves held by the government decline. While the financial market response is striking, the effect on inflation and output is relatively smaller. Surprising increases in global policy uncertainty negatively affect real activity as well as financial market indicators. Industrial production exhibits a persistent drop. The stock market index, government bond rate, and total reserves also decline significantly while the rupee depreciates. Geopolitical risk shocks lead to a delayed appreciation of the rupee, increase in total foreign reserves held by the government, and expansion in the stock market. The effect of this geopolitical risk shock is muted on prices and output. Finally, oil supply shocks act as textbook adverse supply shocks.

After an adverse shock, there is a simultaneous drop in output and increase in prices. Moreover, the effect is persistent.

Overall, the exposure of Indian output to these shocks is lower relative to an index of advanced economies, but comparable to an index of BRICS economies excluding India. To better understand how India performs among peer developing countries, the authors compare the response of Indian output individually to that of China, Russia, Brazil, and South Africa. They find that, with the exception of China, the Indian economy reacts less to these foreign shocks relative to its counterparts. This suggests that, in facing an adverse international shock, the Indian economy is more resilient than other developing countries. But, on the flip side, since the estimated model's effects are symmetric, it is implied that the Indian economy may also miss out on the positive effects of beneficial international shocks. The paper discusses the implications of the results for the design of stabilization policy, with a focus on the role of monetary policy.

Finally, the authors consider what each shock implies about the contribution of the core Indian macrovariables to forecast error variance. Overall, they find that the oil supply shock is the most important shock for explaining variations in industrial production. Specifically, oil shocks appear to create the most disruption in output around a year or two after impact. For the US monetary policy shock, they find more modest effects on both financial market variables and output and prices. Overall, on summing up the contributions of the four main shocks that they consider, they find that just these four shocks can explain from 15 percent to 35 percent of the variation in Indian financial and macrovariables at two- to four-year horizons. They discuss some caveats to this analysis and recommend viewing these numbers as an upper bound.

The objective of the paper is to bring a new set of facts to the macropolicy debate in India. Understanding the quantitative response of the Indian economy to previous international shocks is an important first step in preparing policy responses to future shocks. The authors hope that the econometric tools they have used will be used by researchers in policy institutions to gain a better understanding of the Indian economy.

Four Years after the Base-Year Revision: Taking Stock of the Debate Surrounding India's National Accounts Estimates

In January 2015, the Central Statistical Office (CSO) introduced a new series of national accounts with base year 2011–12, replacing the earlier series with the base-year 2004–05. This was the seventh revision since Independence, a routine affair to account for changing economic structure and relative prices. The revision followed the latest global template, the UN *System of National Accounts* (SNA), 2008, updating from the earlier template of SNA 1994. Rebasing is an opportunity to bring in newer databases and statistical methods to better capture a changing economic reality in the national accounts—the most widely used economic statistics the world over.

In the new series, the absolute GDP size in the base year 2011–12 was smaller by 2.3 percent compared to the earlier series. And annual growth rates were significantly higher for 2012–13 and 2013–14 at both current and constant prices, respectively. Marginal differences in total GDP size are understandable; noticeable variations in growth rates are not. The higher growth rates seem to be at variance with other macroeconomic correlates, sparking an intense debate on the veracity of the new GDP series. In the *IPF 2016–17 Volume*, the paper by Nagaraj and Srinivasan[1] took stock of the debate, recommending the setting up of an independent commission of experts to resolve the problem. The debate, however, continued unabated. Newer data releases and official explanations appear to have only raised more questions rather than offering satisfactory answers. The present paper by one of the original authors, R. Nagaraj, now joined by Amey Sapre and Rajeswari Sengupta, seeks to update the debate.

A significant change in the revised series is to estimate GDP of the private corporate sector directly from financial returns filed with the Ministry of Corporate Affairs (MCA), which is, in principle, a welcome move and in line with SNA guidelines. For the manufacturing sector, MCA data replaced Annual Survey of Industries (ASI) data—factory-based production accounts—on the assumption that financial returns better captured firm output. According to the authors, new research has proven that this claim is untrue.

Following SNA guidelines, the revised series has introduced the concept of "gross saving" in place of "gross domestic saving." For private corporate saving, it has brought in the concept of "quasi corporations" (QCs), i.e. proprietary and partnership companies maintaining a book of accounts, as part of the private corporate sector, apparently boosting gross saving. The authors feel that as there is no clarity in the QC estimates, aggregate saving estimates seem vitiated.

---

1. R. Nagaraj and T. N. Srinivasan. 2017. "Measuring India's GDP Growth: Unpacking the Analytics and Data Issues behind a Controversy that Refuses to Go Away," *India Policy Forum*, 13: 73–128. New Delhi: National Council of Applied Economic Research.

The estimation of GDP of the private corporate sector continues to be the focus of dispute. Briefly, the official procedure is as follows. Of about 1,000,000 "active companies"—defined as those submitting financial returns at least once during the past three years—MCA reportedly has complete and usable data for about 300,000 companies. Although it is a substantial fraction for statistical estimation, the problems lie in the details. The data constitute a self-selected sample, not a random or stratified sample, the completeness and consistency of the data are questionable, and the "blowing-up" factor used for estimation is not made public. Further, there is uncertainty about the size of the universe of working companies.

These problems were highlighted when the National Sample Survey Office's (NSSO's) 74th Round survey of services sector enterprises, conducted in 2016–17, revealed that up to 45 percent of "active" companies in the services sector were non-responsive/closed/out of coverage/non-traceable. These could have been fake/shell/dubious or even dead companies, implying that the universe of real "working companies," that is, those producing goods and services regularly, is likely to be a fraction of the officially claimed universe of "active" companies. The NSSO survey findings have therefore seriously strengthened concerns about the accuracy of the private corporate sector GDP estimate.

Corporate income data in the balance sheet includes revenue from sales as well as non-operating revenues such as treasury operations. The MCA data do not seem to make this distinction. Using CMIE's Prowess database, after excluding non-operating income, the GDP growth rate of the private corporate sector came down by 1 percentage point, pointing to the potential shortcomings of using the MCA database without suitable adjustments.

Price deflators used in the new series have also been a matter of concern. The Wholesale Price Index (WPI) is the dominant deflator used in GDP estimation. The index mainly captures the goods-producing sector and fuels but fails to account for services, which now account for over one-half of GDP. The paper reiterates the need for the Producer Price Index (PPI) to replace WPI. Likewise, the paper shows that the use of the single deflator to obtain real GDP in manufacturing is likely to cause an overestimation of the sector's growth rate.

The 2011–12 GDP series has introduced new challenges in compiling state-level GDP estimates at a time when states' capacity for resource planning and budgeting is becoming more important. Estimates of the organized manufacturing and services sectors are available only at the all-India level from the MCA21 database because enterprise-consolidated financial statements of enterprises are not available by plant locations or products, as used to be the case with the ASI data. As a result, state-level GDP, which had increasingly begun to use state-level data, is now once again largely based on indirect estimation and allocation of shares rather than actual state-level estimation, a method that may not accurately reflect ground realities.

Replacing ASI with MCA data has vitiated other regional estimates for the simple reason that company accounts do not provide for plant location across states. Likewise, the use of all-India parameters of labor productivity by industry in the unorganized/informal sector has severely distorted the value-added capture across geographies. The authors note that the new estimates have boosted the size of wealthier states at the expense of weaker states. Such a change has severe implications for policy; for instance, the distribution of divisible tax revenues among states.

Finally, the authors note that this debate has become more complicated over the last four years as newer problems with the base-year revision have surfaced. They reiterate that the way forward, following the earlier recommendations of the Srinivasan Nagaraj paper, is to (a) make the MCA database public for independent verification of the official estimates and (b) set up an independent expert commission to resolve all disputed issues.

An Inclusive Growth Dividend: Reframing the Role of Income Transfers in India's Anti-Poverty Strategy

Theory and evidence point to several advantages of unconditional universal income transfers as a tool not only for anti-poverty policy but also for achieving development goals more broadly. Such transfers directly reduce poverty and have the following attractive properties: limited administrative costs of targeting and lower risk of exclusion errors (since they are universal); lower leakage of benefits because of fewer intermediaries between fund disbursal and receipt; lower disincentives for work compared to most targeted programs; greater sociological acceptability because of the lack of "rank reversal" in incomes that often happens under targeted programs; improved financial inclusion and formal savings, which can, in turn, mitigate risk and enable consumption smoothing at a lower cost than credit (which is subject to higher costs of financial intermediation); relaxing borrowing constraints for productive investments; and improved female empowerment (especially if transfers to children are sent to their mothers' accounts).

The authors of this paper, Maitreesh Ghatak and Karthik Muralidharan, believe that one reason that policy has moved more slowly despite the endorsement by the government's *2016–17 Economic Survey* is that policy discussions about universal income transfers have been conflated with those about a Universal Basic Income (UBI). Specifically, the term "basic income" connotes an amount sufficient for survival, and most academic and policy discussions of a UBI have focused on transfers large enough to nearly eliminate poverty, ranging from 3.5–10 percent of GDP, so that the fiscal math simply does not work out. It is impossible to implement such a large universal transfer without either cutting other major anti-poverty programs or substantially increasing the tax-to-GDP ratio (currently around 18 percent). Alternatively, a large transfer automatically necessitates some targeting, which negates several key advantages of universality.

Even if one were to believe that income transfers are a more efficient way of achieving the goals of existing welfare programs, it is politically and practically infeasible to cut major categories of government welfare spending. In contrast, it is much more feasible to direct the incremental rupee that is earmarked for welfare spending towards income transfers. This is exactly what is happening with the *Rythu Bandhu*, Krushak Assistance for Livelihood and Income Augmentation, and PM-KISAN schemes. While no existing scheme has been replaced to finance these programs, they still represent a landmark policy pivot to spend the marginal rupee allocated to farmer welfare on direct income transfers as opposed to increases in distortionary subsidies, procurement prices, or loan waivers. The authors' proposed policy follows exactly the same approach.

Specifically, the authors recommend that India adopt an "Inclusive Growth Dividend" or IGD for every citizen that is pegged at 1 percent of GDP per capita to be deposited directly into the bank account of every citizen on a monthly basis. This would provide every citizen with a supplemental benefit of around ₹120 per month (at current estimates). The amounts for children under the age of 18 should be transferred to the accounts of their mothers (or the next responsible guardian). The authors believe that such an approach, which is modest in magnitude but ambitious in reach (by being truly universal), can achieve almost all the benefits of income transfers discussed above while mitigating almost all the concerns raised to date regarding the potential costs of a UBI.

First, the terminology of an IGD sets a very different set of expectations than that of a UBI. The term "dividend" makes it clear that this is one component of a portfolio of income streams that people would have. The word "inclusive" reflects the progressive aspect of the proposal: since the amount is the same for all citizens, the marginal value of the transfer is correspondingly greater for the poor. Finally, the word "growth" captures the idea that the amount will increase in tandem with the overall economic growth. Thus, an IGD would be one component of people's income that reaches all citizens and grows equally for all with the country's growth. It would thus be a powerful practical and symbolic commitment to universally shared prosperity.

The biggest advantage of the proposed scheme is simply that it is affordable enough to actually be implemented. Indeed, the value envisaged by the IGD is quite similar to that of PM-KISAN and so it can be implemented simply by roughly doubling the budget for PM-KISAN and making the program truly universal.

In addition to the well-known benefits of income transfers discussed above, a critical long-term benefit of an IGD may be to improve the quality of all public expenditure by providing an attainable benchmark against which government programs can be assessed.

Income transfers could act as a low-cost "index fund" for development spending, and in-kind programs would need to demonstrate that their targeting, administrative, and implementation costs deliver more value than their cost when compared to the cost–benefit of this index fund. Over time, programs that deliver less value than their costs could be replaced with income transfers, while those that deliver more value can be retained. It may be noted that this approach does not make any blanket assumptions regarding the quality (or lack thereof) of government service delivery. Rather, it raises the accountability of government spending by providing a fiscally equivalent benchmark. This can have major long-term positive implications for the quality of government expenditure, both by scrapping programs whose value is less than their cost and by forcing programs to become more efficient to deliver value in excess of their cost.

An IGD will also promote inter-state equality, equity, and efficiency. First, as an equal payment to all citizens, an IGD clearly meets the equality consideration. Second, because the marginal value of an IGD is much higher in poorer areas, it is progressive by construction. It is also progressive by being directly based on population, which favors poorer states. Finally, since it will be financed through the general tax pool (which the rich contribute more to), it is also progressive in terms of financing. Thus, an IGD could be a powerful tool for promoting equity across the country.

The authors also highlight that it is important to move beyond discussing universal income transfers as a redistributive policy aimed at supporting the poor and recognizing that they can also be a powerful tool for alleviating microeconomic constraints to development, thereby improving productivity and boosting economic growth. The paper concludes by noting that the current moment (the period of the COVID-19 pandemic and associated lockdown) is especially appropriate for an IGD. It would support the vulnerable while also boosting aggregate demand. It would mitigate the elevated risk of social conflict due to an economic contraction by providing a powerful symbol of social solidarity that all Indians experience together regardless of their station. Finally, an IGD would be a portable benefit (accessible anywhere in the country) and, therefore, especially suitable to support migrant workers. Indeed, the existence of an IGD might have mitigated some of the heartrending suffering of migrant workers seen during the COVID-19 crisis.

An Employment Data Strategy for India

Employment statistics are a key input in designing macroeconomic policies and need to be reliably sourced, accurate, and timely for policy responses to be meaningful. Historically, employment estimates in India have been generated using household and establishment surveys. Household surveys capture both the organized and unorganized sectors, particularly the self-employed. They largely satisfy the requirements of completeness. The quinquennial household surveys on employment and unemployment conducted by the NSSO, the last of which was conducted in 2011–12, have been the primary source of various labor market indicators since 1972–73. Establishment surveys, on the other hand, compile data from worksites and provide a more detailed picture of the industry's employment structure and establishments characteristics. The key establishment survey in India is the ASI by the Ministry of Statistics and Programme Implementation, which provides annual data on registered firms.

Much of India's employment data has been generated with a considerable time lag and is often restricted to the formal sector. Recognizing the challenges arising from the paucity of real-time jobs data, the government set up a Task Force in 2017 to revamp the employment data architecture. Significant among the recommendations of the Task Force was the replacement of the NSSO's quinquennial household survey with the Periodic Labour Force Survey (PLFS), an annual household survey with a quarterly module in urban areas, and the introduction of monthly payroll data. A large part of the efforts in this data revamp focused on producing high-frequency data, particularly in the formal sector.

However, given the dualistic nature of India's labor markets and the dominance of low-wage and low-productivity informal jobs, this exercise serves a limited purpose. There is a need to not only understand how key labor market indicators such as unemployment and employment rates vary over time but also to provide insights into how the conditions and quality of employment change over time. This issue assumes even greater significance given recent evidence that the formal sector has witnessed rapid informalization over the years and that new forms of informality are emerging even as old forms of informal employment persist.

In this backdrop, this paper by Radhicka Kapoor examines the current state of labor market statistics and their inadequacies in dealing with the complexities of the Indian setting, and makes a series of recommendations for generating more relevant and comprehensive labor market data. Importantly, these recommendations do not entail conducting new surveys but pertain to more effective use of the data being currently generated.

To begin with, the paper argues that it is imperative to continue with the NSSO's quinquennial household survey while conducting the annual PLFS. With its exhaustive schedule and in-depth comprehensive questions, the importance of the former cannot be overemphasized. Additionally, the collection of data in household surveys needs to be based on all three different approaches, usual status, current weekly status, and current daily status, recommended by the Dantwala Committee (1970). Given that no one-dimensional measure is meaningful in the Indian context, none of these approaches can be dispensed with, as the PLFS has done vis-à-vis the current daily status.

To get a comprehensive picture of the extent of labor underutilization, the paper proposes constructing measures of labor underutilization in line with the recommendations of the 19th International Conference on Labour Statistics (2013). Such measures will capture not just the extent of unemployment but also underemployment and the potential labor force (which includes unavailable job seekers and available potential job seekers). The latter concept assumes particular significance in recent times, given the decline in labor force participation rates and the fact that almost half of the working-age population is outside the labor force (PLFS, 2017–18).

To highlight the quality of employment, it would be useful to include a 'rate of informal employment' as one of the Key Indicators of the Labor Market, or KILM, supposed to be generated by the PLFS, and report this measure in all official reports when survey data are released. Additionally, there is a need to rethink the existing classification of employment status categories and to ask more probing questions about the nature of the employment and the activities undertaken by workers. This will provide deeper insights into the conditions of employment and how these are evolving over time. Given the challenges in creating absolute estimates of the size of the workforce and labor force using population data from the Census (and not the population estimates obtained from the household survey), it would be useful if the NSSO provided an additional summary publication giving absolute estimates of KILM.

The NSSO's decision to include a quarterly module for urban areas in the PLFS is indeed welcome, and the introduction of such a module in rural areas is worth considering. Notably, it is still not clear if the sample size in urban areas is large enough to measure quarterly changes with precision. If this is not the case, there is a need to expand the sample size in both urban and rural areas. A related issue is that of generating more reliable estimates at the state level, where large standard errors of unemployment rates have been observed. Addressing this problem will require greater participation at the state level and the pooling of "central samples" and "state samples" to increase the sample size.

Finally, it is worth noting that enterprise surveys have not been as widely used as household surveys for generating employment data. This is largely because of the absence of an appropriate frame for enterprises. It is critical to implement a national business register and ensure universal coverage in the Economic Census (EC) for obtaining a complete frame for enterprise surveys. This also necessitates conducting the EC at regular intervals.

For implementing any of the suggestions laid out in this paper, the capacity of national statistics systems needs to be strengthened. This entails greater investments not only in data collection machinery but also in addressing the shortage of regular field investigators faced by the NSSO, as well as training them to ensure that they can correctly implement concepts and definitions applied in the survey and leveraging technology to reduce the time lag in data collection and dissemination. These investments are imperative for improving the statistical base of the world of work and achieving accuracy in capturing the different dimensions and nuances of the labor market.

Rural–Urban Disparities in India in the Time of Growth

The period since the 1990s has seen an aggregate growth takeoff in India, during which the rural agricultural sector has gradually ceded space in both employment and output share to non-agricultural sectors. How have agriculture-dependent rural workers and households fared during this episode relative to their urban counterparts? Has growth lifted all boats, or has it induced widening economic disparities between rural and urban households?

Using household-level NSSO survey data, this paper by Sudipta Ghosh, Viktoria Hnatkovska, and Amartya Lahiri finds that rural–urban education gaps have declined significantly between 1983 and 2012. Moreover, occupational choices in the two sectors have become more aligned with an expansion of non-farm occupations in rural India.

The picture on rural–urban consumption differences is more mixed. The paper documents a clear decline in rural–urban consumption gaps for the bottom 45th percentile of households between 1983 and 2004–05. However, some of these gains appear to have reversed between 2004–05 and 2011–12. As a result, from 1983 to 2012, the rural–urban consumption gaps declined for only the bottom 15 percent of households.

In order to uncover some of the mechanisms that could be at work in driving these trends, the authors use state-level data on education, occupation, and consumption gaps across different NSSO rounds to construct a panel. They find that per capita income levels, per capita growth rates, and rural–urban education gaps are all positively correlated with rural–urban consumption gaps. While the effects of income—both levels and growth rates—are counterintuitive, the effect of declining rural–urban education gaps on consumption gaps is reassuring. Indeed, it suggests that a fruitful policy for reducing consumption inequality is to reduce education disparities.

The trends in rural–urban consumption gaps are both insightful and somewhat puzzling. The fact that the gaps have declined for the bottom 15 percentile suggests that the penalty for being really poor has become more severe in urban India relative to rural India. This likely has to do with greater ability to share income risk in larger rural households as opposed to urban households. Another contributing factor for the worsening of consumption outcomes of the urban poor is possibly rising urban food inflation.

The widening of rural–urban consumption gaps since 2004–05 is perplexing, particularly since the Mahatma Gandhi National Rural Employment Guarantee Act (MGNREGA), the employment guarantee scheme for rural workers, was introduced in 2006. One would have expected MGNREGA to have boosted household consumption in rural India. This trend bears closer scrutiny and further investigation.

In separate work, the authors have found that the period 1983–2012 was characterized by sharp reductions in rural–urban wage disparities. In fact, wage gaps declined by much more than what can be explained using standard worker attributes. In combination with the results on widening consumption gaps, this suggests that saving behavior of rural and urban households may have evolved differently over the last couple of decades. Have the saving rates of rural households been rising over this period? If so, why? This is an important issue that deserves deeper probing.

The 2019 T. N. Srinivasan Lecture, IPF Policy Roundtables, the IPF 2019 Lecture, and the Concluding IPF Panel on GDP Estimates

The 2019 IPF featured the Annual IPF Lecture and hosted the first T. N. Srinivasan Memorial Lecture. Srinivasan, who passed away sadly in November 2018, was one of the IPF's most ardent supporters, not missing a single IPF over its 15 years. The Lecture, *Reflections in Memory of TN*, was delivered by his long-time friend and colleague, Professor Pranab Bardhan, at the University of California, Berkeley. Bardhan began by sharing his personal reminiscences of Srinivasan, then discussed Srinivasan's contributions to economics, and finally ended with a detailed discussion of Srinivasan's major preoccupation with data quality and the state of economic statistics in India.

Professor Stanley Fischer, former Vice Chairman of the Board of Governors of the US Federal Reserve, delivered the 16th Annual IPF Lecture on *Modern Macroeconomic Policy*. He started by asking what is causing many macroeconomists to believe that they need a new approach to macro-stabilization policies. He touched upon changes in the global economy, the role of the central bank in financial sector supervision and regulation, and the new thinking about fiscal policy and fiscal deficits. In the second part of his Lecture, he turned to macroeconomic stabilization policy in India.

The IPF Policy Roundtable on "How Will the New National Education Policy Deliver?" was moderated by Devesh Kapur of the School of Advanced International Studies, Johns Hopkins University, with the panelists Rukmini Banerjee of the Pratham Education Foundation, Karthik Muralidharan at the University of California, San Diego, and NCAER, Alok Kumar of NITI Aayog, and Ashish Dhawan of the Central Square Foundation.

The final event of IPF 2019 was a lively panel discussion on *Validating India's GDP Estimates* moderated by T. N. Ninan of the *Business Standard*, with the lead presentation by Arvind Subramanian, former Chief Economic Adviser, Government of India, and joined by panelists Pronab Sen, former Chief Statistician of India, and Sebastian Morris from the Indian Institute of Management, Ahmedabad.

Subramanian emphasized that his objective was to get to the best and most credible GDP data for India. His presentation was built around three critical questions: (a) Can the current GDP growth estimates be validated by looking at other collateral data? (b) If not, is the overestimation of GDP growth figures small or large? And (c) if it is large, could it have serious consequences for the Indian economy, and what could be done to address the issue? Comments from the other two panelists and from the floor made this final closing session of the IPF 2019 one of the most energetic and engaging ones.

Videos, papers, presentations, the Roundtable discussion, the T. N. Srinivasan Lecture, the special IPF Panel Discussion, and the IPF 2019 Lecture are hyperlinked to the IPF 2019 Program available on the NCAER website by scanning this QR code or going to the URL:
https://www.ncaer.org/IPF2019/Agenda/Agenda_IPF_2019.pdf

AEIMIT LAKDAWALA[*]
Michigan State University

SANJAY R. SINGH[†]
University of California, Davis

The Effect of Foreign Shocks on the Indian Economy[§]

ABSTRACT The Indian economy has been increasingly exposed to external shocks with growing financial and trade integration. We examine the effects of four key international shocks: shocks to US monetary policy, oil supply, global economic policy uncertainty, and geopolitical risk. Using the external instruments strategy with Local Projections and Structural Vector Autoregression methods, we document the dynamic causal effects of these shocks on the Indian economy. We find significant effects of these foreign shocks on both macroeconomic and financial variables. Combined, these shocks explain about 15 to 35 percent of the variation in inflation, output, and financial variables at two- to four-year horizons. However, the magnitude of effects on output is lower relative to both global output and output of peer developing countries. While the oil shock behaves like a traditional supply shock, the US monetary policy and economic policy uncertainty shocks look more like domestic demand shocks. We discuss the implications for stabilization policy.

Keywords: Foreign Shocks, Indian Economy, External Instruments

JEL Classification: F4, E5, C3

1. Introduction

In recent years, increases in financial and trade linkages to the rest of the world have exposed India to global economic spillovers. This has occurred through a variety of channels, including reliance on imported oil,

---

[*] *lakdawa@wfu.edu*
[†] *sjrsingh@ucdavis.edu*
[§] The authors are grateful to Barry Bosworth, Ken Kletzer, Mihir Desai, Pami Dua, Karthik Muralidharan, Shekhar Shah, Rajeswari Sengupta, Abhijit Banerjee, Montek Singh Ahluwalia, Rakesh Mohan, Anne Krueger, Nirvikar Singh, and Rajnish Mehra for useful comments and suggestions.

exposure of financial markets to capital flows driven by the global financial cycle, and fluctuations in the exchange rate. These and other channels have contributed to the inclusion of India in the "fragile five" during the recent "taper tantrums" episode (see, e.g., Shin 2014).

While there has been much work studying the transmission of foreign shocks to emerging economies, there has been surprisingly little research that specifically answers these questions for the Indian macroeconomy. In this paper, we document the impact of foreign shocks on the Indian macroeconomy. Our contribution is divided into two parts. First, we focus on estimating the dynamic causal effects of international shocks using the recently developed method of identification through external instruments. Second, we consider a comprehensive set of external shocks that are likely to have played a role in driving economic fluctuations in India.

A key challenge in estimating dynamic causal relationships boils down to finding random variation in the treatment of interest. To address this issue, we rely on the recent progress made in the empirical macroeconomics literature in identifying exogenous macroeconomic shocks using a variety of new methodological innovations (see Ramey 2016 for an excellent recent survey). We incorporate these measures of identified exogenous shocks in a structural framework using both the Local Projections (LP) and Structural Vector Autoregression (SVAR) frameworks. Within these frameworks, we follow the recent modeling innovation of the external instruments approach, where the methodology involves using information outside (or external to) the core model to achieve the restrictions required for estimating causal relationships; see the work of Stock and Watson (2002), Mertens and Ravn (2013), Ramey and Zubairy (2018), and Jordà et al. (2020). Stock and Watson (2018) provide a survey of this literature focusing on the two main techniques of LP Instrument Variables (LP-IV) and SVAR Instrumental Variables (SVAR-IV). Based on the relevance for the Indian economy, our focus is on a core set of shocks that includes US monetary policy, oil supply, commodity prices, uncertainty, and geopolitical risk.

As documented by Miranda-Agrippino and Rey (2018), there is a global financial cycle that is important for driving international flows, and the source of this cycle is the US Federal Reserve. Additionally, new work by Lakdawala (2018) shows that the spillover effects of US monetary policy on Indian financial markets have increased since the early 2000s. We incorporate US monetary shocks into our analysis by using high-frequency changes in future rates around the policy announcements of the Federal Open Market Committee (FOMC). The futures rates incorporate market expectations and, thus, any change in these futures rates within a narrow window around the FOMC announcement is likely due to unexpected changes in the monetary policy announcement. This approach has been widely used in the recent literature studying US monetary policy; see, for example, Gertler and Karadi (2015).

According to the International Energy Agency, as of 2018, India was the third largest importer of crude oil. Hence, another important source of foreign shocks for the Indian economy is the fluctuations in the global price of oil. Since India accounts for a large share of total global oil consumption, changes in India's demand for oil are likely to be an important driver of the global price of oil, making causal identification of oil price shocks problematic. However, India's contribution to global oil production is less than 1 percent and, therefore, supply disruptions in India are unlikely to be a contributor to changes in the global price of oil. Thus, we use an exogenous measure of oil supply shocks to identify the causal effect of disruptions in the global oil market on the Indian economy. While there is a long literature on distinguishing oil demand from oil supply shocks (see, e.g., Kilian 2009), we use the recently developed measure of oil supply shocks in Baumeister and Hamilton (2019). They use a Bayesian approach to rigorously incorporate prior information about supply and demand elasticities to identify oil supply shocks.

Our final two measures of baseline foreign shocks involve uncertainty. In a recent speech, the Bank of England Governor, Mark Carney (2016), outlined an "uncertainty trinity" composed of economic, policy, and geopolitical uncertainty as important factors for economic activity. Recent work has also highlighted the importance of uncertainty and risk aversion for international asset prices and capital flows; see, for example, the work of Rey (2015) and Bruno and Shin (2015). There is also evidence of the substantial effects of US uncertainty on emerging economies; see Bhattarai et al. (2017). For recent work exploring the impact of US uncertainty on the Indian economy, see Ghosh et al. (2017). We proxy uncertainty with two measures that are constructed from newspaper analyses by counting the relative frequency of certain key terms. The first measure proxies for global economic policy uncertainty, constructed by Baker et al. (2016), and the second measure is a proxy for geopolitical risk, constructed by Caldara and Iacoviello (2018).

Our main empirical analysis builds on the recent work of Mishra et al. (2016), who identify monetary policy shocks in India in a SVAR setting.[1]

---

1. They find that shocks to the policy rate do transmit to bank lending rates in India, albeit imperfectly. However, the predicted bank lending rates do not seem to drive aggregate demand in their estimation.

Specifically, we use the Index of Industrial Production (IIP) as a proxy for output and the Consumer Price Index (CPI) to measure inflation. In addition to these macrovariables, we consider a variety of financial market variables. For our measure of interest rates, we use the 10-year Indian government bond rate. While there are a number of short-term rates that could have helped us better assess the response of the Reserve Bank of India (RBI) to foreign shocks, we found that data availability and non-variation over time were issues for several of these measures. Our qualitative results do not change if the short-term repo rate is used instead of the 10-year government bond rate. Moreover, since we want to focus on the aggregate economic effect of foreign shocks, we concluded that a higher interest rate was the best option. We use the nominal exchange rate of the Indian rupee with the US dollar as our baseline measure of exchange rates. We found that using real and nominal effective exchange rates, which are constructed with a broader set of countries, gave similar results. Finally, we also include indicators for the aggregate stock market index and total foreign reserves (excluding gold) measured in US dollars. We believe that total foreign reserves and the 10-year government bond rate indirectly capture the policy stance of the RBI, which uses various tools in its conduct of monetary policy.

Reassuringly, we find similar results using either the LP or SVAR estimation strategy. Here are the key findings. US monetary policy, economic policy uncertainty, and oil supply shocks have substantial disruptive effects on both economic activity and financial markets in India. But the geopolitical risk shock does not have a major discernible effect. Overall, US monetary policy and economic policy uncertainty have effects similar to those of a domestic demand shock, while the oil shock has effects similar to those of a supply shock. From a stabilization policy perspective, this means that there is a trade-off involved in responding to oil shocks but not to US monetary policy or economic policy uncertainty shocks.

For the monetary policy shock, our results corroborate Rajan's (2015) findings that US monetary policy indeed has important financial spillovers to the Indian economy. In response to a contractionary monetary policy shock to US policy rates, the Indian rupee depreciates, and the domestic stock market index and total foreign reserves held by the government decline. While the financial market response is striking, the effect on inflation and output is relatively smaller. The real effects are consistent with the global spillovers of US monetary policy. The peak drop of India's monthly industrial production is –0.3 percent. To benchmark these effects, the peak drop in world industrial production is –0.4 percent, and the peak drop in BRICS (excluding India, 'BRCS' henceforth) industrial production is –0.3 percent.

Second, surprise increases in policy uncertainty, measured with the global Economic Policy Uncertainty Index (EPU) of Baker et al. (2016), negatively affects real activity as well as financial market indicators. Industrial production exhibits a persistent drop, which peaks at −0.3 percent at 16 quarters, and becomes statistically indistinguishable from zero subsequently. The stock market index, government bond rate, and total reserves also decline significantly while the rupee depreciates.

Third, geopolitical risk shocks lead to a delayed appreciation of the rupee, increase in total foreign reserves held by the government, and expansion in the stock market. The effect of this geopolitical risk shock is muted on prices and output. One way to understand these results is a flight to safety story: when global geopolitical risk goes up, the Indian economy becomes an attractive destination.

Finally, oil supply shocks act as textbook adverse supply shocks. After an adverse supply shock, there is a simultaneous drop in output and an increase in prices. Moreover, the effect is persistent. Relative to the BRCS benchmark, we find that Indian output is more adversely affected by oil supply shocks. The shock also causes a general worsening of financial conditions with a reduction in total reserves, depreciation of the rupee, and a fall in stock prices.

Overall, the exposure of Indian output to these shocks is lower relative to an index of advanced economies, but it is comparable to the index of BRCS economies. To better understand how India performs among peer developing countries, we compare the response of Indian output on its own to that of China, Russia, Brazil, and South Africa. We find that, with the exception of China, the Indian economy reacts less to these foreign shocks relative to its counterparts. This suggests that in facing an adverse international shock, the Indian economy is more resilient than the economies of other developing countries. But on the flip side, since the estimated model's effects are symmetric, it implies that the Indian economy may also miss out on the positive effects of beneficial international shocks.

With the growing integration of India into the world economy, one might expect that the responsiveness of the Indian economy to international shocks has changed over time. To test this, we estimate the impulse responses for India by splitting our sample into two halves (pre- and post-December 2005). But for most of the variables (including output), we do not find statistically significant differences in the responses. What explains this phenomenon? A comprehensive analysis of this question would investigate any structural changes in the Indian economy and the response of policymakers. While this exercise lies outside the scope of this paper, our results provide some suggestive evidence on the role that monetary policymakers might have played.

Central banks can respond to international shocks primarily by changing their policy interest rates or intervening in foreign exchange markets, at least in terms of conventional policy tools. A common pattern that also emerges in the analysis is the modest response of the 10-year government bond rate to these adverse global shocks. This has potentially important implications from a policy stabilization perspective. For example, policymakers may consider easing interest rates in response to adverse international shocks. For the oil supply shock, the central bank faces a clear trade-off as output falls while prices rise. Thus, if the central bank is worried more about higher inflation, then it may want to refrain from lowering rates and accept the downturn in economic activity. But the US monetary policy and uncertainty shocks have effects that look like domestic demand shocks. In this case, there is no longer a trade-off and optimal monetary policy from conventional models dictates the central bank to lower rates.

In light of this, we think there are two different ways to interpret our results of the relative nonresponsiveness of the 10-year interest rate. First, it is possible that the RBI is not responding strongly with interest rate changes to international shocks, either because it fails to identify the shocks in a timely manner or because it perceives the trade-off is too costly. Alternatively, the RBI is indeed responding to these shocks by changing interest rates, but the transmission mechanism of monetary policy in India is weak and, thus, there are no substantial effects on the long rate.

But the RBI has also intervened in the foreign exchange market in response to international events. Our results from the split-sample estimation show that in response to adverse monetary and oil shocks, the Indian rupee depreciates less in the more recent sample. One potential factor could be the actions (or anticipated actions) of the RBI becoming stronger in the last decade or so. Our results highlight that disentangling these different channels is important to understand the role of monetary policy in overall stabilization policy.

Finally, we consider what each shock implies about the contribution to the forecast error variance of the core Indian macro variables. Overall, we find that the oil supply shock is the most important shock for explaining variations in industrial production. Specifically, oil shocks appear to create the most disruption in output around a year or two after impact. For inflation, we find that the two uncertainty shocks and the oil supply shocks are important contributors to its variation. For the US monetary policy shock, we find more modest effects on both financial market variables and output and prices. Overall, when we sum up the contributions of the four main shocks that we consider, we find that just these four shocks can explain 15–35 percent of the variation in Indian financial and macro variables at two- to four-year horizons. We discuss some caveats to this analysis and recommend viewing these numbers as an upper bound. Nevertheless, the overall picture that emerges is that these four shocks combined account for a significant source of international fluctuations that are important for the Indian economy.

Our objective is to bring a new set of facts to the macro policy debate in India. Understanding the quantitative response of the Indian economy to previous international shocks is an important first step in preparing the policy response to future shocks. Moreover, our hope is that the econometric tools we have used can be readily applied by researchers in policy institutions to broaden our understanding of the Indian macroeconomy. Finally, the new facts that we document can guide economic modelers in building structural economic models relevant for the Indian economy.

2. Methodology

To estimate dynamic causal effects, we will consider a structural framework that relies on both the LP framework and the SVAR framework. For both these approaches, we will either directly incorporate exogenous measures of shocks or use the instrumental variables framework.

The first strategy is to use a SVAR framework. Consider the SVAR, where y_t is an $n \times 1$ vector of macroeconomic variables and α_i and A are $n \times n$ parameter matrices.

$$Ay_t = \alpha_1 y_{t-1} + \ldots + \alpha_p y_{t-p} + \varepsilon_t \tag{1}$$

The components of the error terms ε_t are assumed to be uncorrelated with each other and interpreted as structural shocks. Pre-multiply by A^{-1} to get the reduced form VAR

$$y_t = \delta_1 y_{t-1} + \ldots + \delta_p y_{t-p} + u_t \tag{2}$$

where

$$u_t = B\varepsilon_t \tag{3}$$

and $A^{-1} = B$. Also note that $E[u_t u_t'] = BB' = \Sigma$. This reduced form of VAR can be estimated in a straightforward manner. However, identification of the impulse responses to structural shocks requires an estimate of the matrix $B = A^{-1}$. This requires further identifying restrictions. If the structural shock of interest is directly observable, we will order it first in the vector y_t and use a Cholesky ordering to identify the structural impulse responses. If we do not directly observe the structural shock but have an instrument for it (Z_t), we will use the external instruments procedure developed by Stock and Watson (2002), as well as Mertens and Ravn (2013). In the external instruments methodology, the key requirements are to find instruments that are (a) correlated with the shocks of interest and (b) uncorrelated with the other structural shocks. Denote the structural policy shocks as ε_t^p and the structural nonpolicy shocks as ε_t^q. The reduced-form residuals from the corresponding policy and non-policy equations are denoted as u_t^p and u_t^q, respectively. For a given set of instruments Z_t, these two conditions can be formally stated as

$$E[Z_t \varepsilon_t^{p'}] = \phi \tag{4}$$

$$E[Z_t \varepsilon_t^{q'}] = 0 \tag{5}$$

With these conditions, it can be shown in a straightforward manner how to identify structural impulse responses; see, for example, Mertens and Ravn (2013).

Jordà (2005) introduced the LP method for directly estimating impulse responses without relying on the assumption that the vector auto regression (VAR) is correctly specified. In an analogy with forecasting, this method involves forecasting future values of a variable using a horizon-specific regression rather than iterating one period ahead on the estimated model. Estimating impulse responses using VAR is analogous to iterated forecasting, while the LP method is analogous to direct forecasting. With a correctly specified VAR and standard assumptions on invertibility, Stock and Watson (2018), and with some generality Plagborg-Møller and Wolf (2019) prove that the impulse responses estimated using SVARs and LP are identical. However, in small samples, it is possible to reach different conclusions using the two different methods. Thus, we explore both of them in this paper.

For incorporating instruments variables into the LP framework, we will follow the recent literature (Jordà et al. 2020; Ramey and Zubairy 2018). This strategy is appropriate if the direct shocks are measured with error or if they capture only part of the shock. We treat the measured macroeconomic shocks e_t as proxy for the true shocks ε_t. Here, we describe the estimation strategy with the LP-IV technique and relegate the discussion of SVAR-IV to the Appendix. In the first stage, we instrument a policy indicator (e.g., the federal funds rate) with the relevant proxy. In the second stage, we run a sequence of predictive regressions of the dependent variable on the instrumented policy indicator for different prediction horizons. The estimated sequence of regression coefficients of the instrumented policy indicator are then the impulse responses.

More specifically, we estimate the following second-stage LP specification for horizons $h \in 0, \ldots H$:

$$y_{t+h} = \alpha^h + \beta^h \hat{x}_t + \Sigma_p \theta^{ph} Z_{t-p} + \nu_{t+h} \qquad (6)$$

$\hat{x}_t$ is the predicted policy instrument from the first-stage regression using instruments for the measured macroeconomic shocks e_t. The set Z_t includes lags of the dependent variable, the policy indicator, the policy instrument, and the current and lagged conditioning variables which identify exogenous fluctuations in the instrument and improve precision of standard errors (see Stock and Watson 2018). The dynamic coefficients of interest are, therefore, the estimates of β^h for $h = 0, 1, \ldots, H$. We compute standard errors based on heteroskedasticity and autocorrelation robust covariance matrix (Newey–West) estimators. We report one standard deviation confidence bands in our estimated impulse responses.

3. Data

3.1. Indian Macroeconomic Data

We consider the impact of external shocks on industrial production, CPI, holdings of foreign reserves, exchange rates, the 10-year government bond rate, and stock prices. We use the data for nominal exchange rate of the Indian rupee with respect to the US dollar, stock price index (measured in constant US dollars), and total foreign reserves from the Global Economic Monitor database of the World Bank, and the International Financial Statistics of the IMF. We use the Index of Industrial Production (seasonally adjusted) from the OECD database, and obtain non-seasonally adjusted CPI from the St Louis Fed's database.

Historically, Indian monetary policy has been conducted using multiple instruments: price-based and quantity-based. Starting from April 3, 2001, the RBI used the repo rate as the price-based instrument. For the preceding years, we follow the BIS in using the bank rate as the price-based policy instrument. Quantity-based instruments such as the Cash Reserve Ratio (CRR) and Statutory Liquidity Ratio (SLR) have also been used regularly. Nonetheless, we measure the overall stance of monetary policy using the price-based instruments.[2] In the main text, we only report the impulse

---

2. In terms of other interest rates and policy indicators, we also looked at the commercial bank lending rate. The results reported here are robust to including the series for the commercial bank lending rate.

FIGURE 1. Indian Interest Rates: Repo Rate and the 10-year G-Sec

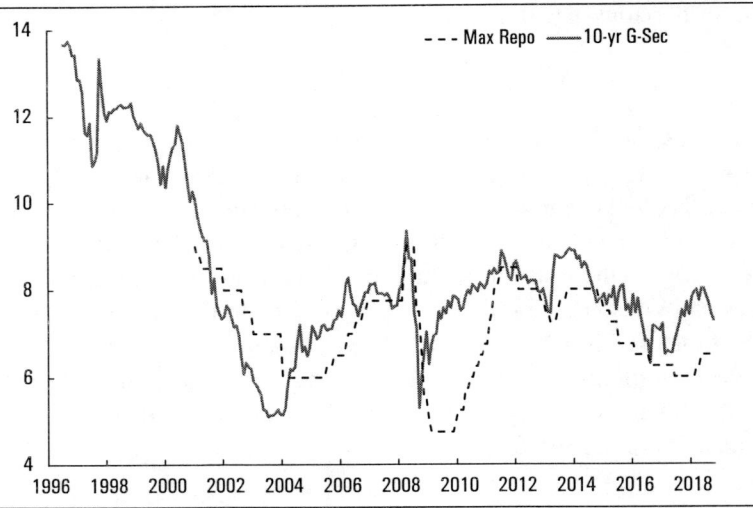

Source: Authors' calculations. RBI data.
Notes: This figure compares the evolution of the repo rate with the interest rate on 10-year bonds issued by the Government of India. Sample: February 1996–December 2018. See text for details.

responses for the 10-year government bond rate. Data for this series are available for the longest duration and exhibit considerable time variation relative to short-term interest rate set by the RBI, as shown in Figure 1. Moreover, the RBI uses a variety of instruments in its conduct of monetary policy. Market-driven variation in the 10-year bond yields would serve as a proxy for variation in other instruments used by the central bank. Impulse responses for other policy indicator variables are available upon request.

We also looked at the responses of nominal and real effective exchange rates. The results are similar to the US dollar/Indian rupee nominal exchange rate. The data for these series came from the Global Economic Monitor database of the World Bank and the International Financial Statistics of the IMF.

Next, we provide the details for our four baseline shock measures that we use in the analysis.

3.2. US Monetary Policy Shocks

For measuring exogenous changes in the stance of US monetary policy, we follow the external instruments (proxy-SVAR) strategy developed by Mertens and Ravn (2013), and Stock and Watson (2002). This methodology involves finding instruments that are correlated with the structural shock of interest (US monetary policy shock here) but uncorrelated with the other structural shocks. We follow the work of Gertler and Karadi (2015) and use changes in futures contracts in a narrow window around FOMC announcements as instruments to identify a structural US monetary policy shock within a standard SVAR. We use both federal funds futures and Eurodollar futures contracts. Specifically, we use the current month's and next month's fed funds futures contracts and the 2, 3, and 4 quarters ahead Eurodollar futures contracts. Following Nakamura and Steinsson (2018), we take the first principal component of the change in these contracts in a 30-minute window around the FOMC announcement. Recent work in the literature has highlighted a potential issue with this approach by finding counter-intuitive effects of monetary policy shocks based on information effects (see, e.g., Lakdawala 2019; Nakamura and Steinsson 2018). To overcome this problem, we take two steps. First, we cleanse the instrument from information effects using real GDP forecasts from a market-based measure of survey forecasts (*Blue Chip*). Specifically, we regress the instrument on four lags of itself, the *Blue Chip* real GDP forecast for the previous quarter, the current quarter, the next quarter, two quarters ahead, and three quarters ahead. Second, we use this instrument to estimate the SVAR model of Gertler and Karadi (2015), and then we use the estimated structural shocks from this SVAR as our baseline measure of monetary policy shocks. This approach ensures that the information contained in the survey forecasts and the SVAR considers any predictability and information effects. Specifically, the SVAR model that we use for the US includes monthly data on industrial production, the CPI, the excess bond premium of Gilchrist and Zakrajek (2012), and the one-year treasury rate as the monetary policy tool. The estimated monetary policy shock is plotted in Figure 2A.

3.3. Economic Policy Uncertainty Shocks

We will use the measure of Baker et al. (2016) of economic policy uncertainty (EPU). This measure is constructed by analyzing newspaper coverage and measuring the relative frequency of words that capture "... a trio of terms pertaining to the economy (E), policy (P) and uncertainty (U)." We use the Global EPU variable that captures economic policy uncertainty for 20 major economies. This measure is plotted in the Figure 2B. To identify the dynamic causal effects of changes in economic policy uncertainty, Baker et al. (2016) use a SVAR with a Cholesky identification strategy by ordering the EPU index first. Recent work by Carriero et al. (2015) has pointed out

FIGURE 2. Foreign Shocks

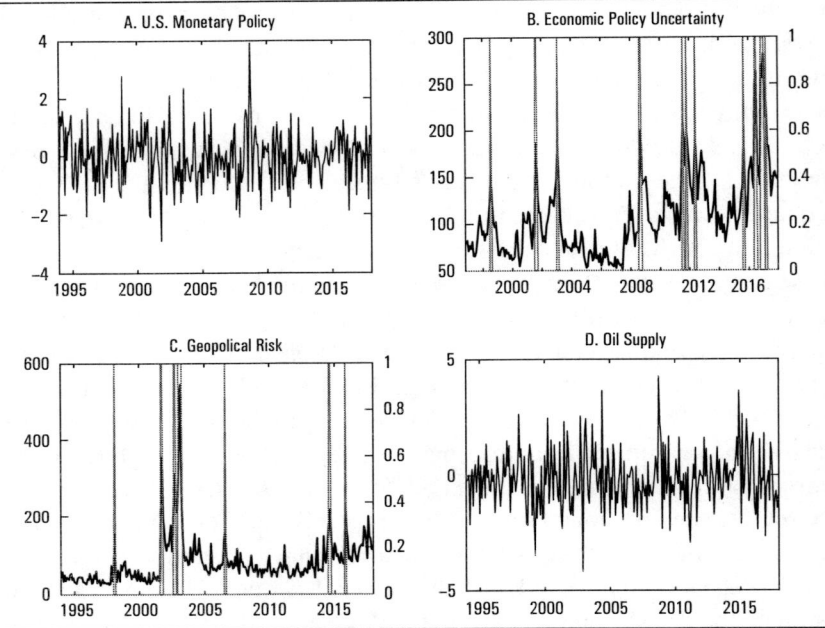

Source: Authors' calculations.
Notes: This figure plots the four main shock measures. The sources for data series are described in the text. The sample is for January 1994 to December 2017, except for the EPU shock for which the sample starts in February 1997 because the EPU measure started only in January 1997. See text for details of the 0-1 dummy variables in Figures 2B and 2C depicted in grey, with the y-axis shown on the right side.

that this approach can lead to attenuation bias due to measurement error. They advocate using a SVAR approach with external instruments. This approach has also been used recently by Caballero and Kamber (2019). Specifically, we construct a dummy indicator that takes the value 1 when the EPU index exceeds 1.65 times the unconditional standard deviation of the Hodrick–Prescott (HP) filtered data. The indicator is also plotted in Figure 2B (y-axis shown on the right side). This dummy indicator is used as an instrument for the structural shock to the EPU index in both the SVAR and LP frameworks.

3.4. Geopolitical Risk Shocks

We will use the geopolitical risk measure of Caldara and Iacoviello (2018). They use a methodology that is similar to Baker et al. (2016), which involves counting the frequency of newspaper articles related to geopolitical risk. They define geopolitical risk as "… risk associated with wars, terrorist acts, and tensions between states that affect the normal and peaceful course of international relations." This measure (GPR) reflects both the risk of these adverse events occurring together and the actual realization of these events. Again, to identify the causal effects of geopolitical risk shocks, Caldara and Iacoviello (2018) use a SVAR identified with Cholesky ordering. Since the same caveat about measurement error and attenuation bias applies, we follow the same approach as above to construct a 0-1 dummy variable. Both the GPR index (y-axis shown on the left) and the dummy indicator (y-axis shown on the right) are plotted in Figure 2C.

3.5. Oil Shocks

Given India's reliance on imported oil, a potentially important source of shocks to the Indian economy involves changes in the price of crude oil. Of course, oil price dynamics are driven by shocks to both oil supply and oil demand. Since India is the world's third largest consumer of oil (after the USA and China), oil demand shocks can be expected to be driven in part by changes in India's economic conditions. On the other hand, India contributes to less than 1 percent of the total global oil production and thus oil supply disruptions originating in India are unlikely to move the global price of oil. Thus, to study the causal effect of changes in oil prices, we rely on an exogenous measure of oil supply shocks. Specifically, we use the newly developed measure of oil supply shocks by Baumeister and Hamilton (2019). They use an SVAR framework to disentangle oil supply shocks from oil demand shocks. While the existing literature has made some strong assumptions about relevant elasticities, their Bayesian framework allows them to incorporate uncertainty about these elasticities in a transparent manner. The estimated oil shock is plotted in Figure 2D.

4. Results

4.1. Benchmark: World and BRCS Industrial Production

We first document the responses of both the world's and BRCS countries' industrial production to external shocks. We believe this is useful for at least two reasons. First, these responses will be helpful to understand the nature of the foreign shock, for example, whether it is contractionary and expansionary, or the persistence of the effects of the shock. Second, it will help us place a benchmark on the quantitative magnitudes we should have in mind when we are looking at India-specific macro and financial variables.

Our sample uses monthly data from January 1994 to December 2017. For the economic policy uncertainty shock, the sample starts in February

FIGURE 3. Response to One Standard Deviation Shock: World Index of Industrial Production

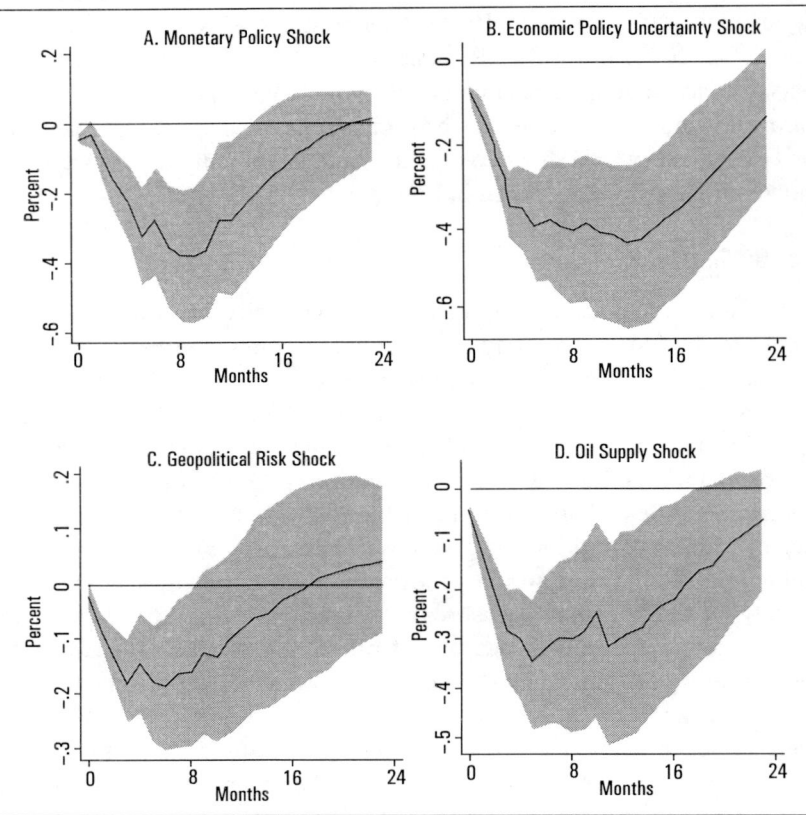

Source: Authors' calculations.
Notes: SVAR estimated response of world industrial production (OECD + BRICS + Indonesia) region to a one standard deviation shock. The shaded areas represent confidence intervals of one standard deviation. Standard errors are bootstrapped as in Gertler and Karadi (2015). The World Index of Industrial Production (WIIP) is an extended version of the OECD's index of monthly industrial production in the OECD and six major other countries developed by Baumeister and Hamilton (2019). The sources for shocks are described in the text. The sample is from January 1994 to December 2017, except for the EPU shock for which the sample starts in February 1997 because the EPU measure started only in January 1997. See text for details.

1997. Figure 3 plots the impulse responses of world industrial production to our four measures of shocks, namely, shocks to US monetary policy, economic policy uncertainty, geopolitical risk, and global oil supply. This measure of industrial production includes all OECD countries plus the six major non-member economies (Brazil, China, India, Indonesia, Russia, and South Africa). As mentioned above, the impulse responses are computed by using a combination of putting our shocks directly in the SVAR or LP framework and using them as instruments in the SVAR-IV or LP-IV framework. Specifically, for monetary policy and oil supply shocks, we use these measures of exogenous shocks directly. For the responses to economic policy uncertainty and geopolitical risk shocks, we use the dummy indicators described above as instruments. Figure 3 displays the responses to a one standard deviation shock from a bivariate SVAR framework, which includes the log of the industrial production index and the relevant shock. The impulse responses from the LP framework are similar and have been included in the Appendix. The shaded areas in the figures represent one standard deviation confidence bands, where standard errors are computed using a bootstrap algorithm.

Figure 3A shows the response to a contractionary US monetary policy shock, or an unexpected increase in short-term interest rate by the Federal Reserve. The response of world industrial production displays an inverse hump-shaped response, with a trough of about –0.4 percent at the one-year mark. The effects of the shock have faded by the two-year horizon. These results are consistent with the hypothesis of the global financial cycle (Miranda-Agrippino and Rey 2018), which finds substantial global effects of US monetary policy. Figure 3B shows the response to an increase in economic policy uncertainty. World industrial production falls on impact, reaching a peak fall of –0.4 percent in around six months; the response stays around this level for about a year before reverting. Figure 3C shows a one standard deviation increase in geopolitical risk. The effects of this shock are also contractionary but somewhat smaller with a peak effect of almost –0.2 percent. Finally, Figure 3D shows the response to an adverse supply shock in the oil market. As expected, we see a contractionary effect on world industrial production with a peak fall of about –0.3 percent. In addition to having quantitatively meaningful effects, for all four shocks the peak effect of roughly around the one-year mark is also statistically significant as indicated by the confidence intervals.

Figure 4 plots the impulse responses of industrial production for the BRCS countries (Brazil, Russia, China, and South Africa). The broad pattern of responses for these countries is similar to that of world industrial production qualitatively. Quantitatively, the responses are slightly smaller. For both the US monetary policy shock and the economic policy uncertainty shock, the peak fall is around –0.25 percent (relative to roughly –0.4 percent for the world index). We do see a notable difference in response to the geopolitical risk shock. After this shock, BRCS industrial production actually rises slightly on impact before falling. However, the magnitude of the fall is quite small and statistically insignificant. Thus, while GPR shocks had a clear adverse effect on OECD countries, they do not appear to have

FIGURE 4. Response to One Standard Deviation Shock: Index of Industrial Production for BRCS Countries

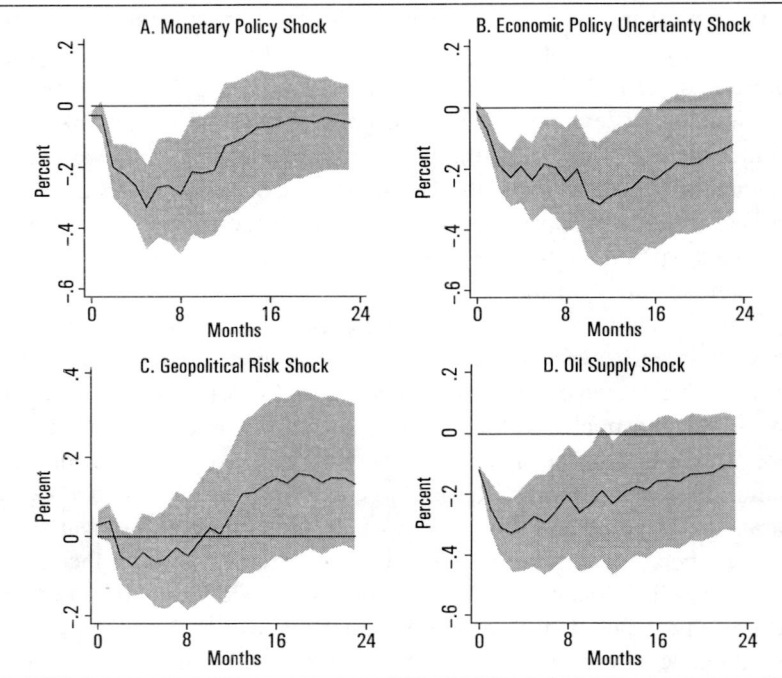

Source: Authors' calculations.
Notes: SVAR estimated response of the monthly seasonally adjusted industrial production in the four-country BRCS (BRICS excluding India) region to a one standard deviation shock. The shaded areas represent one standard deviation confidence intervals. Standard errors are bootstrapped as in Gertler and Karadi (2015). The BRICS industrial production data are from the World Bank Global Economic Monitor. The sample is for January 1994 to December 2017, except for the EPU shock for which the sample starts in February 1997 because the EPU measure started only in January 1997. The sources for shocks are described in the text.

had much of an effect on the BRCS countries. Finally, the response to oil supply shocks is quite similar to the case of world industrial production.

In summary, we have established that adverse increases in our four shock measures have had a substantial and statistically significant effect on world industrial production and a somewhat smaller effect on industrial production in the BRCS countries. This establishes a simple benchmark for comparing the response of Indian economic activity, which we undertake next.

4.2. Impulse Responses for the Indian Economy

In this section, we present the impulse responses for the Indian macroeconomic and financial market variables. We have done the estimation using both the SVAR and LP frameworks outlined above. The results are consistent with both methods. From an econometric perspective, SVAR and LP should give similar results as long as certain conditions about the sufficiency of the information set are met. Overall, we find similar results using both approaches, which is reassuring. For the rest of this section, we present results using the SVAR framework, and the LP results are presented in Appendix A.1, A.2, A.3, and A.4.

We estimate impulse response functions (IRF) for the following six Indian macro and financial variables available at monthly frequency: industrial production, CPI, nominal exchange rate of US dollar/Indian rupee, yields on 10-year government bonds, stock market index, and US dollar value of total foreign reserves (minus gold) as a measure of international liquidity (coded as RAXG_USD in IMF/IFS). Following the recent trend in the empirical macroeconomics literature (see, e.g., Gertler and Karadi 2015), we run the SVAR in log levels. Specifically, we put the 10-year bond rate in levels (percentage points) and for all the other variables we take the log of the variable and then multiply it by 100. We also check the robustness of our results using a "gaps" specification. In this case, we de-trend the seasonally adjusted industrial production using an HP filter with a monthly frequency smoothing parameter of 14,400. Further, we take the year-over-year percentage change in the CPI price index to calculate the inflation rate. This specification is similar to the one used recently by Mishra et al. (2016). We find that the results are similar using this approach and thus do not report these impulse responses in the main draft.

The SVAR is estimated with 12 lags. All figures are presented as responses to a one standard deviation "adverse" shock. This means that based on the responses shown for the world and BRCS industrial production, these shocks are expected to lower economic activity, for example an increase in US interest rates or an increase in the global price of oil. One standard deviation confidence intervals constructed using a bootstrap algorithm are reported on all the impulse response figures.

4.2.1. MONETARY POLICY SHOCKS

Figure 5 presents the impulse response to a contractionary monetary policy shock. On impact the rupee depreciates and reserves and the stock market fall as has been documented in the literature; see, for example, Lakdawala (2018). These variables take about a year to a year and a half to recover from this shock. Overall, these effects are statistically significant and sizeable for reserves and the stock market with a peak fall of around −1.5 percent and −0.75 percent, respectively. The responses of prices, output, and the government bond rate are not significant on impact, but all three variables display a fall at around the 6-month to 1-year mark. The peak fall in Indian

FIGURE 5. SVAR Response of the India Economy to Monetary Policy Shock

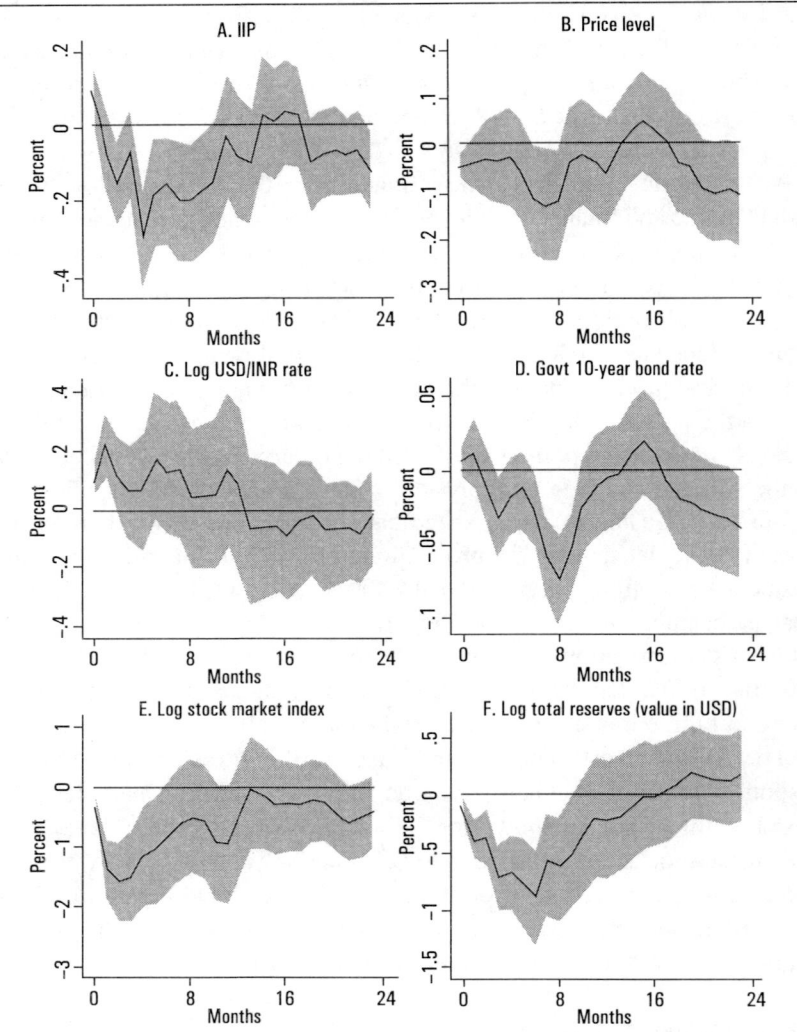

Source: Authors' calculations.
Notes: SVAR estimated response of monthly industrial production, CPI, USD/INR nominal exchange rate, 10-year government bond rate, stock market index, and total reserves (excluding gold) outstanding for India to a one standard deviation identified US monetary policy shock. The shaded areas represent one standard deviation confidence intervals. Standard errors are bootstrapped as in Gertler and Karadi (2015). The sources for data series are described in the text. Sample: February 1994–December 2017. See text for details.

industrial production is around −0.3 percent, which is quite similar to the fall in BRCS industrial production displayed above and slightly smaller than the peak fall in world industrial production. However, Indian industrial production does not display the inertial and persistent response and has almost recovered around the 15-month mark.

These results are consistent with the story of the global financial cycle. Monetary policy shocks originating in the US are propagated throughout the world through the global financial cycle. However, we should note that relative to the size of the effect on the stock market and dollar reserves, the effect on prices and thus, Indian economic activity is, to some extent, shielded from the global financial cycle.

4.2.2. Economic Policy Uncertainty Shocks

The impulse responses to a one standard deviation shock that increases the economic policy uncertainty are shown in Figure 6. Industrial production has a sustained fall for over two years of around 0.2 percent. The size of this effect for Indian industrial production is very similar to the size of the fall in BRCS industrial production. This shock has a larger impact on the financial markets that are persistent as well. The rupee depreciates and dollar reserves and stock market fall. Quantitatively, the stock market index falls more than 1 percent on impact and the peak effect is more than −2 percent after a couple of months. Reserves fall by 0.25 percent on impact and gradually fall to trough at −0.75 percent, staying lower for over a year. The rupee depreciates on impact and then returns around the six-month mark. The government bond rate heads slightly lower around the six-month mark before recovering. Thus, an increase in global economic policy uncertainty is clearly detrimental to the Indian economy, both immediately on impact and in the medium term.

4.2.3. Geopolitical Risk Shocks

Figure 7 presents the impulse responses to a one standard deviation increase in the geopolitical risk shock. With this shock, the SVAR results do not show a clear discernible pattern. The responses of both industrial production and CPI are quantitatively small and statistically insignificant. Thus, the response of Indian industrial production is consistent with the response of BRCS industrial production seen above: neither appears to be substantially affected by the geopolitical risk shock. Even for financial market variables, we notice that the responses are mostly near zero and insignificant. The one exception is the stock market, which falls on impact. Overall, for financial variables, if anything, this adverse shock represents some beneficial effects with an

FIGURE 6. SVAR Response of the India Economy to Economic Policy Uncertainty Shock

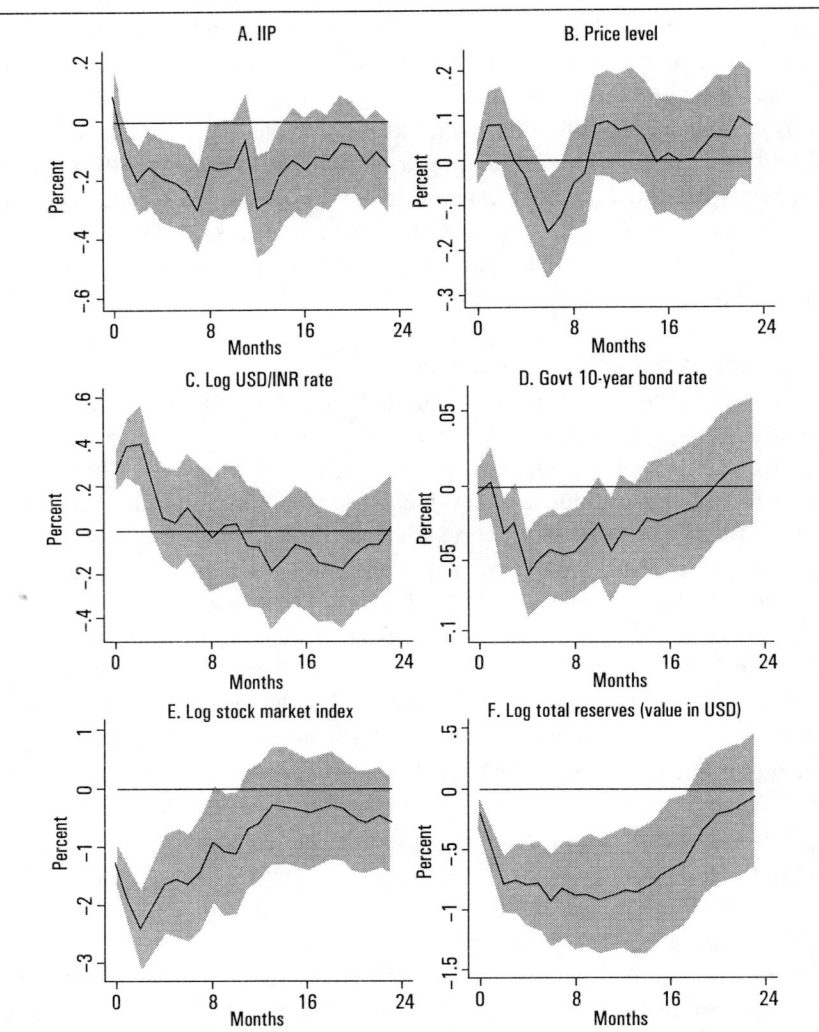

Source: Authors' calculations.
Notes: SVAR estimated response of monthly industrial production, CPI, USD/INR nominal exchange rate, 10-year government bond rate, stock market index, and total reserves (excluding gold) outstanding to a one standard deviation identified shock to global EPU. The shaded areas represent one standard deviation confidence intervals. Standard errors are bootstrapped as in Gertler and Karadi (2015). The sources for data series are described in the text. Sample: February 1997–December 2017. See text for details.

FIGURE 7. SVAR Response of the India Economy to Geopolitical Risk Shock

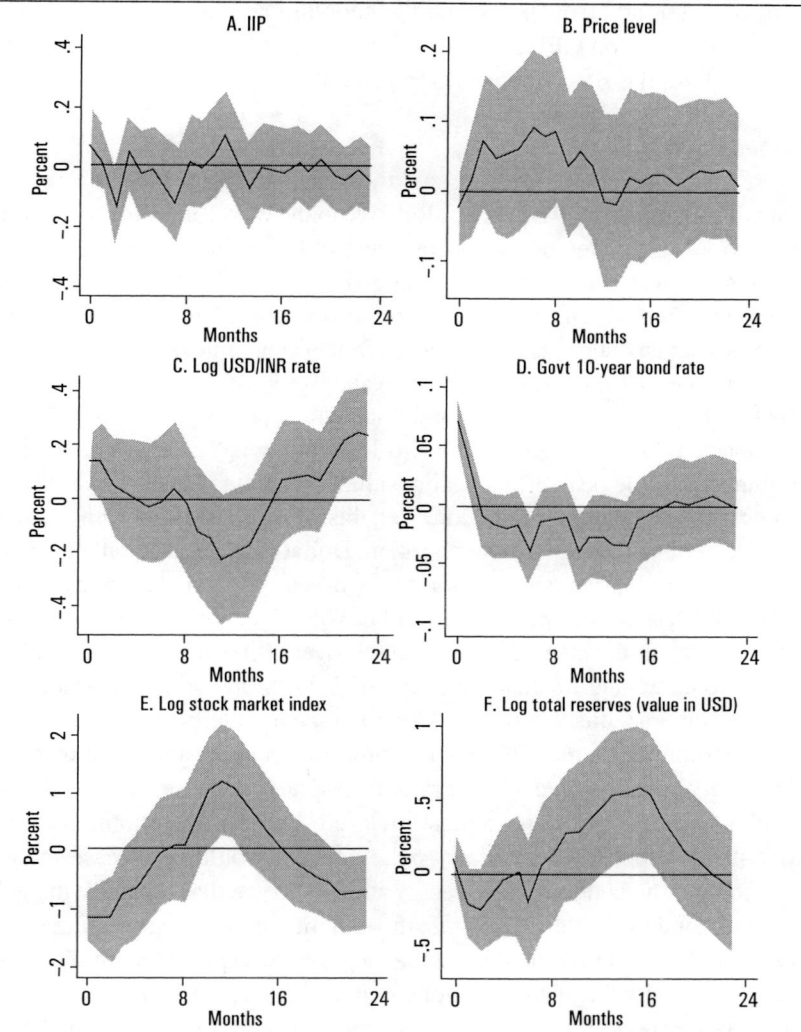

Source: Authors' calculations.
Notes: SVAR estimated response of monthly industrial production, CPI, USD/INR nominal exchange rate, 10-year government bond rate, stock market index, and total reserves (excluding gold) outstanding to a one standard deviation identified shock to GPR measure. The shaded areas represent one standard deviation confidence intervals. Standard errors are bootstrapped as in Gertler and Karadi (2015). The sources for data series are described in the text. Sample: February 1997–December 2017. See text for details.

increase in dollar reserves and a delayed rise in the stock market. Thus, in contrast to the other shocks, while the geopolitical risk shock does have a significant effect on OECD countries, its impact is mostly insignificant for India, as with the BRCS countries in general.

4.2.4. Oil Supply Shocks

Figure 8 shows the impulse response to the oil supply shock. Industrial production falls on impact by 0.3 percent. Relative to the world and BRCS industrial production, this contemporaneous response of Indian industrial production is larger. Moreover, this response stays negative and significant even at the two-year mark. Thus, among the four shocks we have considered, the oil shock has the largest and most persistent effects on Indian economic activity. Consistent with expectations, the oil supply shock responses look like a textbook "supply shock." Output goes down while at the same time prices go up. The CPI rises on impact and is still higher at the two-level horizon. The rupee depreciates on impact and the peak effect is almost half a percent. This is larger than in response to other three shocks. Moreover, this effect is persistent with the rupee being lower even at the two-year horizon. Dollar reserves also fall on impact and stay about 0.5 percent lower at the two-year horizon. The stock market and the 10-year government bond yield fall on impact but recover somewhat faster. Thus, an adverse oil supply shock overall has large effects on both macroeconomic and financial market variables. Moreover, these effects are felt contemporaneously and persist over the medium term.

One common theme emerges from the four shocks about the response of the 10-year government bond rate. In response to these adverse shocks, which cause disruption in financial markets and lower economic activity, the typical response of monetary policymakers would be to ease interest rates to help the economy recover. While we do see that typically the government bond rate tends to decline, the magnitude of the fall is quite small. We think this is an important point that needs to be explored more. There are two reasons why this could be happening. First, it could be the case that the RBI is not responding enough to offset these shocks. But even if the RBI is recognizing these shocks and responding appropriately by changing policy rates, it could be the case that the monetary transmission mechanism is not effective. Indeed, there is corroborating evidence for the latter explanation. For a prominent paper, see the recent work of Mishra et al. (2016).

4.3. Discussion: Resilience versus Integration

Our results suggest that the exposure of Indian output to foreign shocks is lower relative to an index of advanced economies but comparable to an index of BRCS economies. In the Appendix, we make direct comparisons of the

FIGURE 8. SVAR Response of the India Economy to Oil Supply Shock

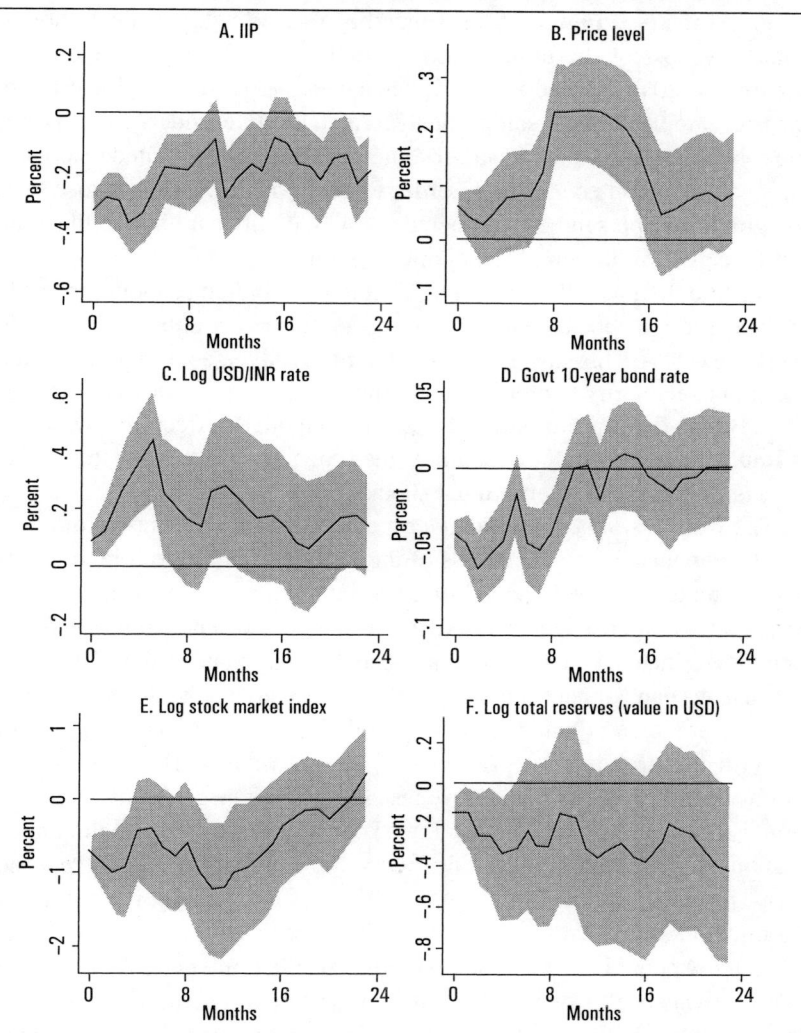

Source: Authors' calculations.
Notes: SVAR estimated response of monthly industrial production, CPI, USD/INR nominal exchange rate, 10-year government bond rate, stock market index, and total reserves (excluding gold) outstanding to a one standard deviation identified shock to oil supply. The shaded areas represent one standard deviation confidence intervals. Standard errors are bootstrapped as in Gertler and Karadi (2015). The sources for data series are described in the text. Sample: February 1994–December 2017. See text for details.

responsiveness of the Indian economy to that of China, Russia, Brazil, and South Africa (see Figure 15 in Appendix A.4). We also evaluate how the responsiveness of the Indian economy may have changed over time (see Figures 16–20 in Appendix A.4). Given the increased financial integration in the later sample, this sub-sample analysis is suggestive evidence for assessing the role of resilience and the lack of integration in the estimated responsiveness of the Indian economy. In order to keep the discussion focused here, the graphs are presented in Appendix A.4. We only summarize the results with the goal of drawing broad policy lessons.

We find that, with the exception of China, the Indian economy reacts less to these foreign shocks relative to these counterpart countries (Figure 15 in Appendix A.4). This suggests that in facing an adverse international shock, the Indian economy is more resilient than those of other developing countries. But on the flip side, since the estimated model's effects are symmetric, it implies that the Indian economy may also miss out from the positive effects of beneficial international shocks.

The word *resilience* is a broad term that may capture a variety of reasons for the attenuated responsiveness of the Indian economy to foreign shocks. For example, lack of financial or trade integration could explain subdued responsiveness. To a first order, we use 'resilience' to denote forces, structural or policy-initiated, which are distinct from the lack of integration. This is done because we can conduct sub-sample analysis to provide suggestive evidence of whether increased integration has implied greater responsiveness or not.

With the growing integration of India into the world economy, one might expect that the responsiveness of the Indian economy to international shocks has changed over time. To test this, we estimate the impulse responses for India by splitting our sample into two halves (pre- and post-December 2005). But for most of the variables (including output), we do not find statistically significant differences in the responses (Figures 16–20 in Appendix A.4). What explains this phenomenon? A comprehensive analysis of this question would investigate any structural changes in the Indian economy and the response of policymakers. While this exercise lies outside the scope of this paper, our results provide some suggestive evidence of the role that monetary policymakers might have played.

Central banks can respond to international shocks primarily by changing their policy interest rates or intervening in exchange rate markets, at least in terms of conventional policy tools. A common pattern that also emerges in the analysis is the modest response of the 10-year government bond rate to these adverse global shocks. This has potentially important implications from a policy stabilization perspective. For example, policymakers may consider easing of interest rates in response to adverse international shocks.

For the oil supply shock, the central bank faces a clear trade-off as output falls, but prices rise. Thus, if the central bank is worried more about higher inflation, it may want to refrain from lowering rates and accept the downturn in economic activity. But the US monetary policy and uncertainty shocks have effects that look like domestic demand shocks. In this case, there is no longer a trade-off and optimal monetary policy from conventional models dictates that the central bank lower rates.

In light of this, we think there are two different ways to interpret our results of relative non-responsiveness of the 10-year interest rate. First, it is possible that the Reserve Bank is not responding strongly with interest rate changes to international shocks, either because they fail to identify the shocks in a timely manner or because they perceive the trade-off as too costly. Alternatively, the Reserve Bank is indeed responding to these shocks by changing interest rates, but the transmission mechanism of monetary policy in India is weak and thus there are no substantial effects on the long rate.

However, the RBI has also intervened in the exchange rate market in response to international events. Our results from the split-sample estimation show that in response to adverse monetary and oil shocks, the Indian rupee depreciates less in the more recent sample. One potential factor could be the actions (or anticipated actions) of the RBI becoming stronger in the last decade or so. Our results highlight that disentangling these different channels is important to understand the role of monetary policy in the overall stabilization policy.

4.4. Variance Decomposition for the Indian Economy

We now consider what each shock implies about the contribution to the forecast error variance of the core Indian macro variables. In principle, these quantities can be calculated from the LP framework. However, we found that in practice, the estimates implied that the total contribution of the shocks would add up to more than 100 percent. This is a finding that is common in the literature; see, for example, Ramey (2016). Thus, we use the SVAR framework to compute the forecast error variance decompositions. We include all four shocks at the same time in the following order: (a) economic policy uncertainty shock, (b) geopolitical risk shock, (c) monetary policy shock, and (d) oil supply shock. While the total share of the forecast error variance to these four shocks is not affected by the ordering, the relative contribution of each shock can be affected by the ordering. We found that, in practice, the relative shares are similar regardless of the ordering that we choose. The baseline sample runs from January 1997 to December 2017.

Table 1 presents these variance decompositions. Panel A in the table shows the contribution of the US monetary policy shock. On impact, this shock has

TABLE 1. Individual Shock Contribution to the Forecast Error Variance 1 to 48 Months After the Shock

	A. Monetary Policy Shock					B. Economic Policy Uncertainty Shock				
Months →	1	6	12	24	48	1	6	12	24	48
Stock market	1.800	3.913	12.282	10.164	9.199	3.103	5.560	4.651	4.879	5.078
USD/INR	0.843	0.654	1.650	2.082	2.568	1.972	1.153	0.746	1.371	5.219
10-year bond	2.572	0.447	8.494	11.728	7.327	0.078	4.169	5.085	3.190	2.516
Dollar reserves	2.013	0.670	8.938	6.387	4.113	0.011	3.938	10.007	13.408	7.207
Inflation	1.835	0.724	3.160	3.680	5.066	0.000	1.557	1.804	1.597	1.046
Ind. Prod.	1.738	0.027	13.506	13.817	12.286	0.080	3.239	4.441	5.066	8.928

	C. Geopolitical Risk Shock					D. Oil Supply Shock				
Months →	1	6	12	24	48	1	6	12	24	48
Stock market	0.679	1.074	1.865	2.058	2.770	1.926	3.044	5.380	6.854	6.189
USD/INR	0.665	0.337	0.565	1.635	1.791	0.497	10.290	10.209	12.324	9.143
10-year bond	1.208	0.633	0.429	0.493	5.498	2.295	9.044	6.500	4.257	4.032
Dollar reserves	0.005	0.160	1.712	2.414	6.543	2.038	2.504	2.002	2.471	3.028
Inflation	0.260	6.009	8.654	9.319	10.237	0.668	0.311	6.475	5.415	3.520
Ind. Prod.	0.003	0.580	0.944	0.953	0.742	4.814	15.524	13.663	16.504	13.027

Source: Authors' calculations.

a small contribution, explaining about 1–2 percent of the movement in macro and financial variables. At longer horizons, we see a substantially bigger effect, explaining 13 percent of the variation in output at the one- to four-year horizon. The US monetary policy shock also has a similar long-term impact on the stock market and the 10-year bond rate, explaining roughly 10 percent at longer horizons. Somewhat surprisingly, the contribution of the monetary policy shock to the exchange rate is smaller. We also note that the shock does not explain much of the contribution to prices.

Panel B of Table 1 shows the contributions of the economic policy uncertainty shock. This shock also does not explain much of the contemporaneous contribution to output or inflation. But it has a more substantial amount of contribution at the one-year horizon, explaining 4 percent of the variation in output and 2 percent in inflation. At longer horizons, the effect on output is even bigger, explaining close to 9 percent of the variation. This shock also has relatively bigger effects on the dollar reserves. At the one-year horizon, it explains 10 percent of the impact on dollar reserves. Finally, this shock also explains around 5 percent of the long-term variation in the exchange rate and stock market.

The geopolitical risk shock is shown in panel C of Table 1. Similar to the policy uncertainty shock, it has small effects on output and inflation at shorter horizons. The peak contribution to output is less than 1 percent. However, this shock has a bigger effect on prices. For inflation, the peak effect in the long run (four years out) is at around 10 percent. This shock also contributes significantly to the long-term variation in dollar reserves and the 10-year government bond rate, with contributions of 7 percent and 5 percent, respectively.

Finally, panel D of Table 1 shows the oil supply shock. Here, we see substantially larger effects for output, even at the short and medium horizons. At the six-month horizon, oil supply shocks explain 15 percent of the variation in output. At longer horizons, the contributions remain sizeable, with 16 percent explained at two years and 13 percent explained at four years. The effects of inflation are largest around the one- to two-year mark, explaining around 5 to 7 percent of the variation. The oil supply shock is also the highest contributor to the US dollar–Indian rupee exchange rate from all the four shocks we have considered, explaining 12 percent of the variation at the two-year horizon.

Table 2 shows the sum of the contributions of the four shocks. They explain around 32 percent of the variation in output at the one-year horizon and over 34 percent of the variation at the four-year horizon. For inflation, these numbers are lower at 20 percent at the one-year and two-year horizons.

TABLE 2. Sum of Contributions of Four Shocks to the Forecast Error Variance 1 to 48 Months After the Shock

Months →	1	6	12	24	48
Stock market	7.507	13.592	24.179	23.955	23.236
USD/INR	3.977	12.435	13.170	17.412	18.721
10-year bond	6.154	14.292	20.509	19.667	19.372
Dollar reserves	4.066	7.272	22.659	24.681	20.891
Inflation	2.763	8.600	20.094	20.011	19.869
Ind. Prod.	6.636	19.370	32.553	36.340	34.983

Source: Authors' calculations.

In the long run, the four shocks combine to explain close to 20 percent of the financial market variables as well. The overall picture emerges that these four shocks form a substantial component of the variation in output and inflation for the Indian economy, especially the monetary policy and oil price shocks.

We think that these numbers should be interpreted as representing an upper bound of the effects of these shocks. As mentioned earlier, we also ran our SVAR and LP estimation by using the IIP gap and year-over-year inflation rate, rather than the log-level specification presented in the baseline results. When we redo the variance decomposition calculations using the "gap" specification for the macro variables, we find that the contribution of the shocks is somewhat diminished. This is especially true for output. The total contribution to industrial production from the four shocks drops to 16 percent at the one-year horizon and 18 percent at the four-year horizon. While still sizeable, these numbers are definitively smaller than the 35 percent range for the baseline specification. The reduction in the contribution comes primarily from the monetary policy and oil supply shocks.

Further, there are two more qualifiers that we should mention with this analysis. First, the usual disclaimer about omitted variable bias about vector autoregressions applies here. In other words, if there are important variables that we are missing, the variance decompositions numbers have the potential to be overstated. We address this concern in the Appendix and show that our results are similar when we include a variety of other Indian macro variables. Second, this analysis looks at the net aggregate effects of these foreign shocks. If there are distributional effects of these shocks, it is possible that those effects cancel out and we are missing important transmission mechanisms. While we do not undertake this disaggregated analysis, we believe it to be a promising area for future research.

5. Conclusion

Recently, there have been increasing concern about the resilience of the Indian economy to international developments. This paper is an attempt to understand the quantitative relevance of foreign shocks for the Indian economy and to shed some light on the transmission mechanisms.

Our analysis finds substantial effects of three main foreign shocks to the macroeconomy: US monetary policy, economic policy uncertainty, and oil. We do not find a major role for geopolitical risk shocks. The spillovers associated with US monetary policy as well as the increase in global economic uncertainty have quantitatively significant bearings on Indian financial markets consistent with the global financial cycle narrative. The effects of these shocks are similar to what we would expect with domestic demand shocks. On the other hand, oil shocks act as textbook adverse supply shocks. After an adverse supply shock, there is a simultaneous drop in output and an increase in prices, and this effect is persistent. The shock also causes a general worsening of financial conditions with a reduction in total reserves, a depreciation of the rupee, and a fall in stock prices. Among the external shocks considered, consumer price inflation is largely driven by uncertainty shocks and oil supply shocks.

These four shocks combined can explain up to 35 percent of the variation in Indian output at business cycle frequencies. Thus, while the size of the effect is substantial, the response of Indian output is lower relative to the response of an index of global output and also lower relative to the output of peer developing countries. This suggests that the Indian economy is relatively more resilient to international shocks. However, this resilience potentially comes at the cost of India not reaping the gains from beneficial global shocks. Our results also highlight an important implication about counter-cyclical policy responses to stabilize the business cycle. In response to adverse foreign shocks, which cause disruption in financial markets and lower economic activity, the main tool of monetary policymakers would be to lower interest rates to help the economy recover. While the government bond rate tends to decline in response to these shocks, the magnitude of the fall is modest. Given that the foreign shocks are quantitatively relevant, our analysis suggests that quantifying the role of counter-cyclical policy should be an important agenda for further research.

We conclude with an important caveat. Our analysis provides insights for the transmission of four key foreign shocks. Since our aim is to use the instrumental variables strategy to guide our analysis, we were limited in the choice of instruments available and, hence, in the nature of foreign shocks that we could investigate. We believe, and have hopefully convinced the reader, that these are quantitatively relevant shocks. Yet there are important transmission mechanisms, particularly through the banking system, variations in foreign currency denominated debt issuances by the private sector, and trade linkages that have not been explored here. We leave it to future research to bring more data and novel econometric techniques that can guide us in understanding the resilience of the Indian macroeconomy.

A. Appendix: Results from Local Projections Estimation Strategy

A.1. Baseline Results for India from LP-IV Estimation

We directly estimate the impulse response functions for six Indian macro variables available at monthly frequency: industrial production, CPI, nominal exchange rate US dollar/Indian rupee, yields on 10-year government bonds, stock market index, and US dollar value of total foreign reserves (minus gold) as a measure of international liquidity (coded as RAXG_USD in IMF/IFS). Following Mishra et al. (2016), we de-trend seasonally adjusted industrial production using an HP filter with a monthly frequency smoothing parameter of 14,400. In the SVAR-IVs, we directly use seasonally adjusted monthly industrial production from the IMF/IFS database along with linear time trends.

One advantage of using LP-IVs instead of SVARs is that we do not need to have a balanced sample across all horizons. We can use more information for estimating the IRFs at shorter horizons. Our sample starts in April 1994 and extends up to December 2017.

The IRFs are computed from the second-stage LP estimation method described in Equation 6. The graphs plot the β^h at each horizon. While the US Federal Reserve has a legal mandate to focus explicitly on three domestic variables, shocks identified for the US economy may be predictable by foreign economy's conditions (Obstfeld 2019). As such, we control for 12 lags of the industrial production gap, consumer price level-based inflation, and the instrument/external shock. Because of the shorter sample length, we only add six lags for the other variables, namely, nominal exchange rate US dollar/Indian rupee, yields on 10-year government bonds, stock market index, US dollar value of total foreign reserves (minus gold), and global industrial production index obtained from Baumeister and Hamilton (2019). The countries included in this index account for 79 percent of the global petroleum product consumption and 75 percent of the IMF World Economic Outlook estimate of global GDP. When estimating IRFs for oil supply shocks, we also control for six lags of global oil production (millions barrels/day), changes in oil inventories as a ratio of last year's global oil production, and the real spot price of West Texas Intermediate oil.

Figures 9–13 report the LP-IV estimated impulse responses to the four main shocks of interest. A caveat with LP estimation is the irregular shape of the impulse responses compared to relatively smooth IRFs obtained with VAR estimation. One could potentially smooth out these IRFs using methods developed in the literature (Barnichon and Brownlees 2018). That requires taking a stand on which turning points are the truth and which are noise. As a result, we chose to report the LP-IV-based IRFs.

A.1.1. MONETARY POLICY SHOCKS

Figure 9 reports the LP-IV-estimated impulse responses to US monetary policy shocks. Consistent with the global financial cycle hypothesis, we find that US monetary policy has important spillovers to the Indian economy. The rupee depreciates on impact and exhibits a persistent depreciation with respect to the US dollar. The Indian stock market index gradually falls, and the stock of foreign reserves declines. The 10-year Indian government bond yields and the consumer price level fall.

A.1.2. ECONOMIC POLICY UNCERTAINTY SHOCKS

Figure 10 reports the LP-IV-estimated impulse responses to increase in global economic policy uncertainty. Industrial production falls, the rupee depreciates, and consumer prices fall. The stock market initially falls to recover after one year.

Since the economic policy uncertainty measure only starts in 1997, we also estimate the IRFs with respect to one standard deviation in VIX (the Chicago Board of Trade's Volatility Index) orthogonalized to past Indian macro variables as well as world industrial production. Figure 11 reports the LP-IV estimated impulse responses to an increase in the VIX measure of uncertainty in global financial markets. The effects are more pronounced with this shock, while we do not claim identification of the exogenous shock in this case. The impulse responses are similar to global economic policy uncertainty shocks, largely because of a high correlation between the two series.

A.1.3. GEOPOLITICAL RISK SHOCKS

Figure 12 reports the LP-IV-estimated impulse responses to the increase in geopolitical risk in the rest of the world. There is no significant effect on industrial production, while the price level falls in response to the global geopolitical risk. Somewhat surprisingly, we find an increase in industrial production roughly 14 months after the shock. However, the financial variables seem to move in India's favor with improvement in the value of foreign reserve holdings. This would be consistent with India being a relatively safe option when there is increase in geopolitical risk in the rest of the world.

A.1.4. OIL SUPPLY SHOCKS

Figure 13 reports the LP-IV estimated impulse responses to the increase in oil prices because of a reduction in supply. The industrial production gap falls and recovers eight months after the shock. Reliance on oil imports implies that consumer prices go up in India, the rupee depreciates, and foreign reserves go down.

A.2. COMPARISON TO THE WORLD AND BRCS

We next document the responses of world industrial production and industrial production in the BRCS block to external shocks. We believe this is useful for at least two reasons. One, the response of WIIP and BRCS-IP is helpful to understand the nature of the foreign shock, whether contractionary or expansionary. Two, it can help place a benchmark on the quantitative magnitudes one should expect when we look at India-specific macrovariables.

Our measure of WIIP is an extended version of the OECD's index of monthly industrial production in the OECD and six major other countries developed by Baumeister and Hamilton (2019). The countries included in this index account for 79 percent of global petroleum product consumption and 75 percent of the IMF World Economic Outlook estimate of global GDP. Our measure of BRCS-IP is the average of industrial production obtained for Brazil, China, Russia, and South Africa from the World Bank's *Global Economic Monitor*. Further, we control for past 12 lags of the instrument and world industrial production in our regression to account for the predictability of these shocks to past lags as well as to improve the precision of our estimates. In addition, we control for 12 lags of the US federal funds rate, US industrial production, and US CPI inflation. When estimating the IRFs for oil supply shocks, we also control for 12 lags of global oil production (millions barrels/day), changes in oil inventories as a ratio of last year's global oil production, and the real spot price of West Texas Intermediate oil. This is important to identify oil supply shocks from oil demand and other confounding factors.

Figure 14 plots the impulse responses to the shocks described earlier, namely, shocks to US monetary policy, economic policy uncertainty, geopolitical risk, and global oil supply shocks.

Consistent with the hypothesis of the global financial cycle (Miranda-Agrippino and Rey 2018), we find that contractionary surprises in the US federal funds rate indeed have contractionary effects on world industrial production and BRCS industrial production. Similarly, surprise increases in economic policy uncertainty and global oil prices cause a reduction in world industrial production.

The magnitude of responses of Indian industrial production is comparable to the average response of Brazil, China, Russia, and South Africa.

A.3. Figures for Local Projections Estimation

FIGURE 9. LP Baseline Responses of the India Economy to One Standard Deviation Monetary Policy Shock

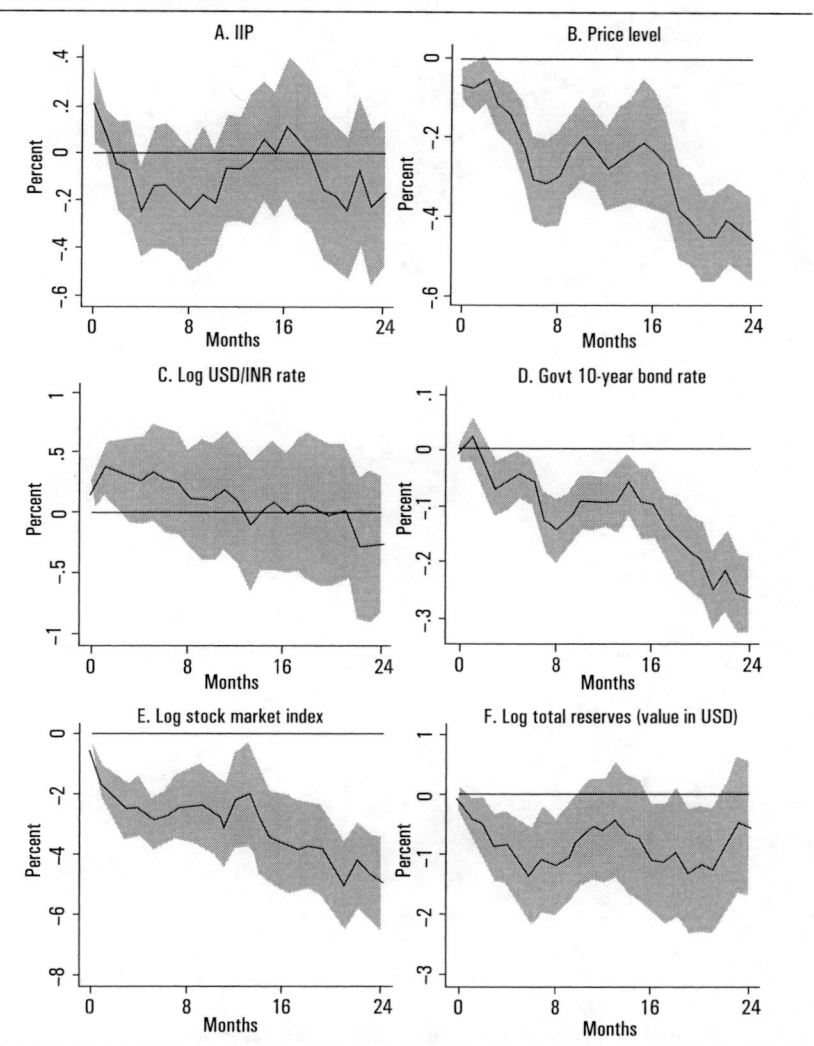

Source: Authors' calculations.
Notes: The response of monthly industrial production, CPI, US dollar/Indian rupee nominal exchange rate, 10-year government bond rate, stock market index, and total reserves (excluding gold) outstanding to a one standard deviation identified shock to the US monetary policy rate. The shaded areas in the figure represent one standard deviation confidence intervals. Standard errors are heteroskedasticity and autocorrelation robust Newey–West standard errors. The sources for data series are described in the text. Sample: April 1994–December 2017. See text for details.

FIGURE 10. LP Baseline Responses of the India Economy to One Standard Deviation Economic Policy Uncertainty Shock

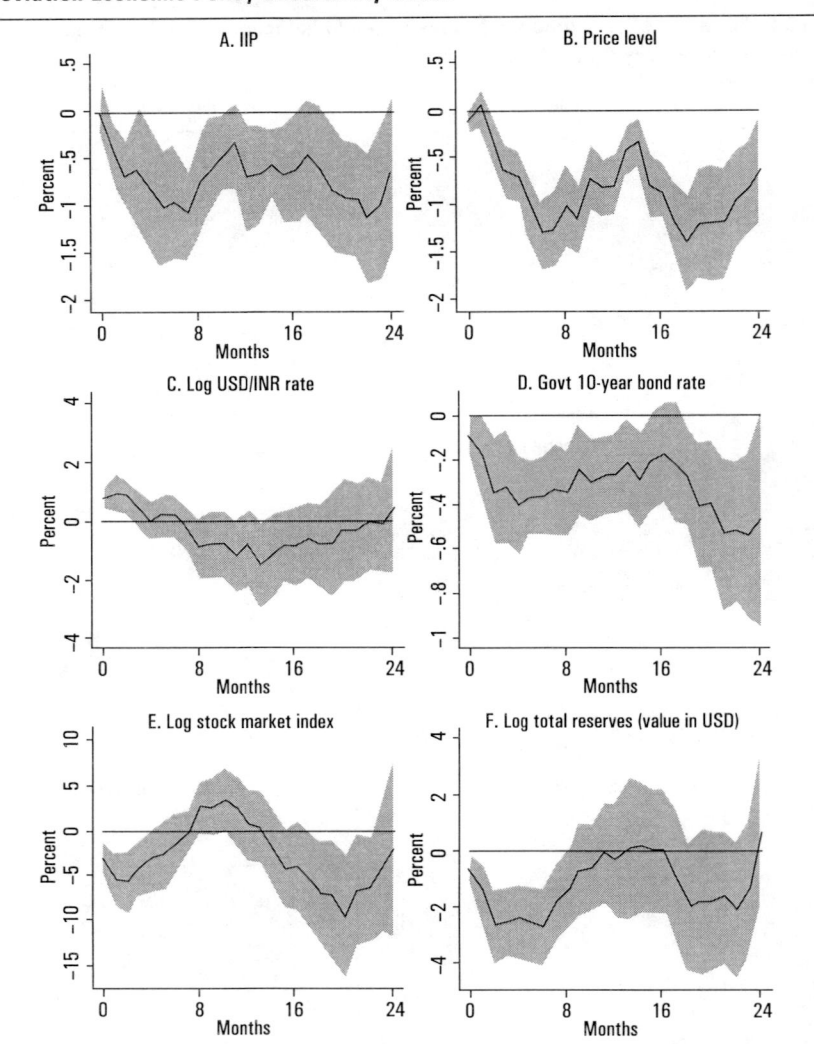

Source: Authors' calculations.
Notes: The response of monthly industrial production, CPI, US dollar/Indian rupee nominal exchange rate, 10-year government bond rate, stock market index, and total reserves (excluding gold) outstanding to a one standard deviation identified shock to global EPU. The shaded areas in the figure represent one standard deviation confidence intervals. Standard errors are heteroskedasticity and autocorrelation robust Newey–West standard errors. The sources for data series are described in the text. Sample: February 1997–December 2017. See text for details.

FIGURE 11. LP Baseline Responses of the India Economy to One Standard Deviation Movement in VIX

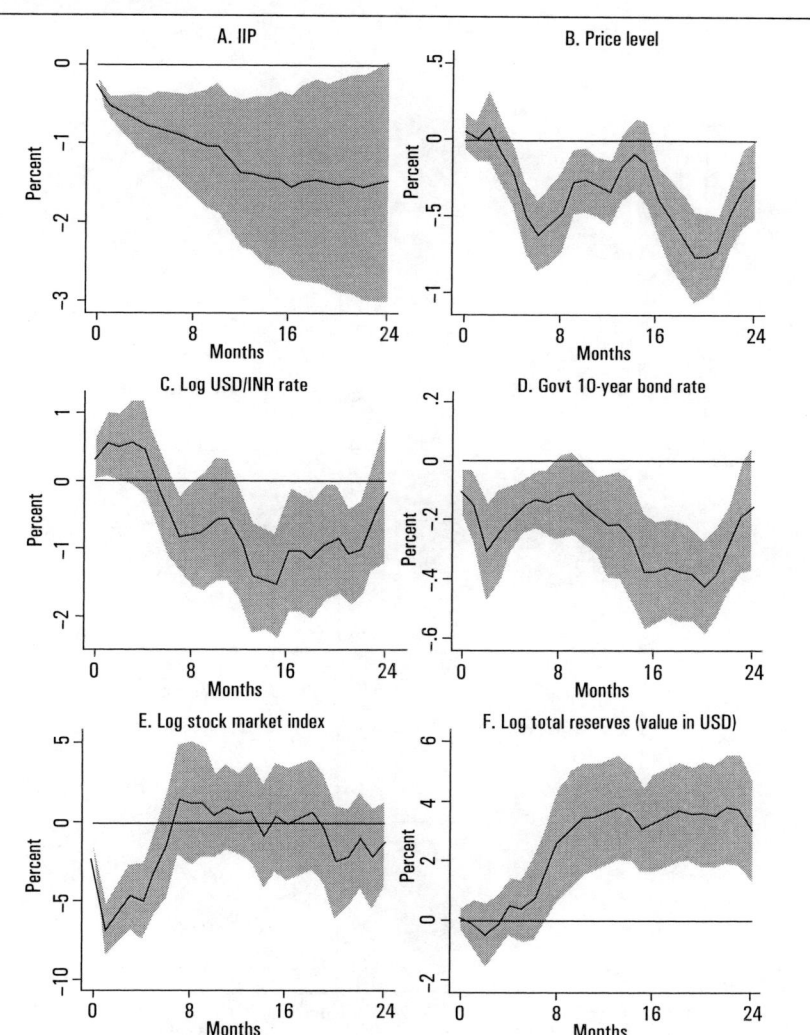

Source: Authors' calculations.
Notes: The response of monthly industrial production, CPI, US dollar/Indian rupee nominal exchange rate, 10-year government bond rate, stock market index, and total reserves (excluding gold) outstanding to a one standard deviation change in VIX. The shaded areas in the figure represent one standard deviation confidence intervals. Standard errors are heteroskedasticity and autocorrelation robust Newey–West standard errors. The sources for data series are described in the text. Sample: April 1994–December 2017. See text for details.

FIGURE 12. LP Baseline Responses of the India Economy to One Standard Deviation Geopolitical Risk Shock

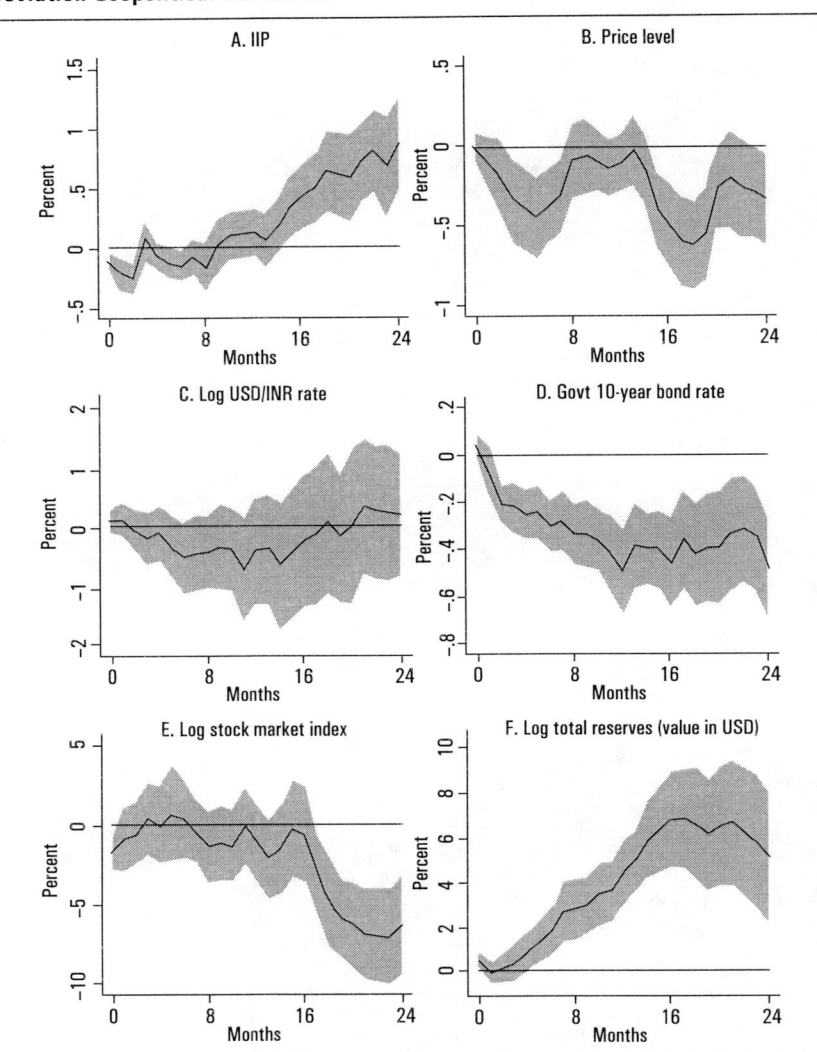

Source: Authors' calculations.
Notes: The response of monthly industrial production, CPI, US dollar/Indian rupee nominal exchange rate, 10-year government bond rate, stock market index, and total reserves (excluding gold) outstanding to a one standard deviation identified shock to GPR measure. The shaded areas in the figure represent one standard deviation confidence intervals. Standard errors are heteroskedasticity and autocorrelation robust Newey–West standard errors. The sources for data series are described in the text. Sample: April 1994–December 2017. See text for details.

FIGURE 13. LP Baseline Responses of the India Economy to One Standard Deviation Oil Supply Shock

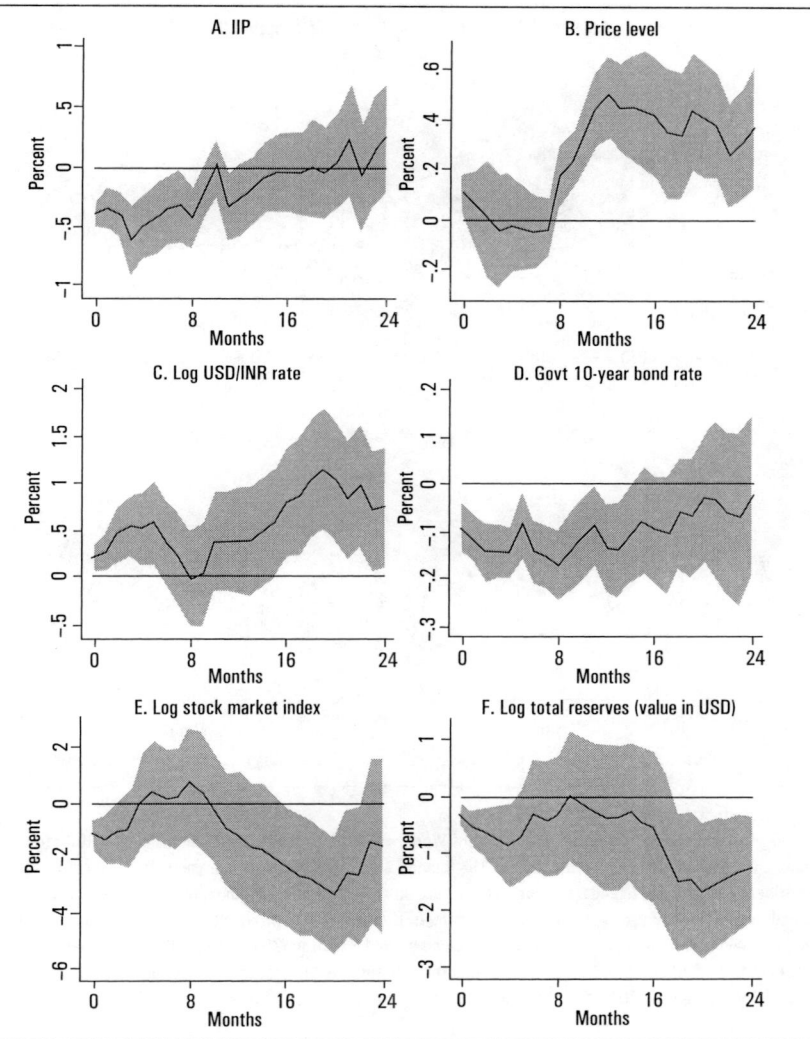

Source: Authors' calculations.
Notes: The response of monthly industrial production, CPI, US dollar/Indian rupee nominal exchange rate, 10-year government bond rate, stock market index, and total reserves (excluding gold) outstanding to a one standard deviation identified shock to oil supply. The shaded areas in the figure represent one standard deviation confidence intervals. Standard errors are heteroskedasticity and autocorrelation robust Newey–West standard errors. The sources for data series are described in the text. Sample: April 1994–December 2017. See text for details.

FIGURE 14. Industrial Production Responses for India, World and BRICS excluding India ("BRCS") to One Standard Deviation Shock

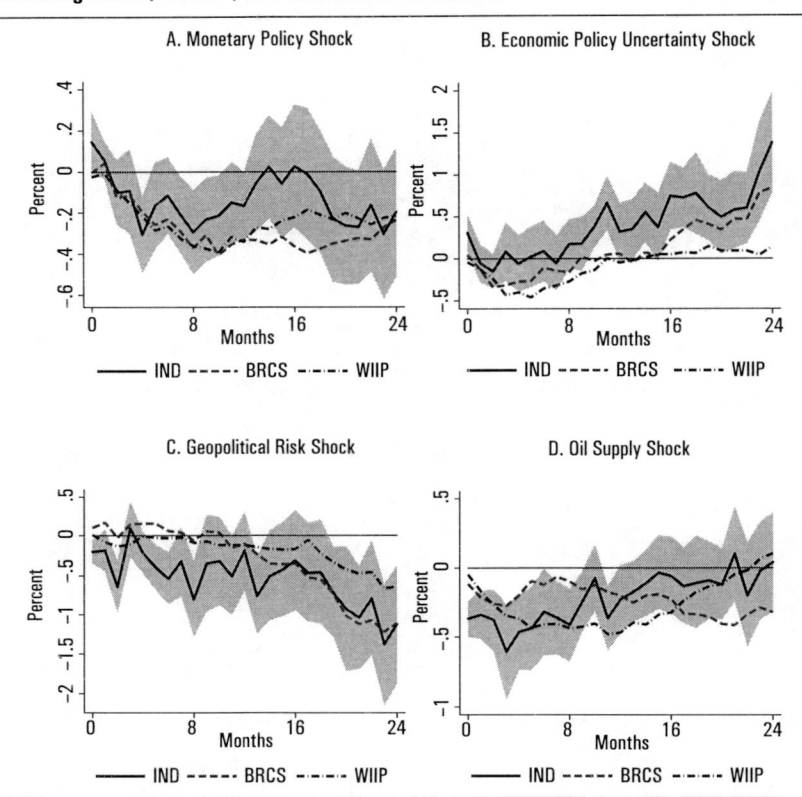

Source: Authors' calculations.
Notes: The response of industrial production of World (OECD + BRICS + Indonesia) region, BRCS region and India to a one standard deviation shock. The shaded areas in the figure represent one standard deviation confidence intervals. Standard errors are heteroskedasticity and autocorrelation robust Newey–West standard errors. WIIP is an extended version of the OECD's index of monthly industrial production in the OECD and six major other countries developed by Baumeister and Hamilton (2019). The BRICS industrial production data are from World Bank Global Economic Monitor. The sources for shocks are described in the text. Sample: April 1994–December 2017. See text for details.

A.4. Additional Figures: BRICS Country Comparisons and Sub-period Analysis

FIGURE 15. Industrial Production Responses for India, Brazil, China, Russia and South Africa to One Standard Deviation Shock

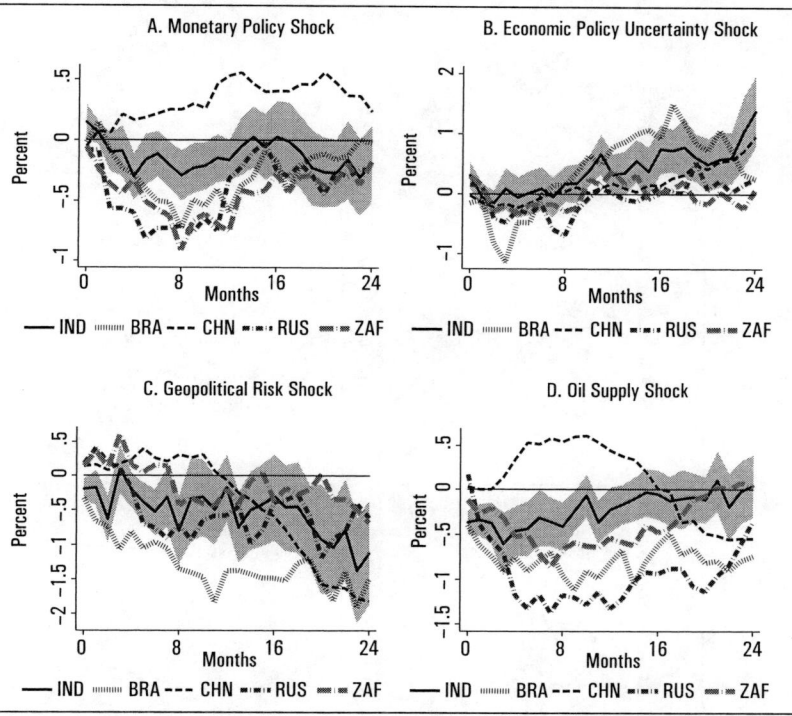

Source: Authors' calculations.
Notes: The response of industrial production of BRICS countries to a one standard deviation shock. The shaded areas in the figure represent one standard deviation confidence intervals. Standard errors are heteroskedasticity and autocorrelation robust Newey–West standard errors. The BRICS industrial production data are from the World Bank Global Economic Monitor. The sources for shocks are described in the text. Sample: April 1994–December 2017.

FIGURE 16. LP Sub-period Responses of the India Economy to One Standard Deviation Movement in Monetary Policy Shock

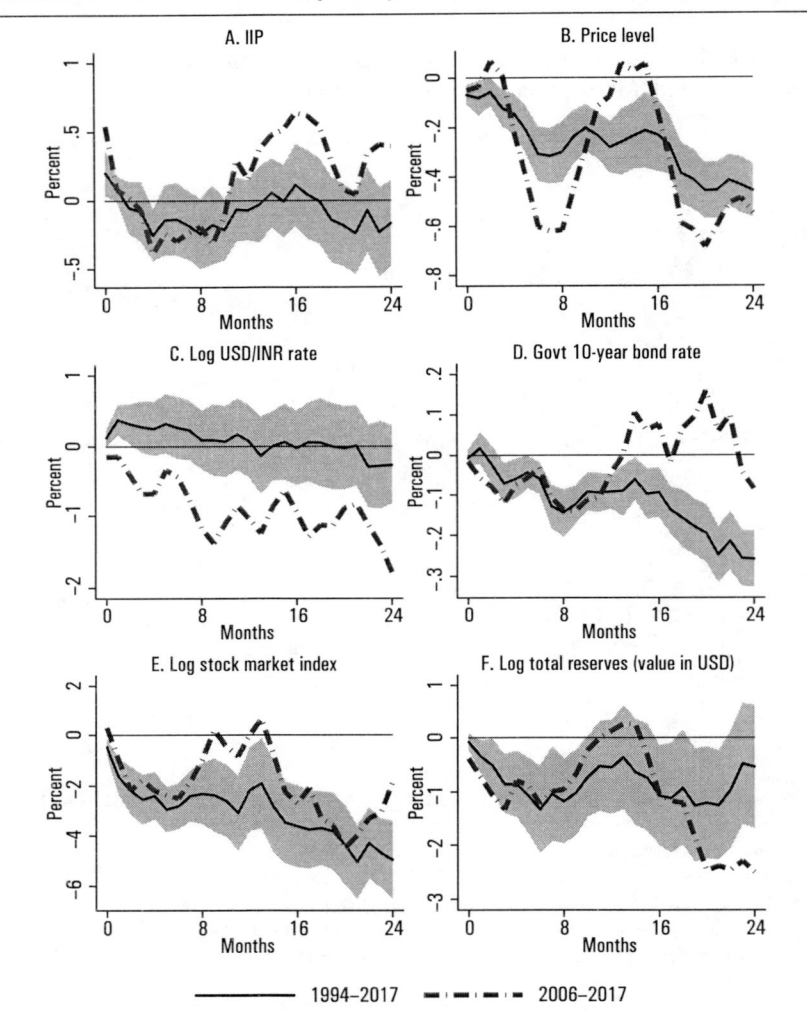

Source: Authors' calculations.
Notes: The response of monthly industrial production, CPI, US dollar/Indian rupee nominal exchange rate, 10-year government bond rate, stock market index, and total reserves (excluding gold) outstanding to a one standard deviation identified shock to US monetary policy rate. The shaded areas in the figure represent one standard deviation confidence intervals. Standard errors are heteroskedasticity and autocorrelation robust Newey–West standard errors. The sources for data series are described in the text. The solid line plots the estimated IRF for full sample from April 1994 to December 2017. The dashed line plots the estimated IRF for post-2005 sample from January 2006 to December 2017.

FIGURE 17. LP Sub-period Responses of the India Economy to One Standard Deviation Movement in Economic Policy Uncertainty Shock

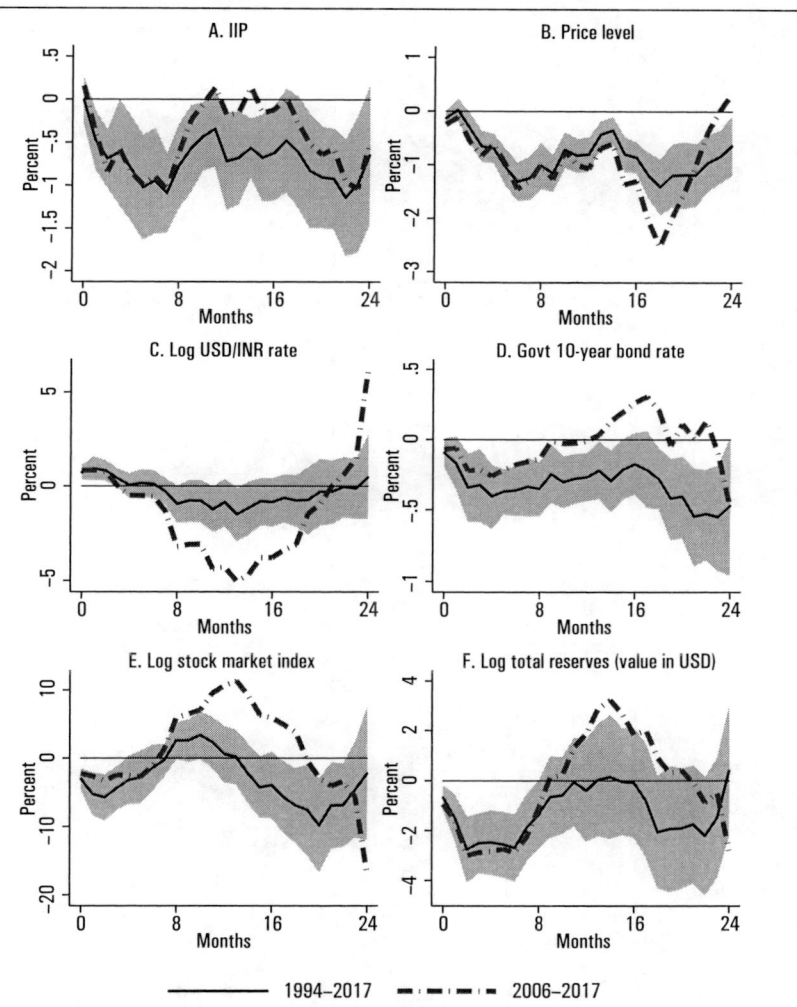

Source: Authors' calculations.
Notes: The response of monthly industrial production, CPI, US dollar/Indian rupee nominal exchange rate, 10-year government bond rate, stock market index, and total reserves (excluding gold) outstanding to a one standard deviation identified shock to global EPU. The shaded areas in the figure represent one standard deviation confidence intervals. Standard errors are heteroskedasticity and autocorrelation robust Newey–West standard errors. The sources for data series are described in the text. The solid line plots the estimated IRF for full sample from April 1994 to December 2017. The dashed line plots the estimated IRF for post-2005 sample from January 2006 to December 2017.

FIGURE 18. LP Sub-period Responses of the India Economy to One Standard Deviation Change in VIX

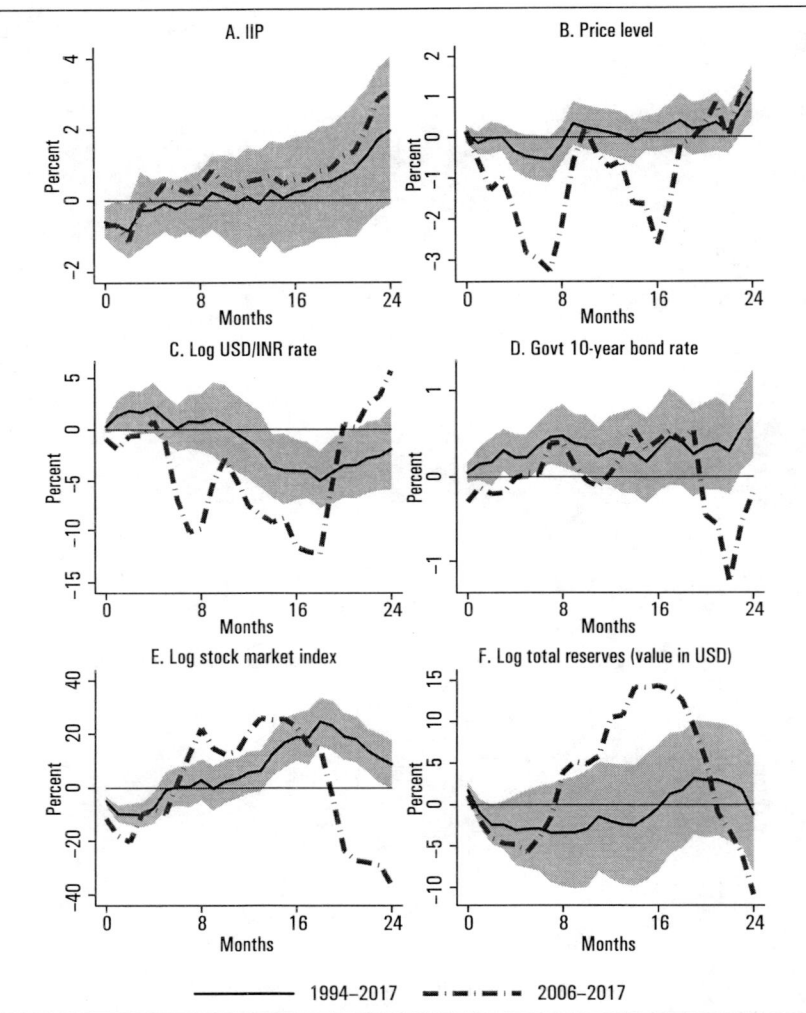

Source: Authors' calculations.
Notes: The response of monthly industrial production, CPI, US dollar/Indian rupee nominal exchange rate, 10-year government bond rate, stock market index, and total reserves (excluding gold) outstanding to a one standard deviation change in VIX. The shaded areas in the figure represent one standard deviation confidence intervals. Standard errors are heteroskedasticity and autocorrelation robust Newey–West standard errors. The sources for data series are described in the text. The solid line plots the estimated IRF for full sample from April 1994 to December 2017. The dashed line plots the estimated IRF for post 2005 sample from January 2006 to December 2017.

FIGURE 19. LP Sub-period Responses of the India Economy to One Standard Deviation Movement in Geopolitical Risk Shock

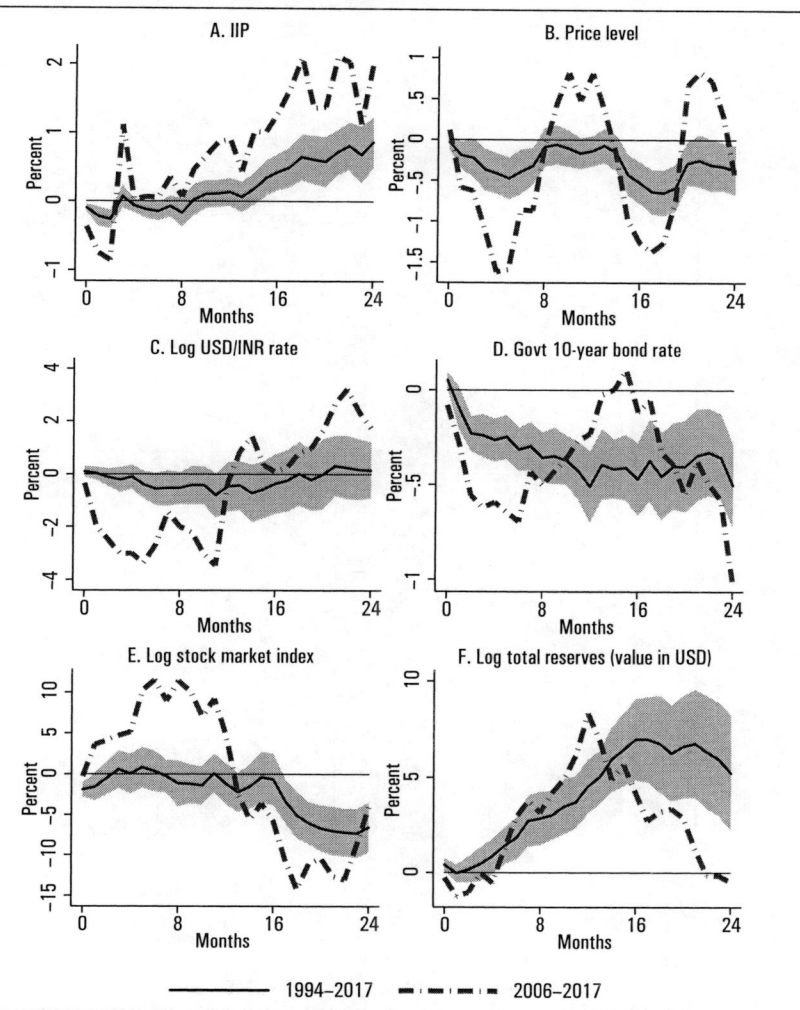

Source: Authors' calculations.
Notes: The response of monthly industrial production, CPI, US dollar/Indian rupee nominal exchange rate, 10-year government bond rate, stock market index, and total reserves (excluding gold) outstanding to a one standard deviation identified shock to GPR measure. The shaded areas in the figure represent one standard deviation confidence intervals. Standard errors are heteroskedasticity and autocorrelation robust Newey–West standard errors. The sources for data series are described in the text. The solid line plots the estimated IRF for full sample from April 1994 to December 2017. The dashed line plots the estimated IRF for post-2005 sample from January 2006 to December 2017.

FIGURE 20. LP Sub-period Responses of the India Economy to One Standard Deviation Movement in Oil Supply Shock

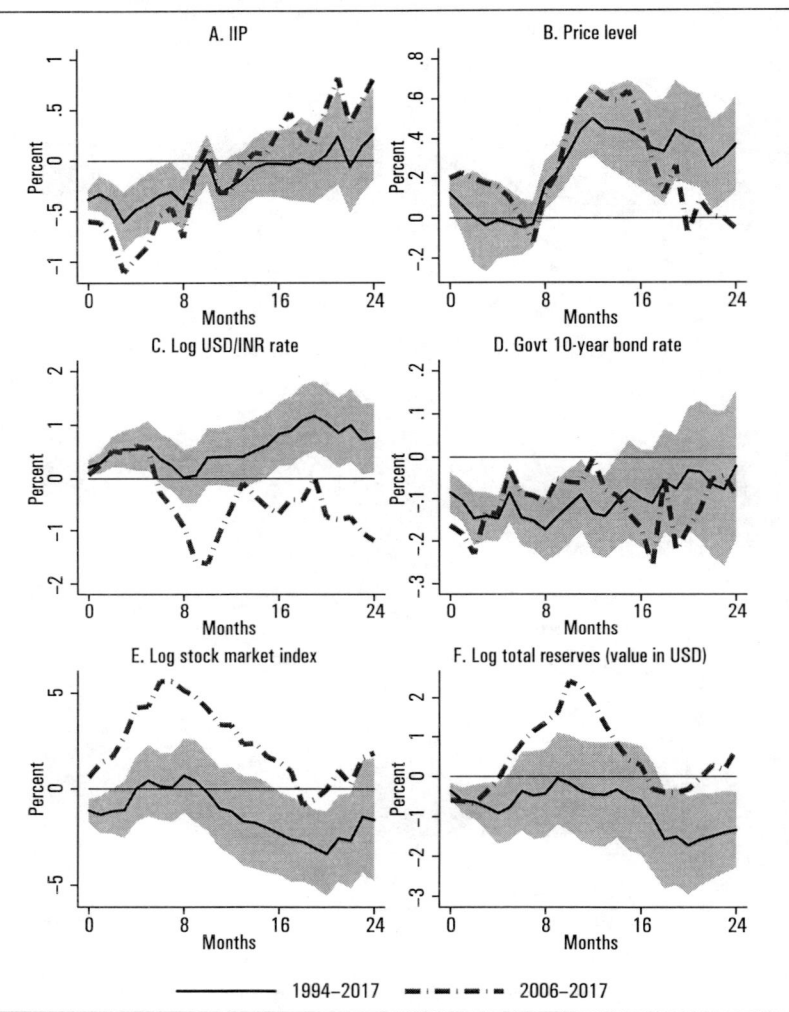

Source: Authors' calculations.
Notes: The response of monthly industrial production, CPI, US dollar/Indian rupee nominal exchange rate, 10-year government bond rate, stock market index, and total reserves (excluding gold) outstanding to a one standard deviation identified shock to oil supply. The shaded areas in the figure represent one standard deviation confidence intervals. Standard errors are heteroskedasticity and autocorrelation robust Newey–West standard errors. The sources for data series are described in the text. The solid line plots the estimated IRF for full sample from April 1994 to December 2017. The dashed line plots the estimated IRF for post-2005 sample from January 2006 to December 2017.

References

Baker, S.R., N. Bloom, and S.J. Davis. 2016. "Measuring Economic Policy Uncertainty." *The Quarterly Journal of Economics,* 131(4): 1593–1636.

Barnichon, R., and C. Brownlees. 2018. "Impulse Response Estimation by Smooth Local Projections." *Review of Economics and Statistics,* 101(3): 522–530.

Baumeister, C., and J.D. Hamilton. 2019. "Structural Interpretation of Vector Autoregressions with Incomplete Identification: Revisiting the Role of Oil Supply and Demand Shocks." *American Economic Review,* 109(5): 1873–1910.

Bhattarai, S., A. Chatterjee, and W.Y. Park. 2017. "Global Spillover Effects of US Uncertainty", *Working Paper.* Available at https://ideas.repec.org/a/eee/moneco/v114y2020icp71-89.html (accessed May 6, 2021).

Bruno, V., and H.S. Shin. 2015. "Capital Flows and the Risk-taking Channel of Monetary Policy." *Journal of Monetary Economics,* 71: 119–132.

Caballero, R.J., and G. Kamber. 2019. "On the Global Impact of Risk-off Shocks and Policy-put Frameworks", *NBER Working Paper No. 26031.* Cambridge, MA: National Bureau of Economic Research.

Caldara, D., and M. Iacoviello. 2018. "Measuring Geopolitical Risk", *FRB International Finance Discussion Paper No. 1222.* Washington, DC: Board of Governors of the Federal Reserve System (US).

Carney, M. 2016, June 30. "Uncertainty, the Economy and Policy", *Bank of England speech.* London: Bank of England.

Carriero, A., H. Mumtaz, K. Theodoridis, and A. Theophilopoulou. 2015. "The Impact of Uncertainty Shocks under Measurement Error: A Proxy SVAR Approach." *Journal of Money, Credit and Banking,* 47(6): 1223–1238.

Gertler, M., and P. Karadi. 2015. "Monetary Policy Surprises, Credit Costs, and Economic Activity." *American Economic Journal: Macroeconomics,* 7(1): 44–76.

Ghosh, T., S. Sahu, and S. Chattopadhyay. 2017. "Households' Inflation Expectations in India: Role of Economic Policy Uncertainty and Global Financial Uncertainty Spillover", *Technical Report.* Mumbai: Indira Gandhi Institute of Development Research.

Gilchrist, S., and E. Zakrajek. 2012. "Credit Spreads and Business Cycle Fluctuations." *American Economic Review,* 102(4): 1692–1720.

Jordà, O. 2005. "Estimation and Inference of Impulse Responses by Local Projections." *American Economic Review,* 95(1): 161–182.

Jordà, O., S.R. Singh, and A.M. Taylor. 2020. "The Long-run Effects of Monetary Policy", *NBER Working Paper No. 26666.* Cambridge, MA: National Bureau of Economic Research.

Kilian, L. 2009. "Not All Oil Price Shocks Are Alike: Disentangling Demand and Supply Shocks in the Crude Oil Market." *American Economic Review,* 99(3): 1053–1069.

Lakdawala, A. 2018. "The Growing Impact of US Monetary Policy on Emerging Financial Markets: Evidence from India", *Michigan State University Working Paper Series*. Available at https://ideas.repec.org/p/ris/msuecw/2018_009.html (accessed May 6, 2021).

———. 2019. "Decomposing the Effects of Monetary Policy Using an External Instruments SVAR." *Journal of Applied Econometrics,* 34(6): 934–950.

Mertens, K., and M.O. Ravn. 2013. "The Dynamic Effects of Personal and Corporate Income Tax Changes in the United States." *American Economic Review,* 103(4): 1212–1247.

Miranda-Agrippino, S., and H. Rey. 2018. "US Monetary Policy and the Global Financial Cycle", *NBER Working Paper No. 21722*. Cambridge, MA: National Bureau of Economic Research.

Mishra, P., P. Montiel, and R. Sengupta. 2016. "Monetary Transmission in Developing Countries: Evidence from India." In Chetan Ghate and Kenneth Kletzer (eds.), *Monetary Policy in India: A Modern Macroeconomic Perspective,* pp. 59–110. Chennai: Springer India.

Nakamura, E., and J. Steinsson. 2018. "High Frequency Identification of Monetary Non-neutrality." *The Quarterly Journal of Economics,* 133(3): 1283–1330.

Obstfeld, M. 2019. "Global Dimensions of US Monetary Policy", *Technical Report*, Conference on Monetary Policy Strategy, Tools, and Communication Practices at the Federal Reserve Bank of Chicago, June 4–5.

Plagborg-Møller, M., and C.K. Wolf. 2019. "Local Projections and VARs Estimate the Same Impulse Responses", *Working Paper*. Available at https://scholar.princeton.edu/mikkelpm/lp_var (accessed May 6, 2021).

Rajan, R. 2015. "Competitive Monetary Easing: Is It Yesterday Once More?" *Macroeconomics and Finance in Emerging Market Economies,* 8(1–2): 5–16.

Ramey, V.A. 2016. "Macroeconomic Shocks and Their Propagation." In John Taylor and Harald Uhlig (eds.), *Handbook of Macroeconomics*, Vol. 2, pp. 71–162. Amsterdam: Elsevier.

Ramey, V.A., and S. Zubairy. 2018. "Government Spending Multipliers in Good Times and in Bad: Evidence from US Historical Data." *Journal of Political Economy,* 126(2): 850–901.

Rey, H. 2015. "Dilemma Not Trilemma: The Global Financial Cycle and Monetary Policy Independence", *Technical Report*. Cambridge, MA: National Bureau of Economic Research.

Shin, H.S. 2014. "The Second Phase of Global Liquidity and Its Impact on Emerging Economies," In Kyuil Chung, Soyoung Kim, Hail Park, Changho Choi, and Hyun Song Shin (eds.), *Volatile Capital Flows in Korea*, pp. 247–257. New York: Palgrave Macmillan.

Stock, J.H., and M. Watson. 2002. "Disentangling the Channels of the 2007-09 Recession", *Brookings Papers on Economic Activity: Spring 2012*. Washington, DC: The Brookings Institution.

———. 2018. "Identification and Estimation of Dynamic Causal Effects in Macroeconomics Using External Instruments." *The Economic Journal,* 128(610): 917–948.

To view the entire video of this IPF session and the General Discussion that ended the session, please scan this QR code or use the following URL:
https://youtu.be/tiDdi9mvGYQ

Comments and Discussion*

Chair: **Anne Krueger**
SAIS, Johns Hopkins University

Mihir Desai
Harvard Business School

I really enjoyed this paper. I have a couple of fairly straightforward quick thoughts about this. Karthik mentioned different models for IPF papers, including the grand synthesis, which is a great model. What we have here is the other kind of IPF paper, which is the 'big facts' kind of paper. So this is an effort to bring together state-of-the-art methods, a big question which is the effect of foreign shocks, and hopefully some big facts. In that sense, the paper is incredibly simple and straightforward. There are four big shocks—US monetary policy, oil supply, economic policy uncertainty, and certainly geopolitical risk—and there is a whole bunch of outcome variables. There is underneath this a sense of having some real variables and then having some prices and some financial markets. I think the paper could benefit from being more distinct and thinking about real versus financial variables in a more concrete way. Then, there is up to a third of the variance in some of these outcome variables over 2–4-year horizons.

Some of my comments are a bit about tone and a bit about content. First, I think the paper might benefit from being reorganized more specifically around real versus financial variables. I would be more interested in some sense in diving more deeply into the elements of industrial production as opposed to doing the kitchen sink on a bunch of financial variables.

The way the paper is written is that the world and the BRCS pictures raise the question, "Are the shocks valid?" We should think about it as a relative measure of Indian vulnerability, which is not really done in the paper currently. I came in with a prior that actually the Indian economy is highly levered to the global economy. It is actually a lot more resilient, and hence the talk about how GDP of 8 percent is possible regardless of what the global economy is going to do.

---

*To preserve the sense of the discussions at the India Policy Forum, these discussants' comments reflect the views expressed at the IPF and do not necessarily take into account revisions to the conference version of the paper in response to these and other comments in preparing the final, revised version published in this volume. The original conference version of the paper is available at www.ncaer.org.

Second, in terms of these actual shocks, the pictures need to be highly annotated and elaborated. I want to know what is going on inside these pictures. As regards US monetary policy, I would blow it out, annotate it, and make sure that the periods being highlighted are actually the interesting periods. I would also want to know a lot more about the relationship between the outcome variables and the geopolitical risk and economic policy uncertainty variables.

The monetary policy uncertainty variable has been carefully constructed. It has futures prices and seems interesting when the innovations in the future prices are regressed against its lags and other possibilities. In contrast, I am skeptical about the economic policy uncertainty and geopolitical risk variables as they do not seem rigorous. I found the risk measure of the oil price shock to be amorphous and unsatisfying, and I am not sure what it is really trying to capture. I think the paper would benefit if this were explained more.

I would also like to see something about time trends and regimes in the paper. I think one of the underlying themes would be that we would become less exposed, and understanding that over time would be really helpful. It is also important to assess if the headline of the paper is substantiated by the underlying data. For instance, the shocks on monetary policy and oil do not necessarily seem large in terms of the magnitudes. In fact, I came away thinking that monetary policy innovations do not reflect a very significant change. I also did not see any large changes in prices and stock market levels, or at least changes I might have expected with a one standard deviation change in these measures. So, to me, the shocks delineated in the paper do not seem nearly as disruptive as one would have expected, and the recoveries have been quick. However, oil supply is an exception. I think the shock pertaining to oil supply on the industrial production is interesting and real but, otherwise, I am not sure if the shocks are big.

I would organize the paper in terms of the world, BRICS, and India, on monetary policy shocks. The big surprise to me is that the world is the most sensitive, the BRCS less so, and India even less so. It is not clear to me why that should be so. Second, these are baskets of countries, but India is a single country, which makes it even more surprising. Also, to cite one example on BRCS, Russia figures in the oil supply shock, which has left me puzzled. If we were to use these as benchmarks, as opposed to just validation that the shocks are real, then it needs to be done at the single-country level: I would want to see what Brazil looks like, what Malaysia looks like, what some of the other countries look like, and then we can talk about the relative resilience or fragility of the Indian economy. Similarly, on the oil supply shock, I would have expected India to be much more sensitive than other parts of the world, but that is not really showing up. We see some sensitivity but not in a significant way. Again, this is more surprising as these are bundles of countries, and not a single country.

So, altogether, I think the headline of the paper should be about the resilience of the Indian economy as opposed to the headline currently given. Finally, I confess that the variance decomposition is hard to interpret. I think, as the authors acknowledge in the paper, that is an extreme upper bound on what these effects are. So when we add them all up, more than a third of the variance at four-year horizons in industrial production is being accounted for by these four shocks. We know that when we do this analysis, they can easily add up to more than a 100 percent. So it is a bit of an unsatisfactory analysis as I, in some sense, reach the opposite conclusion. My instinct is to conclude more about the resilience of the Indian economy than its fragility. However, it is a really interesting paper.

Pami Dua
Delhi School of Economics

In the backdrop of increasing globalization, the susceptibility of the Indian economy to external shocks is expected to rise. In this context, the authors examine the impact of external shocks, including US monetary policy, oil supply, uncertainty in global economic policy, and geopolitical risks on the Indian economy. They analyze the dynamic causal effects of these shocks on the Indian economy, namely, output, inflation, foreign exchange reserves, exchange rate, government bonds, and stock prices. The estimation consists of an external instrument strategy with LP-IVs and SVAR-IVs (Gertler and Karadi 2015). The results highlight the impact of these global shocks on the economy and financial markets of India.

I congratulate the authors for a competent piece of work and for using state-of-the-art econometric techniques. I will divide my comments into three parts. The first has to do with the data that are used and construction of variables. The second part has to do with the estimation methodology, and lastly I will look at the results.

Comments on data and construction of variables

1. In the introduction section, the authors mention that since India accounts for a large share of total world oil consumption, a change in India's demand for oil is likely to be an important driver of the

global price of oil, and so on. The data published by the US Energy Information Administration suggests that India is a significant but small player relative to the USA, which has a 20 percent share, China, with a 13 percent share, and the European Union, with about 15 percent share in the oil market, while India imports only about 5 percent of the total oil production. Therefore, changes in India's demand for oil may not be major drivers of the global price of oil.
2. My second comment is on the construction of the economic policy uncertainty and geopolitical risk measures. Since these are based on news events, these are media perceptions about policy uncertainty and political risks, and it is not very clear whether these indices measure the true underlying uncertainties. The authors recognize that there is a measurement error, and they correct for that using dummy variables. Still, one needs to bear in mind that we are measuring perceptions, and I am not sure whether this correction of the measurement error fixes the problem. My suggestion is that one could try out an alternate measure of uncertainty as a robustness check of the main results.
3. The authors utilize the 10-year government bond rate as an indicator of monetary policy. Normally, studies use rates at the shorter end, such as the call money rate, three-month T-bill rates, or the repo rate, for the monetary policy indicator. The problem with using the 10-year bond is that it is possible to think of cases where the central bank's policy only moves the short end of the yield curve and, therefore, the 10-year bond will not be able to capture this. This might be a possible reason behind weak transmission of monetary policy in the results.

Comments on estimation

4. For constructing the monetary policy instrument, the authors follow Nakamura and Steinsson (2018) by using the first principal component of the change in contracts. However, Gürkaynak et al. (2005) show that monetary policy is captured by two separable dimensions: change in the federal funds rate and change in forward guidance. The Cragg–Donald (1997) test (presented in Gürkaynak's paper) suggests that the two factors should be included in the model. These two factors certainly explain more variation in the surprises than a single factor. It may be useful to see whether these two factors might improve results.

5. The authors utilize an HP filter, but it is known that the filter may create spurious cycles and, therefore, the robustness of results may be checked using alternate filters.
6. The identification strategy for the SVAR is not described in the paper. The authors may also look into the issue of puzzles emerging from the results. The authors use the Cholesky decomposition, and what should be noted are the drawbacks from this decomposition. In particular, these results are order dependent.

Comments on results

7. There is a positive impact of a monetary policy shock on the Indian IIP at t = 0 and then it is negative in the long run, while for other countries it is positive. It would be interesting to understand why the Indian IIP displays this reversal.
8. If we want to study the impact of shocks on the Indian economy, then one could use benchmarks like the episodes of slowdowns or recessions. One can then measure the impact of these shocks against that of these slowdown episodes. One may also utilize the US business cycle/growth rate cycle for this purpose. This will provide a better idea of the impact of the shocks.
9. The results indicate a positive impact of the shocks on the stock and bond markets. However, stock markets do not typically show sensitivity to any shocks in the long run. In the near or medium term, there may be an impact, but it is difficult to explain the sensitivity in the long run for stock markets. As regards bond markets, one can argue that monetary policy can have an effect. A minor point about the bond market is to consider whether the bonds are in the primary or secondary markets. This might also make a difference to the analysis.

References

Gertler, Mark, and Peter Karadi. 2015. "Monetary Policy Surprises, Credit Costs, and Economic Activity." *American Economic Journal: Macroeconomics,* 7(1): 44–76.

Gürkaynak, Refet S., Brian Sack, and Eric Swanson. 2005. "The Sensitivity of Long-term Interest Rates to Economic News: Evidence and Implications for Macroeconomic Models." *American Economic Review*, 95(1): 425–436.

Nakamura, Emi, and Jón Steinsson. 2018. "High-frequency Identification of Monetary Non-neutrality: The Information Effect." *The Quarterly Journal of Economics*, 133(3): 1283–1330.

General Discussion

Anne Krueger, the chairperson, asked whether the effect of domestic shocks would be larger or smaller in an open economy as opposed to a closed economy. She thought that the monsoons were probably the source of the largest domestic shocks, but cyclones had also caused large damage in previous years. How should policymakers respond to reduce output variability in such situations? Would that involve a greater focus on irrigation? She also noted that the government had often acted to stabilize oil prices, but those actions often involved granting greater subsidies. Hence, the economic impact involved both a price effect and the impact of a greater fiscal deficit.

Rajeswari Sengupta focused on the effect of a tightening of monetary policy originating in the US. It would involve a capital outflow from emerging markets, including India, to the US and a depreciation of the rupee. She thought that the role of capital flows as the primary transmission mechanism was missing from the SVAR model. She also noted that the capital outflow and exchange rate depreciation would lead the RBI to increase the interest rate; hence, the repo rate should also be included in the model. Second, she agreed with Pami Dua that the persistence of the effect on financial markets was surprising, given the evidence of a very quick effect on bond and equity markets. Finally, she was concerned that the measure of reserve changes may be affected by valuation changes. She preferred a focus on the RBI's interventions in the exchange market.

Rakesh Mohan pointed to the surprising result that India's economy was more resilient to shocks than the other BRICS countries. He thought it would be interesting to explore further the reasons for that result. Could it be related to measures of capital market or trade openness? He also agreed with Rajeswari Sengupta about the need to incorporate measures of domestic policy responses.

Devesh Kapur argued that the analysis should include the impact of global agricultural prices. Indian farmers gained substantially from the surge in prices between 2006 and 2012. Conversely, they have been very badly hit by the fall in prices in recent years.

Karthik Muralidharan asked if the model could address the question of whether the impacts of shocks were symmetric. He was also concerned that many would draw the conclusion that vulnerability against foreign shocks could best be achieved by not being integrated with the world economy, but that would come at the cost of not benefiting from the upside gains of integration.

Abhijit Banerjee noted that large portions of the Indian economy are largely unconnected to the global economy. A counter-example is provided by oil prices. He suggested that the government often responded to oil price shocks by changing the composition of government expenditures rather than changing the overall budget balance. In effect, the government was sacrificing long-term investment to achieve short-run stability.

Banerjee and Montek Singh Ahluwalia were both concerned about the extent to which the model's coefficients already embodied typical or average policy responses. Thus, they thought it would be difficult to use the model to infer superior policy actions.

Rajnish Mehra expressed a desire to introduce an element of welfare analysis in evaluating the fluctuations in output and the costs of countervailing policy actions. A cost–benefit analysis would be useful to evaluate the net gains of hedging against shocks.

The session video, the paper, and all presentations for this IPF session are hyperlinked on the IPF program available on the NCAER website by scanning this QR code or going to the URL:
https://www.ncaer.org/IPF2019/Agenda/Agenda_IPF_2019.pdf

R. NAGARAJ*
Indira Gandhi Institute of Development Research

AMEY SAPRE†
National Institute of Public Finance and Policy

RAJESWARI SENGUPTA‡
Indira Gandhi Institute of Development Research

Four Years After the Base-Year Revision: Taking Stock of the Debate Surrounding India's National Accounts Estimates§

ABSTRACT In 2015, with the release of the 2011–12 base-year GDP series, the Central Statistics Office (CSO) substantially revised the way GDP is calculated in India. According to the new series, India is the fastest growing large economy in the world. However, other trusted measures of the state of the economy convey a discordant picture. This discrepancy has led to an active debate over the last few years. Numerous studies by academic scholars have identified, analyzed, and documented the problems with the kind of data used in the new series as well as with the specific methodologies applied. The criticisms have cast persistent doubts on the new GDP series and have dented the credibility of India's National Accounts Statistics. The debate seems at an impasse. In this paper, we provide a comprehensive summary of the issues surrounding the new GDP series as highlighted by academic experts and outline recommendations for a possible way forward to resolve India's GDP data crisis.

Keywords: GDP Measurement, National Accounts Statistics, National Income, Manufacturing, Gross Value Added, Base-Year Revision

JEL Classification: E01, E11

---

* nag@igidr.ac.in
† amey.sapre@nipfp.org.in
‡ rajeswari@igidr.ac.in
§ The authors are thankful to Pramod Sinha for contributing to the discussion and offering suggestions.

1. Introduction

Gross domestic product or GDP is one of the most important macroeconomic indicators of the level of economic activity in the country.[1] It drives economic policies, is a crucial input in the fiscal calculations of the government, affects investor confidence, and conveys a comprehensive picture about the health of the economy to the rest of the world. In India, while policy outcomes and the performance of the economy are debated extensively using GDP growth numbers, evaluation of the quality of data and assessment of the soundness of the methodology used for making the GDP estimates do not get as much attention. The last few years have been an exception in this regard. In January 2015, the Central Statistics Office (CSO) released the 2011–12 base-year series of the National Accounts Statistics (NAS) to replace the earlier 2004–05 series.[2] Since then, issues in the measurement of GDP have taken center stage in academic and policy debates.

The 2011–12 series, apart from changing the base year of the NAS, also introduced several methodological changes in GDP computation. These changes were done primarily to align the methods with the most recent international guidelines of the United Nations System of National Accounts (UNSNA), 2008 (SNA 2008). New data sources, particularly for the private corporate sector (PCS, which includes organized manufacturing as well as service sector enterprises), were also introduced. As a result of these changes, the growth rates at the aggregate level, as well as for some sectors, changed significantly under the 2011–12 series as compared to the 2004–2005 series, particularly for the years for which data were available in both the series.

In a paper presented at the 2016 India Policy Forum, Nagaraj and Srinivasan (2017) highlighted some of the core issues in the measurement of the 2011–12 series. They summarized the arguments made in studies published after the release of the NAS in 2015. According to Nagaraj and Srinivasan (2017), while a base-year revision usually leads to a marginal rise in the absolute size

---

1. GDP, or gross value added (GVA), is a measure of goods and services produced in an economy in a year, net of intermediate inputs. Broadly speaking, it is a statistical construct based on innumerable estimations of value addition taking place in an economy. GDP is estimated following the United Nations System of National Accounts (UNSNA)—a global template, revised periodically to account for evolving economic activities.

2. GDP is re-based regularly to account for changing production structure, relative prices, and better recording of economic activities. Crucially, the re-basing also allows for introducing newer methodologies and improved databases. Such changes often expand the absolute GDP size because we are able to more accurately capture output. However, annual growth rates usually do not vary too much with re-basing of GDP, implying that the underlying pace of economic expansion has remained the same.

FIGURE 1. Nominal and Real Growth Rates of GDP at Factor Cost (GDPfc) and GVA at Basic Prices (GVAbp) under the Old and New Series for Comparable Years

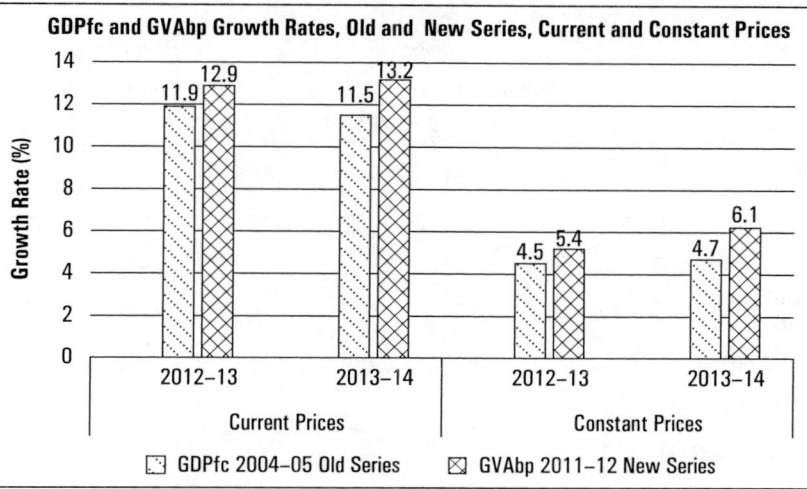

Source: CSO (2014), CSO (2015b).

of the economy owing to better representation, it does not cause a big change in the annual growth rates of GDP estimates. However, the latest base-year revision significantly changed growth rates. It resulted in a 2.3 percentage point *shrinkage* of the absolute size of GDP in the base year (2011–12) and *higher* aggregate GDP growth rates in the subsequent years.

Since the new NAS was released, the biggest doubt has been about the increase in GDP growth rates for the overlapping years for which data on both old and new NAS were available. This led to suspicion about the overestimation of growth rates for the subsequent years. Changes took place in both real and nominal GDP growth rates, as shown in Figure 1.

Changes in the sectoral real growth rates are presented in Table 1 for the overlapping set of years before the 2004–05 series was discontinued. For instance, the changes in the manufacturing sector led to a revision in growth rates from 1.14 percent to 5.45 percent in 2012–13, and from –0.71 percent to 4.9 percent in 2013–14. Similarly, growth rates for the trade, hotels, and transport sector were significantly revised from 3.02 percent to 6.51 percent for 2013–14 as compared to the 2004–05 series. The revision also altered the institutional composition of India's GDP. In particular, the size of PCS was enlarged, while the unorganized/informal/household (HH) sector got contracted, with the share of the public sector remaining the same.

The methodological changes responsible for these comprehensive revisions have since then been questioned by a number of academic experts and continue to capture the attention of mainstream media, both domestic and

TABLE 1. Growth Rates of GDP at Factor Cost (2004–05 Series) and GVA at Basic Prices (2011–12 Series), Constant Prices for Comparable Years

Sector	2004–05 Series Constant Prices GDP at Factor Cost			2011–12 Series Constant Prices GVA at Basic Prices		
	2011–12	2012–13	2013–14	2011–12	2012–13	2013–14
Agriculture, forestry, and fishing	5.02	1.42	4.71	6.4	1.49	5.57
Mining and quarrying	0.1	−2.16	−1.38	−17.53	0.60	0.19
Manufacturing	7.41	1.14	−0.71	3.13	5.45	4.97
Electricity, gas, and water supply	8.38	2.26	5.92	8.56	2.66	4.16
Construction	10.8	1.11	1.64	13.14	0.35	2.66
Trade, hotels, transport, storage, and communication	4.33	5.07	3.02	6.36	9.77	6.51
Financing, insurance, real estate, and business services	11.35	10.92	12.87	4.49	9.74	11.15
Community, social and, personal services	4.9	5.31	5.55	7.28	4.26	3.85
Total	**6.69**	**4.47**	**4.74**	**5.22**	**5.42**	**6.05**

Source: CSO (2014), CSO (2015b).

international. Over the last four years, a large number of analytical studies have identified and analyzed specific problems in the data and methodology used in the 2011–12 GDP series, over and above those highlighted by Nagaraj and Srinivasan (2017). The common question in these studies has been about the extent to which the revised growth rates paint a true picture of the economy as opposed to being an outcome of problems in the underlying methodology and data used for estimation.

In addition, new controversies related to the 2011–12 series have cropped up in recent times such as: (a) release of two contradictory back series that paint diametrically opposite pictures of the historical performance of the economy, (b) release of first revised estimates for 2016–17, which showed a staggering 8.2 percent growth rate in the year of demonetization when more than 80 percent of the cash in the economy was removed from circulation overnight, dealing a severe blow to the unorganized segment of the population, and (c) release of an NSS service sector survey report (74th Round) in May 2019, which showed several gaps in the sample of firms used for GDP estimation by the CSO.

Despite growing skepticism and the wide range of questions raised by the academic community following the release of the new series, the CSO has defended the series (see, for instance, CSO 2015e; 2018a) citing reasons such as adoption of international best practices, improvements in methods of estimation, and wider coverage of the economy through new datasets.

The findings of the research studies put out in the public domain since June 2016 have raised new questions about the quality of the underlying data sources used in computing the new GDP series, the accuracy of the methods applied, and hence about the credibility of the estimates. It is perhaps time to take stock of all the issues that have been raised in various research studies and explore plausible solutions to the problem. That is what we aim to achieve in this paper.

We approach the issue in a two-step manner. First, we describe the basic changes brought about in the size and composition of various sectors by the new GDP series. Some of these issues were also discussed by Nagaraj and Srinivasan (2017) and we take off from where they had left. We attempt to understand the repercussions of these changes on the sectoral as well as aggregate GDP growth rates. We conclude that a majority of the changes affect the estimates for the private corporate sector, or PCS.[3]

Next, we undertake an examination of the changes in data and methodology used to compute the PCS estimates and discuss the problems therein. Most of these problems seem to stem from the usage of the MCA21 database. In particular, there are three main issues, all of which are related to the way sampling is done by the CSO for estimating the output of the PCS: (a) Which companies are included in the sample? (b) How can we deal with companies that are outside the sample but form a part of the larger universe of companies? (c) How can we deal with companies that cannot be sampled but are included in the PCS? It appears that there are problems in each of these aspects of sampling and we present a detailed discussion of these issues. In addition, we also analyze the problems in GDP growth estimation arising from deflator-related issues, problems in the regional accounts, and issues with the release of two contradictory back series.

We base our analysis largely on the findings of academic experts who have written extensively on these problems. We also take stock of the findings of different committee reports that have dealt with various issues regarding GDP estimation (CSO 2015c; 2015d). Our goal here is to present a

---

3. The PCS includes companies (both financial and non-financial) from the manufacturing and services sectors. MCA21 is an e-Governance initiative of Ministry of Corporate Affairs (MCA), Government of India, that enables secure access to MCA services for corporate entities, professionals and Indian citizens. The MCA21 application is designed to automate processes related to the proactive enforcement and compliance of the legal requirements under the Companies Act, 1956, New Companies Act, 2013 and Limited Liability Partnership Act, 2008.

comprehensive summary of major issues in the new NAS in order to provide deeper insights into the GDP debate, assess the severity of the problem at hand, and discuss a way forward.

The rest of the paper is organized as follows. In Section 2, we discuss the changes in the shares of various sectors and in the institutional composition of GDP under the new series. In Section 3, we present a detailed analysis of the problems affecting the estimates of the PCS. In Section 4, we discuss issues related to the deflators. In Sections 5 and 6, we talk about the issues with the estimation of the regional accounts and issues with the release of the two back series, respectively. Finally, in Section 7, we summarize the main points and provide recommendations for the way forward.

2. Size, Structure and Evaluation of the Economy as Seen through the NAS

The new NAS has brought about many changes that have altered our image (or understanding) of the structure of the economy. We describe some of the prominent changes with regard to the institutional and sectoral composition of GDP as follows.

1. In terms of institutions, the share of the PCS increased by about 11–12 percentage points of GDP (as of 2011–12), with a corresponding decline in the share of the HH/unorganized sector. This was mostly on account of shifting of the proprietary/partnership enterprises from the HH sector to the PCS under a new category, quasi corporations (or QCs), defined as those maintaining accounts. The share of the public sector—defined as general government, public financial enterprises, and public non-financial enterprises—in GDP remained the same across the old and new NAS. This is shown in Figure 2.
2. Within the PCS, the share of private financial enterprises in GDP remained roughly the same in the new NAS, whereas the share of non-financial PCS went up significantly from 21.1 percent to 31.9 percent (Figure 3).[4]

---

4. The PCS constituted 34–35 percent of GDP in 2015–16. Financial PCS accounts for 2–3 percent of GDP. Non-financial PCS consists of: (a) public limited companies (13.4%), (b) private limited companies (11.9%), and (c) QCs (9.6%; their GDP shares are mentioned in parentheses). Roughly speaking, public limited companies represent larger companies, private limited companies are smaller companies, representing medium-sized enterprises, and QCs are smaller enterprises, mostly partnership and proprietary concerns.

FIGURE 2. GDP Shares by Institutional Sector for Base Year 2011–12 in Old and New Series

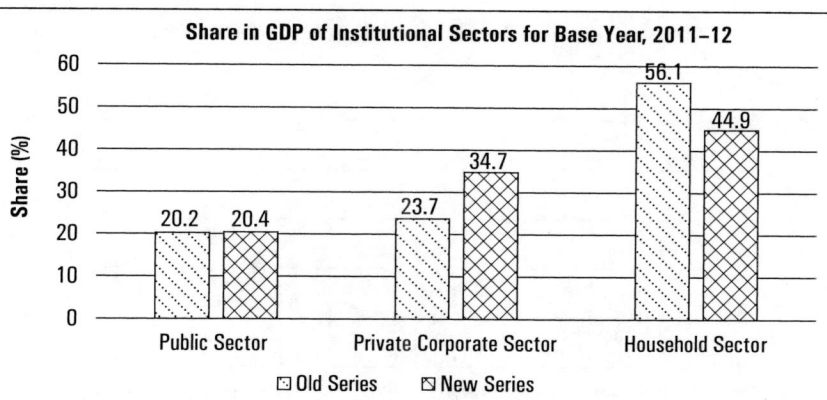

Source: CSO (2014), CSO (2015b).

FIGURE 3. GDP Shares of Sub-sectors of PCS for Base Year 2011–12 in Old and New Series

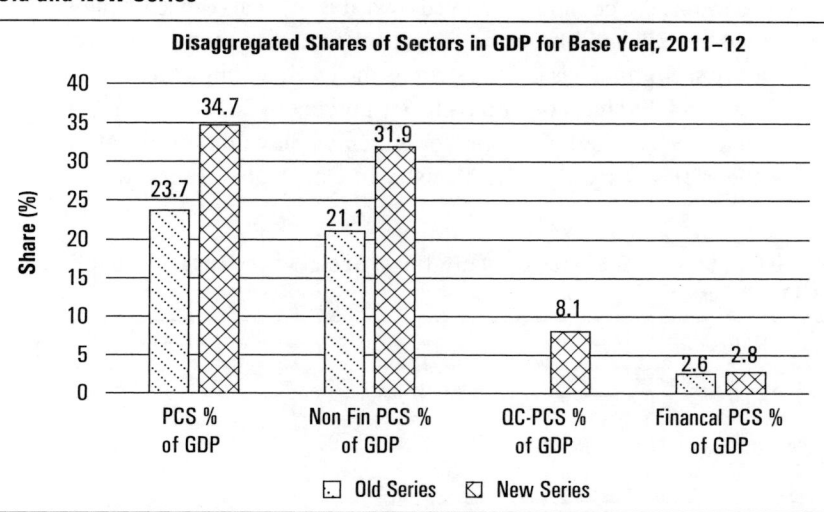

Source: CSO (2014), CSO (2015b).
Note: PCS = Private Corporate Sector; Non-Fin = Non-financial; QC = Quasi corporations.

3. In terms of output sectors or industries, in 2011–12, the share in GDP of industry (consisting of mining, manufacturing, electricity, gas and water, and construction) went up, somewhat with a corresponding decline in the share of the services sector. The increase in industry's share was mainly on account of manufacturing (Figure 4).

FIGURE 4. Sectoral Composition of GDP for Base Year 2011–12 in Old and New Series

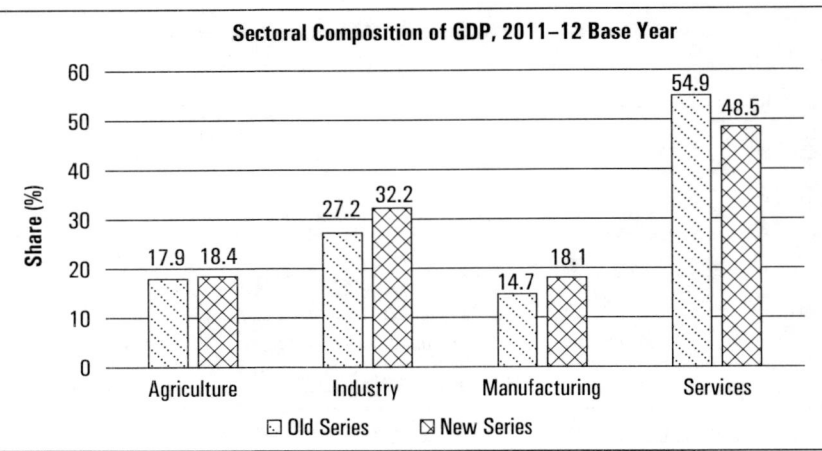

Source: CSO (2014), CSO (2015b).

4. How has the economy evolved over the six years since the new NAS was introduced? In terms of institutions, as shown in Figure 5, the only sector that has gained share is the PCS, within which the share of QCs in GDP has gone up from 8.1 percent in 2011–12 to 9.6 percent in 2015–16, the latest year for which we have the information from the RBI's analysis of the Ministry of Corporate Affairs (MCA) data.

FIGURE 5. GVA Shares by Institutional Sectors over Time, Current Prices, 2011–12 Series

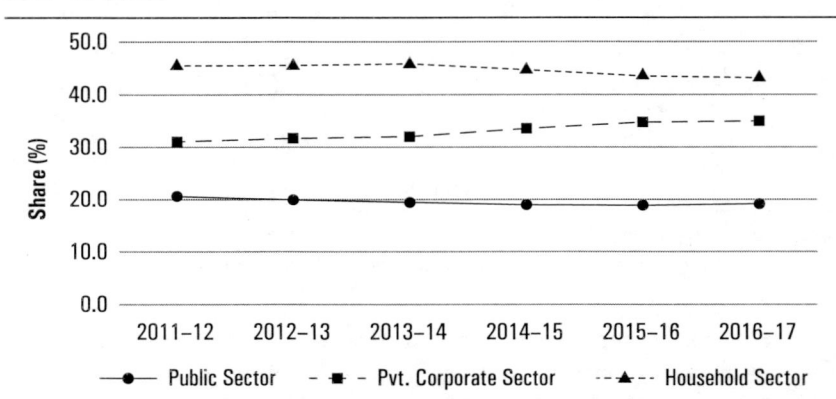

Source: CSO (2018c).

FIGURE 6. GVA Shares by Major Sectors over Time, Constant Prices, 2011–12 Series

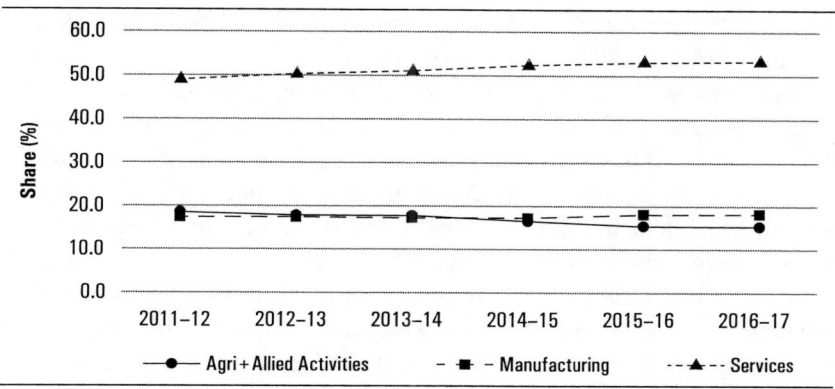

Source: CSO (2018c).

In terms of output, as shown in Figure 6, the shares of agriculture and industry have declined slightly, with a compensating rise in the share of the services sector.

The two big changes introduced in the new NAS are as follows:

1. Shifting the QCs from the HH sector to the PCS; and
2. Use of a new database (MCA21) to compute GVA estimates for the PCS.

If the changes in the shares of sectors and institutions in the aggregate output in the new NAS are an outcome of a mere reshuffling of economic activities, then these should not affect aggregate growth rates. For example, the shifting of QCs to PCS should not increase the aggregate GDP growth rates, given that QCs were already accounted for in the old NAS as part of the HH sector. Yet as we see from Table 1, in the overlapping years for which data on both the old and new NAS are available, the aggregate GDP growth rates were revised upwards in the new series. In terms of coverage, no new sector was captured by the new NAS either, which could have potentially explained the increase in growth rates.

The very fact that the new series reported significantly higher growth rates at the aggregate level for the overlapping years points to the possibility that the changes in methodology and data played a role. Since there has been no substantial change in the methodology used to measure GVA of the public sector and the HH sector, it may be concluded that the increase in the growth rate of aggregate GDP is mainly due to changes in the PCS, primarily the non-financial PCS since the financial PCS constitutes a small fraction of overall GDP (see Footnote 4).

As shown above, the PCS consists of non-financial companies, financial companies and QCs. Net of QCs and financial companies, the size of the PCS in the new GDP series is higher by 2.9 percent of GDP. This can be attributed to the changes in methodology and introduction of the MCA21 database. The main question here is: Is it a case of more comprehensive capture of the contribution of the PCS, or does it represent an over-estimation?

A number of academic experts have identified and documented multiple problems with the MCA21 database, which under some scenarios might lead to over-estimation of the growth rate of the PCS and of the aggregate GDP growth rate, given the high share of the PCS in overall GDP. Moreover, given the infirmities in the estimation of output of QCs under the new NAS, shifting these entities to the PCS could have potentially contributed to boosting the level and growth rate of PCS GVA and hence aggregate GDP. We discuss these problems in detail in the next section.

3. Issues with Estimates of PCS

The PCS, especially the manufacturing sector, continues to be at the heart of the GDP measurement debate. Since Nagaraj and Srinivasan (2017), a number of new issues concerning the PCS have come up in public debates and these have been chronicled by several academic scholars over the last few years. The bulk of the problem in estimation seems to stem from the shift to the MCA21 database from the Annual Survey of Industries (ASI) database. In what follows we discuss three major issues with regard to the PCS estimates that have surfaced after the introduction of the MCA21 database. These issues, listed below, are primarily related to the manner in which sampling is done by the CSO for the PCS–GVA estimation:

1. What companies are included in the sample?
2. What method is used to account for companies not in the sample but in the larger universe of all companies?
3. What about the companies that cannot be sampled but are included in the PCS?

Below we discuss these issues in detail. In addition, we also analyze the validity of the rationale behind the shift from ASI to the MCA21 database, issues of misclassification of companies in the PCS, and the problems associated with the shift from an "establishment" to an "enterprise" approach.

3.1. Sample of Companies Used for Estimation

Companies belonging to the PCS, that is, manufacturing as well as services sector companies, file their financial returns in the MCA21 database but not all companies file in every year. The set of companies that file returns at least once in three years is called an "active" set.[5] This is regarded by the CSO as the "universe" of companies for estimating the GVA of the PCS. Within the "active" set, only a fraction of the companies file returns in any given year. For the GVA estimation of any given year, the CSO first considers those companies that have filed their returns in that specific year. This is the "filing" set which constitutes the sample for that year.[6] They then use a blow-up factor to estimate the GVA of the non-filing, active companies.

The first big question with regard to sampling is whether the companies in the sample considered by the CSO are working companies. It would be problematic if the "filing" set consisted of say shell companies that engage in fictitious transactions for the purpose of evading laws and falsely report their returns. The GVA estimates computed on the basis of the returns of these companies are likely to be erroneous. In this context, two key issues are worth looking into. We discuss them sequentially.

3.1.1. DOUBTS ABOUT THE UNIVERSE AND SAMPLE OF COMPANIES

In 2016–17, the National Sample Survey Office (NSSO), in its 74th Round, conducted a survey of services sector enterprises, on the way to launching an annual survey of services (on the line of the ASI). With the release of the NSSO's technical report on the services sector survey (hereafter, the

---

5. We do not know the exact definition of "active" companies in the MCA database. When the MCA passes on the "active" list to the CSO, as per the official documents, the latter considers this "active" set to consist of companies that have filed returns at least once in the last three years. This may not necessarily be the case and there does not seem to be any verification process in place to ensure that this definition indeed correctly identifies the "active" companies given to CSO by the MCA. This itself introduces a layer of uncertainty about the universe of companies that is being considered for the estimation of GVA.

6. The "filing" companies, which constitute the sample set used by the CSO for GVA estimation, vary from year to year because they self-select to file returns. As shown in Table 4B later in this paper, the absolute number of "filing" companies changes every year and so does the ratio of "filing" and "active" companies. This implies that the sample used by the CSO for GVA estimation changes every year. This raises doubts about the comparability of the sectoral GVA estimates over multiple years and the statistical soundness and stability of the estimates obtained.

NSS report) in May 2019, new questions arose regarding the quality and reliability of the MCA21 database, in particular, about the soundness of the sample of companies used by the CSO for its estimation. Official press notes of May 10, 2019, issued by the Ministry of Finance, and May 30, 2019, issued by the Ministry of Statistics and Programme Implementation (MoSPI) have sought to dismiss the doubts, claiming that the MCA database is in fine order for GDP estimation. But if anything, these have raised further doubts about the sample of companies.

One of the three list frames (or universes of enterprises) used for the NSS survey was the list of "active" companies—companies that are said to have filed their statutory returns at least once during the previous three years—obtained from the CSO (called the MCA frame). After due verification of a sample of about 35,000 non-financial companies, the non-response to the survey was found to be as high as 45.5 percent; 21.3 percent of the sampled companies were found to be mis-classified, and 24.2 percent of the companies refused to provide information, or were found to be closed or were non-traceable. Considering the severity of the non-response, NSSO abandoned its project of bringing out two volumes of survey results, and instead settled for a modest technical report. NSSO cautioned data users that "the estimates from the sample are therefore, not likely to be robust over the domains" (NSSO 2019: 16).

Arguing that the non-responding companies could be shell/fake/dubious/non-existent companies that do not produce goods and services on a regular basis, but perhaps serve as conduits to hide profits or circumvent regulations, critics contended that such companies represent non-working companies. MoSPI defended their GDP estimation procedure (in the May 30 press note) saying that every year MCA has been weeding out an increasingly larger number of companies that are not operating, implying that "active" companies in the MCA's register represent genuinely working companies. Further, the missing/fake/shell companies are outside the set of "active" companies, and hence the database and methodology used by the CSO are correct. MoSPI's May 30 press release also said the following:

…from the 35,456 companies included in the NSS 74th Round, around 34,834 (86.5%) companies had filed their returns in the MCA database and only 622 were untraceable in MCA. In the context of GVA estimation in respect of private corporate sector (PCS), out of the 4,235 units categorised as not traceable at the given address in the 74th Round, around 3,154 units had actually filed returns online on the MCA portal.... For the purposes of National Accounts Estimates, the returns actually filed by the corporates under MCA is duly taken into account and the scaling up factor for the Paid-Up-Capital for the non-response is low.

MoSPI is therefore implying that the above record of filing of returns holds for the PCS as a whole too. This would imply that, say out of about 10.9 lakh "active" companies (as of 2015–16), a majority are filing returns. Non-filing companies form a small fraction of "active" companies whose output is estimated by blowing up the parameters prepared for a majority of the companies. Hence, MoSPI claims that the GDP estimates and its growth rates are valid.

Shortcomings of MoSPI's Contention

The May 30 press note classifies the MCA database into: (a) active companies, and (b) others. An "active" company is taken to mean a working company as it files its financial returns at least once in three years. So, by definition, "others" are non-working companies, whose status, as per the press release, could be "amalgamated," "converted," "unclassified," "under process," "under liquidation," "dissolved," "dormant," etc. There are several problems with MoSPI's claims.

First, contrary to the May 30 press release, the NSS report clearly states that its sample is drawn from the list of *active companies* obtained from the CSO. To quote it, "From the MCA frame *active* private non-financial companies of 2013–14, as available from National Accounts Division was taken into consideration" (p. 3; emphasis added). Hence, all the non-responding/untraceable companies in the sample must also be "active" companies. This means that the active list includes non-working or "others" as well, and hence CSO's list of "active" companies is not watertight, as claimed.

Second, as per MoSPI's note, there are missing companies *within* the set of "active" companies as well as in the set of "filing" companies. Table 2 (abridged from the press note) shows that 2,242 "active" companies belonged to the "casualty" category and 1,845 of these were filing returns. Likewise, 1,357 "active" companies were found to be closed and of these, 990 were filing returns, whereas 3,928 "active" companies were non-traceable and 3,141 of these were filing returns. In other words, both the universe (active) and the sample (filing) of companies used by the CSO for the PCS–GVA estimation appear to be faulty.

Third, as pointed out by MoSPI in the press note, the companies in the "Others" category are also filing returns. Yet by definition "Others" are non-active companies, as explained earlier. This implies that for obtaining the sample GVA estimates (even before blowing up for the universe of "active" companies), the CSO is using financial data of non-active companies, which is theoretically incorrect.

Fourth, MoSPI's (May 30) press release claimed, "In the last few years, nearly 6.3 lakh entities have been de-registered." However, we do not know the distribution of such companies between (a) "filing" companies,

TABLE 2. Status of Companies in the NSS 74th Round Survey

Category	Number of Companies in NSS Survey	In MCA in 2016–17, Active Companies	
		Active Companies	Companies Filing Returns
Surveyed	19,317 (54.5)	18,818 (55.5)	17,612 (57.6)
Casualty (i.e., refused information)	2,428 (6.9)	2,242 (6.6)	1,845 (6.0)
Closed during survey	1,579 (4.5)	1,357 (4.0)	990 (3.2)
Out of coverage, i.e., misclassified	7,573 (21.4)	7,291 (21.5)	6,755 (22.0)
Non-traceable units at the address provided	4,235 (12.0)	3,928 (11.6)	3,141 (10.3)
Total	35,456	33,912	30,583

Source: NSSO (2019).
Note: Figures in brackets refer to percentages of the column total. Percentages do not add to 100 percent, as this is an abridged version. See text for details.

(b) "active" companies, and (c) "others." There is no a priori reason to believe that the act of de-registering companies would remove the unresponsive companies (as highlighted by the NSSO report) from the sample.

Generalizing from the NSS services sector survey results, we now present a fuller picture of the shortcomings of the MCA database for the entire PCS, with the help of Table 3 and a Venn diagram given in Figure 7, using the MCA data for 2015–16. Out of 15.5 lakh companies registered with the MCA, 10.9 lakh or 70 percent were "active" companies (see Table 3) and the rest were "others" (belonging to categories mentioned above). Legally, all "active" companies are said to be working companies. Only 58 percent of the "active" companies filed returns in 2015–16 (i.e., these constitute the "filing" companies). The "filing" companies constitute 85–87 percent of the paid-up capital (PUC) of "active" companies, and hence, MoSPI claims that GDP estimates for the PCS are reliable.

TABLE 3. Details of the MCA 21 Database for 2015–16

Number of registered companies	15.5 lakh
Number of active companies	10.9 lakh
Number of companies filing returns	6.3 lakh
Ratio of active to registered companies	70.1%
Ratio of filing to active companies	58.3%
Ratio of filing to registered companies	40.7%

Source: Ministry of Finance (2019).

However, as described above, the sets of "active" as well as "filing" companies, that is, the universe as well as the sample of companies, appear defective. While the boundaries of various categories of companies in the MCA database are claimed to be watertight, as shown in Figure 7, there seems to be a grey area consisting of shell/fake/dubious/non-existent companies (shaded portion in the figure), whose contours and quantitative dimensions are unknown.

Given that the sample of companies used by the CSO for GVA estimation appears to contain shell companies that engage in fictitious transactions, the sectoral as well as aggregate growth estimates obtained from such a sample are likely to be biased upwards.

3.1.2. FILING VERSUS WORKING COMPANIES

As reported by the CSO (2015b; 2015c), close to 5 lakh "active" companies were a part of the sample used for estimation in the NAS for the initial years of the 2011–12 series. Over the last few years, the number of "active" companies has increased more than 11 lakh (see MCA 2019, for details), while the number of "filing" companies has increased to more than 7 lakh. Tables 4A and 4B show the numbers of registered, active, and filing companies for the years for which data is available. Table 4A tabulates the figures of the total registered and active companies available in the MCA21 database and Table 4B shows the number of "filing" companies in each year. The tables show a steady rise in the numbers of "active" companies and those filing returns. The reality, however, may be different as gleaned from various official documents.

It appears that the CSO uses a set of "common" companies instead of the entire "filing" set for preparing the sample estimates. Common companies are those that have data on returns for the previous year and the current year.

TABLE 4A. Details of the MCA21 Database: Number of Registered and Active Companies, 2013–19

Year	Total Registered Companies (in lakhs)	Active Companies (in lakhs)	% Active of Total Registered Companies
2013 (October)	13.45	9.06	67.37
2014 (April)	13.95	9.51	68.20
2015 (April)	14.65	10.26	70.04
2016 (April)	15.47	10.85	70.14
2017 (April)	16.50	13.15	79.73
2018 (April)	17.59	11.76	66.82
2019 (January)	18.50	11.34	61.27

Source: *Monthly Information Bulletin*, Ministry of Corporate Affairs.

TABLE 4B. Number of Active and Filing Companies in the MCA21 Database, from 2012–13 to 2016–17

Year	Active Companies (in lakhs)	Number of Companies that Filed Returns (in lakhs)	% Filed out of Active
2012–13	8.8	5.6	63.64
2013–14	9.5	6.1	64.21
2014–15	10.1	6.0	59.41
2015–16	10.8	6.3	58.33
2016–17	11.6	7.1	61.21

Source: Ministry of Finance (2019).

This set has remained stable at around 3 lakh companies, a figure just around one-half of the companies touted to be the number of companies filing returns. Ramana Murthy (2018) mentioned,

> Accounts of about 5.5 lakh companies (covering both the manufacturing, mining and services sectors) have been analysed and incorporated in the estimation of national accounts series for the above mentioned sectors whereas there are some 11 lakh active companies. The estimates based on the available data were blown up to cover all companies using the active population and ratio of paid-up capital for them. A common company growth based on over 3 lakh companies was used when the data on the whole complement of 5.5 lakh companies were not available.

Therefore, it seems that even though the set of "filing" companies was 5.5 lakh, CSO uses a common set of 3 lakh companies for GVA estimation. It is not clear why this is the case and what happened to the remaining companies. Similarly, the set of companies used by the RBI (as obtained from the MCA) for estimating savings has also remained stable at around 3 lakh companies, as shown in Table 5 (all figures for 2015–16).[7]

TABLE 5. RBI Database of Companies (Obtained from MCA)

No. of NGNF public limited companies	19,602 with 39.9% of PUC
No. of NGNF private limited companies	2.92 lakh with 32.9% of PUC
Total	3.11 lakh companies (whose PUC would be the weighted average of the PUCs mentioned above)

Source: *Reserve Bank of India Bulletin*, May and June 2017.
Note: NGNF—Non-government, Non-financial.

---

7. MCA shares the corporate database in its entirety with RBI, as per an agreement in 2015. RBI has been publishing summary results of the MCA data analysis for NGNF public and private limited companies separately.

From the foregoing discussion, we are inclined to infer that an "active" company is merely a legal definition. It does not represent the *economic concept of a working company*, which produces goods and services on a regular basis. Our contention is that the working companies form a subset of: (a) "active" companies and (b) "filing" companies, and perhaps are only 3 lakh in number (the RBI set as well as the set of "common" companies as mentioned by Ramana Murthy [2018]). This is what we show in Figure 7. This anomaly also raises the question as to whether the remaining companies in the "filing" set are shell/fake/dubious/non-existent companies. Moreover, if the actual set used by the CSO for PCS–GVA estimation is only 3 lakh companies, then the reasoning offered by the CSO to defend the use of the MCA21 database based on a comprehensive capture of a larger number of companies is also doubtful.

Until we have a reasonable estimate of the size and composition of working companies, there is no meaningful way of drawing a sample and preparing GVA estimates. If one claims that the difference between the GVA estimates based on the set of working companies and the set of "active" companies is a mere level difference, it would be a leap of faith to say that this does not affect the growth rate.

FIGURE 7. Venn Diagram for Type of Companies in the "Private Corporate Sector" Category in 2015–16 based on Information from MCA, RBI, and MoSPI

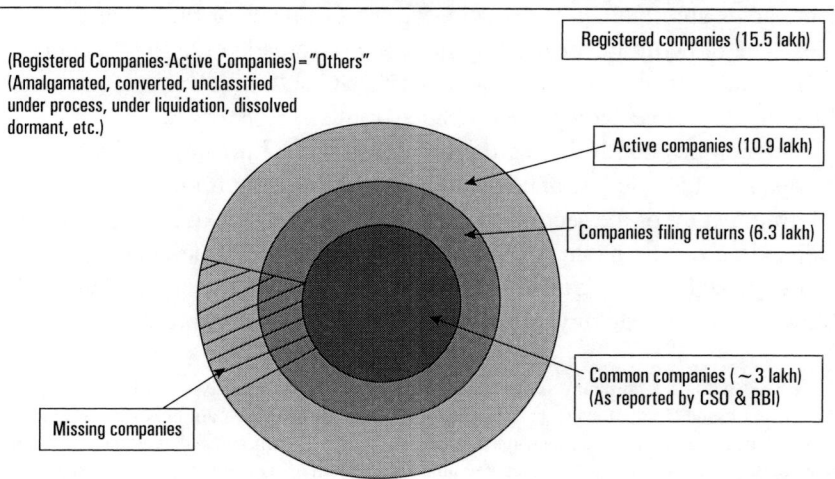

Source: CSO (2015b); *Monthly Information Bulletin*, March 2016, Ministry of Corporate Affairs; *Reserve Bank of India Bulletin*, May 2016, June 2016, May 2017 and June 2017.
Note: See Table 3 and text for explanations.

3.2. Accounting for Companies Not in the Sample

Under the old NAS, GDP of PCS was not estimated directly. It used to be derived indirectly, as a residual. The saving and investment of the PCS were estimated by the RBI using the balance sheet of selected companies. The RBI sample consisted of about 4,500 large public limited companies and a smaller number of private limited companies. For public limited companies, the PUC of the selected large companies was said to be around 45 percent of the total PUC of public limited companies (as provided to RBI by MCA). Likewise, for private limited companies, the estimates of the selected companies were blown up to cover the entire universe of companies. Separate blow-up factors were used for public and private limited companies.

There was a concern that RBI's blowing up procedure was problematic because the size and composition of the PCS had changed substantially during the last three decades. To overcome the problem, the National Statistical Commission headed by C. Rangarajan recommended conducting a census of working companies. This was not taken up. Instead, MCA's e-filing initiative was seen as a solution to the problem of obtaining the universe of working companies.

Under the new NAS, the CSO does not have data on the returns of the companies that are part of the universe but not part of the sample, that is, the non-filing, active companies. So they use a *blow-up* methodology to calculate the GVA of these companies. The estimates for the non-filing companies are obtained by blowing up the estimates of the filing companies. The blow-up factor used by the CSO (also called the PUC factor) is computed as the reciprocal of the ratio of PUC of "filing" companies to the PUC of all "active" companies (CSO 2015a; 2015c).[8]

This implies that if there are problems in the "non-filing, active" set of companies, then the estimates obtained after blowing up may not convey the true picture of the sectoral growth and hence, of the aggregate growth. Depending on the nature of the problems, there could be overestimation of the growth rates. Several studies have pointed out problems with this blowing up methodology. Here we discuss the two main problems.

---

8. The PUC of a company is the amount for which shares are issued to shareholders. According to the Companies Act, 2013 (Section 64), paid-up share capital is such aggregate amount of money credited as paid-up as is equivalent to the amount received as paid-up in respect of shares issued and includes any amount credited as paid-up in respect of shares of the company. There is a reliance on PUC because in the absence of information on actual production, a physical indicator is required that is closely related to production (or production capacity).

3.2.1. LACK OF CORRESPONDENCE BETWEEN PUC AND GVA

The use of PUC in computing the blow-up factor is based on the assumption that the GVA and PUC have a one-to-one correspondence, and that one can directly infer a company's value addition by analyzing its PUC.

Sapre and Sinha (2016) replicated the process of blow-up of GVA for a comparable sample of firms (from the CMIE Prowess database) that qualify for filing in the XBRL format in the MCA21. They find that GVA and PUC have little or no correspondence, especially in cases where GVA is negative (i.e., a loss-making company). The PUC of a company is by definition always positive. This means that it is possible that by using a PUC-based blow-up factor, estimates are scaled up for companies that are, in reality, loss-making companies with negative GVA. This would potentially lead to an overestimation (see Box 1 for details).[9]

The application of the blow-up methodology requires a detailed analysis of the GVA and PUC of registered companies in the MCA21 database. In response to this problem, NSC (2018) recommends:

Cross-validation study on data on corporate bodies with single manufacturing unit available from the two sources, MCA and the ASI. Additionally, a study of plants covered in ASI data belonging to non-reporting but active companies in the MCA list should be undertaken. In the same vain, the ratio of GVA to PUC should be compared between companies that submit their returns by the specified due date and those that submit their returns after the due date. A related research that may be undertaken using ASI and MCA data is to identify plant covered in ASI data which belong to active but not reporting manufacturing companies in the MCA list. The ratio of GVA to invested capital for such plants should be studied in comparison with plants that belong to companies in the MCA list which are active and reporting. (NSC 2018, III 6.5)

At present the PUC based blow-up factor is determined on the basis of the data of firms that have submitted their data in the required forms by a specific date. Some of the non-reporting firms submit their data later. The ratio of GVA to PUC should be compared between the firms that submit their returns within the specified date and those that submit later. Such research may provide an answer to the question whether the ratio of GVA to PUC is lower for later filers or non-filers as compared to the firms that file their returns in time. (NSC 2018, III 3.3.11)

---

9. Manna (2017) corroborates this finding by highlighting that a common blow-up factor for all companies would be inappropriate and separate blow-up factors ought to be computed for different size classes of PUC. Both Sapre and Sinha (2016) and Manna (2017) have argued in favor of exploring alternatives other than PUC for blow-up of GVA. Manna (2017) proposed the use of gross fixed assets, and Sapre and Sinha (2016) explored the possibility of using industry-wise growth rates for scaling up GVA of non-filing companies.

3.2.2. ISSUES WITH THE UNAVAILABLE COMPANIES

One key issue in using the MCA21 dataset is in dealing with the problem of non-filing. Given the process of data extraction from the MCA21 database, the non-filling points to a case of potential overestimation. If there are sufficient reasons to consider that non-filing firms are (a) wound up, or de-registered, (b) loss-making, or (c) are fictitious shell companies that exist only on paper and are not undertaking any service or production activities, then scaling up the estimates of the "filing" companies to account for the "non-filing" ones is likely to lead to overestimation of GVA, of the PCS, and possibly of the overall level of GDP as well. As discussed earlier, the NSS report of May 2019 showed that there are indeed serious problems of missing companies in the "active" set and in the set of "non-filing" companies.

The problem with the blowing-up methodology is, therefore, an inevitable consequence of inappropriate sampling where in the set of "non-filing" companies: (a) there could be shell companies with fake accounts, showing growth rates that never happened, (b) there could be dead companies (i.e., companies that have shut down) with zero GVA, whose imputed growth rates will be higher than actual, and (c) there could be loss-making companies, whose value added is overstated, because the PUC is used as a blow-up factor. Since these companies are actually shrinking, the overall growth rates will be overstated because positive growth rates will be imputed to them.

In summary, the main point as discussed in Sections 3.1 and 3.2 is that the extent to which the MCA21 database problems distort the sectoral and aggregate GDP growth rates depends on: (a) the blow-up ratio for the "non-filing" companies, and (b) the nature of the problems (low growth rates, no growth, decline in GVA, negative GVA, etc.), with the "non-filing" companies. Problems would also arise if the "active" set contains shell companies. Unless there is concrete evidence that the "non-filing" set consists of proper companies with positive GVA and growth rates, and that the "active" set does not contain shell companies, it is hard to dismiss the doubts of overestimation, given the sampling and methodological issues outlined above.

3.3. Companies That Cannot Be Sampled

A portion of the PCS under the new NAS consists of entities that cannot be sampled. They do not file returns in the MCA21 database, which means that they are not part of the usual sample of "filing" companies used by the CSO for GVA estimation. The manner in which their growth rate is estimated raises questions about possible overestimation. These entities are QCs. They are perhaps the least understood part of the PCS in the new

NAS, as disaggregated information on the PCS is not available. Here, we piece together the available information on the PCS, and the size and composition of QCs.

In Figure 3, the size and structure of the PCS in the old and the new NAS are discernible (as discussed in Section 2). The size of the PCS relative to GDP in the new series increased substantially, mainly on account of QCs, which in 2011–12, constituted 8.1 percent of GDP.

WHAT ARE QCS?

A QC is an enterprise not registered under the Companies Act, yet said to behave like a company. It is a partnership or proprietary enterprise maintaining books of accounts. The underlying idea is that such enterprises are akin to limited liability, profit maximizing firms, as against own-account or HH enterprises engaged in subsistence activities, and often employing family labor. The new NAS, following the SNA 2008 guidelines, introduced the concept of QCs by bifurcating unorganized/HH/informal sector enterprises into QCs, and clubbing them with the non-financial PCS, leaving HH/own-account enterprises in the HH/informal sector. As per the new NAS, QCs consist of:

1. Crop production in plantations, other than those covered in the PCS.
2. Unincorporated enterprises covered in ASI.
3. Unincorporated enterprises of manufacturing that are not covered under the ASI but maintain accounts.
4. Cooperatives providing non-financial services.
5. Unincorporated enterprises providing non-financial services maintaining accounts.
6. Unorganized financial enterprises.[10]

In the earlier NAS, items (1), (2), and (4) were included in the non-financial PCS. The remaining three are the new additions clubbed together under QCs. Table 6 provides the share of institutions in GDP as of 2015–16 (based on the RBI's analysis of MCA data).[11] The QCs' share in GDP was 9.6 percent in 2015–16 and their share in the non-financial PCS GDP was 27.5 percent.

10. It is not clear how unorganized financial enterprises, essentially, informal moneylenders, are included in QCs.
11. It is to be noted that the RBI's analysis of the MCA database provides summary results separately for Non-government Non-financial (NGNF) public and private limited companies. The QCs' share is obtained by subtracting the share of public and private limited companies from the PCS.

TABLE 6. Disaggregation of Non-financial PCS Companies and their Percentage Shares in GDP for 2015–16

Institutional Sector	Share in GDP (%)	Share in Non-financial PCS GDP (%)
Public limited companies	13.4	38.5
Private limited companies	11.9	34.0
Quasi-corporations	9.6	27.5
Non-financial PCS	34.9	100

Source: *Reserve Bank of India Bulletin*, May and June 2017.

TABLE 7. Percentage GVA shares of QCs by Industry or Sector for 2011–12

Sector	Distribution of QCs (%)
Agriculture and allied	4.2
Mining and quarrying	1.7
Manufacturing	28.3
Electricity, gas, and water	–0.6
Construction	–1.0
Trade, hotel, and restaurants	40.0
Transport and communication	5.7
Community, social, and personal services	9.2

Source: CSO (2015b).
Note: The columns do not add up to 100% as this table excludes QCs from financial services.

Table 7 shows the industry or sectoral distribution of the QCs' output for 2011–12 (more recent data is not available). Evidently, two sectors, namely, manufacturing, and trade, hotels and restaurants accounted for 68.3 percent of the QCs' output in 2011–12. Incidentally, these are also the sectors which had witnessed a significant boost in their growth rates after the GDP revision.

Methodologically, the shift of QCs from the unorganized sector to the PCS is questionable. The SNA (2008) lays down conditions under which such a shift may be done. To quote the SNA, QC is "an unincorporated enterprise that has sufficient information to compile a complete set of accounts as if it were a separate corporation and whose de facto relationship to its owner is that of a corporation to its shareholders" (as mentioned in Subba Rao 2015).

In contrast, what is done in India is the following:

The enterprise survey collects information on whether the enterprise is maintaining books of accounts or not. As recommended by SNA 2008, all these unincorporated enterprises have been classified as QCs, if they are maintaining accounts, and otherwise as household enterprises. The estimate of GVA from QCs has been added to the GVA of incorporated enterprises in the case of non-financial corporations. (CSO 2015b; 11).

In the GDP revision, proprietary and partnership firms in the ASI, and non-HH enterprises in NSS surveys were *deemed* to maintain accounts, and hence were categorized as QCs. There is no evidence of the NAS revision committees verifying if the QCs, in fact, maintained accounts and whether "…it were a separate corporation and whose de facto relationship to its owner is that of a corporation to its shareholders."

As mentioned in the previous section, the mere shifting of QCs from the unorganized/HH sector to the PCS should not change the aggregate growth estimates. But the concern is that along with the shift, the methods of estimating their output have also undergone some changes, which may have affected the growth rates (Subba Rao 2015). Since the QCs do not form a part of the sample used by the CSO for PCS–GVA estimation, to the best of our knowledge, their growth rate is estimated in two different ways, depending on which sector they belong to. The growth rate for the QCs engaged in manufacturing activities is taken from the ASI data on partnerships and proprietary entities. The growth rate for the QCs engaged in services is taken to be the same as that of the rest of the private corporate sector, which would be an exaggeration given the nature of the QCs. This may have boosted the growth rate of the QCs and, accordingly, of the PCS and aggregate GDP.

The issue really is whether the QCs are growing at the rate of other companies in the PCS. For most periods, we do not have enough information to assess this. They may be more dynamic since they are smaller, or they may be stagnant in which case their growth would be overestimated. It is possible that some are the former, and some the latter. We have no idea what the aggregate situation is for the QCs. It is possible however, that post-demonetization and post-GST, these companies are growing much more slowly than the big companies in the PCS. In that case, the maintained assumption will lead to an overestimation of growth.

3.4. Comparability of MCA21 with ASI-based Estimates

The discussion in Sections 3.1–3.3 shows that there are myriad problems with the MCA21 database used by the CSO to compile the estimates for the PCS under the new NAS. Both the universe and the sample of companies used for the estimation of GVA seem to be riddled with holes and given the manner in which blowing up of estimates is undertaken, there is ample room for overestimation of sectoral and aggregate growth rates.

As mentioned earlier, under the old NAS, for much of the non-government and non-agricultural activities, data used to be collected for the factory sector from the ASI. In addition, various unorganized sector surveys by the NSS were establishment-based surveys. However, there has been a concern that the ASI was increasingly missing out value addition taking place outside of the factory premises, in sites such as service centers, R&D laboratories, and company headquarters. Hence, a view prevailed that the ASI was underestimating the output growth in the manufacturing sector, given its specific approach to data collection.

The replacement of ASI with the MCA21 database for the manufacturing sector was predicated on the foregoing views. The problems with the MCA database that have been uncovered over the past few years by various academic experts raised the following question: Is it really true that the ASI captured value addition taking place only inside the registered premises, ignoring the related or auxiliary activities? Dholakia et al. (2018) examined the question by closely looking at: (a) the ASI schedule, (b) its field investigators' manual (which provides detailed instructions to investigators on how to post the information in the questionnaire), and (c) discussions with the concerned officials responsible for the data collection.

The investigation revealed that the ASI, in fact, gathers information on all activities of a factory, and the data gathered are apportioned to different factories of an enterprise as per standardized procedures. The argument that a shift to the enterprise approach increased the capture of value addition is not entirely correct. In light of this research, the premises of the changeover from an establishment approach to an enterprise approach for GDP estimation and, hence, the use of the MCA database itself appears questionable and unwarranted.

In the face of all the criticisms, the CSO has continued to defend the use of the MCA21 database. In 2015, after the release of the new series, the then Chief Statistician of India, T. C. A. Anant claimed that the use of the new database for the PCS captures the production that was left out in the earlier ASI series. To quote him,

> There is a large invisible corporate segment, which we were not adequately describing in the earlier series. We were partially describing it in manufacturing through the ASI. So, there is recognition that there is a need to get better information on this segment as a large part of government policies are aimed at this segment. The 5,000 listed companies are typically not the principal focus of promotional policies. (Sidhartha and Gupta 2015).

While the MCA database may have technically increased the coverage of companies, it is worth noting that more data need not necessarily mean better data, as has been analyzed in the previous sections.

3.5. Other Problems with the MCA21 Database

3.5.1. Shift from an Establishment to an Enterprise Approach

The 2011–12 series makes a conceptual shift by capturing value addition at an "enterprise" level instead of at an "establishment" level. In economic terms, the distinction between the two can be understood as the difference between a factory (or a plant) and a firm (or an enterprise). The former is a technical unit of production, and the latter is an organizational unit of production. Various authors (Nagaraj 2015a; 2015b; 2015c; Nagaraj and Srinivasan 2017; Rajakumar et al. 2015; Sapre and Sinha 2016) have looked into several aspects of the estimation process in detail. In the new series, the GDP of the private corporate sector is estimated using the financial statements of enterprises as a whole as opposed to the earlier method of using the industrial output of factory establishments. This shift leads to a direct comparison with the ASI-based estimates.

Sapre and Sinha (2016) point out that lack of clarity on measures of output and costs at the enterprise level can lead to imprecise estimates of GVA for various sectors. For instance, the activities of enterprises can be much more diverse than those of factories, and not all of these functions would qualify as "manufacturing." Yet under the enterprise approach, all sources of value added of enterprises classified as "manufacturing companies" are included in the calculation of the manufacturing sector's GVA. This approach inflates the level of manufacturing output and possibly also the growth rate of the sector if the ancillary activities are growing faster than the manufacturing ones. To get a sense of the magnitude, we can compare the level of output based on industrial sales, that is, only considering manufacturing output with the total revenue, which includes the overall enterprise activities. Using data from CMIE Prowess, Sapre and Sinha (2017) show the difference in value addition based on two different measures of output for a set of companies.

As can be seen from Table 8, in comparison to industrial sales, total revenue shows a considerable increase in the level estimates of GVA. Total

TABLE 8. Comparison of GVA Using Industrial Sales and Total Revenue as Measures of Output, from 2011–12 to 2013–14

Year	Based on Sales (₹ crores)	Growth Rate (%)	Based on Dis. Revenue (₹ crores)	Growth Rate (%)	Difference (₹ crores)
2011–12	701,896.6		767,311.7		65,415.1
2012–13	742,237.2	5.74	819,228.5	6.76	76,991.3
2013–14	780,371.1	5.13	872,178.0	6.46	91,806.9

Source: Sapre and Sinha (2016).
Note: "Dis. Revenue" represents fields of disaggregated revenue adding up to total revenue of the company.

revenue fields include revenues from ancillary and related manufacturing activities and other non-operating revenues like treasury operations. The change in the measure of output possibly explains the large upward revisions in levels and on average, it corresponds to a 1 percent increase in growth rate for the manufacturing sector.

In comparison to the establishment-based estimation, the enterprise approach has also complicated the process of GVA estimation to some extent. Conventionally, subtracting the cost of production (of manufactured items) and taxes from the value of output gives an estimate of value addition. However, with diversified activities under one roof in case of an enterprise, identifying the costs of manufacturing activities from financial statements poses serious challenges (see Sapre and Sinha 2016, for details on the process of GVA estimation). Lack of proper identification of cost components can lead to imprecise GVA estimates.

3.5.2. IDENTIFICATION OF FIRMS IN THE MCA21 DATABASE

In the MCA21 database, the CSO relied on using company identification (CIN) code to identify manufacturing companies. The decision to use the CIN was made as the ITC-HS codes of products were either unreported or unavailable in the XBRL forms (see CSO 2015c, for details).[12] However, in absence of the ITC-HS codes, using the CIN code can potentially lead to a mis-classification of companies in identifying their business activity. Sapre and Sinha (2016) find that within the manufacturing sector, several companies operate as wholesale traders or service providers. These companies may have changed their line of business after they were originally registered (this was reported in the NSS survey of services as discussed earlier). These changes do not get reflected in the CIN code assigned to the companies. Such misclassification of companies will distort the manufacturing estimates, though not the overall GVA. The Sapre and Sinha paper and Table 9 illustrate how firms registered in manufacturing can also be in other activities.

Companies may change their primary activities over time as part of their usual business strategy and even repeatedly. Hence, lack of a proper identification system poses serious challenges for classification and estimation of value addition at the sectoral level. Sapre and Sinha (2016), and Pandey et al.

---

12. The Indian Trade Classification Harmonized System (ITC-HS) is an eight-digit code system used for product identification for import, export operations. XBRL is an Extensive Business Reporting Language e-platform used for filing annual financial statements with the MCA. Companies that have: (a) turnover greater than ₹100 crores, or (b) PUC greater than ₹5 crores, or (c) are listed, file in the XBRL format (see http://www.mca.gov.in/XBRL/pdf/ITC_HS_codes.pdf for details, accessed on May 7, 2021).

TABLE 9. Sample of Firms with CI Registered in Manufacturing Activities but Operating as Services Companies (2011–12)

Industry Activity (2-digit NIC 2008)	Number	Industry Activity (2-digit NIC 2008)	Number
Trade in other manufacturing goods	362	Financial services including leasing	328
Other asset financing services	279	Securities investment services	275
Renting services	163	Services	128
Software services	81	Commission agents services	76
Trade in electrical machinery	76	Trade in manufactured products	63
Trade in chemicals	59	Trade in minerals and energy sources	57
Real estate infrastructural services	54	Trade in transport equipment	49
Trade in drugs and medicines	48	Business services	43
Trading in food products	43	Trade in agricultural crops	40
Tech. consultancy and engineering services	31	Info. tech-enabled service/BPO	21
Hotel and restaurant service	22	Other consultancy	17
Fund-based financial services	19	Trade in non-electrical machinery	15
Finance-related allied activities	15	Shipping services	13
Printing and related services	13	Research and development	10
Storage and warehousing services	11		

Source: CMIE Prowess, see Sapre and Sinha (2017) for details.

(2019) show the extent of misclassification that can arise in the absence of a system of identification and classification, and present an illustrative exercise on the frequency of changes in economic activity. They contend that it is of crucial importance to build and use the history of economic activity of companies so as to correctly classify companies into respective sectors based on their primary economic activities. As an illustrative case, Table 9 shows a sample of companies with economic activity different from their CIN-based activity.

In principle, the misclassification is a year-on-year problem and requires a detailed scrutiny of their product schedules. While the problem in using the CIN code was briefly raised in CSO (2015c), no systematic recourse was mentioned to solve this problem. NSC (2018, III 3.3.9) had taken a critical view of the problem by stating:

Moreover, the MCA21 dataset has serious quality issues. The economic activity or activities (NIC codes) perused by a company is extracted out of the CIN (Corporate Identification Number), assigned to the company at the time of registration. The NIC code reported at time of registration is likely to undergo change in due course of time. The MCA21 dataset is not designed to include all the economic activities pursued by a company. However, it may be possible to tackle this difficulty by using the MGT-7 forms, which contain information regarding activity-mix of the companies.

The extent of distortion in GVA estimates due to misclassification cannot be assumed to be negligible. There are two main concerns: (a) misclassification introduces spurious volatility in levels and growth rates, and such volatility does not represent actual movements, and (b) it distorts the GVA-to-Output (GVA/GVO) ratio, which is significantly different for manufacturing and services. Identification of economic activity remains among the finer aspects of measurement and accuracy of macroeconomic aggregates. The case of the manufacturing or services sector is no different and deciphering information from a large dataset like MCA21 is a challenging task.

4. Deflator-Related Issues

The issues discussed in the previous section pertain to nominal GDP estimation. When it comes to real GDP growth rate estimation under the new NAS, a major issue is related to the kind of deflators that are being used to convert the nominal values to real estimates. There are two main issues in this regard, and we discuss them below.

4.1. Single versus Double Deflation

To get to the heart of the problem, one needs to understand how GDP figures or, almost equivalently, GVA figures are calculated. In the broadest terms, the procedure followed by the CSO is the same as that followed all over the world. It obtains data on the nominal values of output produced in various sectors of the economy from the financial accounts of firms. Then, it deflates these figures by price indices to arrive at estimates of real GDP. The CSO's methodology differs from what is followed in other countries in two specific areas: the deflating procedure it follows and the price indices it uses.

In terms of the deflating procedure, the standard international practice, followed by nearly every major country with the exception of China and India, is to use a methodology called "double deflation." Under this procedure, output prices are deflated by an output deflator, while raw material prices are deflated by a raw material deflator. Then the real input value is subtracted from the real output value to obtain real GVA estimates. The CSO's methodology is different in that it first computes the nominal

GVA, and then deflates this number using a single deflator to obtain the real GVA. If input prices move in tandem with output prices, there is no problem and both methodologies will give similar results. But if the two price series diverge—as they did in India for the first few years after the release of the new GDP series—single deflation can overstate growth by a big margin.[13]

The reason is not difficult to see. If input prices fall sharply, profits will increase, and nominal value added will go up. Since real GDP is supposed to be measured at "constant prices," this increase needs to be *deflated away*. Double deflation will do this easily. But single deflation will not work. In fact, if a commodity-weighted deflator like the Wholesale Price Index (WPI) is used as the single deflator, as is the case under the current methodology, nominal growth will be inflated whenever commodity prices are falling. In this case, real growth will be seriously overestimated.

As the gap between input and output inflation starts to close, the problem will diminish. But that could also send a misleading signal because it might seem that growth is slowing, when only the measurement bias is disappearing. This can be best explained using a numerical example as given in Box 1.

Globally, major developed countries have moved to a double deflator method, particularly for the manufacturing sector. In India, the issue of the deflator regained importance in the 2011–12 series for two reasons. First, while under the old NAS, the real growth rate was calculated largely using volume-based measures, under the new NAS, it is calculated using value-based measures. As a result, the deflating procedure has become more critical than before. Second, starting 2012–13, the WPI and the CPI series diverged substantially from each other, owing to a dramatic fall in global oil prices, which pushed the WPI significantly lower than the CPI. For example, in 2015–16, while WPI inflation fell to –3.7 percent, CPI inflation was 4.9 percent. This divergence continued till 2017–18. Considering that the WPI is the main deflator used by the CSO, this gap between input prices and output prices would have led to an overestimation of the real GDP growth rates under the new series, irrespective of the problems with data and methodology described in the previous section.

The introduction of the MCA21 database has led to new challenges in the construction of a double deflator method in the case of the manufacturing

---

13. For more details about how lack of a double deflation practice may have overstated real GDP growth under the new series, see the article in *LiveMint*: https://www.livemint.com/Opinion/58qihTaOIRd3rPyf1eK09L/Real-GDP-is-growing-at-5-not-71.html (accessed on May 7, 2021).

> **BOX 1. Single versus Double Deflation: An Illustrative Example**
>
> Consider a case where actual production is stagnating at, say 100 units, in years 2014–15 and 2015–16, but output and input prices are changing. Assume that a firm raises its output price by 5 percent, in line with general Consumer Price Index (CPI) inflation, whereas the price of its raw materials falls by 5 percent since WPI is down by 5 percent. In this example, the nominal value added defined as the value of sales less value of raw materials will increase by 8 percent from 2014–15 to 2015–16. Since this increase arises entirely from price changes, it needs to be deflated away in order to obtain "real GVA at constant prices."
>
> | | 2014–15 | 2015–16 | 2015–16 | 2015–16 | 2015–16 |
> |---|---|---|---|---|---|
> | | Nominal | Nominal | Real | Real | Real |
> | | | | Estimated Using Double Deflation | Estimated Using Single Deflation and WPI | Estimated Using Single Deflation and CPI |
> | Sales | 100 | 105 | 100 | | |
> | Raw materials | 20 | 19 | 20 | | |
> | Value added | 80 | 86 | 80 | 91 | 82 |
> | CPI inflation (%) | | 5 | | | |
> | WPI inflation (%) | | –5 | | | |
> | Growth (%) | | 8 | 0 | 13 | 2 |
>
> As the above table shows, using the double deflation methodology, real GVA growth is zero. In other words, production has remained unchanged, which is correct by construction. If instead the CSO's method of single deflation were applied to this example, one would simply take the nominal value added and deflate it by the WPI. Since nominal growth is 8 percent and the WPI has fallen by 5 percent, real GVA growth is estimated at 13 percent, which is clearly way off the mark. It conveys the impression of a boom when none, in fact, exists.
>
> Source: Authors' estimates.

sector. MCA21 is a database of financial statements (such as profit/loss statements and balance sheets) that does not provide information on input or output prices at a commodity level. These are necessary ingredients for constructing a double deflator that can deflate the values of inputs and outputs separately. In most countries, nominal production is deflated by the Producer Price Index (PPI). India lacks a PPI, so the CSO uses the WPI instead. To ensure that the GDP numbers accurately reflect developments in the economy, the CSO needs to develop proper PPIs, and then employ them using the double deflation methodology. The NSC Real Sector Committee recommended that ASI data should be used together with the MCA data to develop a procedure for processing the data, including use of a double deflation procedure.

4.2. WPI versus CPI as Deflator

It will take some time to develop PPIs, and even longer to calibrate double deflation for each sector. There is, however, an interim solution that can be much more easily applied, which would also deal with the other problem with CSO's deflation procedure, in that the WPI suffers from several drawbacks. For one, it does not measure the price of services, and services constitute the bulk—around two-thirds—of India's economy. Instead, the WPI is heavily weighted towards commodities, especially oil. So when oil prices fall, the WPI falls, and this leads to measured deflation in the services sectors (notably finance and trade) even if service costs could actually be rising. As a result, growth in services could be overstated by a large margin.

One interim solution to this problem, till the time a proper PPI is developed and data on input prices are collected, is to start using the CPI series for the whole of the services sector, instead of the WPI. The change to CPI makes even more sense in the services sector because the CPI has extensive information on price movements in the various services sub-sectors.

Using the CPI would not solve the problems caused by single deflation as that can only be resolved through the introduction of a double deflation methodology, especially for the manufacturing sector, but it would nonetheless help, as shown in the table in Box 1. The main reason is that the CPI at least has the correct sign for the deflator. It is increasing when the deflator needs to increase, rather than falling like the WPI. The result, of course, is not perfect. Using the CPI to deflate the nominal value added leads to an estimated real GVA growth of 2 percent in our example, when the correct answer is zero. But this is much closer to reality than the 13 percent real growth rate obtained by using the WPI as the deflator.

The better "fit" of the CPI is not just an accident of the particular example chosen. It is perfectly general because when commodity prices (such as oil prices) fall, GVA tends to increase, at least in commodity importers such as India (in this case, one should think of GVA as firm profits, which will go up when input prices fall). Since this increase needs to be deflated away to arrive at a real GVA estimate at constant prices, one needs an index that will increase when commodity prices fall, rather than decrease, as the WPI tends to do. The CPI will also tend to decrease, but by much less than the WPI, since commodities constitute a much smaller share of the consumer basket.[14]

---

14. As shown in Sengupta (2016), for the year 2015–16, official statistics showed that nominal growth was 8 percent, and real growth was 9 percent in the manufacturing sector. If the correct deflator was actually around 3 percent, in line with CPI manufacturing inflation, then real growth was only around 5 percent.

5. Issues in Compiling Regional Accounts (Gross State Domestic Product)

The 2011–12 GDP series has led to new challenges for compiling state-level GDP estimates. After the introduction of the MCA21 database, estimates of the organized manufacturing and services sectors are available only at the all-India level. This constraint occurs because the consolidated financial statements of enterprises are not available as per geographical regions, plant locations, and products. As a result, state-level GDP for the organized manufacturing and services sectors is driven largely by allocation rather than by actual estimation done in each state. Relying on an allocation method (e.g., using ASI shares of value added) causes serious measurement issues as such estimates may not entirely reflect ground realities.

For instance, Manna (2018) shows the bias arising out of allocating state-wise GVA based on shares of each compilation category in the total GVA available from ASI. Instead, Manna (2018) argues that a more appropriate allocation method would be to use the shares of the respective compilation category in the total GVA of private companies, as per the ASI. The issue with such an allocation method is that both the MCA21 and ASI frames have different coverage of units and GVA, thus leading to mismatches in growth rates. The problem has also been acknowledged by the Committee on Real Sector Statistics when it stated:

> The most important gap in MCA21 data relates to the information at the regional (State) level. For the companies operating in more than one State, there is no way of ascertaining the distribution of GVA of such a company over its States of operation. (NSC 2018, III 3.3.7)

Adding another dimension to the problem, Dholakia and Pandya (2017) in the context of the unorganized services argued that the effective labor input (ELI) method does not take into account variations in productivity at the state level. They argue that labor productivity in sectors such as trade and freight transport services would be necessarily different across states and ignoring such differences can lead to imprecise estimates. In the old labor input (LI) method, although category-wise labor productivity was not explicitly considered, interstate variation was taken into account as the output per worker varied across states. Thus, on theoretical grounds, the new ELI method cannot be assumed to be superior as compared to the simple LI method.

The revised GDP methodology has affected Gross State Domestic Product (GSDP) estimation, with a sharp rise in "apportionments" and "projections," and a decline in the share of estimates based on state-level primary data, as demonstrated by Dholakia and Pandya (2017) for Gujarat. This amounts to a regression in the quality of estimation of the GSDP series. It has happened at a time when a greater share of fiscal resources is being managed by the states. In response to the problems in compiling the regional accounts, NSC (2018) clearly outlined that the major issue with regional accounts apart from existing problems was due to the data gap in MCA21. To quote:

In absence of details of a company's State-wise activities, the national-level GVA estimates are allocated to States in proportion to (i) State-level GVA estimates obtained from ASI for manufacturing activities, (ii) the indicators for allocating services sector estimates have been mentioned in para IV.2.4.3 above. [IV. 3.3.6 NSC (2018).]

Given the complexity of the problem at the regional level, lack of credible GSDP estimates could adversely affect the states' ability for resource planning and budgeting. The recommendations of the NSC (2018) for resolving these issues would require a series of policy and regulatory efforts so as to rely less on voluntary compliance by companies and more on data validation and scrutiny checks.

6. Issues with the 2011–12 Back Series of GDP

While data and methodology problems remained unresolved, new controversies related to the 2011–12 series have also cropped up in the last one year. Since its release, the 2011–12 NAS did not have a "back-casted series," that is, estimates at 2011–12 prices beginning from 1950–51. The release of a back series of any new base-year series is a routine exercise. Given the substantial changes in data sources and methods of estimation in the 2011–12 NAS series, which introduced inconsistencies with the sources and methods used in the older series, compiling a back series was a major challenge.

However, in 2018, two separate sets of back series based on two different approaches were released, one official and another unofficial, for varying time lengths, leading to an inconclusive debate on the historic growth performance of the economy. First, the Committee on Real Sector Statistics presented its own estimates from 1994–95 to 2013–14 (henceforth, the NSC back series). Subsequently, the CSO released the official version of the back series for only seven years from 2004–05 to 2011–12 (henceforth, the CSO back series).[15] These two series showed different growth rates for 2005–06 to 2011–12. (CSO 2018a; NSC 2018). This is clearly demonstrated in Figures 8 and 9.

15. See NSC (2018) and CSO (2018b) for details and documentation.

FIGURE 8. Comparison of the NSC and the CSO Back Series Growth Rates: Current Prices, 2011–12 Series

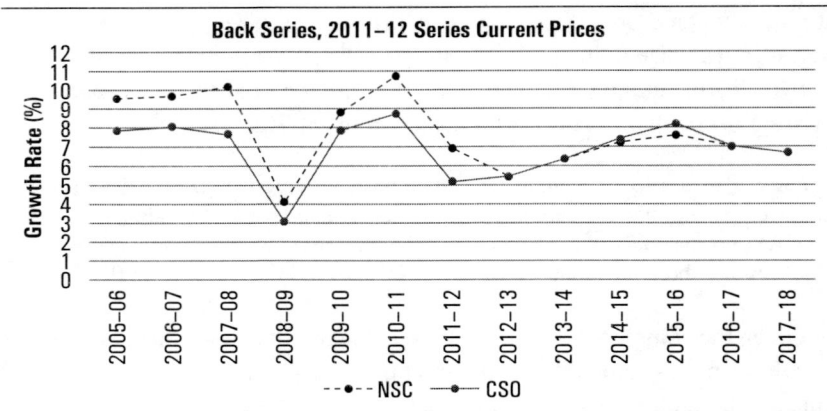

Source: CSO (2018b).

FIGURE 9. Comparison of Average GDP Growth Rates during 2005–12 from the 2004–05 Series, NSC Back Series and CSO Back Series

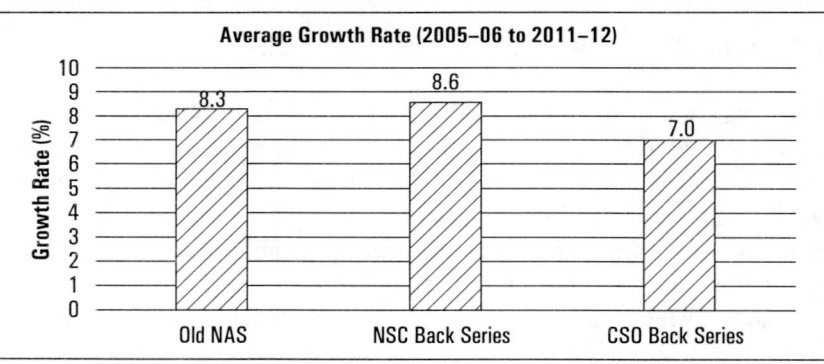

Source: CSO (2018b).

The CSO back series showed lower annual growth rates for all the years from 2005–06 to 2011–12. For the seven-year period, most of which had been so far considered to be an economic boom period for India, the CSO back series reported an average annual growth rate of 7.0 percent, as opposed to the 8.3 percent growth rate reported in the 2004–05 base-year series.

The significant downward revision of growth rates and the diametrically opposite picture painted by the CSO back series compared to the NSC back series raised suspicion about the veracity of the estimates. This was especially because, as mentioned earlier, by most popular accounts, these seven years recorded unprecedented economic growth, an export boom, a credit boom, and an investment boom when India was hailed as one of the fastest growing economies in the world. The CSO back series changed this piece of Indian economic history.

In addition to changes in the aggregate growth rates, the CSO back series also changed the overall composition of GDP in the following ways:

1. Reduction in the share of the services sector for this seven-year period;
2. A rise in the shares of primary and secondary sectors (corporate manufacturing in particular); and
3. A reduction in the size of the unorganized/informal sector and expansion of the size of the private corporate sector.

The CSO has so far not released the details of all the methods, procedures, and adjustments made in preparing the back series. We can obtain some understanding of how this series was put together from its press release of November 28, 2018. While the NSC back series applied a "production-shift" technique to obtain previous years' growth rates, it seems the CSO back series used a concoction of methods and data sources.

For example, as claimed by the CSO in its press note, till the time the MCA21 database was available, they used this data to calculate the GVA of the PCS. For all the previous years when the MCA data on corporate filings were not available, they resorted to the ASI data (that was used in the older NAS series). They further mention in the same press note:

The methodology for preparing the back-series estimates for the years 2004–05 to 2010–11 is largely the same as the methodology followed in the new base (2011–12). In certain cases, owing to the limitations of the availability of data, either splicing method or ratios observed in the estimates in base year 2011–12 have been applied. …Splicing method has been applied for preparing the estimates in Construction Sector entirely and applied partially in Agriculture and Allied Sectors, Gas Trade, Repair, Hotels and Restaurants, Real Estate, Ownership of Dwelling and Professional Services, Public Administration and Defence and Other Services.

This shows that the CSO back series was estimated using different databases for different periods and different methods for different sectors. This raises serious doubts about the comparability and continuity of the back series with the new 2011–12 GDP series and hence, about the reliability and usability of the back series.

Moreover, as discussed in detail in the previous sections of this paper, many infirmities in the new methodologies and data sources used by the CSO have come to light in the GDP measurement debate and none of these has been resolved so far. The use of the MCA database, in particular, could have misleadingly enlarged the PCS's share in the Indian economy and its growth rate. Therefore, using the same methods and data sources to backcast the 2011–12 series is likely to result in incorrect estimates as well. In this context, it is worth asking how correct and prudent it is to selectively use some of the contested methods for preparing the back series.

7. Conclusion and Way Forward

In 2015, the CSO introduced a new series of National Accounts Statistics with 2011–12 as the base year, replacing the earlier 2004–05 base-year series—a routine matter for statistical authorities of most countries. The re-basing was carried out to account for changes in the structure of the economy and in relative prices, always following the global template of the UNSNA, the latest one being the 2008 edition. It is also an occasion for statistical authorities to introduce newer databases and better methodologies to improve the data quality.

Typically, as seen in the past, re-basing leads to a slight enlargement of the absolute GDP size, as output that was previously left out or inadequately captured gets recorded after the revision. This does not usually lead to changes in the growth rates, implying that the underlying trend remains the same. The latest NAS revision, however, defied these usual patterns, and reported a slight contraction of the GDP size in the base year, as well as a faster growth rate in the subsequent years. As the growth trends in the new series did not square with related macroeconomic aggregates, widespread skepticism emerged questioning the veracity of the new GDP series. The statistical authorities responded, saying that the newer estimates are sound because they have used the latest UN guidelines, larger databases, and improved methodologies but this failed to carry conviction.

In their IPF paper, Nagaraj and Srinivasan (2017) unpacked the issues and recorded the state of affairs as they were till mid-2016. Since then, fresh research and data releases have uncovered newer problems, thereby strengthening the earlier doubts about the new GDP's veracity and reliability. This has made it imperative to assess the issues, which is the objective of the present paper. Given that much of the newer research and questions are centered on the PCS output estimates, our paper has paid most attention to this aspect of the revision.

A major change in GDP estimation in the new series was the use of regulatory filings of financial returns (in the MCA database) to estimate output of the PCS, replacing the production accounts obtained under the ASI for manufacturing firms (which account for nearly one-half of the overall corporate sector output). This change was predicated on the view that the production accounts did not capture output outside the factory premises given *its approach* to data collection. The *enterprise approach* used the company balance sheet, which is considered as a solution to this problem. Research undertaken to closely examine the ASI data revealed that the assumption for the shift in approach is factually incorrect, thereby undercutting the very basis of the innovation introduced in the new NAS. Since the manufacturing sector growth rate has been persistently higher in the new series as compared to the picture painted by other macroeconomic indicators, there are apprehensions that the change in approach to data collection may be at the source of the problem.

While the universe of registered companies may have increased substantially, the state of "active" and "filing" companies in the database has serious implications for GVA estimation. The structure of the PCS is such that a small number of large companies contribute a large share to GVA. Limited information from the MCA database suggests that a large number of small companies are unavailable for estimation on an annual basis. Their estimates are obtained through a blowing-up procedure, the details of which have not been released by the CSO. The GVA estimates can be imprecise, especially when the sample size, its fraction, and the universe of working companies are indeterminate.

A recent official data release gave credence to the above suspicion. In 2016–17, NSSO conducted a survey of non-government and non-financial services sector enterprises on its way to launch a full-fledged series of annual survey of services on the lines of the ASI. One of the list frames (i.e., the universe) for drawing the sample, expectedly, was the MCA's list of "active" (i.e., deemed working) companies—a part of the universe of companies CSO uses for estimating the PCS GDP. After due verification, when NSSO launched the survey, it failed to get a response from up to 45 percent of the sampled companies. Admittedly, some of the non-responses could be due to misclassification (which, in principle, could be rectified). But the fact that 24 percent of the sample companies were non-traceable/failed to respond suggests that the universe of "active" companies used for PCS GDP estimation is unreliable and riddled with holes. This raises doubts about the magnitude and reliability of output estimates (prepared using the same list frame) accounting for over one-third of the economy's GDP.

Another problem with the GDP measurement, which is a legacy issue but became prominent when the new NAS was released, is the manner in which nominal GDP or GVA values are deflated to obtain the real GDP growth rates. The global best practice is double deflation where different price indices are used for inputs and outputs because if their prices are changing at different rates, then using the same price deflators would yield distorted estimates of value addition. This has not been done for the new GDP series. A single deflator is used in generating the GVA series for a given sector. In the absence of the double deflator method, whenever there is a divergence between output and input prices, the real growth rates would tend to be overestimated. This is exactly what happened in the period 2013–2016 when WPI inflation was significantly lower than the CPI inflation, the net result being a potential overestimation of the real GDP growth rates under the new NAS.

Regional accounts are an integral part of the system of national accounts. The NAS revision process has apparently paid scant attention to the implications of methodological and database changes for the estimation of GSDP estimates. The problem arises because the newer databases used—such as the corporate filings in the MCA database mentioned above—are not geared for producing state-level (let alone at the district level) output estimates. As a result, the state-level estimates are mostly apportionments of the national estimates, grossly distorting the statistical picture of underlying economic reality. With increasing economic decentralization, distorted state income accounts end up affecting the distribution of resources and probably even aggravating inter-regional inequalities.

After claiming for three years that the GDP back series could not be prepared due to the substantial methodological changes in the latest GDP revision, in 2018 the statistical establishment, in quick succession, came out in with two back series with diametrically opposite trends. While the series by a committee of the National Statistical Commission boosted growth rates for the last decade (from 2004–05 to 2011–12), CSO's officially accepted series reversed the trends, drastically lowering growth trends for the previous decade. The conflicting trends and lack of transparency in the methodology used, especially in the official back series confounded data users, and further dented the credibility of the statistical establishment.

Recommendations

If the foregoing analysis is sound and substantial, then it casts a serious doubt on the new GDP series. In response, many private and international financial firms have apparently resorted to their own devices to find proxies for GDP. Some are apparently using World Bank's night lights data as a measure of economic activity, or high-frequency industry- and sector-specific data, all of which, at best, are second-best solutions.

Going forward, we consider two sets of recommendations, one short run or intermediate remedies, and the second, a longer term and lasting solution. Since the MCA database and the methodologies are the heart of the problem, authorities should immediately release the data in a suitable form for independent verification of the official GDP estimates. As corporate filing is a statutory requirement, the data should, in principle, be easily accessible in the public domain. However, considering its sheer size and complexity, the database needs to be made public in a suitable format via public institutions. MCA could set up data laboratories in leading research institutions and universities, similar to the Census Commission's initiative, to encourage policy-oriented research on the corporate sector. More specifically and immediately, the MCA/CSO can release the following data from 2011–12 onwards:

- Yearly information on the sample size, sample fraction, and the size of universe of "active" companies and their PUCs;
- A break-up of financial and non-financial companies, by various categories; and
- List of companies filing returns with information on selected variables, which could help data users to independently verify data quality.

The MCA and CSO should also create a suitable institutionalized forum for regular and sustained interaction with data users to address the numerous issues that have come up in the course of the GDP measurement debate.

To address the problems arising out of the single deflator issue, till the time producer price indices are generated, which may enable the move towards a double deflator method, the CSO may consider using the WPI as a deflator for the industrial sector and the CPI as a deflator for the services sector. This will help deal with some parts of the problem arising from the deflator issue.

For a lasting overall solution—reiterating Nagaraj and Srinivasan's 2017 recommendation—a statistical audit and a credible expert committee need to be set up to invite the best expertise available globally to review the GDP revision process. Some of the core issues that the expert body may examine are the following:

1. Appropriateness of replacing the establishment approach to data collection with the enterprise approach for the non-farm sector, given

the present level of India's development, and quality and reliability of the available statistical bases;
2. Shifting of QCs from the HH/unorganized sector to the PCS, and its many ramifications for macroeconomic aggregates, and policy; and
3. Critical examination of the incompleteness and unreliability of the MCA database, given the limited state capacity to enforce laws governing private enterprises. There is an urgent need for a thorough investigation to ascertain its suitability for estimating domestic output for an emerging market economy like India.

The objective of the audit/committee would be to investigate in detail the problems in the sources and methods of the new NAS and help come up with the best alternative estimates, preferably before the next base-year revision is conducted, otherwise we may end up perpetuating the defects in the current base-year series and India's GDP will continue to be marred in controversy.

References

CSO. 2014. *National Accounts Statistics - 2014*. New Delhi: Ministry of Statistics and Programme Implementation.

———. 2015a. *Report of the Sundaram Committee on Unorganised Manufacturing and Services Compilation of National Accounts Statistics with Base-Year 2011-12*. New Delhi: Central Statistics Office, Ministry of Statistics and Programme Implementation, Government of India.

———. 2015b. *Changes in Methodology and Data Sources in the New Series of National Accounts, Base Year 2011–12*. New Delhi: Central Statistics Office, Ministry of Statistics and Programme Implementation, Government of India.

———. 2015c. *Final Report of the Sub-Committee on Private Corporate Sector including PPPs*. New Delhi: National Accounts Division, Central Statistics Office, Ministry of Statistics and Programme Implementation, Government of India.

———. 2015d. *Report of the Sub-Committee on System of Indian National Accounts*. New Delhi: National Accounts Division, Central Statistics Office, Ministry of Statistics and Programme Implementation, Government of India.

———. 2015e, "No Room for Doubts on New GDP Numbers." *Economic & Political Weekly*, 50(16): 86–89.

———. 2018a. *Proceedings of Awareness Workshop on "Challenges and Issues of Official Statistics" for Senior ISS Officers during 18th–19th May, 2018 at Bengaluru* (Part I and II). New Delhi: National Statistical Systems Training Academy, Ministry of Statistics and Programme Implementation, Government of India.

———. 2018b. *Back-series Estimation Base 2011–12 Methodology Document*. New Delhi: Central Statistics Office, Ministry of Statistics and Programme Implementation, Government of India.

CSO. 2018c. *National Accounts Statistics - 2018*. New Delhi: Ministry of Statistics and Programme Implementation, Government of India.

Dholakia, Ravindra, and Manish B. Pandya. 2017. "Critique of Recent Revisions with Base Year Change for Estimation of State Income in India." *Journal of Indian School of Political Economy,* 29(1–2), January–June.

Dholakia, Ravindra H., R. Nagaraj, and Manish B. Pandya. 2018, September 1. "Manufacturing Output in New GDP Series: Some Methodological Issues." *Economic & Political Weekly,* 53(35): 10–13.

Manna, G.C. 2017. "An Investigation into Some Contentious Issues of GDP Estimation." *Journal of Indian School of Political Economy,* 29(1–2), January–June.

———. 2018, January. "A Study on the Likely Magnitude of Bias in the Estimates of Gross State Domestic Product for the Private Corporate Segment of Manufacturing Sector as per the New Methodology." *Journal of Indian School of Political Economy,* 30(3–4): 455–468.

Ministry of Finance. 2019. *GDP Estimation: A Clarification*. New Delhi: Press Information Bureau, Government of India, May 10.

Nagaraj, R. 2015a. "Seeds of Doubts on New GDP Numbers: Private Corporate Sector Overestimated?" *Economic & Political Weekly,* 50(13): 14–17.

———. 2015b. "Seeds of Doubt Remain: A Reply to CSO's Rejoinder." *Economic & Political Weekly,* 50(18): 64–66.

———. 2015c. "Growth in GVA in Indian Manufacturing." *Economic & Political Weekly,* 50(24): 117–120.

Nagaraj, R., and T.N. Srinivasan. 2017. "Measuring India's GDP Growth: Unpacking the Analytics and Data Issues behind a Controversy that Refuses to Go Away." In *India Policy Forum*, 13: 73–128. New Delhi: National Council of Applied Economic Research.

NSC. 2018, May. *Report of the Committee on Real Sector Statistics*. New Delhi: National Statistical Commission.

NSSO. 2019. *Technical Report of Services Sector Enterprises in India*. New Delhi: Ministry of Statistics and Programme Implementation, Government of India.

Pandey, Radhika, Amey Sapre, and Pramod Sinha. 2019, January. "What Do We Know about Changing Economic Activity of Firms?" *Working Paper No. 249*. New Delhi: National Institute of Public Finance and Policy.

Rajakumar, Dennis J., Vijayata B. Sawant, and Anita B. Shetty. 2015. "New Estimates of Saving and Capital Formation." *Economic & Political Weekly,* 50(12): 64–66.

Ramana Murthy, S.V. 2018. "Base Change 2011-12 and Implications on GSVA." *Journal of Indian School of Political Economy,* 30(3–4), July–December.

Sapre, Amey, and Pramod Sinha. 2016. "Some Areas of Concern about Indian Manufacturing Sector GDP Estimation", *Working Paper No. 172/2016*. New Delhi: National Institute of Public Finance and Policy.

———. 2017. "Some Unsettled Questions about Indian Manufacturing GDP Estimation." *Journal of Indian School of Political Economy,* 29(1–2), January–June.

Sengupta, Rajeswari. 2016. "Why Inflation Targeting Works." *LiveMint*, August 16. Available at https://www.livemint.com/Opinion/YZFLeMeRm0U94zQzwDVBIK/Why-inflation-targeting-works.html (accessed August 30, 2020).

Sidhartha, and S. Gupta. 2015. "There Is More Acceptance, Credibility of New GDP Data: Chief Statistician." *Times of India*, June 2.

Subba Rao, K.G.K. 2015. "Mystery Private Corporate Saving." *Economic & Political Weekly,* 50(2): 158–162.

To view the entire video of this IPF session and the General Discussion that ended the session, please scan this QR code or use the following URL:
https://www.youtube.com/watch?v=xl0H1a4bEyI

Comments and Discussion*

Chair: **Rakesh Mohan**
Yale University

Sudipto Mundle
NCAER

Before getting to the paper itself, let me first give a little bit of the background regarding the report of the committee that the National Statistical Commission (NSC) had set up on real sector statistics (henceforth, the Real Sector Committee). This is partly for reasons of full disclosure, as I happened to be the Chair of that committee, the findings of which are discussed in several parts of the paper and because I will refer to some of the recommendations of the Real Sector Committee in my comments on the present paper.

When I was asked by the NSC to chair the Real Sector Committee, which was supposed to look at different ways of improving real sector statistics in the country, I said I would be prepared to do that only if the terms of reference of that committee included generating the GDP back series because this had become quite urgent by then. There is a convention that whenever a new, rebased GDP series is released, a corresponding GDP back series for earlier years is also released subsequently to enable comparison of what was there before with what came after the rebasing. However, this was not done when the 2011–12 base GDP series was issued and several years had since passed. This left all analysts, whether for policymaking or in the private sector or in academic research, in quite a quandary because tools of time series analysis could not be applied to the new GDP data without the back series.

Fortunately, the terms of reference of the Real Sector Committee were revised as requested and our work proceeded. I should mention that the secretariat for this committee was the CSO, the part of the Statistics Ministry that produces India's national accounts. The member secretary of the committee was the then director general of the CSO, Shri Srivastava, who is now the Chief Statistician and Secretary of the Ministry. When the

---

* To preserve the sense of the discussions at the India Policy Forum, these discussants' comments reflect the views expressed at the IPF and do not necessarily take into account revisions to the conference version of the paper in response to these and other comments in preparing the final, revised version published in this volume. The original conference version of the paper is available at www.ncaer.org

report was completed, it was reviewed by the committee page by page, line by line, and it was unanimously approved, including by the representative of CSO who also signed off. The report was then submitted to the NSC. In other words, there was strong ownership of the Real Sector Committee report by CSO. In fact, once this report was submitted, it was prominently posted among the new releases of the Ministry on the MoSPI website. This was around July 2018. About a month or so after that, a journalist used the Real Sector Committee's GDP back series to show that the growth rates during the Congress period ending in 2014 were higher than the growth rates after 2014, which is the Bharatiya Janata Party (BJP) period. This was, of course, well known, as the Congress period was one of strong policy stimulus the world over following the 2008 financial crisis. In fact, this growth spurt was evident even in the old 2004–05 base GDP. But once the journalist provocatively politicized the GDP back series issue, politicians got into the act. The Congress spokespersons said that theirs was a much better period. The BJP representatives started saying that the Congress period was one of fiscal profligacy leading to high inflation. With the controversy rising, MoSPI gradually distanced itself from the report, which till then it had fully owned. It was shifted from the prominent "recent reports" section of the Ministry's website to the NSC reports section. Subsequently, the back series that CSO had not been able to produce for the previous four years or so was suddenly completed and released within 2–3 months as the new "official" back series. This "official" back series reversed the comparison, now showing that the growth rates were actually lower during the Congress period than during the BJP period.

I will not go further into this back series issue, but I will use some of the recommendations from other parts of the Real Sector Committee Report while commenting on the present paper.

Let me now get to the paper itself. Most of my comments will focus on issues where I am not on the same page as the authors of this paper, mainly in order to induce discussion. Hence, let me state clearly at the outset that I think this is really an excellent paper, it is very comprehensive and drills down to the details of what has been done in the new national accounts series. That is what is needed to unravel all the puzzles we have been living with for the past few years, ever since the new 2011–12 base GDP series was released.

Following the release of this new series in 2015, doubts were expressed right from the beginning about the reliability of the new series. This was partly because for the three common years for which the old series numbers were given along with the new series, the new series estimates lowered the growth rate for the first common year, compared to the old series, but made it higher for the subsequent two years. Also, the new growth estimates did not gel with other macroeconomic indicators. Subsequently, a lot of analysis has been undertaken of the possible sources of error, including by the authors of this paper—most famously in the Nagaraj–Srinivasan paper presented at the 2016 IPF (Nagaraj and Srinivasan 2017) and in more work subsequently. All of this is well summarized in the present paper.

There seems to be a general consensus that there is a problem of overestimation in the new GDP series, especially relating to the MCA data for the industrial sector. Generally, I think it is fair to say that there is a broad consensus that there is growth overestimation, and this paper presents an updated and comprehensive critique of the new GDP series. Certainly, the critique is important and has to be there, but from my perspective, the really important question is about how to fix the problem. The availability of reliable, usable GDP statistics is essential for all economic and other important decision-making in both the public and private sectors, and it is through that lens that I am making my observations.

I think the problems with the new series fall into two broad groups. One has to do with the data itself, especially the MCA data, and how it has been used to generate the GDP numbers as detailed in the paper. The other part is the deflation method that has been used. That is also discussed in the paper. It is useful to compare the new GDP series with the old series or the Real Sector Committee back series with the official back series and see how much of the difference can be explained by differences in the data source and how much by the deflation procedure. I am emphasizing this because while there are differences in nominal growth rates between the two series, these differences are relatively small. The big differences appear when we compare the real GDP growth rates. This suggests that the real problem lies more with the deflation procedures used and not so much with the data. My main reservation with the present paper is that it focuses more on the problem with the MCA data and its unreliability rather than on the problem of the deflation procedure used.

But that being said, let me now first talk about the MCA database, some of the points raised in the paper are regarding the MCA database and the blow-up method that has been used in the new GDP series. As the paper mentions, and illustrates with a Venn diagram, there are at present about 18 lakh companies in the MCA database. Of these, about 12 lakh are the companies which are described as "active," in the sense that they have submitted accounts at least once in the last three years. Of these, about half or 6 lakh companies are described as "filing" companies in the sense that they filed their accounts with the MCA in the last year. When the NSS tried to use the MCA list of 12 lakh active companies as a sample frame, it found that a large proportion of these companies was either misclassified or non-existent. So the paper concludes that this database is not robust enough to be usable. But the paper also notes that CSO subsequently clarified that a lot of companies reported as missing or non-existent had, in fact, filed their accounts electronically. It was eventually found that just 622 companies were missing, which amounts to about 2 percent of the universe of active companies. Obviously, this error needs to be fixed but it is not such a drastic defect that it calls for the entire MCA database to be junked.

A potentially more serious problem in my view is that the sample of companies filing reports in the current year, the "filing" companies, changes from year to year. It is not the same set of companies which are filing reports every year. So if the set of companies filing accounts this year is different from that which did so last year, *even if the output level has not changed at all*, it could still appear as either an increase or decrease in output. That would obviously be an error. The way CSO has dealt with this is to use the data for what are called "common" companies, which is a subset of 3 lakh companies that have filed accounts with MCA in both years. The paper cites the fact that only 3 lakh companies belong to the set of "common" companies as further weakness of the MCA database. But to me, it is a source of strength because these 3 lakh companies, which form the core of the Venn diagram, comprise a set of companies for which we have robust, comparable data over the years. It is, in fact, still a very large sample, amounting to 25 percent of the universe of active companies.

The blow-up method used by CSO, another weakness cited by the paper, is a genuinely serious problem. The ratio of PUC of the active companies to that of the common companies is used as the blow-up factor to arrive at GVA estimates for the universe of active companies from the data relating to common companies. However, there is no correlation between GVA and paid-up capital, PUC, and this is a genuine weakness in the new GDP series. The Real Sector Committee had suggested that the ASI data should be used together with the MCA data to get more reasonable estimates of GVA.

To sum up on the data side, the MCA data was released and used prematurely in the new GDP series. A lot more homework needed to be done on how to calibrate it better, how to clean it up with the help of ASI data, and so on. I think this can be done by adopting some of the recommendations made by the NSC Real Sector Committee.

Let me now quickly come to the deflation problem, which I think is the main problem with the new 2011–12 base GDP series. As I indicated earlier, the differences between the different GDP series are quite modest in nominal terms. The major differences appear in the real estimates after deflation. The global best practice is double deflation where different price indices are used for the inputs and outputs because if their prices are changing at different rates, then using the same price deflators would yield distorted estimates of value addition. This has not been done for the new GDP series. A single deflator is used in generating the GVA series for a given sector. The reason is that the MCA data does not lend itself easily to this kind of double deflation because it is enterprise data and not establishment data, and it cannot be classified by products or location of production. Here again, the NSC Real Sector Committee recommended that ASI data should be used together with the MCA data to develop a procedure for processing the data, including use of the double deflation procedure. However, switching to these new procedures will take time, mainly because India still does not have a producer price series and CSO still makes do with the CPI and WPI price indices. This is a major gap in India's price statistics. Pending the generation of producer price indices, the paper offers an excellent suggestion and makes a compelling case for using WPI indices for the industrial sector and CPI for the services sector in the interim period. I think that is a good way to go.

Reference

Nagaraj, R., and T.N. Srinivasan. 2017. "Measuring India's GDP Growth: Unpacking the Analytics and Data Issues behind a Controversy That Has Refused to Go Away." *India Policy Forum*, 13: 73–128. New Delhi: National Council of Applied Economic Research.

N. R. Bhanumurthy
NIPFP

I will try to limit my comments on the back series work that I have done for the Mundle Committee. I will also highlight and show some of the issues that Dr Mundle has already pointed out in terms of what the difference is between the new official back series and the National Statistical Commission's back series numbers. The main contention of the paper is that the base year revisions should not cause big changes in the growth rates. For this, we need to look at the nominal GDP numbers. When the revision happens, it does so on the nominal series. If you compare the old and new nominal series as the paper has already pointed out, there was a decline in the nominal GDP numbers in 2011–12, not an increase as many of us believe. In fact, there was also a decline in the years 2012–13 and 2013–14.

The paper talks about sharp revisions in the shares of the private corporate sector and the shifts in the shares of overall manufacturing as well as trade. The authors feel that the revised growth rates do not actually reflect the kind of changes that are happening in the Indian economy. They have not highlighted in their presentation but mention in the paper issues related to two contradicting back series data. The paper also raises concern about high GDP growth during the demonetization period in 2016–17, and it takes the help of the NSS survey to highlight the issue of use of MCA21 data. The paper also questions the quality and accuracy of the methods as well as the databases that have been used in GDP estimation.

The authors conclude that there seems to be overestimation of the growth rates, especially in one particular sector, that is, PCS, and within the non-financial component. The paper raises a lot of issues regarding the reasons for the upward bias in the growth rates. The paper also discusses the relation between the paid-up capital and the GVA, especially that being used for the blow-up. Another issue raised in the paper concerns non-filing companies and the issue related to shifting of the entire methodology from establishment to enterprises as well as the double-deflation problem, which is very useful for further research.

I believe that the paper is very comprehensive. The authors have summarized most of the issues that have been raised since 2015, and in fact, those who have read their IPF July 2016 paper (Nagaraj and Srinivasan 2017) will know that this new paper has updated most of the issues that have been raised since then. In many places, the paper also makes very strong recommendations and attributes those recommendations to a government committee. In a sense, these recommendations are already there in the public domain and I am sure MoSPI is also aware of this.

As regards the use of WPI and CPI in the new series, it has been observed that mostly CPI is used instead of WPI. At one place, the paper says that the NSC back series actually boosted up the growth rates. I believe that if you take the numbers from 1993–94, the difference between the old series and new series, on an average, is higher by only 0.2 percent. The paper also points out that we have done splicing. We have been opposing this method and suggesting that it should not be used mechanically. We have basically used the *production shift approach*, which is very different from splicing. Again, at one place, the paper says that estimation of the NSC back series is not really transparent. My view is that many people have read our committee report and in fact some have re-estimated and they are getting the same numbers as ours. So, in that sense, the Mundle Committee report recommendations on back series is replicable and is much more transparent than any other method.

The paper also recommends the creation of a *credible* expert committee, thus in a sense appearing to question the integrity of committees and their members. As part of the Advisory Committee on National Accounts Statistics, we do not even get to see the numbers. We only discuss the method and suggest the methodology that should be adopted, and we have not really seen the original databases that have been used. It seems that the paper repeatedly wants to show that GDP is overestimated. Most of the examples in the paper (Box 1) aim to show how the MoSPI figures have been overestimated. However, one can flip back the examples and say that GDP can also be underestimated. For example, the paper assumes a CPI of 5 percent and WPI of –5 percent. But if one assumes that these figures can be taken to be the other way round, one can find that you will be underestimating the GDP numbers. I thought that may be looked at.

The paper is ostensibly saying that the past method was more accurate than the current method. However, let us look at some of the issues. In terms of the nominal GDP growth estimates, the old series and new series are almost the same. I think it is very clear from the two graphs in my presentation that there is no change in the nominal GDP growth. But if you look at the real growth rates, you see that the new series is slightly lower in the pre-2011–12 period but in the post-2011–12 period, you will see a completely different trend. This is exactly what Dr Mundle pointed out in terms of the deflators. I do have some estimates on the deflators that are derived from the new back series.

So what we did as part of the Mundle Committee was basically that we tried to adopt a production shift approach. If we look at both GVA growth rates and GDP growth rates from this approach, we get a smooth series as compared to what we had in the past. In fact, one of the basic objectives of GDP estimation when you look at the back series is that we would like to have something free of artificial breaks and free of deflator issues. In fact, the revision happened only on the production side, not on the prices side. So I don't know why we should see the change in the deflators when we revise the GDP series.

In terms of deflators, the new series of CPI is used instead of CPI-AL agricultural laborer or industrial worker, but for GDP data prior to 2010, we are not clear what kind of CPI numbers have been used as there was no comparable back series for the new CPI estimates. Ultimately, the problem arises when MoSPI does not provide us details about what exactly is getting into the estimation of their new back series numbers. So as regards the lower growth in the new series as compared to the old series, as seen in the graph, the nominal seems to be fine but there is a problem with real numbers. I think that is where we are seeing some kind of *deflated* growth in the new back series.

The alternative could have been to retain the old deflators, which would have prevented any controversy. If you look at the deflators, we tried to estimate the deflators for the period 2004–11, and it is very clear that actually it is the new deflators that are higher than the old ones, while there should not be any change in the way CPI or WPI or price has been estimated in the pre-2011–12 series. So the entire difference between the new back series and the NSC back series can be explained by the changes in the deflator numbers. This is also true at the sectoral level by looking at the sectoral deflators.

The last question I want to raise is: Has the past method given consistent numbers? Basically, IIP numbers are used to estimate manufacturing sector growth. If you look at the IIP numbers, you will see almost a flat kind of a curve in the recent period. In fact, even in 2016–17, the year of demonetization, the IIP series did not show any dip as compared to the previous year. We use these IIP numbers to estimate the manufacturing sector growth in the past. On the other hand, if you look at ASI as well as MCA21 data, the pattern seems almost similar. But when you use IIP numbers, you do not really get a real picture of the manufacturing sector. Here, I am trying to say that the IIP numbers we had in the past and the way we estimated the manufacturing sector value addition in the past were also flawed. I think that we were perhaps underestimating past growth.

At present, we get the ASI numbers with a lag of two years. Now if you look at the final numbers, after two years, you should be seeing a sharp revision between the ASI numbers and the numbers that have been generated by IIP. We don't see those kinds of sharp revisions when we get the final numbers on the manufacturing sector.

Let me conclude by saying that the paper has raised many relevant issues. I am sure these will be useful for the future. But as Dr Mundle pointed out, we need to really work with NSO, and I hope MCA will release the database for researchers so that more work can be done. In terms of methodology, the past method is very different from the current method. Hence, comparing the past and the present may not really help much when you want to come up with credible GDP numbers.

General Discussion

Rakesh Mohan, the chair, initiated the discussion by stressing that GDP estimation is a serious issue for the country for the interpretation of what is going on in the economy and how it impacts thinking about what to do in the future. He asked that since it is only CSO that knows which companies are included in the MCA21 and which establishments in the ASI, why is it not possible for CSO to do a complete correspondence to clarify what is going on?

Bishwanath Goldar clarified why 2012 and 2013 manufacturing growth rates in the old series were much lower than the growth rates in the new series. He explained that the standard practice is to estimate growth rates initially on the basis of the Index of Industrial Production and then to revise them subsequently. However, the shift to the new series meant that the revisions for 2012 and 2013 never took place, so the growth rates for these two years remained low. On double deflation, he pointed out that using data available on the RBI website, it is possible to compute the double-deflated GVA series for manufacturing or for any other sector and compare it with the single-deflated series from the national accounts.

Goldar talked about how factory-based growth numbers from the ASI would typically be lower than company-based growth numbers simply because companies include more activities beyond production, and these may be growing faster. He noted that factory data from the ASI could now be compared with the corresponding MCA company data since the ASI now has a field for the CIN number of its associated company. He also pointed to the need to resolve the new difficulty of apportioning GVA national estimates (estimated using MCA company data) to the states (using the ASI data). This was not a problem in the past when the ASI was also being used for GVA.

Arvind Subramanian noted that the discussion on GDP estimates was taking place in a very narrow way because of lack of access to expenditure side estimates of GDP; we should be looking in parallel at estimates of investment, consumption, and exports. He asked a question about the size of the sample of companies in the MCA database that was being used to calculate GVA and thought it was much less than the 3 lakhs that the paper spoke about and was more like 3,000–6,000 firms.

Ramana Murthy, the head of CSO's Economics and Statistics Wing, and until recently the head of its Industrial Wing handling the ASI, noted that the report in the paper that NSSO, in preparing for the Annual Survey of Services, had found that 45 percent of the service companies in MCA's list of active companies were untraceable or did not respond was a misrepresentation. He explained that a total of 35,456 companies were sampled out of

1,100,000 supposedly active companies (of which 700,000 were companies filing returns). Hence, the NSSO had taken a small portion of companies belonging to the services sector covered by the NSS 74th Round. Financial enterprises, air transport, and many other service sector enterprises were excluded. Some 21 percent of these were "out-of-survey" units because their NIC codes, the National Industrial Classification codes, fell outside the coverage of the survey, so that constituted a portion of the 45 percent. Further, there were closed units. There were also establishments in the MCA database that were dropped since we were following an enterprise approach, but that did not mean that they were fake or non-existent units. Then there were "non-traceable" units that could not be found at the given addresses, but that again did not mean they were closed, since they could have shifted to a new location and were in operation. There were also about 6 percent "casualty units" that declined to share their data even though they were operational. All of these categories added up to 45 percent, but that did not mean that they did not exist. But that should not be the reason to drop the MCA data, which is much larger than what was used for the NSSO survey.

He also noted that "quasi corporations," mostly proprietary, partnership enterprises maintaining accounts, unincorporated units that are nonetheless counted in the ASI under the Factories Act, are organized sector units and should be treated as part of the PCS in the national accounts according to the best-practice recommendations of the UNSNA. That is exactly what the CSO had done.

Srinivas Murthy, also from the CSO, adding to Professor Goldar's explanation, pointed out that Professor Nagaraj's first slide comparing growth rates for GDP, manufacturing, and trade/hotels had been repeated elsewhere and creates confusion because it does not distinguish between the many stages of finalizing GDP/GVA estimates, ranging from First and Second Advance Estimates, then the second stage Provisional Estimate, and the final First, Second, and Third Revised Estimates. All three have different coverage as more data becomes available. This is all made clear on the MoSPI website. So it is really important to compare like with like.

As regards the use of the MCA21 data, there is a conceptual difference between the First Revised and the Second Revised Estimates of the nominal national account numbers. The common sample of 350,000 companies from the MCA21 cited in the paper relates to the First Revised Estimate, but it is a truncated sample. The Second Revised Estimate uses a larger sample of companies from the MCA21 and uses the provisional ASI data. It is not the number of companies that matters but the PUC of the sample vis-à-vis the universe that matters, and we may be covering some 85 percent of that by the Second Revised Estimate, which is where the blow-up factor matters.

He agreed that PUC and GVA may not be highly correlated, but that is the metric put out by the MCA in public, and even the RBI has used it.

Brijender Singh from MoSPI gave some examples to counter the charge of potential overestimation; he suggested that comparing the ASI manufacturing growth rate and private corporate manufacturing growth rate over time does not always point to overestimation in the case of manufacturing for private corporates. Further, the divergence between First Revised Estimate, which is based on the growth rate of common companies, and the Second Revised Estimate, which is based on the scaling-up factor, does not indicate that the scaling-up factor systematically leads to an increase in the growth rate, and in fact, it sometimes actually leads to a downward revision.

Kaushik Basu pointed out that the share of registered but non-active companies in total companies jumped a lot during individual years. For instance, there was a precipitous drop in 2017–18, but the figure remained more or less constant during the period 2013–16. These fluctuations may provide insights about the identity of these companies, and the impact on growth rates.

Arvind Virmani noted that it is unfair to blame MoSPI for lack of access to the MCA21 data since it belongs to MCA. He highlighted the need for making the data public. He also stressed that while there is a standard methodology for estimating the SNA, there is no standard methodology for the back series. So it is important to distinguish between problems with the back series and those with the estimation.

Dilip Mookherjee said that double deflation versus single deflation seemed to account for most of the difference in the growth rate. So it was not clear why, from an economic standpoint, double deflation was the right way to go. What we are interested in ultimately is national income and not physical production.

Rakesh Mohan concluded the session by urging the government, CSO, and MCA to jointly clarify the doubts being raised about the GDP figures. He noted that since confidence in India's national accounts has fallen, these figures need to be corrected. He suggested that NCAER and CSO could hold a meeting to discuss and clarify these doubts.

The session video, the paper, and all presentations for this IPF session are hyperlinked on the IPF program available on the NCAER website by scanning this QR code or going to the following URL:
https://www.ncaer.org/IPF2019/Agenda/Agenda_IPF_2019.pdf

MAITREESH GHATAK[*]
London School of Economics

KARTHIK MURALIDHARAN[†]
University of California, San Diego

An Inclusive Growth Dividend: Reframing the Role of Income Transfers in India's Anti-Poverty Strategy[§]

ABSTRACT   Both theory and evidence suggest that unconditional universal income transfers can not only reduce poverty, but also improve productivity and achieve development goals more broadly. Given recent policy initiatives in India to support farmers with income transfers (at an estimated cost of around 0.4 percent of GDP), we propose an expansion of this approach to cover *all* citizens, as one component of India's portfolio of social protection programs. Specifically, we propose that India implements an inclusive growth dividend (IGD), pegged at 1 percent of GDP per capita, which reaches all citizens and grows equally for all with the economy's growth. This will be both fiscally feasible and practically implementable and would be a powerful practical and symbolic commitment to universally shared prosperity. We review global evidence on the impact of income transfers and argue that an IGD would be a highly cost-effective way of directly reducing poverty, with limited administrative costs of targeting, reduced risk of exclusion errors, lower leakage of benefits, and *lower* disincentives for work compared to most targeted programs. It would also improve financial inclusion and formal savings, relax borrowing constraints for productive investments, and improve female empowerment. Further, successfully delivering an IGD would augment the capacity and credibility of the Indian State. Over time, it could create an attainable benchmark against which to evaluate (and improve) the quality of public expenditure. Finally, we note that an IGD could be a powerful tool for the Government of India to promote the objectives of equity and efficiency given the vast differences in income levels and state capacity among Indian states.

[*] m.ghatak@lse.ac.uk
[†] kamurali@ucsd.edu
[§] The authors thank Abhijit Banerjee, Pranab Bardhan, Timothy Besley, Xavier Jaravel, Renana Jhabvala, Vijay Joshi, François Maniquet, Paul Niehaus, Arvind Subramanian, Sandip Sukhtankar, and Jeff Weaver for conversations over the years that have shaped their thinking. In some cases, they draw directly on their joint work. They thank discussants Abhijit Banerjee and Arvind Subramanian, and IPF participants for helpful comments, Hannah Blackburn and Ramya Raghavan for excellent research assistance, and Ophira Shalev for editorial assistance. They remain responsible for all errors and omissions.

Keywords: Income Transfers, Targeting, Inclusive Growth Dividend, Anti-Poverty Strategy

JEL Classification: D63, H24, H53, I38

1. Introduction

There has been a global surge in academic and policy interest in using universal basic income (UBI) to alleviate poverty and enable inclusive prosperity.[1] In the Indian context, several scholars and policy commentators have argued over the past decade that inefficient and poorly implemented welfare schemes should be replaced with direct income transfers to the poor.[2] The 2016–17 *Economic Survey of India* gave further policy salience to the idea of a UBI for India by recommending its active consideration. Parallel investments in the *Jan-Dhan, Aadhaar*, Mobile (JAM) infrastructure required to implement direct benefit transfers (DBT) into beneficiary bank accounts, have also made it feasible to implement the idea.

The move to income transfers as a component of India's anti-poverty strategy has also been reflected in actual policy in the last two years, especially in the context of farmers' welfare. The State of Telangana's early 2018 launch of the *Rythu Bandhu* Scheme (RBS), which gave farmers an unconditional payment of ₹4,000 per acre, pioneered this approach. Since then, such policies have been replicated at both the state level (as in the Krushak Assistance for Livelihood and Income Augmentation (KALIA) program

---

1. While the discussion in developed countries has been motivated mainly by concerns of needing to find policy responses to rapid automation and job destruction, the discussion in developing countries has focused more on the benefits of income transfers relative to targeted in-kind transfers because of weak state capacity for implementation (seen, for instance, from considerable targeting errors and leakage in benefits).

2. A non-exhaustive list of references making this argument includes Kapur, Mukhopadhyay, and Subramanian (2008a; 2008b), Bardhan (2011; 2016; 2018), Banerjee (2016), Ghatak (2016), Joshi (2016), Mundle (2016), and Ray (2016). Note that not all of these pieces call for universality in income transfers, with some like Kapur, Mukhopadhyay, and Subramanian (2008a; 2008b) putting more emphasis on replacing in-kind benefits with cash transfers for program beneficiaries. Davala *et al.* (2015) make the argument for basic income without explicitly calling for the substitution of other programs. Critics of income transfers in India primarily worry that it will lead to a substitution of in-kind welfare programs and an abdication of the responsibility of the government to guarantee minimum levels of basic goods and services. Representative references include Shah (2008), Dreze (2018), and Roy (2019a). Khosla (2018) provides an excellent summary of the key issues with a focus on the Indian context.

in Odisha) and the national level (through the PM-KISAN program). The *Pradhan Mantri Kisan Samman Nidhi Yojana* (PM-KISAN) was launched in December 2018. At first, it provided ₹6,000/year per family with cultivable landholding up to two hectares, subject to some exclusions. The first Cabinet meeting of the NDA Government after re-election in 2019 extended the scheme to *all* farmers, regardless of landholdings. Today, it is likely the world's largest income transfer scheme. With the extended coverage, it aims to reach 14.5 crore farming households (or roughly half the country) with an estimated cost to the Central Government of ₹75,000 crores for the year 2020–21, or roughly 0.4 percent of GDP at current prices.[3]

As a result, the relevant questions regarding the role of income transfers in India's anti-poverty strategy have shifted from whether to have them at all to how to think about the design, coverage, and scope of such a policy. This paper, therefore, focuses on the following main questions: Should these income transfers be made universal, covering all citizens regardless of whether they are farmers? Should income transfers supplement other programs, or should they substitute existing welfare programs? Considering both the broad development strategy and also the opportunity cost of resources, how might such a policy fit in with other anti-poverty and social welfare policies? How can such a policy be both fiscally viable and mitigate the concerns regarding UBI raised by skeptics? How can the needs and preferences of beneficiaries be taken into consideration accounting for heterogeneity in these over time and space?

While much has been written about income transfers in recent years, this paper is motivated by: (a) the need for this debate to reflect recent evidence on actually implementing income transfer policies in India as well as data on beneficiary preferences and experiences, (b) the greater political willingness to implement income transfers at scale (seen in the PM-KISAN program), which makes it especially policy-relevant to provide both conceptual clarity and a practical roadmap forward, and (c) the urgency of strengthening India's social protection architecture in light of the economic hardship induced by COVID-19 and the associated lockdowns to slow the spread of the virus. In addition to providing a concise discussion of the conceptual issues, we offer a specific policy proposal that we believe is implementable at scale and will deliver almost all the benefits of UBI while mitigating

---

3. PM-KISAN was launched during the 2019 Interim Union Budget of India and came into effect from December 1, 2018 (Government of India 2019a; 2019b). For the year 2019–20, the estimated cost of the scheme was ₹87,217.50 crores, which amounts to roughly 0.5 percent of GDP at current prices (Source: https://www.indiabudget.gov.in/doc/eb/sbe1.pdf).

several of the concerns that have been raised by skeptics. We summarize the core argument below.

Theory and evidence point to several advantages of unconditional universal income transfers as a tool not only for anti-poverty policy but for achieving development goals more broadly. Such transfers directly reduce poverty and have the following attractive properties: limited administrative costs of targeting and lower risk of exclusion errors (since they are universal); lower leakage of benefits because of fewer intermediaries between fund disbursal and receipt; *lower* disincentives for work compared to most targeted programs;[4] greater sociological acceptability because of the lack of "rank reversal" in incomes that often happens under targeted programs; improved financial inclusion and formal savings, which can, in turn, mitigate risk and enable consumption smoothing at a lower cost than credit (which is subject to higher costs of financial intermediation); relaxing borrowing constraints for productive investments, and improved female empowerment (especially if transfers to children are sent to their mothers' accounts).

However, we believe that one reason that policy has moved more slowly despite the endorsement by the *Economic Survey* is that policy discussions of universal income transfers have been conflated with those of a UBI. Specifically, the term "basic income" connotes an amount sufficient for survival, and most academic and policy discussions of a UBI have focused on transfers large enough to nearly eliminate poverty, ranging from 3.5 to 4 percent of GDP (Government of India 2017; Joshi 2016) to 10–11 percent of GDP (Bardhan 2016; Ghatak 2016). As a result, the fiscal math simply does not work out.[5] It is impossible to implement such a large universal transfer without either cutting other major anti-poverty programs or substantially increasing the tax to GDP ratio (currently around 18 percent). Alternatively, a large transfer automatically necessitates some targeting, which negates several key advantages of universality.

As we discuss in detail, even if we were to believe that income transfers are a more efficient way of achieving the goals of existing welfare

---

4. This point is not well understood by many commentators who continue to believe that unconditional income transfers will reduce work incentives. As we discuss in Section 2, the need to phase out targeted benefits with income growth usually leads to a high marginal tax rate on income just in the range where people are climbing out of poverty. This is typically a much bigger disincentive to work than the income effect of a universal unconditional transfer that is not phased out.

5. Not all proposals of UBI involve committing such a large amount to UBI only. For example, Bardhan (2018) argues that about 10 percent of GDP is potentially mobilizable by eliminating regressive subsidies and imposing some fresh taxes and that should be equally allocated to fresh public expenditures on health, education, infrastructure, and UBI.

programs, it is politically and practically infeasible to cut major categories of government welfare spending. In contrast, it is much more feasible to direct the *incremental* rupee that is earmarked for welfare spending towards income transfers.[6] This is exactly what is happening with the *Rythu Bandhu,* KALIA, and PM-KISAN schemes. While no existing scheme has been replaced to finance these programs, they still represent a landmark policy pivot to spend the *marginal rupee* allocated to farmers' welfare on direct income transfers as opposed to increases in distortionary subsidies, procurement prices, or loan waivers. Our proposed policy follows exactly this same approach.

Specifically, we recommend that India adopt an "inclusive growth dividend" or IGD for every citizen that is pegged at 1 percent of GDP per capita to be deposited directly into the bank account of every citizen on a regular monthly basis.[7] This would provide every citizen with a supplemental benefit of around ₹120 per month (at current estimates).[8] The amounts for children under 18 should be transferred into the accounts of their mothers (or the next responsible guardian). We believe that such an approach, which is modest in magnitude but ambitious in reach (by being truly universal), can achieve almost all the benefits of income transfers discussed above while mitigating almost all the concerns raised to date regarding the potential costs of a UBI, as we discuss further below.

First, the terminology of an IGD sets a very different set of expectations than a UBI. The term "dividend" makes it clear that this is one component of a *portfolio* of income streams that people would have. The word "inclusive" reflects the progressive aspect of the proposal: since the amount is the same for all citizens, the marginal value of the transfer is correspondingly greater for the poor. Finally, the word "growth" captures the idea that the amount will grow along with the growth of the overall economy. Thus, an IGD would be one component of people's income which reaches all citizens and

---

6. A similar point was made by former Chief Economic Adviser, Arvind Subramanian, in conversation with one of us (see Muralidharan and Subramanian 2015 for more details).

7. The specific terminology and proposal were introduced by one of us in a joint op-ed with Paul Niehaus and Sandip Sukhtankar (Muralidharan, Niehaus, and Sukhtankar 2018a) and in short internal notes for the Ministry of Finance put together by Muralidharan in 2017–18. One of the main goals of this paper is to flesh out the full details of such a proposal and place the recommendation in the larger policy context and more fully distinguish it from the related but distinct discussions of a UBI.

8. This is obtained by taking the latest estimate of GDP per capita at current prices (2018–19), which is ₹142,963 (see Government of India 2020, Statement 2, p. 5). Taking 1 percent of this gives a monthly figure of ₹119, which we round off to ₹120.

grows equally for all with the economy's growth. It would, thus, be a powerful practical and symbolic commitment to universally shared prosperity.

We now discuss the various benefits of such an approach. The biggest advantage of our proposed scheme is simply that it is affordable enough to actually be implemented. Indeed, the value envisaged by the IGD is quite similar to that of PM-KISAN (which works out to ₹500/month per household or ₹120/month per person) and so it can be implemented simply by roughly doubling the budget for PM-KISAN and making the program truly universal.[9] This would allow benefits to also reach landless laborers, who are typically more likely to be destitute and needy than farmers who own land. It would also reduce the likelihood that farmers continue to engage in economically unviable cultivation just to get the PM-KISAN benefit. It would be easier to implement by further reducing eligibility and verification costs. Also, by being at the individual level, it would limit the potential for gaming the scheme (by households splitting to double the value of the transfer). Further, as we discuss in Section 3, an IGD would advance several other social goals, including female empowerment, financial inclusion, and savings (and be a complement to the *Jan-Dhan* Scheme). It would also augment both the capacity and the credibility of the Indian State by building and demonstrating the ability to deliver a benefit to every citizen—a first in independent India.

In addition to the well-known benefits of income transfers discussed above, we believe that a critical long-term benefit from an IGD may be to increase the quality of *all* public expenditure by providing an attainable benchmark against which government programs can be assessed. As we document in Section 2.1, evidence suggests that there is a lot of "value destruction" in public service delivery in India because the government incurs large costs in providing services of such low quality that people opt for paid market solutions despite the public services being "free". Credibly delivering an income transfer every month to every citizen will, over time, allow the government to consider whether it is more cost-effective to directly provide a service or simply provide a fiscally equivalent income transfer directly to intended beneficiaries (to use on market-provided solutions). In many cases, beneficiaries themselves can exercise this choice (as suggested

---

9. As we discuss later, we do not envisage any exclusions from eligibility at this point simply because we believe that it is a powerful symbol of inclusive development and state capacity for the government to demonstrably reach every citizen credibly month after month. One option for excluding the affluent would be to have a "give it up" equivalent option at the time of filing tax returns, whereby citizens who earn above the income tax exemption limit can indicate on their tax returns if they would prefer to forgo their IGD.

by Muralidharan, Niehaus, and Sukhtankar 2018b, in the context of the public distribution system (PDS)).

In other words, income transfers would become a low-implementation cost "index fund" for development spending and in-kind programs would need to demonstrate that their targeting, administrative, and implementation costs deliver more value than their cost. Over time, programs that deliver less value than their cost could be replaced with income transfers while those that deliver more value can be retained. Note that this approach does not make any blanket assumptions regarding the quality (or lack thereof) of government service delivery. Rather, it raises the accountability of government spending by providing a fiscally equivalent benchmark.[10] This can have major long-term positive implications for the quality of government expenditure, both by scrapping programs whose value is less than their cost and by forcing programs to become more efficient to deliver value in excess of their cost.

An IGD will also promote inter-state equality, equity, and efficiency. First, as an equal payment to all citizens, an IGD clearly meets the equality consideration. Second, because the marginal value of an IGD is much higher in poorer areas, it is progressive by construction.[11] It is also progressive by being directly based on the population, which favors poorer states. Finally, since it will be financed out of the general tax pool (which the rich contribute more to), it is also progressive on the financing side. Thus, an IGD is a powerful tool for promoting equity across the country.

The IGD's contribution to efficiency is more subtle. A vexing challenge for the Government of India is that economically disadvantaged states also have weaker governance. For instance, teacher and doctor absence rates in public schools and clinics are consistently higher in states with lower per capita income (Chaudhury et al. 2006). Similarly, welfare programs

---

10. To continue the analogy from investing, the powerful insight of John Bogle was that fund managers all claim to have "alpha" (i.e., they claim to be able to beat the market). But most actively managed funds deliver less value over time than low-cost index funds because the fees of the former destroy considerable value. Of course, in the case of public spending, it is possible that many projects have positive "alpha" (which they will if they are true public goods), but it is also true that many programs have negative "alpha" where beneficiaries are better off with an income equivalent. Our point is simply that an IGD will make these trade-offs clear.

11. We estimate that it would increase per capita income by 16 percent for the poorest 5 percent of the rural population, and by 13 percent for those between the 6th to 10th percentiles. The corresponding figures for the urban population are a 12 percent increase for the poorest 5 percent and a 9 percent increase for those between the 6th and 10th percentiles. At the top end of the distribution, the IGD would increase per capita income by 2 percent for the top 5 percent of the rural population and by 1 percent for the top 5 percent of the urban population. See Table 1 in Section 3.3 for details.

like the NREGS disproportionately benefit better-off states because poorer states lack the administrative capacity to effectively avail of Government of India funds (Aiyar 2014). Thus, to the extent that the Government of India's expenditure on welfare programs aims to reduce inter-regional inequality, direct transfers to citizens may be more efficient than in-kind programs because of weaker governance in poorer states.

Our proposed scheme is a specific version of the idea of a universal basic share (UBS) scheme proposed by Ray (2016), where a share of GDP as opposed to an absolute amount is committed to a universal basic income scheme.[12] Two key benefits of a UBS relative to a UBI highlighted by Ray (2016) are that it is inflation-proof and automatically indexed, and also that it is a flexible, not fixed, commitment that co-moves with GDP.[13] Our proposal also builds on a very similar idea mooted even earlier by Sunil Khilnani, who made the case for a "Citizen's Growth Dividend".[14] Khilnani (2010) emphasizes that the political case for such an approach is recognizing citizens as individuals as opposed to groups (which are the de facto basis on which political mobilization takes place). Both Ray (2016) and Khilnani (2010) emphasize the shared solidarity and "equity-like" sharing in a country's prosperity, which we also highlight here. A similar argument has been made in the context of the US by Shiller (2009).

Thus, our primary contribution is to expand on the conceptual framework described in short essays by Shiller (2009), Khilnani (2010), Ray (2016), and Muralidharan, Niehaus, and Sukhtankar (2018a) and provide a more comprehensive treatment of the relevant issues from a broad development policy perspective, with an emphasis on the Indian policy context. In particular, we move beyond discussing universal income transfers as a redistributive policy aimed at supporting the poor, to highlight that they can also be a powerful tool for alleviating micro-economic constraints to development, and thereby improving productivity and boosting economic growth. In practical terms, we also note that the adoption of universal income transfers may be sub-optimally delayed if discussed alongside the question of which in-kind programs to substitute away from. While some substitution will likely make

---

12. Ray (2016) proposes a benchmark of close to 9 percent of GDP for UBS, which would be fiscally impossible without substantially raising tax revenue or cutting other expenditure. However, he also notes that it is possible to start with a smaller amount and increase it over time.

13. Ray (2016) and Moene and Ray (2016) also discuss additional possible advantages of a UBS scheme, such as creating a broad-based support for tax collection capacity and economic growth among citizens.

14. We thank Pranab Bardhan for pointing out this reference to us, which was not known to us at the time of writing the first draft.

sense over time, we emphasize that this should happen gradually, only after credibly building and demonstrating the capacity of the government to consistently deliver income transfers to all Indians, and ideally based on beneficiary choice. We also ground our discussion of the IGD with evidence on the quality of public expenditure and the track record of implementation of income transfers and other social programs in the Indian context and present a very specific idea that is feasible to implement in the near future.

The rest of the paper is organized as follows. In Section 2, we review the broad conceptual issues involved in thinking through the trade-offs regarding various aspects of the design of income transfer programs as well as the relevant evidence from India and other developing countries. In Section 3, we flesh out the IGD approach in detail and provide specific illustrations of the general aspects of income transfer programs discussed in Section 2 in the Indian context. Section 4 provides an implementation roadmap, and Section 5 has some concluding observations.

2. Key Conceptual Issues

In this section, we review the various arguments and related evidence from India and other developing countries regarding the role of unconditional income transfers as a tool of development policy. We focus on the key conceptual arguments and broadly review the evidence. In particular, we consider the argument regarding the relative value of spending the marginal rupee spent on anti-poverty policies on income transfers as opposed to the direct provision of goods and services aimed at the poor; supplementation versus substitution; the pros and cons of targeted versus universal programs, and the potential impact of an unconditional income transfer scheme such as the IGD on wasteful consumption, work incentives, gender empowerment, relaxing borrowing constraints, providing partial mitigation of consumption risk, and facilitating saving for the poor.

2.1. Income Transfers versus Direct Provision of Goods and Services

A key consideration in assessing the case for income transfers is the question of opportunity costs and whether the same resources could be spent better. Critics of income transfers have argued that it would crowd out resources for spending on other important categories of public expenditure, such as education and health, which may have a greater long-term impact on improving citizens' welfare (see, for instance, Aiyar 2019; Roy 2019a). As some critics have put it, the move towards income transfers represents giving up on the idea of a "developmental state" and moving towards a "compensatory state" (Roy 2019a). Taken to the extreme, such an approach could lead to the abdication of core responsibilities of the state.

How should we assess this criticism? There are two key concepts to keep in mind while assessing the opportunity cost of funds that may be allocated to an income transfer program. The first is expenditure on public goods versus redistribution, where redistribution includes publicly provided private goods (like education, health, or food) where the government provides free or highly subsidized services to make them accessible to the poor. The second is the quality and effectiveness of public expenditure on redistribution and publicly provided private goods.

Most economists (including us) believe that the returns to spending on public goods and infrastructure significantly exceed the costs, especially in countries like India. Examples of such investments include transportation and market integration (such as roads, railways, and ports), communications (Internet cables), public health (anti-vector campaigns, water, and sanitation), and basic research. The return to these public goods likely exceeds their costs because their social benefit is the sum total of private benefits across millions of individuals. Moreover, since the market on its own is unlikely to provide the socially optimal amount of these public goods, the case for public leadership in ensuring adequate provision is clear.

However, in practice, the patterns of public expenditure in India suggest that substantial funds are allocated to further broadly redistributive goals. These include subsidies to make items (such as food, fuel, and fertilizer) cheaper for the poor, as well as investments in publicly provided private goods (such as government-run schools, clinics, and fair-price shops that distribute subsidized food under PDS). Here, an important rationale for public provision is the ability to offer the service at low or no cost to the poor (which is a redistributive goal).[15]

Analysis of public expenditure in India suggests that a much larger fraction of social sector spending goes to redistribution rather than public goods. For instance, in agriculture, public expenditure on interest, fertilizer, and electricity subsidies is much greater than spending on public irrigation or agricultural research and extension.[16] Similarly, in health, expenditure on

---

15. The National Rural Employment Guarantee Scheme (NREGS) has elements of both public good creation (through construction of rural assets) and redistribution (through creating jobs for the rural poor).

16. Interest subsidies alone account for ₹21,175 crores in the budget for the Ministry of Agriculture and Farmers' Welfare in the 2020–21 Union Budget. Further, fertilizer subsidies under the Ministry of Chemicals and Fertilizers are worth ₹71,309 crores. Together, expenditure

curative services (a private good) is greater than that on public goods with substantial positive externalities such as vector control and immunizations. This is also true in education, where the majority of expenditure is on teacher salaries (for providing education) rather than on public goods such as setting standards and syllabi and running public examination systems.[17]

Thus, to assess the relative value of expanding income transfers versus expanding public provision of goods and services, we need to assess the quality of public expenditure in doing so. This is an area where a considerable amount of research has been done in the past 15 years, and several pieces of evidence suggest that the quality of expenditure on public services under the status quo is quite poor.

Take the example of schooling, where the public spending per student in government schools is over three times higher than the total cost per student in affordable private schools. Yet high-quality evidence finds that private schools are still at least as effective at improving student learning (Muralidharan and Sundararaman 2015).[18] The main drivers of greater productivity of spending (defined as learning outcomes produced per rupee spent) in private schools are much lower teacher salaries (allowing them to hire more teachers, which leads to smaller pupil–teacher ratios and less multi-grade teaching) and better accountability (which leads to lower teacher absence rates and greater time on task). Millions of parents choose to pay out of pocket for these private schools—even though public schools are available for free or even at a *negative* cost (because they provide students with free books and mid-day meals).

---

on just these two subsidies is over 11 times the total budget for the Department of Agriculture Research and Education (₹8,363 crores). In addition, state budgets also spend more on electricity subsidies for groundwater than on investments in public irrigation.

17. The reasons for this pattern of expenditure are beyond the scope of this paper, but one broad explanation is that India adopted universal adult franchise-based democracy at a much lower level of per capita income than most other OECD countries. Thus, India faced political pressure for redistribution and subsidized or free access to services at a much lower level of development compared to historical norms (see Muralidharan and Subramanian 2015, for a more extended discussion).

18. Note that a naive comparison of student learning outcomes across public and private schools will yield an incorrect impression that private schools are better. This comparison does not account for the fact that parents of children attending private schools are typically more educated and affluent than those of parents attending government schools. Muralidharan and Sundararaman (2015) address this concern using a large-scale randomized experiment where randomly selected students (using a lottery) in government schools were provided a voucher to enable them to attend a private school of their choice. Tracking outcomes over time for lottery winners and losers allows for a more accurate comparison of the effects of attending private versus government schools.

The health care situation is even more striking. Over 70 percent of primary health care visits in rural India are to fee-charging private providers, even when the village has a public health clinic. Private providers are less qualified but exert more effort (Das et al. 2016). Further, Das et al. (2016) show that private providers with lower qualifications deliver comparable quality of care as in the public sector but at less than one-fourth the cost per patient seen. Just like in education, an important mechanism for the greater cost-effectiveness of private providers is lower pay and higher effort.

The flight of the poor towards market solutions is at least in part a consequence of the poor accountability of public sector service providers. This is starkly illustrated by the high rates of teacher and doctor absence across India (25 percent and 40 percent, respectively). Overall, the government incurs large costs in providing services that are of such low quality that most people do not want them. In other words, there is considerable "value destruction" in the status quo of public service delivery since the service provided is valued considerably lower than the cost of providing it. Thus, while there is a strong need to improve the quality of government services, the evidence suggests that value for money under the status quo is low and that the returns to simply increasing spending along existing patterns are likely to be low. Further, evidence from multiple studies suggests that improving governance can be many more times more cost-effective at achieving the same level of effective increase in the presence of a program on the ground than spending more on the program itself.[19]

One way of doing this is to improve top-down governance, which is what the existing evidence is based on. However, another way of forcing the public sector to improve its efficiency is by eliminating the captive market of poor households by enabling the poorest to avail of services from both public and private providers.

The above discussion highlights that providing some income support should be seen as a *complement to public services and not a substitute*. Over time, once the state shows that it can credibly reach the poorest through income transfers, it opens up a set of policy options whereby the poor can choose between status quo public services and an equivalent cash transfer.[20]

This approach makes no assumptions regarding the relative merits of provision of services by the state or the market. We recognize that there is

---

19. See Muralidharan, Niehaus, and Sukhtankar (2016) for evidence in the context of NREGS, Muralidharan et al. (2017) for evidence from education, and Muralidharan et al. (2019) for evidence from a cash transfer scheme for farmers.

20. Such an approach has been outlined in the case of the PDS by Muralidharan, Niehaus, and Sukhtankar 2018b.

enormous heterogeneity in both provider quality and beneficiary preferences across time and space. Rather, our point is that having income transfers be part of the portfolio of policy options to reach the poor can empower beneficiaries to have a stronger voice in how social sector funds (spent in their name) are actually spent. Over time, the public sector would need to show that it can deliver more value than an equivalent income transfer and compete for the business of the poor who will be empowered with more options after their incomes are augmented.

To summarize this section, we believe that expenditure on pure public goods—especially productivity-enhancing infrastructure—should not be crowded out to make fiscal space for income transfers. However, we believe that at least one component of the budget allocated for poverty alleviation and publicly provided private goods could fruitfully be used for income transfers instead. This informs our view of income transfers as one key component in a portfolio of social protection policies. Such an approach will empower citizens to choose from a broader menu of service providers (including private and non-government providers) and to increase the accountability of public provision through greater choice and competition.

2.2. Substitution versus Supplementation

Most of the existing discourse on the UBI has assumed that the fiscal space for UBI/income transfers would come from existing programs, which would be replaced with income transfers. However, this has almost never been successfully done in practice. There are several reasons for this including the considerable political economy challenges of shutting down existing programs that benefit millions of people, and the risk of imperfect implementation of cash transfers.

Recent evidence illustrates how implementation challenges are non-trivial. Starting in 2015, the Government of India attempted a pilot in the three Union Territories of Chandigarh, Puducherry, and Dadra and Nagar Haveli. The government replaced PDS entitlements (subsidized foodgrains) with DBT into bank accounts.

However, a process monitoring study with over 10,000 household surveys (Muralidharan et al. 2017) reported that though government records showed that over 99 percent of transfers had been made successfully, *nearly a third of households reported not having received their transfers*. This likely reflected a combination of funds going to an inactive account, passbooks not being updated, and no outbound notification of fund transfer.

In ongoing work with other co-authors, one of us has found similar issues in the flagship Prime Minister's Maternity Benefits Scheme or *Pradhan*

Mantri Matru Vandana Yojana (PMMVY), where we monitored implementation quality in Jharkhand.[21] Officials at more senior levels (district and above) indicated that no eligible woman was being excluded. However, at more junior levels, 30 percent of supervisors and 50 percent of Anganwadi workers reported cases of beneficiaries not being registered and hence not receiving their payments. This is corroborated by our survey of actual eligible beneficiaries, where less than 40 percent of eligible women reported receiving their most recent payment. Since payments may arrive late, this should be interpreted as the fraction of women receiving benefits on time. However, given the goal of providing funds to pregnant and lactating mothers during the key stages of child development, delayed payments are still a significant marker of weaknesses in last-mile delivery.

This field experience highlights how non-trivial it is to ensure that all beneficiaries have bank accounts that are seeded with *Aadhaar* details as well as eligibility details, and that transfers are made reliably. Given the implementation issues that we have documented across sectors and states, we feel that for political and ethical reasons, it is not prudent to embark on income transfers based on mandated substitution of other benefits.

Further, given the political difficulty of scrapping or replacing existing programs that have millions of beneficiaries, the many benefits of having predictable income transfers comprise one part of the portfolio of anti-poverty strategies that are not getting realized. In part, this is because there is no way to make the fiscal space for the large transfers (envisaged under most UBI proposals) that would be needed to eliminate poverty without also replacing existing programs.

So, from a practical policy perspective, we feel that "less is more." Starting with a modest supplementary income transfer to all citizens will allow us to get started on the path towards realizing the many benefits of income transfers while mitigating several concerns that have been raised by critics. We refer to this approach as an inclusive growth dividend or IGD (which we explain in more detail in the next section).

Our recommended approach is also consistent with how income transfers are playing out in practice in India. The political economy of expenditure reform is that it is much more difficult to change existing spending than it is to improve the quality of new spending (Muralidharan and Subramanian 2015). We see this playing out in the introduction of income transfers as the preferred policy instrument for supporting farmers over the past 15 months, starting with the RBS in Telangana, and then followed up by the KALIA

---

21. This is based on ongoing work by Muralidharan with Paul Niehaus, Sandip Sukhtankar, and Jeff Weaver.

program in Odisha and the PM-KISAN program on a nationwide basis. Note that these are all *supplemental* programs that do not replace any existing programs or subsidies. However, they do considerably improve resource allocation at the margin because the marginal rupee earmarked for farmer support was spent on these transfers rather than the much more distortionary default options of farm loan waivers and increases in minimum support prices (MSPs).

2.3. Targeted versus Universal Income Transfer Programs

The pros and cons of targeted versus universal social welfare programs have been discussed extensively in the public economics and development economics literature (see, for instance, the discussions in Banerjee, Niehaus, and Suri 2019; Currie and Gahvari 2008; Ghatak and Maniquet 2019; Hanna and Olken 2018). This section summarizes the key trade-offs.

Compared to targeted income or benefit transfer schemes that are aimed at the poor and are therefore subject to means-testing, IGD is an unconditional stream of cash income paid by the government to every member of society—it is paid regardless of whether an individual is working, of his or her existing income, and whoever he or she lives with.

There are three aspects of the design of such a program. First, it is an income transfer as opposed to an in-kind transfer like food, housing, or fuel.[22] Second, it is universal, that is, it is not targeted to any specific group based on socioeconomic or demographic criteria (such as age, gender, marriage or family status, and family composition), and it is provided at the level of the individual as opposed to the household. Third, it is unconditional and not contingent on the recipient satisfying any compliance criteria or being deemed as deserving. This makes an IGD distinct from conditional transfer schemes that are contingent, for example, on parents sending their children to school.

From the economic point of view, the absence of means-testing or targeting is the most salient aspect of programs like a UBI or an IGD.[23] The main reasons for this design are explained as follows.

Any program that is not universal has substantial direct and indirect administrative costs of targeting the relevant group (Hanna and Olken 2018). It also creates scope for errors of inclusion and exclusion (namely those who are not eligible but get it, and those who are eligible but not get

---

22. We use the term income transfer rather than cash transfer to capture the idea that the income will go into a bank account and not be handed out as cash, which may be more susceptible to impulsive spending.

23. See Hanna and Olken (2018) and Ravallion (2016) for excellent reviews on different forms of targeting.

it, respectively).[24] Also, other than the standard inefficiencies associated with subsidies of any kind, targeted schemes create scope for corruption and leakage in the implementation process. Additionally, citizens' efforts to be added to the list of beneficiaries, legitimately or illegitimately, are another set of costs.[25] Finally, scholars and practitioners have argued that "programs meant for the poor" become "poor programs". Specifically, the argument is that universal programs tend to have broader political support and are therefore better funded and implemented.[26] As we show in Section 3, an IGD would augment consumption by 7–8 percent for the median rural household and 4–5 percent for the median urban household, which are non-trivial increases even for the median recipient.

Universal schemes are more expensive than targeted schemes for the same total level of benefits, and so, for a given budget constraint, they require scaling down benefits. Also, being lumpsum in nature, they cannot respond differentially to specific needs of individuals or groups, which may vary over time or across individuals. However, given weaker state capacity as well as the problem of a lot of people living on the margins of subsistence, the case for a universal income transfer scheme is stronger in a developing country like India than in developed countries since the welfare consequences of exclusion errors are higher (see Ghatak and Maniquet 2019, for a more detailed discussion).

To illustrate the argument in the Indian context, suppose we extend the PM-KISAN to all citizens. Assuming an average family size of 4.6 and a population of 132.7 crores, we get 29 crore additional families, which is almost exactly double the current coverage of the scheme. In per capita terms, a transfer of ₹6,000 per family per year translates to approximately

---

24. There is a trade-off between inclusion (Type I error) and exclusion errors (Type II error). If the goal is to minimize exclusion errors (e.g., in the spirit of "no one left behind"), then it is likely that inclusion errors will go up. Conversely, attempts to reduce leakage and inclusion errors will typically be accompanied by an increase in exclusion errors, as shown in ongoing work by Muralidharan, Niehaus, and Sukhtankar (2020). Hanna and Olken (2018) carry out a simulation exercise, using data from Indonesia and Peru, about the trade-off between these two types of errors.

25. See Khosla (2018) for a good review of the various kinds of costs associated with targeting. From an economists' perspective, the deadweight losses associated with these efforts are a substantial cost that is rarely accounted for in discussing the costs and benefits of targeting.

26. In the Indian context, this point has been raised by Jean Dreze, who argues, for instance, that the PDS in Tamil Nadu works better than in other states, in part because it is universal and, therefore, has broader political support (Dreze 2010). In the US context, a similar point has been made to explain why Medicare (which is universal above age 65) is better financed and politically more secure than Medicaid (which caters only to the poor). See Brown and Sparer (2003) for a discussion.

₹1,300 per person per year, or around ₹110 per person per month. This is roughly the same figure for the IGD we obtain from using a benchmark of 1 percent of GDP (₹120 per person/month). At current prices, this would translate to around 9.5 percent of total Central Government expenditure or about 13.2 percent of tax revenue.

A good example of a contrasting proposal based on larger transfers to fewer (poorer) people is the idea of *Nyuntam Aay Yojana* (NYAY) floated by the Congress Party in the run-up to the 2019 Parliamentary elections. NYAY would have given ₹6,000 per month (as opposed to per year, as under PM-KISAN) to the poorest 20 percent of families. This works out to be about 2.5 times the amount that would be needed if PM-KISAN was extended to all families, and accordingly, the total expenditure would have amounted to 2.5 percent of GDP and nearly 25 percent of total government expenditure. Even if the amount of the financial support is scaled down to say, 1 percent, of GDP, the key feature of NYAY is that it is targeted at the poor, which raises the problems of targeting mentioned above, as well as the problems of reduced work incentives due to the phase-out period (described in Section 2.5).[27]

PM-KISAN is also a targeted income transfer scheme—it is aimed at all landholding farmers (subject to some exclusion criteria such as having a family member who pays income tax or is a professional) and so excludes all those who are involved with agriculture but do not own land (such as agricultural laborers and tenants), and of course, those who are not engaged with agriculture. PM-KISAN is a substantial improvement over input subsidies and loan waivers, and targeting based on landholding is easier than doing so based on income. Yet it will still have non-trivial costs of targeting, including costs of verifying landholdings and costs of gaming (by households that choose to split landholdings to take advantage of the non-linear features of the benefits schedule). Making the scheme universal would avoid these costs.

2.4. Will People Spend Cash Transfers Badly?

One frequently raised paternalistic concern about income transfers relative to the in-kind provision of benefits is that people may squander the cash on inessential consumption. All else equal, beneficiaries should prefer income transfers as they allow individuals freedom of choice to spend the money based on their specific needs and priorities. However, if the preferences of

---

27. See Ghatak (2019a) and Muralidharan (2019) for discussions on the design weaknesses of NYAY.

the individual are different from that of the policymaker (which can be due to behavioral biases, or insufficient intergenerational altruism, or gender bias), there may be grounds for paternalistic intervention. If so, unconditional income transfers may not be the most efficient intervention, and there may be a case for other policy instruments that restrict how the value of the benefits may be spent.

While there is some evidence that people spend more when they receive windfalls (like lottery winnings, as suggested by Imbens, Rubin, and Sacerdote 2001), there is no such evidence on small steady streams of income. Indeed, evidence from developing countries suggests that, on average, cash transfers to the poor do not cause them to work less or spend their money on inessential consumption. Evans and Popova (2017) review evidence from 19 studies with quantitative evidence on the impact of cash transfers on expenditure on temptation goods (mainly, alcohol and tobacco), as well as 11 studies that surveyed whether respondents reported that they used transfers to purchase temptation goods (these 30 studies span Latin America, Africa, and Asia). They find either no significant impact or a significant negative impact of transfers on expenditures on alcohol and tobacco. Restricting attention to randomized trials, they find a negative but statistically insignificant effect.

Bastagli et al. (2016) reviewed evidence on the effects of cash transfers on individuals and households through a literature review from 2000 to 2015, covering 201 studies and reporting increases in household food expenditure, school attendance, use of health services, dietary diversity, savings, livestock ownership, and purchase of agricultural inputs. A pilot study of UBI in eight Indian villages in Madhya Pradesh reports similar findings (Davala et al. 2015).

In addition to giving beneficiaries freedom of choice, by not making the transfers contingent on any behavioral norms of recipients, universal income transfer schemes would enable us to avoid setting up entire administrative machinery aimed at monitoring compliance. This not only avoids the direct and indirect costs of running such a bureaucracy, but it also removes the patron-client relationship that is inherent in any system of monitoring and rewards between the state and its citizens that is undesirable in a democracy.

2.5. Effect on Work Incentives

A major concern about any income transfer program is the potentially negative effect on work incentives. Using a standard labor-supply framework where individuals choose between income and leisure, an increase in non-wage income would increase the demand for leisure. This informs the standard view that income transfers will reduce labor supply.

However, this theoretical argument is not robust to allowing for subsistence considerations or market frictions (Ghatak and Maniquet 2019). In situations where income levels are so low that subsistence considerations matter, which is the case with low wages and low levels of non-labor income, a good proportion of the population will be working very hard (i.e., using up all their available time endowment on work) to earn a minimum income level to meet their subsistence needs. For them, an income transfer that is not large will not affect their labor supply but can push them above subsistence, resulting in potentially large welfare gains.

Once we allow for frictions in the labor, credit or insurance markets, the likelihood of a potentially negative effect of income transfers on labor supply will be further reduced (Baird, McKenzie, and Özler 2018). To the extent to which greater income allows better nutrition, which, in turn, leads to greater productivity, there could be an increase in labor supply due to a higher effective wage rate. Also, to the extent to which income transfers relax liquidity constraints or enable individuals to take greater risk given access to a steady stream of income, there could be an increase in labor supply in self-employment, an issue we discuss in detail in Section 3.

While we do not have much direct evidence regarding the effect of unconditional income transfer scheme on labor supply yet, Banerjee, Karlan, and Zinman (2015) re-analyze the results of seven randomized controlled trials of government-run cash transfer programs from six countries worldwide to examine their impacts on labor supply. Across the seven programs, they find no systematic evidence of an impact on either the propensity to work or the overall number of hours worked, for either men or women. Baird, McKenzie, and Özler (2018) also review the evidence on adult labor market outcomes in response to cash transfers, and the general picture that emerges is that these generally had little or no effect on overall labor supply, and to the extent to which there was an effect, it was positive with some substitution away from wage labor to work in self-employment.

One of the very few long-standing nationwide cash transfer programs that most closely resembles a UBI was introduced in Iran in 2011. It faced political criticism for its alleged disincentive for work, especially for the poor. However, careful analysis shows that there was no evidence of reduced labor supply, and if anything, the labor supply of women and self-employed men actually went up (Salehi-Isfahani and Mostafavi-Dehzooei 2018).

Evidence on the labor supply effect of cash transfer programs in developed countries does not appear to suggest a potentially large negative effect, either. For example, Marinescu (2018) reviews empirical results from the US and Canadian negative income tax experiments, the Alaska Permanent Fund Dividend, and the Eastern Band of Cherokees casino dividend program, as well as a few other assorted studies and finds that, overall, the programs analyzed suggest either no effect on labor market supply or a slight reduction in work and earnings. Taken together, there is no systematic evidence across various cash transfer programs that they have a negative effect on labor supply.

Finally, comparing across potential designs of income transfer programs, a small universal unconditional transfer will likely have smaller adverse effects on work incentives compared to a larger transfer to fewer (poorer people) for at least two reasons. First, the smaller transfer implies a lower-income-effect-based increase in the demand for leisure. Second, under targeted schemes, the benefits decrease with means. This may create strong negative incentive effects due to a potentially high marginal tax rate in the range of income where the benefits are phased out.

To take a concrete example of the problem of targeted schemes in the Indian context, let us consider the NYAY proposal, which targeted families in the bottom 20 percent of the population. The proposal was to either pay the eligible families the difference between ₹12,000 and their actual income or simply a flat amount of ₹6,000 per month. However, there is no way to directly verify the incomes of the poor (e.g., via payroll or income tax) as they work in the unorganized sector. As a result, both versions of the scheme create strong incentives to under-report income since the marginal tax rate as someone crosses the threshold of qualifying for this scheme is 100 percent (every rupee hidden is one rupee gained in benefits) or more (crossing from below the threshold to above the threshold entails losing the entire benefit).

This illustrates that while income effects of unconditional cash transfers may deter effort in theory, targeting can actually exacerbate poverty due to the disincentive to climb out of official poverty (since the phasing out of benefits with increasing income is equivalent to a high effective marginal tax rate on incomes earned by the poor).[28]

---

28. While the theoretical argument is clear, there is less direct evidence on the incentive effects of targeting in developing countries (Banerjee, Niehaus, and Suri 2019). One piece of indirect evidence is from a field experiment that finds that households try to appear poorer when participation in surveys is incentivized (Stecklov, Weinreb, and Carletto 2018). Hanna and Olken (2018) provide a brief and useful review of this literature. One interesting point they make is that in developing countries that use proxy-means tests for eligibility for benefits programs, the greater the noise in these formulas, the lower the implied labor supply distortions

2.6. Female Empowerment and Improved Intra-household Targeting

A large literature shows the positive effects of cash transfer schemes on female empowerment (see, e.g., Bastagli et al. 2016; Duflo 2012, for reviews). Direct recent evidence on this point is presented by Field et al. (2020), who randomize whether NREGS payments for women's work in Madhya Pradesh are paid into the account of the head of household (typically male) or of the female worker herself and find that sending money into female accounts (combined with training on how to use the accounts) significantly raises the labor supply of women on both NREGS and the open market. The authors interpret this result as direct evidence of increased female empowerment from depositing money into their accounts.[29]

Giving women control over more resources may also improve the intra-household targeting of anti-poverty programs. Most targeted schemes attempt to reach poor individuals by targeting poor households, but as Brown, Calvi, and Penglase (2019) show, intra-household inequality may mean that many poor individuals live within non-poor households. Using data from Bangladesh, they apply a new approach to calculating individual-level poverty rates that takes intra-household inequality into consideration. They find that women, children, and the elderly are at risk of living in poverty even within households with per capita expenditure levels that exceed the poverty threshold. Thus, universal untargeted income transfers (with the allowance for children going to mothers) may actually *improve* targeting to the most vulnerable members of society relative to a system that targets transfers based on mean household income.

2.7. Relaxing Borrowing Constraints for Productive Investments

Critics of income transfers often caricature them as band-aids for poverty, diverting resources from policies and programs that would have enhanced productivity and provided a more long-term sustained pathway out of poverty (e.g., Aiyar 2019; Roy 2019a). There are two problems with this argument. First, what may seem like a "band-aid" to policymakers can be quite substantial for those living on the margins of subsistence. Second, and more importantly, in contrast to the standard trope of income transfers

---

due to the phasing out, for the same reason that incentive schemes are less effective when performance is noisily measured. However, there is no direct evidence regarding this point.

29. Additional recent evidence on increased female empowerment from being the recipient of income transfers is provided by Almås et al. (2018), who used a randomized experiment from Macedonia that varied the gender of the parent who received a conditional cash transfer for secondary school attendance.

reducing incentives for work, there are several theoretically sound reasons to believe that they may *increase* the productivity of the poor by providing an important source of working capital. Also, having a source of consumption insurance will enable the poor to make risky investments. In this section and the next, we discuss these two channels in detail, where having a regular income flow can relax borrowing constraints as well as provide a threshold level of insurance, outlining the theoretical arguments and providing supporting empirical evidence.

An extensive literature on returns to capital in developing countries suggests very high rates of return that often exceed prevailing interest rates (see Banerjee and Duflo 2005, for a review). For example, in a well-known study, de Mel, McKenzie, and Woodruff (2008) consider the effect of one-time randomized capital grants worth at most 10–20 percent of the capital stock of microenterprises in Sri Lanka and estimate the returns to capital to be 60 percent per year, which is substantially higher than market interest rates, and conclude from this that these enterprises are indeed credit-constrained. Experiments with similar-sized grants were carried out in other countries, such as Mexico, Ghana, and India, and yielded similar rates of return (see Banerjee, Niehaus, and Suri 2019, and Baird, McKenzie, and Özler 2018, for reviews of the literature).[30]

Despite these high rates of return to capital, only a small fraction of individuals in developing countries have access to bank loans—Banerjee, Niehaus and Suri (2019) report a figure of 12 percent for India from the most recent financial inclusion surveys. For the poor in India, a well-known survey of the economic lives of the poor (Banerjee and Duflo 2008) suggests that among those who have at least one loan (about 66 percent of the rural poor and 70 percent of the urban poor), a very small fraction comes from bank loans (6 percent in rural and 7 percent in urban areas).

However, despite high returns to extra capital for existing business owners, the *average* returns across all potential borrowers may not be as high. This, in fact, is the general conclusion that emerges from experimental evidence from microfinance from six countries (Banerjee, Karlan, and Zinman 2015). In a study based in India (Banerjee et al. 2015), there was no significant effect on business earnings, on average, but a strongly positive and persistent impact on those who had a pre-existing business. Even in the

---

30. There are also experimental studies that look at the effect of large capital grants, such as Bandiera et al. (2017) and Blattman et al. (2016). In the former study, the average capital transfer was 90 percent of the per capita annual consumption expenditure of the group that was targeted for the intervention. Because of our focus on IGD, which involves much smaller amounts, we do not discuss these.

aforementioned studies on capital grants to microenterprises, which found high average rates of return, returns vary considerably. The key implication of this finding is that lenders need to exert considerable costly effort to screen borrowers to identify those who are likely to have high returns on capital and are able to repay their loans.

These intermediation costs may help explain why even microcredit interest rates are not low. The India study mentioned above had an annual interest rate of 24 percent, which is considerably higher than bank interest rates, largely reflecting the costs of intermediation to poor borrowers with small loan amounts. It is not surprising then that several microfinance studies have take-up rates of less than 20 percent. Further, microfinance seems to have a limited impact on consumption in most studies, suggesting that credit expansion might not be enough to effectively reduce poverty.

Rather than take a pessimistic view on microcredit, a more optimistic implication of the above results is that people have either investment or consumption smoothing opportunities that generate an internal rate of return of around 25 percent, but that these returns are mainly absorbed by interest costs (which in turn, reflect intermediation costs). In this view, an IGD offers the potential of delivering similar returns to the capital since there is no intermediation cost or interest. More generally, it may help poor households move from a "credit cycle" where they borrow first for a consumption event and then repay in installments (at high-interest cost) to a "savings cycle" where they first pay themselves (through automatic savings of their IGD) and then use their savings to finance consumption or investments. Repeated over several cycles, moving out of a "credit cycle" to a "savings cycle" can generate very high rates of return.

Finally, an IGD may also make it easier for the poor to access formal credit. Recent evidence from developed country contexts suggests, in contrast to many models of credit constraints, that lenders assessing borrowers' creditworthiness care more about their cash flow (since this determines their capacity to service the loan) than about their collateral (since this is typically illiquid; Drechsel 2019). In such a setting, the presence of an IGD may considerably increase the assessed creditworthiness of the poor, which may crowd in formal credit at lower interest rates than the status quo.

The final point worth noting regarding an IGD and credit is that most lenders require repayment on a rigid schedule, which may prevent borrowers from undertaking investments with a delayed pay-off (Field et al. 2013). An IGD can help alleviate this problem by providing a stream of income that can help to make interest payments while the loan is deployed to undertake productive investments that may have a delayed payoff schedule.

2.8. Mitigating Risk to Enable Productive Investments

In their book *Portfolios of the Poor,* Collins et al. (2009) highlight that the poor (defined as those who live on no more than $1.90 a day) face considerable risk and seasonality in their income streams. Thus, they may live on $3 one day, $1 the next day, and nothing the day after. Yet, beyond informal risk-sharing, the poor in developing countries have little access to formal insurance systems. Banerjee and Duflo (2008) report that only 10–11 percent of households had access to any kind of insurance, whether for health or life.

From this point of view, financial inclusion of the poor with even a small fixed periodic transfer to their bank accounts can go a long way in mitigating risk. This risk not only imposes significant welfare costs but also constrains the ability of the poor to undertake income-generating activities because of the extreme risk aversion that comes from living on the margins of subsistence. Banerjee, Niehaus, and Suri (2019) review the experimental evidence on the degree to which small enterprises or farms may be constrained by lack of insurance (as entrepreneurs or farmers do not want to expose themselves to the risk that comes with additional investment, whether it is their own money or borrowed money). The evidence, mostly in the context of agriculture, suggests that with insurance, farmers choose crops that are riskier but have higher average returns, and there is a higher investment.

A particularly striking example of how small the relevant investments might be for generating substantial returns is provided by the experimental study of Bryan, Chowdhury, and Mobarak (2014). Working with a sample of poor households in rural Bangladesh, which suffer considerable hardship in the lean season, they offered a randomly selected subsample a payment of 600 taka in 2008 (around $8.50) conditional on migrating to nearby urban areas, and an additional bonus of 200 taka (approximately $3) if the migrant reports to the survey team at the destination. This, effectively, is the cost of a bus ride. They find that 22 percent of the selected households send out a seasonal migrant, and family members of migrants have significantly higher food expenditure (30–35 percent), which, in turn, improves their caloric intake by 550–700 calories per person per day. They also find that treated households are more likely to remigrate after incentives are removed in subsequent years. This raises the question as to what was stopping these households from taking advantage of migration opportunities given that the costs are relatively small. Their favored answer is risk-aversion. Since there is uncertainty about the returns to migration, and there is the potential for a downside (as the authors find in the data), households at the margin of subsistence (as these were) may not be willing to pay the "search" cost to take advantage of the opportunity.

The lesson from this study that is particularly relevant from our point of view is that relatively small sums of income transfers can have potentially large effects on income generation, other than contributing towards providing some subsistence support.

2.9. Alleviating Savings Constraints

Irrespective of access to credit and insurance, savings can help both to smooth consumption and to accumulate resources for productive investments. Yet in the absence of access to formal banking, saving is difficult due to the risk of theft, demands by friends and extended family, and the temptation to spend on inessential consumption.

There is indeed a demand from the poor for institutional savings opportunities. In an experimental study on expanding access to bank accounts to small enterprise owners in rural Kenya, Dupas and Robinson (2013) find a very high take-up rate (nearly 87 percent), which is in sharp contrast to the lower take-up rates for microfinance (of around 30 percent across studies). Not only that, they found that women (as opposed to men) used bank accounts more actively, increased their total savings, and invested in their businesses.

With the significant progress in financial inclusion through the *Jan-Dhan Yojana* in recent years, many more among the poorer sections now have access to saving opportunities than what earlier studies suggested.[31] Further, recent evidence suggests that payments into bank accounts in India boosted savings. Specifically, Somville and Vandewalle (2018), using a randomized controlled trial in Chhattisgarh, show that savings increased significantly when earnings were directly deposited in beneficiary bank accounts, as opposed to being given out in cash. Thus, an income transfer program combined with bank accounts is likely to meaningfully boost formal savings of the poor.

3. An Inclusive Growth Dividend for India

Based on the discussions above, we now introduce the main policy idea of this paper and our specific recommended way to incorporate income transfers into the portfolio of anti-poverty strategies for India. Specifically, we recommend that India should adopt an "Inclusive Growth Dividend" or IGD

---

31. In a review published a decade ago, Banerjee and Duflo (2008) reported that only 6.4 percent of households in the rural areas and 24 percent in the urban areas of India in their sample had a savings account.

for every citizen, pegged at 1 percent of GDP per capita, to be deposited directly into the bank account of every citizen on a regular monthly basis. At current estimates, this translates to a benefit of around ₹120 per person per month. The amounts for children under 18 will be transferred into the accounts of their mothers (or the next responsible guardians). We believe that such an approach, which is modest in magnitude but ambitious in reach (by being nearly universal), can achieve almost all the benefits of income transfers alluded to in the previous section while mitigating almost all the concerns raised to date regarding the potential costs of a UBI. We also believe that it can be an effective policy not just for social protection, but for broader economic growth by alleviating several constraints to productive investments. We discuss these as follows.

3.1. Terminology

As mentioned above, many of the advantages of income transfers as an anti-poverty strategy have been discussed extensively in the context of a UBI. However, there are important ways in which an IGD is different, which is reflected in the terminology.

Perhaps, most important is the fact that the term "basic income" connotes an amount that is adequate to live on. This sets the expectation that the amount of the transfer will be large enough to eliminate poverty. This, in turn, means that the amounts involved are large enough that they would be infeasible to implement without either eliminating other schemes or substantially increasing tax collections—both of which are practically and politically daunting tasks. Thus, setting the expectation of the value of the income transfer too high may have had the negative consequence of delaying progress on using income transfers as one component of an anti-poverty strategy.

In contrast, an IGD sets a very different set of expectations. The most important word here is "dividend", which makes it clear that this is one component of a portfolio of income streams that people would have. The word "inclusive" captures the built-in progressivity of the idea: since the amount is the same for all citizens, the marginal value of the transfer is correspondingly greater for the poor. Finally, the word "growth" captures the idea that the amount will grow along with the growth of the overall economy. Thus, an IGD would be one component of people's income that reaches all citizens and grows equally for all with the country's growth. It would thus be a powerful practical and symbolic commitment to universally shared prosperity. We now discuss the various benefits of such an approach.

3.2. Affordable Enough to Be Feasible

As discussed above, most of the existing discussions of a UBI in India, including those by Pranab Bardhan, Vijay Joshi, Arvind Subramanian (in the *Economic Survey*), and one of us (Ghatak), have had a benchmark value ranging from 3.5 percent to 10 percent of GDP per capita. In practice, it will be impossible to find the fiscal space to reach this value of transfer without eliminating other programs, which, as discussed above, is both politically and practically difficult. This may be one important reason as to why there has been limited policy traction for a UBI in India.

In contrast, at 1 percent of GDP per capita, the total cost of an IGD (with no exclusions whatsoever) would be in the range of ₹190,000 crores. While this is a non-trivial amount, it is entirely feasible to fund such an allocation. As we mentioned earlier, this is 2.5 times the budget allocated for PM-KISAN, whose estimated cost to the Government of India is ₹75,000 crores for 2020–21. Also, recall that the per capita allocation of PM-KISAN (₹6,000 per household) is quite similar to that of the IGD for an average-sized household (with 4.6 members). Thus, the amounts envisaged here are more likely to be in the realm of fiscal feasibility for a *supplemental* transfer.

Further, while PM-KISAN is a substantial improvement over NYAY in terms of design (as discussed in Section 2), using the funds allocated to PM-KISAN for an IGD would be even better. First, and perhaps most important, it would also reach landless laborers and those without formal title to land, who are typically more destitute and needy than farmers who own land. Second, by being independent of occupation, it would reduce the likelihood that farmers continue to engage in economically unviable cultivation just to get the PM-KISAN benefit. Third, from a practical perspective, by being at the individual level and not the household level, it would limit the scope for gaming the scheme by households splitting to double the value of the transfer. Further, as we discuss below, an IGD would advance several other social goals, including female empowerment, financial inclusion, and savings.

Finally, if the limited fiscal capacity for a universal IGD makes some targeting necessary, it would make sense to target on the basis of region (say district or block) and make the transfer universal within that region. This way, most of the practical benefits of being a universal program will be achieved (especially low-targeting cost) with benefits availing to the most economically disadvantaged regions of the country. Thus, it would be feasible and sensible to start with an IGD in the 20 percent of the lowest-income districts at a cost of 0.2 percent of GDP. Such an approach is similar to how programs such as NREGS or aspirational districts have been initially rolled out in the most disadvantaged parts of the country.

3.3. Progressive, Inclusive, and Sustained Poverty Reduction

By construction, an IGD is a highly progressive program. An amount of ₹120 per month per person may seem like a pittance to someone living in Delhi or Mumbai, but the same amount can augment the consumption of the very poor by a non-trivial amount. Based on our calculations, Table 1 depicts the distribution of per capita expenditures at various percentiles of the income distribution for rural and urban India.

TABLE 1. Rural and Urban Monthly Per-capita Consumer Expenditure (MPCE) at Percentile Distributions of Household Consumption Expenditures, 2018–19

Percentile	Rural		Urban	
	MPCE (monthly, ₹ at current prices)	IGD as a percentage of MPCE (%)	MPCE (monthly, ₹ at current prices)	IGD as a percentage of MPCE (%)
0–5	734	16	986	12
5–10	937	13	1,279	9
10–20	1,102	11	1,573	8
20–30	1,273	9	1,917	6
30–40	1,432	8	2,286	5
40–50	1,598	8	2,656	5
50–60	1,782	7	3,068	4
60–70	2,008	6	3,585	3
70–80	2,315	5	4,310	3
80–90	2,825	4	5,477	2
90–95	3,597	3	7,528	2
95–100	6,305	2	14,468	1
Average	**2,012**	**6**	**3,700**	**3**

Source: Authors' calculations.
Note: This calculation is based on the percentile distribution of household average per capita expenditure using NSS 2011–12 figures (68th Round, NSS 2013), adjusted for inflation. We use an annual 5 percent inflation rate to get the 2018–19 figures so as to be comparable to the IGD figure based on the 2018–19 per capita GDP. The IGD as a percentage of MPCE is Rs 120 divided by MPCE. In the Appendix, we present an equivalent table (Table A.1) based on NSS 2017–18 figures (adjusted for inflation) taken from Subramanian (2019).

As Table 1 makes clear, the 5th percentile rural household has an MPCE of ₹734. Thus, while ₹120/month per head will not eliminate poverty, it is large enough to allow the poorest households to augment their basic consumption by a highly meaningful 16 percent in rural areas and 12 percent in urban areas.

The IGD would augment monthly consumption by 9 percent or more for the bottom 30 percent of the rural population and by at least 8 percent or more for the bottom half of the rural population. These are non-trivial amounts.

This may not seem significant at first glance, but one should take two facts into account. First, while about 22 percent of the population is below the poverty line (according to 2011–12 estimates), there is a great deal of heterogeneity among the poor, and so a monthly sum of ₹120 will not be trivial. Second, these figures are for India as a whole, and once one takes into account the great heterogeneity among states, this sum will be especially meaningful for poorer states and districts.

For example, in Table 2, we present the MPCE in rural areas by state (at current prices) according to National Sample Survey (NSS; Table T4 NSO Draft Report on Consumer Expenditure, 75th Round, 2017–18). Even though for India as a whole, the IGD as a fraction of the MPCE is 6 percent, for the eight poorest states, the figure is at least 7 percent.

Further, by being universal, IGD minimizes the risk of exclusion errors, which represent an important way in which existing programs do not deliver on their goals of alleviating poverty. In addition, if benefits are linked to *Aadhaar*, the benefits would be portable, which is something that very few programs are able to do at present (though this has recently been announced for the PDS). The importance of portability of benefits will only grow as migration and urbanization grow in the coming years. The universal coverage would also make an IGD a powerful symbolic program of national unity as perhaps the only program to date that equally reaches every citizen of the country in a reliable and predictable manner.

Finally, by pegging the value of the transfer to a fraction of GDP per capita, the structure of the IGD has built-in indexation and will grow over time at the rate of *nominal* GDP growth, which will account for both inflation and real economic growth. Critics of income transfers with respect to income-based anti-poverty programs as opposed to in-kind benefits point out that the real value of the former is often allowed to be eroded by inflation for fiscal reasons in a way that the latter is less susceptible to. For instance, the value of the National Old Age Pension Scheme had a nominal value of ₹200/month in

TABLE 2. Rural Average MPCE by State, 2018–19

	Rural	
States	MPCE (monthly, ₹ at current prices)	IGD as a percentage of MPCE (%)
Odisha	1,411.32	9
Jharkhand	1,415.54	8
Chhattisgarh	1,445.09	8
Bihar	1,585.80	8
Madhya Pradesh	1,620.98	7
Uttar Pradesh	1,626.61	7
Assam	1,715.26	7
West Bengal	1,816.57	7
Gujarat	2,161.31	6
Karnataka	2,196.48	5
Rajasthan	2,248.55	5
Maharashtra	2,278.10	5
Tamil Nadu	2,382.22	5
Andhra Pradesh	2,468.05	5
Haryana	3,061.85	4
Punjab	3,299.65	4
Kerala	3,755.55	3
All India	**2,012.15**	**6**

Source: Authors' calculations.
Note: States are arranged in ascending order in terms of rural MPCE based on 2011–12 NSS data (adjusted for inflation, using the adjustments noted for Table 1). In the Appendix, we present an equivalent state-specific table (Table A.2) based on 2017–18 NSS data. The state-specific NSS data for 2017–18 was kindly shared by Himanshu.

2006 but was not adjusted upwards for over a decade, prompting concerned economists (including one of us—Ghatak) to write to the finance minister to request an increase of this amount in 2018. In contrast, by being linked to a fraction of GDP, the IGD makes these increases automatic and will ensure a sustained impact on poverty reduction over time.[32]

---

[32]. As noted earlier, the IGD is a variant of the idea of a "universal basic share" put forward in Ray (2016). The approach is also similar to how social security benefits in the USA are indexed to the rate of wage growth in the economy, capturing not only inflation but growth in real worker earnings over time.

3.4. Rank Preservation and Psychological Well-being

There is an important sociological problem with targeted programs, which is that they can often cause "rank reversals" on the ground. This was a major shortcoming of NYAY. For instance, by providing transfers to people who are in the poorest 20 percent of the population but not those who are right above, this design would reverse the prosperity order between households just below and just above the threshold. Given the well-established evidence that people care about relative income and status as well as absolute income and poverty (Veblen 1899), such ranking reversals can be quite unpopular and may also be a cause for the targeting errors that happen in targeted programs. Further, there is also evidence of negative psychological effects on non-recipients of transfers when some of their neighbors do receive transfers (Haushofer, Reisinger, and Shapiro 2015).

An IGD elegantly avoids all such sociological and psychological challenges by being both universal and not excluding anyone, and also by preserving relative ranking of economic status within communities. Of course, the net distributional impact of an IGD will depend on the structure of the tax system that finances it. But since people do not directly map sources of tax revenue to specific expenditure categories, the salience of these issues is mainly a function of the nature of the expenditure.

3.5. Female Empowerment and Improved Intra-Household Targeting

Consistent with the evidence reviewed in Section 2, it is reasonable to expect that an IGD where the allowance for children under 18 is transferred into the bank accounts of their mothers would, over time, increase female empowerment. Women would have greater control over household resources and will also gain increased autonomy to travel to visit banks and ATMs to access the money (which they will have to do in person to authenticate themselves using *Aadhaar*).

This aspect considerably strengthens the appeal of income transfer schemes like the IGD as they can be aimed at individuals rather than families, and mothers can be given the transfers intended for children. Further, as discussed in Section 2, intra-household inequality is a non-trivial concern in India (highlighted, for instance, by Jayachandran and Pande 2017), and thus, an untargeted universal income transfer with the IGD for children going into their mothers' accounts may do a better job of targeting *individual* poverty.

3.6. Work Incentives

Another advantage of the IGD approach is that the value of the transfer is too small to have any adverse impacts on incentives to work, especially compared to the higher potential disincentives from making larger transfers to fewer people. Adjusting for inflation, the amount of ₹120 per person per month is 8.9 percent of the rural poverty line and 6 percent of the urban poverty line. While non-trivial, this is unlikely to have serious effects on work incentives.

Further, as discussed in Section 2, an important attraction of an IGD is that there is no phase-out of the benefits, which means that there is no disincentive to work during that period. Even if there is a phase-out at a high level of income (say, high enough to be above the threshold for income tax payments of ₹5 lakhs/year) at that point, the marginal tax rate from losing the IGD is under 0.2 percent.

More importantly, an IGD could actually increase worker productivity. Estimates of migration in India suggest that rural to urban migration is sub-optimally low given the disparities in earnings in rural and urban areas (Munshi and Rosenzweig 2016). However, there is also credible evidence from Bangladesh that people often do not invest in profitable opportunities like migration because they are so poor that they cannot afford to invest in "searching" for a better job in an urban area, including transportation and sustenance costs to conduct such a search (Bryan, Chowdhury, and Mobarak 2014). In such a setting, even very modest income transfers to people that are predictable and reliable can significantly improve productivity by increasing their ability to search for better opportunities and take on the small risks needed to "invest" in such a search.

3.7. Financial Inclusion, Savings, Credit, Risk, and Insurance

An IGD would also directly promote financial inclusion in the country and help the poor build savings in a secure bank account. Some sense of how important a development goal this would be is provided by Badarinza, Balasubramaniam, and Ramadorai (2016), who show, using the All-India Debt and Investment Survey of 2012, that households at the 25th percentile of the Indian wealth distribution and below had *zero* financial assets/savings. Even at the median, the financial savings were only ₹2,200 per household.

This figure has likely improved in recent years with the large-scale expansion of *Jan-Dhan* bank accounts. Yet a large number of accounts remain dormant with a zero balance. As of December 2018, the finance minister responded to a Lok Sabha Parliamentary question saying that out of 33.6 crore *Jan-Dhan* accounts created, 23 percent were dormant.

In the World Bank's 2017 Global Findex, 80 percent of Indians surveyed reported having accounts at formal financial institutions; 77 percent of rural Indians reported having accounts (Demirgüç-Kunt et al. 2018). However, among those with accounts, 48 percent did not make any deposits or withdrawals in the previous 12 months. Such inactivity, in turn, leads to banks automatically deeming the accounts dormant, which makes them unusable without reactivation. Thus, a large fraction of the enormous efforts undertaken by banks and governments to boost financial inclusion is wasted because the accounts that are opened under these schemes get deactivated due to lack of activity in them.

There is almost no doubt that having a regular inflow of funds into these accounts will lead to greater usage of these accounts, and, by definition, these accounts will be active due to the monthly deposits they will receive.

3.8. Creating Broad-based Demand

In addition to supporting increased productivity at the micro-level for the reasons noted above, an IGD could also be an engine for broader economic development by boosting aggregate demand. Commentators on the Indian economy have highlighted that India has mainly had top-down economic growth over the past two decades (see Chawla 2016; Roy 2019b for illustrative discussions on this point). Specifically, they have argued that the top 10 percent of the population earns enough to drive consumption. This demand trickles down to sustain the next 30–40 percent working in smaller (mostly informal) enterprises, while the bottom 50 percent lead a hand-to-mouth existence.

By putting more money in the hands of the poor, an IGD could help reverse this pattern and provide a bottom-up boost to the economy. Not only will it increase income, but it will also provide predictability of future income—a key driver for demand. Recent evidence on unconditional income transfers provided to entire communities in Kenya finds an economic multiplier of 2.7 (Egger et al. 2019). More generally, both theory and evidence suggest that a broader consumption base promotes economic development by allowing firms to recover the fixed costs of investing in more productive capital and technology (Matsuyama 2002).

In the Indian context, experimental evidence has found that improving implementation of the Mahatma Gandhi National Rural Employment Guarantee Act (MGNREGA) (by reducing leakage, payment delays, and uncertainty) led to a substantial reduction in rural poverty (Muralidharan, Niehaus, and Sukhtankar 2020). The study also finds longer-term benefits, including increases in credit, assets, the number of non-agricultural enterprises, and employment in these enterprises. These results suggest that improving wages and incomes of the poor, through social protection, can have large positive multiplier effects on the economy through boosting credit and demand. Thus, in addition to the direct benefits to the poor, an IGD is likely to have a substantial multiplier effect on the economy by boosting domestic demand, and thereby delivering a high public return on investment. Boosting demand may be especially important in times of constrained demand, like the current scenario where incomes of the poor have been severely reduced by the lockdowns to contain the spread of COVID-19.

3.9. Augmenting State Capacity and Credibility

Implementing an IGD would involve identifying every citizen, matching him or her to a bank account (or to a parent or guardian's bank account), and being able to reliably send monthly transfers to over 1.3 billion people. Simply doing this would be a tremendous achievement. It would have the indirect benefit of developing demonstrable state capacity to credibly reach every citizen and reliably deliver a benefit for the first time in independent India.

Building such capacity, in turn, opens up an entire range of tools for better policy going forward. In the longer term, the IGD infrastructure may enable a strengthening of tax collection capacity by connecting every citizen to the state and vice versa. Also, there are several critical policy areas for citizens' welfare that require scarce resources to be priced, including water and air (the lack of pollution in the latter instance). Most economists believe that a policy that increased, say, carbon taxation or water pricing, and rebated the proceeds to all citizens would be welfare enhancing. Yet such policy instruments cannot be feasibly implemented right now. Successfully implementing an IGD will make such instruments feasible and thereby augment state capacity to better price scarce resources to reflect their social cost while using income transfers to mitigate the effect of such price increases on the poor.

Remarkably, building such state capacity is no longer a pipe dream and would be a logical culmination of the investments in the past decade in the *Aadhaar* platform combined with *Jan-Dhan* accounts and mobile seeding. The final key step in making this capacity universal is to strengthen the "plumbing" of financial inclusion by making the pipes transport funds every month to keep them from becoming rusty. In this sense, the IGD would be a fitting next step for the broader vision of augmenting state capacity to better identify citizens and deliver benefits to them.

Building the capacity to deliver an IGD would also improve the options available to the government to deal with crises and natural disasters. This point is clearly seen in the context of the current crisis caused by COVID-19 and the lockdowns to prevent its spread. The main policy response to protect the poor and vulnerable has been to increase the allowance of free foodgrains through the PDS and to increase the budgetary allocation to NREGS. This is in large part because these are the existing programs where budgets can be allocated without needing to also build an all-new system to deliver resources to the vulnerable. Implementing an IGD would necessitate having a database of citizens and bank accounts (including a mapping into various benefits they are eligible for), which will make it easy for governments to respond to future crises by augmenting income transfers.

Finally, delivering an IGD would augment not only state capacity but also state credibility by consistently delivering a benefit to every Indian every month, which would be a first in independent India. As discussed in Khilnani (2010), it would be a policy that puts the individual citizen at the center of at least one government policy and be an instrument that puts the government in the service of every citizen.

3.10. IGD as a Benchmark for Development Spending and Enabler of Choice

Finally, an important long-term benefit of building the infrastructure to deliver an IGD is that it can improve the accountability of *other* government programs by making cash transfers an attainable benchmark against which they can be evaluated. There has been an increasing push from policymakers to consider replacing poorly performing programs with income transfers instead. This was the spirit of the pilot of replacing PDS with DBT in three union territories. In a similar vein, the NITI Aayog and the Ministry of Women and Child Development have been preparing for pilot studies that would substitute take-home rations (THR) in the Integrated Child Development Services Scheme, which are believed to be poorly implemented, with DBT.

However, as the discussion in Section 2.2 highlights, the recent field experience in monitoring the implementation of these schemes suggests that there are non-trivial challenges with the quality of last-mile implementation of income transfers. These are meaningful enough that we do not feel comfortable endorsing any attempt to mandatorily replace existing in-kind benefits with an income equivalent—whether this be for the PDS or THR or any other such program.

Further, data collected from ongoing work reveal that there is considerable heterogeneity in beneficiary preferences regarding income versus in-kind benefits.[33] For instance, we asked beneficiaries in Jharkhand to state the value of income transfer at which they would be willing to forego their THR entitlements and found substantial variation, with some beneficiaries willing to accept an amount that was much below the fiscal cost of the program (suggesting that the in-kind program was destroying value relative to the cost), whereas others stated an amount that was considerably above (suggesting that in-kind provision was providing more value than the cost). Similar heterogeneity is observed in both stated and revealed preference in the PDS.

The combination of implementation challenges with income transfers and the demonstrated heterogeneity of beneficiary preferences over income versus in-kind transfers has convinced us that the only politically and ethically prudent way of proceeding with any kind of substitution is by offering beneficiaries a choice between in-kind benefits (which is the default in most cases) and a fiscally equivalent income transfer. This is an approach that we have recommended in the PDS (see Ghatak 2019b; Muralidharan, Niehaus, and Sukhtankar 2018b) and is one that may be applicable in other cases of publicly provided private goods as well.

However, embarking on a choice-based framework itself requires the state to have demonstrated the capacity to credibly deliver income transfers. This is why we think that an IGD can be a foundation for improving the quality of expenditure in several other areas of social sector spending. Once income transfers are credibly established as a feasible option that the poor can depend upon, it opens the possibility of offering program-level choices to beneficiaries between income and in-kind assistance.

It is possible that in-kind provision may deliver more value than market options (because the government does not have a profit motive, marketing costs, and can procure in bulk). But it is also possible that market options may do better (because costs are higher under government provision and accountability of front-line personnel is low). Again, though on average the data in India suggest that the market is more efficient, we do not prejudge the outcome (both because of heterogeneity and because it is possible for the government to get more efficient).

---

33. This ongoing work is being conducted by Muralidharan jointly with Paul Niehaus, Sandip Sukhtankar, and Jeff Weaver.

The point, rather, is that allowing the choice allows much more accountability in government programs and will empower beneficiaries by providing them with one more option. For instance, in ongoing work in Maharashtra, where we are studying the impact of providing a choice between PDS grains and income transfers via DBT, we see that the take-up rate for DBT is around 25 percent.[34] Yet nearly all beneficiaries *value having the option.*

These data also highlight why the default discussion of a UBI that simply assumes that existing welfare programs can be folded into an income transfer is both naïve and unrealistic. People do value their in-kind benefits and often prefer them to income transfers. Conversely, in cases where the performance of the in-kind benefit is poor, they highly value having the option of an income transfer.

In the long term, both public and market provision of goods and services are important, especially for each to keep a check on the other through choice and competition. The problem with the status quo is that the poor constitute a captive market for government provision where they have limited options for both voice and exit (Hirschman 1972). Empowering them with choice improves both their outside options, and thereby their ability to drive improvements in public delivery.

Thus, income transfers would become a low-implementation cost "index fund" for development spending and in-kind programs and subsidies would need to demonstrate that their targeting, administrative and implementation costs deliver more value than their cost. Over time, programs that deliver less value than their cost could be replaced with income transfers while those that deliver more value can be retained.

4. Making It Happen

In practice, making an IGD happen requires two main things: the money for the transfers and ensuring implementation capacity to actually deliver the transfers credibly and reliably. For the purpose of this paper, we assume that the main constraint is the former and assume that the investments in *Aadhaar, Jan-Dhan* bank accounts, and mobile seeding provide enough of a foundation for implementation to happen if there is political will behind the program. Since the political will for large-scale income transfers to nearly half the Indian population has already been demonstrated in the context of

---

34. This is based on ongoing work by Muralidharan with Paul Niehaus, Sandip Sukhtankar, and Jeff Weaver.

PM-KISAN, this seems like a reasonable assumption. This section will, therefore, focus on financing, and considers the case for an IGD being driven at both the level of the Central and state governments.

4.1. Central Government

Constitutionally, most service delivery functions (including primary education and health) are primarily in the domain of state governments. Yet the Government of India plays a large role in the design and delivery of public services as well as welfare programs. It does the former through Centrally Sponsored Schemes (CSS) such as *Sarva Shiksha Abhiyan* for education and the National Rural Health Mission for health, as well as central schemes such as PDS and NREGS. In the case of CSS, the Government of India makes funding conditional on matching contributions by states and spending according to guidelines established at the national level. In the case of PDS and NREGS, the funding is primarily from the Government of India, though implementation details vary across states.

The main rationale for the Government of India playing such an active role in welfare and service delivery programs is that it seeks to achieve an element of national parity and common minimum standards in the delivery of these programs. Thus, the principles that govern the active intervention of the Government of India in these areas are equality (treating every citizen equally), equity (providing additional resources to more disadvantaged areas), and effectiveness (which is why these schemes prescribe minimum standards and guidelines).

An IGD would satisfy all three principles. The equality principle is built into the IGD by construction, by virtue of being the same amount for all citizens. The IGD also satisfies the equity principle as shown in Section 3.3. It is highly progressive, with a higher marginal impact on consumption for the poorest.

The subtle point is the one about effectiveness (or efficiency) and, in particular, the tension between equity and efficiency. Since a key principle for the Government of India (and also for the Finance Commissions) is equity across regions, several programs have provided additional funding for economically and socially disadvantaged states to help reduce regional inequalities, especially in key areas of human development such as health and education.

The problem, however, is that we have fairly robust evidence that the quality of governance is weaker in the poorer states. This point is clearly illustrated by Figure 1 from Chaudhury et al. (2006), who show that states with lower per capita income have significantly higher rates of teacher and health worker absence in the public sector.

FIGURE 1. Absence Rate of Teachers and Health Workers in the Public Sector in Indian States

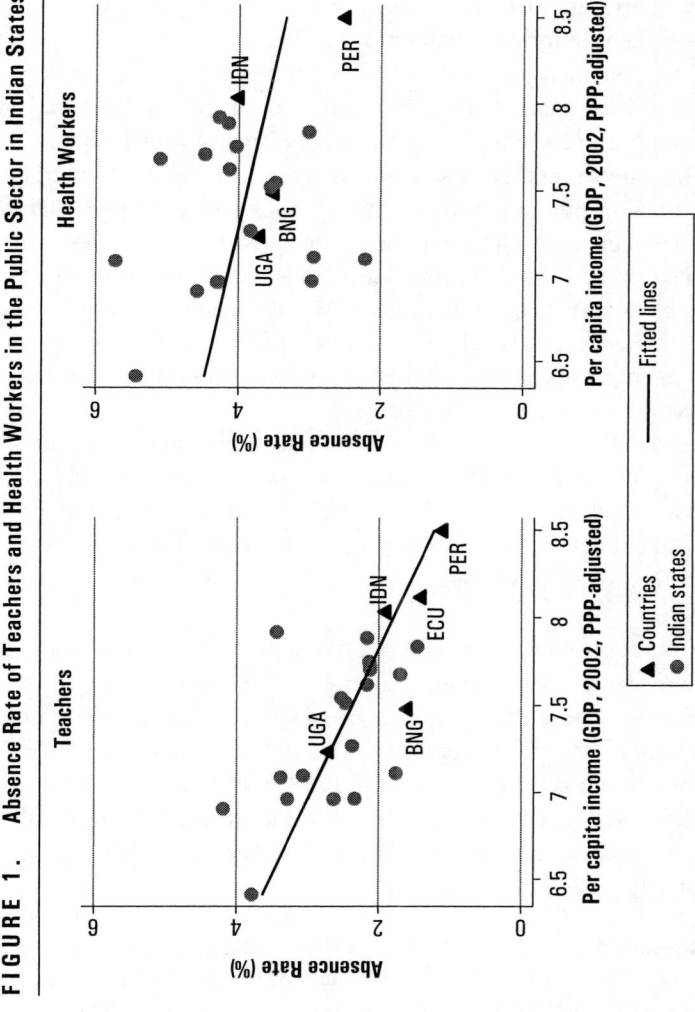

Source: Chaudhary et al. (2006).
Note: BNG = Bangladesh; ECU = Ecuador; IDN = Indonesia; PER = Peru; UGA = Uganda. India's national averages are excluded due to the inclusion of the Indian states. For Indian states, income is their official per capita net state domestic product.

Given that teacher and health worker salaries are the largest component of public expenditure on education and health, this is a direct measure of the leakage of public expenditure. Calculations from follow-up research on teacher absence in India indicate that the fiscal cost of teacher absence alone is over ₹10,000 crores/year (Muralidharan et al. 2017). These figures are based on salaries in 2010 and are likely to be much higher when we use salary figures after the implementation of the 7th Pay Commission.

Another way of seeing the problem of weak public service delivery is to look at the private market share of health and education. Using all-India data on the presence of a private school in villages, Muralidharan and Kremer (2008) show that private schools are more likely to exist in villages with higher rates of public school teacher absence and also show that the correlation between state GDP per capita and private school presence is *negative*. The relationship also turns out to be negative *within* states, with a greater share of private schools in districts with lower consumption per capita (estimated with state fixed effects). In other words, the flight to private options is not simply a function of growing income, but rather likely to be a direct consequence of poor public provision.

Turning to health, Das et al. (2020), using all-India data on the quality and availability of healthcare providers in rural India, show that states such as Uttar Pradesh and Bihar deliver lower-quality healthcare at a higher per-unit cost than better-performing states like Tamil Nadu. The high unit cost is in part a reflection of low usage, which, in turn, is driven by low quality and reliability.

The tension between equity and effectiveness is also seen in the case of the NREGS, which is a flagship program of the Government of India. While it is meant to be a pro-poor program, a key challenge is that implementation quality varies considerably across states. Evidence on NREGS suggests that while it is progressive within states, it is actually *regressive* between states, with better-off states availing more NREGS funds than poorer states. For instance, calculations by the Accountability Initiative show that in 2011–12:

Poorer States such as Uttar Pradesh, Bihar, West Bengal, and Madhya Pradesh, which together account for 59 per cent of the country's rural BPL population, generated only 34 per cent of employment through MGNREGA. On the other hand, Andhra Pradesh and Tamil Nadu, which house eight per cent of the BPL population, accounted for 23 per cent of the total employment generated that year. (Aiyar 2014)

These results highlight the vexing challenge that the Government of India faces in terms of satisfying the equity goals of public expenditure. On the one hand, the poor states need more assistance to help meet horizontal equity goals across the country. On the other hand, the quality of public expenditure is systematically lower in these states, and weak state capacity in poorer states makes it more difficult to even complete the procedures needed to obtain the Government of India's funds in the first place (as seen in the NREGS example). This creates a "Samaritan's dilemma" where the marginal reach and quality of the Government of India's expenditure on welfare is lower in places that need it the most.

An IGD is especially attractive in such a setting by allowing the Government of India to promote equity while circumventing (at least for one component of funding) the weaknesses in governance in the poorer states. In other words, since the "wedge" between the cost of provision and on-the-ground delivery of services is higher in poorer states, sending one component of funds earmarked for equity directly to citizens will improve the efficiency of those funds relative to the counterfactual of sending all the additional "equity" funds through state governments.

It is important to clarify that an IGD does not, in any way, suggest giving up on improving the quality of governance in poorer states. Rather, it is consistent with our portfolio approach whereby one component of funding for India's anti-poverty and development strategy is allocated to direct income transfers. Recommending an IGD does not, in any way, preclude the Government of India from introducing other performance-based metrics for transfers.[35]

However, we strongly believe that an IGD provides a more broadly acceptable way for the Government of India to redistribute resources to poorer states (which will happen because it is based on population, which is greater in poorer states). In particular, because it so transparently satisfies the principles of equality and equity, and directly contributes to poverty alleviation, we believe that citizens in high-income states will be more supportive of this form of redistribution relative to those that go through governments (as in the case of other Centrally Sponsored Schemes).

Of course, fiscal space is tight, and there are several competing demands for funds (including say for implementing the New Education Policy or health initiatives like *Ayushman Bharat*). At the same time, there is clearly a political demand for direct alleviation of poverty, as seen by the major commitment to the PM-KISAN program. Implementing an IGD is a natural extension of this approach at a similar cost per beneficiary.

---

35. Indeed, the terms of the reference of the Fifteenth Finance Commission include making recommendations regarding performance-based funding to states.

Recognizing the importance of political messaging and that good economics needs to also be good politics, implementing an IGD would also be directly consistent with Prime Minister Narendra Modi's stated goal of leading a government that is characterized by *Sabka Saath, Sabka Vikas, Sabka Vishwaas* (with everyone, for everyone's progress, and enjoying everyone's trust). However, while this is a laudable goal, it is not easy to achieve in practice. An IGD provides a practical and implementable way of doing so through its combination of universality (*Sabka Saath*), promoting broad-based development (*Sabka Vikaas*), and building public confidence in the government by credibly delivering a benefit to every Indian every month (*Sabka Vishwaas*). While implementing a scaled-up IGD may take some time, it should be feasible to do so in a couple of years at most, which will provide enough time for the IGD to be taken back to the voters as a demonstrable achievement.

If short-term fiscal constraints are binding, it would also make sense to start an IGD in the most disadvantaged districts (or even blocks) in the coming year and assess and evaluate its performance before scaling up over the next three years to achieve universal coverage before the next elections. Given potential fuzziness in targeting at the district level, it may even be possible to randomize the roll-out within a universe of districts or blocks identified as eligible over a three-year period and use a lottery to phase the program in. This would allow the generation of credible estimates of impact—including general equilibrium effects and multipliers—prior to scaling up.

4.2. State Governments

Even if the Government of India chooses not to make a fiscal commitment to an IGD for the entire country in one shot, there is nothing that prevents a state government from implementing an IGD on its own volition, potentially targeting the poorest districts or blocks within the state with a similar approach as identified above. The simplicity of the idea means that any state can implement it on its own without needing to explicitly coordinate with the center.

One promising option may be for mining-rich states such as Odisha, Jharkhand, and Chhattisgarh to make use of funds in their "District Mineral Foundations" (DMFs) for an IGD pilot and evaluation. The DMFs were created to ensure that a fraction of the royalties from natural resources were returned to the citizens of mining districts. In practice, however, DMFs have accumulated large amounts of unspent funds, in part, because of onerous requirements for projects to be designed and approved for using DMF funds. An IGD using DMF proceeds would be especially appropriate for a pilot and evaluation given that it would pay citizens a "dividend" based on the mining resources that the citizens have a natural claim over.

It is worth recalling that the leadership of the State of Telangana in designing and implementing the RBS and its demonstrated practical and political success is what led to the rapid replication of the idea across the country. The idea of an IGD is similarly ripe for state-level leadership if the Center decides to wait.

5. Conclusion

We have made the case for an IGD pegged at 1 percent of GDP per capita, to be paid unconditionally to every Indian citizen as a modest (in amount) but ambitious (in reach) way of making income transfers a part of the portfolio of anti-poverty strategies in India. The amount of the transfer is very similar to the amount being offered under PM-KISAN, and the fiscal impact is, therefore, within the realm of practical feasibility. We have argued how it avoids some of the criticisms that can be applied to a more generous UBI scheme, that there is a strong case for such a scheme in India, and that it is consistent with key principles that guide our inclusive growth strategy: equality, equity, and efficiency.

At the time of revising the paper for publication, the country is dealing with the COVID-19 crisis, and the role of income transfers in the relief package is very much at the center of discussion. One key lesson from the unique nature of this crisis is its twin demand- and supply-side problems, which make income transfers and in-kind transfers more of complements than substitutes. After all, what good is only income when supply chains are disrupted? Similarly, how does it matter if shops are well-stocked when a person has no money? Cash versus in-kind transfers is a reasonable debate in normal times, but given the current crisis, these are complementary measures. This complementarity between income and in-kind transfers strengthens the case for our view of income transfers as one component in a larger portfolio of social protection programs.

The current moment (June 2020) is especially appropriate for an IGD for several reasons. First, there has been a sharp reduction in incomes resulting from the lockdowns to slow the spread of COVID-19. The Indian economy is highly demand constrained, suggesting that the economic multiplier from an infusion of purchasing power may be especially high, even higher than the multiplier of 2.7 estimated recently in Kenya by Egger et al. (2019). Second, historical evidence suggests that times of economic hardship can lead to increased conflict as people compete over a shrinking economic pie (see, for instance, Miguel, Satyanath, and Sergenti 2004). An IGD can mitigate this risk and provide a powerful symbol of social solidarity that all Indians experience together regardless of their station. Third, an IGD would be a portable benefit (unlike NREGS or the PDS under the status quo), accessible anywhere in the country, and therefore, especially suitable to support migrant workers. Indeed, the existence of an IGD might have mitigated some of the heart-rending sufferings of migrant workers seen during the COVID-19 crisis.

Responding to the hardship caused by COVID-19 and the lockdown imposed to slow its spread requires us to both support and reform the Indian economy. The policy should aim to both support the vulnerable and the broader economy in the short run and promote long-term development goals. An IGD-led nationally portable social protection architecture would do exactly this.

Appendix

TABLE A.1. Rural and Urban Monthly Per Capita Expenditure (MPCE) at Percentiles of Household Consumption Expenditure, 2018–19

	Rural		Urban	
Percentile	MPCE (monthly, ₹ at current prices)	IGD as a percentage of MPCE (%)	MPCE (monthly, ₹ at current prices)	IGD as a percentage of MPCE (%)
0–10	616	19	945	13
10–20	782	15	1,326	9
20–30	913	13	1,595	8
30–40	1,028	12	1,858	6
40–50	1,136	11	2,140	6
50–60	1,257	10	2,463	5
60–70	1,405	9	2,843	4
70–80	1,598	8	3,381	4
80–90	1,899	6	4,189	3
90–100	3,058	4	7,425	2
Average	**1,363**	**9**	**2,816**	**4**

Source: Authors' calculations based on Table 2 in Subramanian (2019), which he reports is based on Tables T3 and T4 of the 2017–18 NSO draft Report on Consumer Expenditure (75th Round). We use an annual 5 percent inflation rate to get the 2018–19 figures, so as to be comparable to the IGD figure calculated based on the 2018–19 per capita GDP. The IGD as a percentage of MPCE is obtained as ₹120 divided by the MPCE.

As Table A.1 makes clear, the 10th percentile rural household has a monthly per capita expenditure (MPCE) of ₹616. Thus, a sum of ₹120/month per head allows the poorest households to augment their basic consumption by 19 percent in rural areas and 13 percent in urban areas. The IGD would augment monthly consumption by 13 percent or more for the bottom 30 percent of the rural population, and by at least 11 percent or more for the bottom half of the rural population.

Although for India as a whole the IGD as a fraction of the MPCE is 7 percent, for the eight poorest states, the figure is at least 8 percent.

TABLE A.2.   Rural Average MPCE by State, 2018–19

	Rural	
States	MPCE (monthly, ₹ at current prices)	IGD as a percentage of MPCE (%)
Chhattisgarh	1,093.86	11
Odisha	1,209.87	10
Jharkhand	1,246.18	10
Bihar	1,282.55	9
Madhya Pradesh	1,293.33	9
Uttar Pradesh	1,331.69	9
West Bengal	1,569.11	8
Maharashtra	1,571.19	8
Karnataka	1,624.08	7
Gujarat	1,699.60	7
Rajasthan	1,736.24	7
Assam	1,780.26	7
Haryana	1,945.87	6
Andhra Pradesh	2,044.61	6
Tamil Nadu	2,313.94	5
Kerala	2,772.31	4
Punjab	2,840.14	4
All India	**1,600.28**	**7**

Source: Authors' calculations based on 2017–18 state-level MPCE data kindly shared with us by Himanshu, who collected these from a single, three-part question on consumption expenditures carried in the PLFS July 2017–June 2018 Round. These are not comparable to the usual consumption survey rounds that the NSO collects. We use an annual 5% inflation rate to get to the 2018–19 figures so as to be comparable to the IGD figure calculated based on the 2018-19 per capita GDP. The IGD as a percentage of MPCE is obtained as ₹120 divided by MPCE.

References

Aiyar, Y. 2014. "Re-framing the MGNREGA Debate." *The Hindu*, November 8. Available at https://www.thehindu.com/opinion/lead/reframing-the-mgnrega-debate/article6575483.ece (accessed May 7, 2021).

Aiyar, S.A. 2019. "Why Universal Basic Income Is a Bad Idea." *The Economic Times*, February 27. Available at https://economictimes.indiatimes.com/news/economy/policy/why-universal-basic-income-is-a-bad-idea/articleshow/68175296.cms (accessed May 7, 2021).

Almås, I., A. Armand, O. Attanasio, and P. Carneiro. 2018. "Measuring and Changing Control: Women's Empowerment and Targeted Transfers." *The Economic Journal*, 128(612): F609–639.

Badarinza, C., V. Balasubramaniam, and T. Ramadorai. 2016. "The Indian Household Finance Landscape." *India Policy Forum 2016–17*, 13:1–55. New Delhi: National Council of Applied Economic Research.

Baird, S., D. McKenzie, and B. Özler. 2018. "The Effects of Cash Transfers on Adult Labor Market Outcomes." *Policy Research Working Paper No. WPS 8404*. Washington, D. C., WA: World Bank Group.

Bandiera, O., R. Burgess, N. Das, S. Gulesci, I. Rasul, and M. Sulaiman. M. 2017. "Labor Markets and Poverty in Village Economies." *The Quarterly Journal of Economics*, 132(2): 811–870.

Banerjee, A. 2016. "The Best Way to Welfare." *The Indian Express*, June 18. Available at https://indianexpress.com/article/opinion/columns/swiss-voted-against-the-idea-of-a-universal-basic-income-but-the-debate-continues-2859528/ (accessed May 7, 2021).

Banerjee, A. and E. Duflo. 2005. "Growth Theory through the Lens of Development Economics." In P. Aghion and S. Durlauf (eds.), *Handbook of Economic Growth*, Vol. 1, pp. 473–452. London: Elsevier.

———. 2008. "Economic Lives of the Poor." *Journal of Economic Perspectives*, 21(1): 141–167.

Banerjee, A., E. Duflo, R. Glennerster, and C. Kinnan. 2015. "The Miracle of Microfinance: Evidence from a Randomized Evaluation." *American Economic Journal: Applied Economics*, 7(1): 22–53.

Banerjee, A., P. Niehaus, and T. Suri. 2019. "Universal Basic Income in a Developing World." *NBER Working Paper No. 25598*. Cambridge, MA: National Bureau of Economic Research.

Banerjee, A.V., D. Karlan, and J. Zinman. 2015. "Six Randomized Evaluations of Microcredit: Introduction and Further Steps." *American Economic Journal: Applied Economics*, 7(1): 1–21.

Bardhan, P. 2011. "Challenges for a Minimum Social Democracy in India." *Economic and Political Weekly*, 46(10): 39–43.

———. 2016. "Basic Income in a Poor Country." *Ideas for India*, September 26. Available at https://www.ideasforindia.in/topics/poverty-inequality/basic-income-in-a-poor-country.html (accessed May 7, 2021).

Bardhan, P. 2018. "Universal Basic Income—Its Special Case for India." *Indian Journal of Human Development,* 11(2): 141–143.

Bastagli, F., J. Hagen-Zanker, L. Harman, V. Barca, G. Sturge, T. Schmidt, and L. Pellerano. 2016. "Cash Transfers: What Does the Evidence Say? A Rigorous Review of Programme Impact and of the Role of Design and Implementation Features." *Oxford Development Institute Papers.* Available at https://odi.org/en/publications/cash-transfers-what-does-the-evidence-say-a-rigorous-review-of-impacts-and-the-role-of-design-and-implementation-features/ (accessed May 7, 2021).

Blattman, C., E.P. Green, J. Jamison, M.C. Lehmann, and J. Annan. 2016. "The Returns to Microenterprise Support among the Ultra-poor: A Field Experiment in Postwar Uganda." *American Economic Journal: Applied Economics,* 8(2): 35–64.

Brown, C., R. Calvi, J. Penglase. 2019. "Sharing the Pie: Undernutrition, Intra-household Allocation, and Poverty." *Working Paper.* Available at https://as.nyu.edu/content/dam/nyu-as/econ/documents/2020-Spring/Sharing%20the%20Pie%20%20Undernutrition,%20Intrahousehold%20Allocation%20and%20Poverty_Calvi.pdf (accessed May 7, 2021).

Brown, L.D. and M. S. Sparer. 2003. "Poor Program's Progress: The Unanticipated Politics of Medicaid Policy." *Health Affairs,* 22(1): 31–44.

Bryan, G., S. Chowdhury, and M.A. Mobarak. 2014. "Under-investment in a Profitable Technology: The Case of Seasonal Migration in Bangladesh." *Econometrica,* 82(5): 1671–1748.

Chaudhury, N., J. Hammer, M. Kremer, K. Muralidharan, F.H. Rogers. 2006. "Missing in Action: Teacher and Health Worker Absence in Developing Countries." *Journal of Economic Perspectives,* 20(1): 91–116.

Chawla, H. 2016. "How India's Digital Economy Can Rediscover Its Mojo." *Founding Fuel,* August 30. Available at https://www.foundingfuel.com/article/how-indias-digital-economy-can-rediscover-its-mojo/ (accessed May 7, 2021).

Collins, D., J. Morduch, S. Rutherford, and O. Ruthven. 2009. *Portfolios of the Poor: How the World's Poor Live on $2 a Day.* Princeton, NJ: Princeton University Press.

Currie, J. and F. Gahvari. 2008. "Transfers in Cash and In-Kind: Theory Meets the Data." *Journal of Economic Literature,* 46(2): 333–383.

Das, J., B. Daniels, M. Ashok, E. -Y. Shim, and K. Muralidharan. 2020. "Two Indias: The Structure of Primary Health Care Markets in Rural Indian Villages with Implications for Policy." *Social Science and Medicine* (1982): 112799.

Das, J., A. Holla, A. Mohpal, K. Muralidharan. 2016. "Quality and Accountability in Health Care Delivery: Audit-Study Evidence from Primary Care in India." *American Economic Review,* 106(12): 3765–3799.

Davala, S., R. Jhabvala, G. Standing, and S.K. Mehta. 2015. *Basic Income: A Transformative Policy for India.* London: Bloomsbury.

de Mel, S., D. McKenzie, and C. Woodruff. 2008. "Returns to Capital in Microenterprises: Evidence from a Field Experiment." *The Quarterly Journal of Economics,* 123(4): 1329–1372.

Demirgüç-Kunt, A., L. Klapper, D. Singer, S. Ansar, and J.R. Hess. 2018. *The Global Findex Database 2017: Measuring Financial Inclusion and the Fintech Revolution*. Washington, D.C., WA: World Bank Group.

Drechsel, T. 2019. "Earnings-based Borrowing Constraints and Macroeconomic Fluctuations." *Working Paper*. London School of Economics. Available at https://economics.nd.edu/assets/307008/jmp_drechsel.pdf (accessed May 7, 2021).

Dreze, J. 2010. "The Task of Making the PDS Work." *The Hindu*, July 8. Available at https://www.thehindu.com/opinion/lead/The-task-of-making-the-PDS-work/article16115247.ece (accessed May 7, 2021).

———. 2018. "Decoding Universal Basic Income." *Indian Journal of Human Development*, 11(2): 163–166.

Duflo, E. 2012. "Women Empowerment and Economic Development." *Journal of Economic Literature*, 50(4): 1051–1079. Available at https//doi.org/10.1257/jel.50.4.1051 (accessed May 7, 2021).

Dupas, P. and J. Robinson. 2011. *Savings Constraints and Microenterprise Development: Evidence from a Field Experiment in Kenya*. Mimeo, University of California, Los Angeles.

Egger, D., J. Haushofer, E. Miguel, P. Niehaus, and M. Walker. 2019. "General Equilibrium Effects of Cash Transfers: Experimental Evidence from Kenya." *NBER Working Paper No. 26600*. Cambridge, MA: National Bureau of Economic Research.

Evans, D.K., and A. Popova. 2017. "Cash Transfers and Temptation Goods." *Economic Development and Cultural Change*, 65(2): 189–221.

Field, E., R. Pande, N. Rigol, S. Schaner, and C.T. Moore. 2020. "On Her Account: Can Strengthening Women's Financial Control Boost Female Labor Supply?" *Working Paper*. Yale University. Available at https://epod.cid.harvard.edu/sites/default/files/2018-05/on_her_account.can_strengthening_womens_financial_control_boost_female_labor_supply.pdf (accessed May 7, 2021).

Field, E., R. Pande, J. Papp, and N. Rigol 2013. "Does the Classic Microfinance Model Discourage Entrepreneurship among the Poor? Experimental Evidence from India." *American Economic Review*, 103(6): 2196–2226.

Ghatak, M. 2016. "Is India Ready for a Universal Basic Income Scheme?" *Ideas for India*, September 28. Available at https://www.ideasforindia.in/topics/poverty-inequality/is-india-ready-for-a-universal-basic-income-scheme.html (accessed May 7, 2021).

———. 2019a. "Not Long-term Solution to Poverty but Useful 'First-aid'." *Ideas for India*, May 2, Available at https://www.ideasforindia.in/topics/poverty-inequality/nyay-e-symposium-not-long-term-solution-to-poverty-but-useful-first-aid.html (accessed May 7, 2021).

———. 2019b. "Social Protection." In A. Banerjee, R.G. Rajan, G. Gopinath, and M.S. Sharma (eds.), *What the Economy Needs Now*, New Delhi: Juggernaut Books.

Ghatak, M. and F. Maniquet. 2019. "Some Theoretical Aspects of a Universal Basic Income Proposal." *Annual Review of Economics,* 11: 895–928.

Government of India. 2017. *Economic Survey 2016–17.* New Delhi: Department of Economic Affairs, Ministry of Finance.

———. 2019a. *Union Budget 2019-2020.* Ministry of Finance, New Delhi. Available at https://www.indiabudget.gov.in/ (accessed May 7, 2021).

———. 2019b. "PM KISAN Scheme Extension to Include All Eligible Farmer Families Irrespective of the Size of Land Holdings." Ministry of Agriculture and Farmers Welfare, Press Information Bureau. [Press release].

———. 2020. *Press Note on Second Advance Estimates of National Income 2019–20 and Quarterly Estimates of Gross Domestic Product for the Third Quarter (Q3) of 2019–20.* Available at http://mospi.nic.in/sites/default/files/press_release/PRESS_NOTE_SAE_Q3_%202019-20_28022020.pdf (accessed May 7, 2021).

Hanna, R., and B. Olken. 2018. "Universal Basic Income versus Targeted Transfers: Anti-Poverty Programs in Developing Countries." *Journal of Economic Perspectives,* 32(4): 201–226.

Haushofer, J., J.H. Reisinger, and J.J. Shapiro. 2015. "Your Gain Is My Pain: Negative Psychological Externalities of Cash Transfers." *Working Paper.* Available at https://files.givewell.org/files/DWDA%202009/Interventions/Cash%20Transfers/Haushofer_Reisinger_and_Shapiro_2015.pdf (accessed May 7, 2021).

Hirschman, A.O. 1970. *Exit, Voice, and Loyalty; Responses to Decline in Firms, Organizations, and States.* Cambridge, MA: Harvard University Press.

Imbens, G.W., D.B. Rubin, and B.I. Sacerdote. 2001. "Estimating the Effect of Unearned Income on Labor Earnings, Savings, and Consumption: Evidence from a Survey of Lottery Players." *American Economic Review,* 91(4): 778–794.

Jayachandran, S., and R. Pande. 2017. "Why Are Indian Children So Short? The Role of Birth Order and Son Preference." *American Economic Review,* 107(9): 2600–2629.

Joshi, V. 2016. "Universal Basic Income for India." *Ideas for India,* October 21. Available at https://www.ideasforindia.in/topics/poverty-inequality/universal-basic-income-for-india.html (accessed May 7, 2021).

Kapur, D., P. Mukhopadhyay, and A. Subramanian. 2008a. "The Case for Direct Cash Transfers to the Poor." *Economic and Political Weekly,* 43(15): 37–41, 43.

———. 2008b. "More on Direct Cash Transfers." *Economic and Political Weekly,* 43(47): 85–87.

Khilnani, S. 2010. "An Idea for India." *Mint,* November 19. Available at https://www.livemint.com/Leisure/gTnUezEaP7Izd7USQBI3TO/An-idea-for-India.html (accessed May 7, 2021).

Khosla, S. 2018. *India's Universal Basic Income: Bedeviled by the Details.* Washington, D.C.: Carnegie India.

Marinescu, I. 2018. "No Strings Attached: The Behavioral Effects of U.S. Unconditional Cash Transfer Programs." *National Bureau of Economic Research*

Working Paper Series No. 24337. Cambridge, MA: National Bureau of Economic Research.

Matsuyama, K. 2002. "The Rise of Mass Consumption Societies." *Journal of Political Economy,* 110(5): 1035–1070.

Miguel, E., S. Satyanath, and E. Sergenti. 2004. "Economic Shocks and Civil Conflict: An Instrumental Variables Approach." *Journal of Political Economy,* 112(4): 725–753.

Moene, K.O., and D. Ray. 2016. "The Universal Basic Share and Social Incentives." *Ideas for India*, September 30. Available at https://www.ideasforindia.in/topics/poverty-inequality/the-universal-basic-share-and-social-incentives.html (accessed May 7, 2021).

Mundle, S. 2016. "Universal Basic Income: An Idea Whose Time Has Come?" *Mint,* September 16. Available at https://www.livemint.com/Opinion/6KbaEPNHIpfdpoloXwb69O/Universal-basic-income-an-idea-whose-time-has-come.html (accessed May 7, 2021).

Munshi, K., and M. Rosenzweig. 2016. "Networks and Misallocation: Insurance, Migration, and the Rural-Urban Wage Gap." *American Economic Review,* 106 (1): 46–98.

Muralidharan, K. 2019. "Getting Targeting Right." *Ideas for India,* May 2. Available at https://www.ideasforindia.in/topics/poverty-inequality/nyay-e-symposium-getting-targeting-right.html (accessed May 7, 2021).

Muralidharan, K., and M. Kremer. 2008. "Public and Private Schools in Rural India." In P. Peterson and R. Chakrabarti (eds.), *School Choice International*, pp. 2–27. Cambridge, MA: MIT Press.

Muralidharan, K., J. Das, A. Holla, and A. Mohpal. 2017. "The Fiscal Cost of Weak Governance: Evidence from Teacher Absence in India." *Journal of Public Economics,* 145: 116–135.

Muralidharan, K., P. Niehaus, and S. Sukhtankar. 2016. "Building State Capacity: Evidence from Biometric Smartcards in India." *American Economic Review,* 106(10): 2895–2929.

———. 2018a. "Go for an 'Inclusive Growth Dividend' in India". *Hindustan Times,* November 6. Available at https://www.hindustantimes.com/columns/an-inclusive-growth-dividend-for-india/story-UiP98IQzxVprnZXBToGrjJ.html (accessed May 7, 2021).

———. 2018b. "We Need a Choice-based Approach in the Public Distribution System." *Hindustan Times,* October 3. Available at https://www.hindustantimes.com/columns/we-need-a-choice-based-approach-to-the-public-distribution-system/story-RY7jEYDmXfsxOMEsZguxmJ.html (accessed May 7, 2021).

———. 2020. "General Equilibrium Effects of (Improving) Public Employment Programs: Experimental Evidence from India." UC San Diego. Available at https://econweb.ucsd.edu/~pniehaus/papers/SmartcardsGE.pdf (accessed May 7, 2021).

Muralidharan, K., P. Niehaus, S. Sukhtankar, and J. Weaver. 2019. "Improving Last-Mile Service Delivery using Phone-Based Monitoring." *National Bureau of Economic Research Working Paper Series No. 25298*. Cambridge, MA: National Bureau of Economic Research. Available at https://www.nber.org/papers/w25298 (accessed May 7, 2021).

Muralidharan, K. and A. Subramanian, A. 2015. "Charting a Course for the Indian Economy." *Ideas for India,* August 5. Available at https://www.ideasforindia.in/topics/governance/charting-a-course-for-the-indian-economy.html (accessed May 7, 2021).

Muralidharan, K. and V. Sundararaman. 2015. "The Aggregate Effect of School Choice: Evidence from a Two-Stage Experiment in India." *The Quarterly Journal of Economics,* 130(3): 1011–1066.

Ravallion, M. 2016. *The Economics of Poverty: History, Measurement and Policy.* Oxford Scholarship Online, Oxford University Press.

Ray, D. 2016. "The Universal Basic Share." *Ideas for India*, September 29. Available at https://www.ideasforindia.in/topics/poverty-inequality/the-universal-basic-share.html (accessed May 7, 2021).

Roy, R. 2019a. "A Tale of Two Disenchantments." *Business Standard*, March 5. Available at https://www.business-standard.com/article/opinion/a-tale-of-two-disenchantments-119030500024_1.html (accessed May 7, 2021)

———. 2019b. "A Common Economic Programme for India." *Business Standard*, May 3. Available at https://www.business-standard.com/article/opinion/a-common-economic-programme-for-india-119050300026_1.html (accessed May 7, 2021).

Salehi-Isfahani, D. and M.H. Mostafavi-Dehzooei. 2018. "Cash Transfers and Labor Supply: Evidence from a Large-scale Program in Iran." *Journal of Development Economics,* 135(C): 349–367.

Shah, M. 2008. "Direct Cash Transfers: No Magic Bullet." *Economic and Political Weekly,* 43(34): 77–79.

Shiller, R. 2009. "A Way to Share in a Nation's Growth." *New York Times,* December 26. Available at https://www.nytimes.com/2009/12/27/business/economy/27view.html (accessed May 7, 2021).

Somville, V., and L. Vandewalle. 2018. "Saving by Default: Evidence from a Field Experiment in Rural India." *American Economic Journal: Applied Economics,* 10(3): 39–66.

Stecklov, G., A. Weinreb, and C. Carletto. 2018. "Can Incentives Improve Survey Data Quality in Developing Countries? Results from a Field Experiment in India." *Journal of the Royal Statistical Society,* 181(4): 1033–1056.

Subramanian, S. 2019. "Letting the Data Speak: Consumption Spending, Rural Distress, Urban Slowdown, and Overall Stagnation." *The Hindu Centre for Politics and Public Policy*, December 11. Available at https://www.thehinducentre.com/the-arena/current-issues/article30265409.ece (accessed May 7, 2021).

The Wire. 2018. "60 Economists Send Wake-up Call to Arun Jaitley on Maternal Benefits." December 21. Available at https://thewire.in/rights/make-pensions-maternity-benefits-priority-in-budget-2019-economists-to-arun-jaitley (accessed May 7, 2021).

Veblen, T. 1899. *The Theory of the Leisure Class: An Economic Study in the Evolution of Institutions*. New York: Macmillan.

To view the entire video of this IPF session and the General Discussion that ended the session, please scan this QR code or use the following URL:
https://www.youtube.com/watch?v=fH3vxNfKtGo

Comments and Discussion*

Chair: **Ashok Lahiri**
Member, 15th Finance Commission

Abhijit Banerjee
MIT

Thank you for having me here. Ashok Lahiri already did most of the job. So I get to say irresponsible things because all the responsible fiscally wise stuff has been said. I like this paper and that is probably not surprising. Let me start by agreeing with your conclusion since, I guess as is my duty, I will disagree with many of the specific points. The idea of an inclusive growth dividend is very much what we call Universal Ultra Basic Income in our new book, *Good Economics for Hard Times*. First, it does have the advantage of putting your money where your mouth is. Unlike Ashok, I am actually not particularly concerned about the fiscal side: Either we are going to become a ₹5 trillion economy soon, and therefore there is nothing to worry about, or else this is not happening, and then maybe we really should be thinking about potential social tensions that that particular prospect might unleash and what we need to deal with it. Therefore, either way this might be a good idea.

I will also emphasize the two big selling points that Karthik said right at the end. One is that the IGD does create a useful benchmark. I think asking the question as to whether any proposed scheme is better than giving cash is always a good idea. I also like the argument that this is the way to substitute for extremely inefficient transfers, at least in the longer run. I think establishing a credible mechanism for delivering cash is central to that project. To have a conversation about removing distortionary subsidies, we have to have good mechanisms for compensating the losers. With a credible mechanism, we actually probably do not need a one-for-one compensation. I think of the amount of electricity that gets used by farmers because of the form of the subsidy: some of it turns out to be not very useful for them and is costly for

---

* To preserve the sense of the discussions at the India Policy Forum, these discussants' comments reflect the views expressed at the IPF and do not necessarily take into account revisions to the conference version of the paper in response to these and other comments in preparing the final, revised version published in this volume. The original conference version of the paper is available on www.ncaer.org.

the country. I think all those ideas will play out soon, but I think having a good compensation mechanism in place is a good idea.

Let me now come to where I think more thought is needed. There are three questions that we will have to think about. One is how much? I think the idea they have that it should be roughly consistent with what PM-KISAN has suggested, is one way to go. I think our job as social scientists is not to take the political economy too literally. I do not know where this number came out of, but I would not guess that it came out of a great deal of deep thinking about exactly where the marginal returns are. So I am going to assume that the figure of ₹6,000 per year per family is just a guess, and some other guess could have been as good. Let me now proceed to argue that it is too little. So I think the first order point is that this is not just a supplement to income, it is more than that, it is going to do additional good things and that is why we can justify it. Let me take that proposition seriously. Is 120 rupees just 120 rupees, or more than that, as Karthik is claiming elaborately, talking about insurance and credit and all those things?

I think there are three mechanisms that he talked about: One is through insurance, one is through human capital investment, and one is through income-raising opportunities. Let me say that ₹120 per month provides almost no insurance. It is a tiny amount of money, even for very poor people. The real risks are much bigger, and I think the government is aware of it. Think of the *Fasal Bima Yojana*, which hasn't really taken off yet, but the amount of losses they are covering in principle are more of the order of many thousand rupees. As regards the idea that this is going to be compensation for either large income loss because of price variation, weather shocks, and health shocks, all those things have to be dealt with in other schemes. They are just too big. They are relatively rare, thankfully, and very large. I don't think that this is the scheme to do that. The amount of money is too small. For most of the people affected by it, this is 5–7 percent of their consumption at most and that is a loss people absorb all the time. That loss is not what ruins people, it is things like when, suddenly, you have to spend ₹5 lakh on a surgery. I think there are other schemes, like *Ayushman Bharat*, that will be needed to deal with that. I don't think insurance is a big argument here.

As for human capital investment, there is just not much evidence. I think the evidence is that human capital investment moves kind of linearly. So, spending for a while scales linearly with consumption. Hence, if you give people ₹6,000, and they spend 10 percent of that on health and education, they will spend 10 percent more. Therefore, you are going to get ₹600 more, and this is not going to be transformative.

The more positive evidence is the idea that when people get some extra cash in their hand, they actually make investments that have very high returns. The returns are sometimes quite stunning: 5–7 percent per month or more, up to 20 percent+ per month. I think that is where the really optimistic ideas come from. And they come in two flavors. A bunch of them come from conditional cash transfers across the world (mainly Latin America), and the rest from lumpsum transfers, again across the world. Both have been studied extensively. There have been lots of randomized control trials (RCTs), lots of other evaluations that are quite credible. If I look at the amount that is being proposed in this paper and compare it to the amounts in the studies that have positive results (which are the ones they cite), all those are basically bigger, much bigger, than the amount they are talking about. Just to give you some examples, in Latin America, the minimum, across 16 countries, was $6 per month in 2008 dollars, and the average is substantially higher. So that is a much bigger number than the one that they are talking about, which is roughly a quarter of the $6 minimum. In Kenya, there is another conditional cash transfer of $21 per month. In Malawi, it is actually closer to what they are proposing, but Malawi is an incredibly poor country. Ethiopia is another example, and the median there is $12 per month. So the amounts are much bigger, 5–10 times bigger. That is something to keep in mind.

It is hard to do this comparison quite right because, on the one side, these are not PPP-adjusted and that is sort of across the board. But India is a bit cheaper than the other countries. Thus, maybe the PPP adjustment would make the Indian number a little bigger. It is also not GDP per capita-adjusted; some inputs that you buy are priced relative to income per capita. For instance, land is more expensive in Mexico than in Malawi. I don't know how to do those adjustments, but the order of magnitude of the inclusive growth dividend seems smaller in general.

Now, why should I worry about it? If it is linear in investment, then you still get returns. But there is no evidence that the returns are necessarily linear. In fact, Maitreesh and co-authors have a very nice paper for Bangladesh where they estimate the threshold at which people get out of poverty and the necessary lumpsum payment to enable people to do so, and the lumpsum they are suggesting is of the order of $165 in 2007. That is probably now a much bigger number. We did a similar estimate for India, and there we said that the critical investment is of the order of ₹7,400 in 2008, so that is again a much bigger number.

Is the IGD amount enough to have some positive impacts on earnings? One possibility is that maybe you have to make a lumpsum investment (i.e., it is not linear), but you can get to the lumpsum by saving a little at a time. Here it is worth noting that despite all the talk about savings and how *Jan-Dhan* has increased savings, the numbers are remarkably small. An RCT shows that *Jan-Dhan* increased savings from 1–2 percent of annual income. So there is no evidence that people are going to save enough, that if you give them a very small amount of money per month, they are going to get $200 by saving. In fact, in a whole bunch of studies, the savings rates are between 0 and 2 percent across the board—none of them has found low-income people saving a lot. I don't believe that what is going to happen is that if you give them this money, they are going to save it all up and then start their business. Therefore, I don't see a very obvious mapping from this intervention to the kind of income growth opportunities suggested in the paper. I think this is going to be just an income supplement.

What then are the design choices? One is to spend more. The second is that if we do not want to spend more, we have to think about whether we want to lump it up for people. So do you want to make yearly payments rather than monthly payments? It seems to me that that would avoid the problem of saving, and might very well be valuable. So one design choice may be to make one-yearly or even two-yearly payments. One advantage of that would be that you could still think of the IGD basis being an individual, and then offer each individual the option of choosing whether they would take one two-yearly payment over these monthly payments. I suspect a bunch of people would. That also has the advantage that you do not have to worry about what a family is. If a group of people say that they will give up monthly transfers and take one lumpsum transfer, then that group of people can be defined to be a family.

Some targeting would be another solution. Given that this amount is actually very small, it should be easy to limit its take up, for example, by insisting that a person has to go and sign every week to get the money, so that most middle-class people will not do it. That is extreme, but the general point is that you can limit take up quite easily and therefore get the amount up. These are interesting design choices to think about.

Another set of issues we should think about is whether it is worthwhile to consider some geographical targeting—there could be greater coverage in some areas because poverty is extremely geographically concentrated in India. We know where it is, so we could target those areas, which is easy because it does not require individual data. Another thing we could do is make it conditional on outcomes. For example, when a mine closes, do you want to increase transfers? Or when environmental policies are drafted, do you want to do something so that the losers are at least partly compensated?

Finally, should we have conditionalities? I personally like the idea of making age at marriage a requirement. If you violate the law, you do not get it.

So I think this is a great launching pad, a great way to start a conversation. I am sure we will have an interesting conversation here, but we should continue it further.

Arvind Subramanian
Harvard Kennedy School and former Chief Economic Adviser, Government of India

First, it's great to be here and I enjoyed the paper very much. When I read it, I felt the paper was pitching not to the converted but the converter himself, and it was great to see that. I want to make just two or three big points.

The first is that I agree with what Abhijit said, but for completely different reasons, I think that the amounts involved in the growth dividend, in my view, are not politically incentive-compatible. The authors mentioned PM-KISAN, but I think we have to leave that aside for a second because it came late, and it came as a response to other things. So it is a little bit more complicated.

But let us start with the revealed preference of four such schemes in the last few months. Let us just talk about *Rythu Bandhu* and the Congress proposal. What is for me fascinating about *Rythu Bandhu* was that, first, it was a scheme that was highly regressive, even to those within the farming community, and second, it excluded all non-farmers, that is, it was almost completely non-universal. Just a very small set of people were getting this. Yet, why did the Chief Minister of Telangana, K. Chandrashekar Rao, think that this was politically incentive-compatible? By excluding a lot of people, why wouldn't jealousies be raised, questions be raised? In fact, because of non-universality, he was able to give more money than the scheme proposes. So I think that big amounts for beneficiaries are absolutely politically necessary. If you take the Congress scheme as well, it is targeted in order to make the numbers big for the beneficiary. So, the numbers have to be big for beneficiaries to be politically incentive-compatible.

Going back to *Rythu Bandhu*, we can broadly agree that it was "successful" because they did very well in the election, and everyone said *Rythu Bandhu* was part of this. So here is a scheme that is regressive and excluded a lot but was able to give a lot of money to beneficiaries and therefore proved very popular. So, in that sense, the two lessons I take away from this are (a) the amounts have to be big, and (b) what I think allowed the Chief Minister to do this was the political opportunity created by the agrarian crisis, which gave rise to the perception that there is a community deserving of this and so a lot of people were willing to not get this in order so that the few others could get it. Thus, it is the combination of opportunity plus relatively big amounts which seemed to work despite regressivity and exclusions.

Hence, if you want to push this idea it seems to me that you need some kind of political opportunity. I do not think giving this meagre amount of ₹120 a month is going to cut political ice with people. Of course, it is going to be politicians who create this political opportunity, but I suspect the sums are still far too small for a politician to say, "Vote for me because I am going to give you ₹120 a month."

My second point is on implementation. I do not think the Finance Commission can decree such a growth dividend. However, one way forward for these kinds of policies is a cooperative federalism framework on the expenditure side, just as GST was the result of cooperative federalism on the tax side. I think it is desirable for the states and the Center to come together because (a) the magnitudes can be bigger, and (b) the scope of what can be eliminated is correspondingly greater. For example, I have had these discussions with state finance ministers where they have said, "I want to do a UBI, and I am willing to cut, but leave it to me what to cut." So why do we not have mechanisms where, from the existing Centrally Sponsored Schemes, the Center says, "I am not going to tie the aid by saying you must do MGNREGA"; instead suppose that the schemes could be untied, so that state governments could have the freedom to decide what they want to cut in order to finance a UBI.

In the current political conjuncture, GST worked in part, or in large part, because there was the BJP at the Center and 17 BJP states sitting around the table to achieve consensus. We still have that configuration today, maybe even more. So why do we not use this cooperative federalism model, but on the expenditure side?

The problem with what I am proposing is that we will have to have an option or a menu-based approach where states can do it on their own. By definition, cooperative federalism means that no one party can appropriate the political benefit from doing a UBI. So there is a political incentive-compatibility challenge. But if the Center were to untie some of the schemes, and perhaps have some conditionality, linking the untying to a UBI, it could perhaps work.

My last point is about universality. Since there are resource constraints, we should be open to thinking of models of quasi-universality where you target out rather than target in. I think there are many ways in which you can do it. For example, my colleagues and I proposed that one version of PM-KISAN would be to give it to the entire rural population, but take out the top 10 percent or 15 percent based on the Socio Economic and Caste Census data. Implementation-wise, targeting out could be easier than targeting in and could also be politically acceptable because the very rich (those targeted out) would be excluded.

The last point relates to this whole debate on the compensatory state versus the redistributive state. In terms of politics, this is a choice only in la-la land. I don't think any state government really says, "Because I am going to do UBI, I will implement my education schemes any worse or any better." So, the debate becomes a little bit of a theoretical argument, and I have less sympathy for that.

General Discussion

The Chair, Ashok Lahiri, provided some initial comments and questions. He was primarily concerned about the cost of the program and how it would be financed. The Government's fiscal deficit has remained at over 3 percent of GDP for the past 11 years, and revenues have declined from a peak of 11 percent to 9.1 percent in 2018–19. Thus, he was skeptical about implementing the program without an offsetting reduction in other programs. He believed that it represented a premature move from a focus on development to a welfare state. He also argued that giving up on efforts to improve targeted income schemes in favor of a universal program was a counsel of despair. However, he thought that the suggestion of initially introducing the program in the most disadvantaged districts with an opportunity to assess its performance had merit.

Indira Rajaraman was unconvinced that a negative correlation between the States' per capita income and teacher absentee rates provided a measure of governance that was a sufficient basis for abandoning efforts to provide public goods and services in favor of more generalized transfers. She suggested that the same correlation would exist for the supply of paved roads and water supply without suggesting that efforts to supply those public goods should be abandoned.

Rajnish Mehra and Rakesh Mohan both questioned the assertion that the IGD, the inclusive growth dividend, would not crowd out other programs.

Government expenditures were 10.6 percent of GDP in 2018–19. Three major items, viz. interest (3.1 percent), subsidies (1.6 percent), and defense (1.5 percent) totaled over 6 percent. Thus, the IGD, as free cash to all citizens, would represent a quarter of the remaining program funds. Given the magnitude of the need for public services, they thought the program would require a tax increase or greatly expanded foreign borrowing. Mehra also argued that the program's efficacy could only be resolved by beginning with a test program along the lines of that suggested by Ashok Lahiri.

Dilip Mookerjee was enthusiastic about the proposal, but he was concerned that a universal scheme is not targeted at the poor and, thus, somewhat ineffective as an anti-poverty scheme. Second, he was worried about the reliance on bank account transfers as the primary delivery mechanism. About 35 percent of the population does not have functioning bank accounts. They are among the most vulnerable to corruption schemes. Also, he thought that the program needed a means of responding to localized crises, like droughts. In some cases, in-kind transfers are more effective than income payments.

Pranab Bardhan argued that from a political perspective, the amount of the transfer was too small to induce workers in informal sectors to mobilize behind the scheme. Further, the suggestion that the program be indexed to a percentage of GDP would intensify the current debate over the accurate measurement of GDP growth. He also agreed with the concerns about substitution with other important public goods. He believed that the addition of a universal basic income would necessitate tax increases, and the country cannot continue to ignore the failure to tax wealth in all its different forms.

Kaushik Basu argued that it was important to broaden the tax base to include wealth, particularly with an inheritance tax. He also agreed with Dilip Mookherjee that, initially, the delivery of the transfer to everyone would be costly, but it would decline as more people began to use bank accounts. He thought it would be useful to introduce a degree of targeting by inducing the wealthy to forego the program.

The session video, the paper, and all presentations for this IPF session are hyperlinked on the IPF program available on the NCAER website by scanning this QR code or going to https://www.ncaer.org/IPF2019/Agenda/Agenda_IPF_2019.pdf

RADHICKA KAPOOR*
Indian Council for Research on International Economic Relations

An Employment Data Strategy for India[§]

ABSTRACT Following the recommendations of the Task Force set up by the Government of India in 2017 to revamp the employment data architecture, India's employment statistics have undergone an overhaul. Two significant changes have been the replacement of NSSO's quinquennial Employment and Unemployment Surveys with the annual Periodic Labour Force Survey (PLFS) and the introduction of monthly payroll data. Given the dualistic nature of India's labor markets and the dominance of low-wage and low-productivity informal jobs, this exercise will serve a limited purpose. Against this backdrop, we examine the inadequacies of the existing data architecture, identify the gaps in data collection, and make recommendations for generating more relevant and comprehensive labor market data. We argue that it is imperative to continue with NSSO's quinquennial household survey and supplement it with the annual PLFS. The collection of data in household surveys needs to be based on all three different employment approaches, usual status, current weekly status, and current daily status. None of these can be dispensed with. We propose constructing measures of labor underutilization and informal employment to help us understand the nature and enormity of the employment challenge. We argue that there is a need to rethink the existing classification of employment status categories and to ask more probing questions about the nature of employment and activities undertaken by workers. We also highlight the importance of establishing a Business Register, as enterprise surveys face the problem of an incomplete frame. Instead of simply conducting new surveys, we believe it would be more prudent to strengthen the existing data machinery and ensure that state governments are equal partners in this exercise.

Keywords: Labor Force, Employment, Employment Data, Household Surveys, Enterprise Surveys

JEL Classification: J21, J29, J40, J46, J60

---

* radhicka.kapoor@gmail.com
[§] The author is extremely grateful to Ajit Ghose, G. C. Manna, P. C. Mohanan, Rinku Murgai, R. Nagaraj, and participants at the India Policy Forum for their insightful comments and suggestions. Ashulipi Singhal provided excellent research assistance.

1. Introduction

Statistics on the economically active population, employment, and unemployment are a key input in designing macroeconomic policies. They are an essential base for the design and evaluation of government programs geared towards employment creation, income enhancement, and poverty reduction. For policy responses to be meaningful, labor market statistics need to be reliably sourced, accurate, and timely. Typically, these statistics are generated from various sources. Data on employment can be obtained from establishment sample surveys, establishment or economic censuses, social security records, and public sector payrolls. Data on unemployment can be derived from administrative records on registered job seekers or recipients of unemployment benefits.

In India, historically, employment estimates have been generated using household and establishment surveys. Household surveys capture both the organized and unorganized sectors, particularly the self-employed. They largely satisfy the requirements of completeness. The quinquennial household surveys on employment and unemployment conducted by the National Sample Survey Office (NSSO), the last of which was conducted in 2011–12, have been the primary source of various labor market indicators since 1972–73. Establishment surveys, on the other hand, compile data from worksites and provide a more detailed picture of the industry structure of employment and characteristics of establishments. The key establishment surveys include the Economic Census (EC), the Annual Survey of Industries (ASI), and NSSO's "Unincorporated Non-agricultural Enterprises (excluding construction)." While the EC provides the most comprehensive database of non-agricultural economic establishments in the country, the latter two are follow-up enterprise surveys of the EC. The ASI database is an annual one compiling information on the growth, composition, and structure of "registered" or formal sector firms, while NSSO's Unincorporated Enterprise Survey is a quinquennial survey which provides data on unregistered firms.

Much of India's employment data has been generated with a considerable time lag and often focuses on the organized sector. Recognizing the challenges arising from the paucity of real-time jobs data, the government set up a Task Force in 2017 to revamp the employment data architecture (NITI Aayog 2017). Significant among the recommendations of the 2017 Task Force was the introduction of the use of high-frequency administrative data (relating to payrolls, social security systems, and provident fund) and the discontinuation of NSSO's quinquennial Employment and Unemployment

Surveys (EUS). NSSO's EUS have been replaced with the Periodic Labour Force Survey (PLFS), a household survey that will generate Key Indicators of the Labour Market (KILM), such as the labor force participation rate, worker population ratio, and unemployment rate (UR) at an annual frequency in rural areas and quarterly frequency in urban areas.

The revamp of employment data needs to be seen against the backdrop of the fact that employment in India is dominated by low-wage and low-productivity jobs in the unorganized sector. In addition to the dominance of the unorganized sector, evidence suggests that the organized sector has witnessed rapid informalization over the years through the contractualization and casualization of the workforce. What is more, many of the new jobs being created in the platform economy are also non-standard in nature and are outside the ambit of labor regulations. Thus, as old forms of informal employment persist, new forms are also emerging and there is an urgent need to improve statistics on the informal economy so that we have a nuanced understanding of the dynamics underlying this sector.

Additionally, India's jobs challenge is not just one of unemployment but also of underemployment. The UR, by itself, is an insufficient metric to anchor the policy discourse. In developing countries, due to the lack of sufficient unemployment benefit schemes, labor underutilization less often takes the explicit form of unemployment, showing up more among the employed (time-related underemployment) and persons outside the labor force (the potential labor force; International Labour Organization 2018). In order to have a comprehensive picture of the state of the labor market, particularly of the extent of labor underutilization, it is crucial to complement the analysis on labor market indicators with indicators on the quality of employment.

Given this backdrop, this paper will begin by examining the key characteristics of India's labor markets in Section 2. In Section 3, we examine the current state of data collection on employment and unemployment. Thereafter, in Section 4, we discuss the inadequacies of the existing data architecture in dealing with the complexities of the Indian setting. While we identify the gaps in data collection and analysis, we also make a series of recommendations for generating more reliable and relevant labor market data. Through these recommendations, we hope to move towards a more appropriate framework and better protocols to collect employment data— one that is cognizant of the formal and the informal sides of the labor market. Strengthening the statistical base of the world of work and achieving accuracy in capturing the different dimensions and nuances of the labor market are essential for shaping sound economic policy.

2. Characteristics of India's Labor Markets

Before delving into a discussion on labor market statistics, it is important to have a conceptual understanding of the nature of India's labor market conditions and how these have evolved over time. This has directional implications for both data collection and analysis. Many are inclined to think that all we need to know about the employment situation in an economy is how many are employed and how many are unemployed. And that we need to know these with high frequency. However, given the complexities of the Indian labor market, we need to know much more. Unemployment and employment rates are inadequate metrics to understand India's labor markets for multiple reasons. We will now examine why this is the case.

To begin with, open URs in India have typically been quite low. Table 1 reports the URs for India since 2004–05. It is worth noting that barring the recent PLFS, URs have fluctuated in the range of 2–3 percent, suggesting that India does not face a significant employment challenge. However, a disaggregated look at the UR suggests that this is not the case. An examination of the UR by education levels in Table 2 shows that for those with relatively higher education, the UR is quite high. For instance, for urban males and females who had received secondary education and above, the UR stood at 4 percent and 10 percent, respectively, in 2011–12, jumping to 9.2 percent and 19.8 percent, respectively, in 2017–18. This is largely a result of the fact that in an economy where the cost of remaining unemployed is very high, in the absence of social security, unemployment is a luxury enjoyed by the relatively well-off and educated individuals who can afford to remain unemployed (Ghose 2016). In contrast, the UR of those who were not literate

TABLE 1. Percentage Unemployment Rates according to Usual Status (Principal Status (PS) + Subsidiary Status (SS)) and Current Weekly Status (CWS)

	Rural				Urban			
	Male		Female		Male		Female	
Round (Year)	Usual Status (PS + SS)	CWS	Usual Status (PS + SS)	CWS	Usual Status (PS + SS)	CWS	Usual Status (PS + SS)	CWS
PLFS (2017–18)	5.8	8.8	3.8	7.7	7.1	8.8	10.8	12.8
68th (2011–12)	1.7	3.3	1.7	3.5	3.0	3.8	5.2	6.7
66th (2009–10)	1.6	3.2	1.6	3.7	2.8	3.6	5.7	7.2
61st (2004–05)	1.6	3.8	1.8	4.2	3.8	5.2	6.9	9.0

Source: Ministry of Statistics and Programme Implementation (2019, Statement 31).

TABLE 2. Percentage Unemployment Rates according to Usual Status (PS + SS) for Persons Aged 15 Years and above by Educational Attainment

General Education Level	2004–05	2009–10	2011–12	PLFS 2017–18	2004–05	2009–10	2011–12	PLFS 2017–18
	Rural Male				Rural Female			
Not literate	0.3	0.3	0.5	1.7	0.2	0.0	0.2	0.1
Literate & up to primary	1.0	1.0	1.0	3.1	1.1	0.5	0.3	0.6
Middle	1.6	1.8	1.8	5.7	3.4	2.3	2.5	3.7
Secondary & above	4.4	3.5	3.6	10.5	15.2	11.8	9.7	17.3
All	1.6	1.6	1.7	5.7	1.8	1.6	1.6	3.8
	Urban Male				Urban Female			
Not literate	1.0	1.0	0.7	2.1	0.3	0.9	0.4	0.8
Literate & up to primary	2.1	1.6	1.9	3.6	2.9	0.5	1.3	1.3
Middle	4.2	2.6	2.2	6.0	8.0	3.7	3.0	5.1
Secondary & above	5.1	3.6	4.0	9.2	15.6	12.2	10.3	19.8
All	3.7	2.8	3.0	6.9	6.9	5.7	5.3	10.8

Source: Ministry of Statistics and Programme Implementation (2019, Statement 32).

fluctuated at around 1 percent. These are the poor who cannot afford to remain unemployed. They are compelled to resort to low-productivity and low-paying work in the unorganized sector. In 2017–18, 81.3 percent of all workers were estimated to be working in the unorganized sector.[1] While employment in the unorganized sector has declined over time, from 88.7 percent in 2004–05, it continues to be large. In fact, labor markets in India can be best characterized by their dualistic structure with the prevalence of an organized sector that co-exists with a large "unorganized sector."

Importantly, self-employment and casual wage employment are the main forms of employment in the unorganized sector.[2] Data from the NSS household surveys and the PLFS indicate that these two forms of employment have continued to account for a disproportionately large share of total employment. As of 2017–18, over 75 percent of the total workers were engaged in these two forms of employment and were thus outside the ambit of standard employer–employee relationships. A mere 23.3 percent were in Regular Wage Salaried (RWS) employment. Ghose (2016) attributes the dominance of self-employment and casual wage employment to the fact that they facilitate work-sharing arrangements. In self-employment, the working members of the household share the work and income from the household enterprise, while in casual wage employment, workers share the amount of wage employment available. It is "this feasibility of work sharing that makes it possible for the unorganized sector to function as a reservoir of surplus labor, which exists in the form of underemployment of many workers rather than in the form of unemployment of some workers" (Ghose 2016, p. 21). In a situation where most workers are underemployed, escaping unemployment

---

1. Using information on enterprise type reported in household surveys, estimates on the unorganized sector are computed by including all enterprises other than government establishments and public enterprises, all enterprises in the private corporate sector and those private non-corporate enterprises that employ at least 10 regular employees. As defined in Section 4, informal or unorganized enterprises include the household sector as household enterprises or, equivalently, unincorporated enterprises owned by households.

2. In the NSSO, persons who operate their own farm or non-farm enterprises or were engaged independently in a profession or trade on own account or with one or a few partners were deemed to be self-employed in household enterprises. The essential feature of the self-employed is that they have autonomy (decide how, where, and when to produce) and economic independence (in respect of choice of market, scale of operation, and finance) for carrying out their operation. A person who is casually engaged in others' farm or non-farm enterprises (both household and non-household) and, in return, receives wages according to the terms of the daily or periodic work contract is considered as a casual laborer. RWS employees are persons who work in others' farm or non-farm enterprises (both household and non-household) and, in return, receive salary or wages on a regular basis (i.e., not on the basis of daily or periodic renewal of work contract). This category includes not only persons getting time wage but also persons receiving piece wage or salary and paid apprentices, both full-time and part-time.

means little. We need to have a better and deeper understanding about conditions of employment and whether the jobs they are engaged in are decent jobs. In other words, do these jobs provide for satisfactory working and living conditions and are people in employment necessarily better off than the unemployed.

Apart from its dualistic nature, another striking feature of India's labor markets has been the increasing informalization of the organized sector over time. Although the share of the organized sector has increased, albeit at a modest pace, the share of formal employment (defined by a worker having access to at least one social security benefit) has declined. In 2004–05, the share of regular formal employment in total employment in the organized sector stood at 51.3 percent. It declined to 47.4 percent in 2017–18.[3] Trends from the ASI also corroborate this phenomenon. Between 2000–01 and 2016–17, approximately half the increase in total employment, from 7.7 million to 13.7 million, was accounted for by the increasing use of contract workers. The share of contract workers in total employment increased sharply from 15.5 percent in 2000–01 to 27.9 percent in 2015–16, while the share of directly hired workers fell from 61.2 percent to 50.4 percent during the same period. It is worth mentioning that even amongst RWS workers, conditions of employment leave much to be desired. As of 2017–18, 71.1 percent of RWS workers had no written job contract and 49.6 percent were not eligible for social security benefits. The contractualization, casualization, and informalization of the workforce point to the need for capturing changes in the quality of employment data.

In such a scenario, simply having a count of how many people are unemployed and employed, and what the employment status of the latter is, is clearly inadequate. Neither the current state of employment conditions nor the changes over time can be discerned simply from observed changes in employment and unemployment rates. To know if employment conditions are improving, we need to know if workers are moving from low-productivity to high-productivity work and if the level of underemployment is declining.

3. The Current Data Architecture

At present, the sources of statistics on India's employment indicators can be grouped into three broad categories: household sample surveys;

---

3. Regular formal employment is defined as RWS employment that offers at least one social security benefit.

establishment censuses and establishment sample surveys; and various types of administrative records. These sources differ in the type and detail of information they provide; in coverage and periodicity; in concepts, definitions, and measurement units; and in cost of operation, quality, and timeliness of the results. We will briefly describe each of these.

3.1. Household Surveys

To get a holistic picture of India's dualistic labor markets, household surveys are the most widely used to generate employment estimates. Given their ability to capture both the organized and unorganized sectors, particularly household enterprises, they provide the most comprehensive data on the employment situation in the country. The main objective of EUS, which have been conducted by NSSO at periodic intervals since 1972–73, is to get estimates of level parameters of various labor force characteristics at the national and state/Union Territory (UT) levels. The participation of people is not only dynamic but also multidimensional—it varies with region, age, education, gender, industry, and occupational category. These aspects of the labor force are captured in detail in NSSO's EUS and estimates are generated for the labor force participation rate, worker population ratio, UR, extent of underemployment, and wages of employees. The key indicators of the labor market and how they are derived are depicted in Table 3. The indicators of the structural aspects of the workforce, such as status in employment, industrial distribution, and occupational distribution are also derived from these surveys.

The detailed activity statuses under each of the three broad activity statuses (viz., "employed," "unemployed," and "not in the labor force") and the corresponding codes used in the survey are reported in Table 4.

Following the recommendations of the "Expert Committee on Unemployment Estimates" (popularly known as the Dantwala Committee 1970), which noted that no one-dimensional measure was meaningful in the

TABLE 3. Key Indicators of the Labor Market Used by NSSO

1. *Labor force participation rate (LFPR):* [(No. of employed persons + No. of unemployed persons) / Total population] × 1,000
2. *Worker Population Ratio (WPR):* [No. of employed persons / Total population] × 1,000
3. *Proportion of Unemployed (PU):* [No. of unemployed persons / Total population] × 1,000
4. *Unemployment Rate (UR):* [No. of unemployed persons / (No. of employed persons + No. of unemployed persons)] × 1,000

Source: National Sample Survey Office (2015).

TABLE 4. NSSO Activity Status Codes for Employed, Unemployed, and Not in Labor Force Categories

	Working (Employed)	
Self-employed	Regular Wage/ Salaried Employee	Casual Labor
11: Worked in household enterprises (self-employed) as own-account workers; 12: Worked in household enterprises (self-employed) as employers; 21: Worked in household enterprises (self-employed) as helpers	31: Worked as regular wage/salaried employees	41: Worked as casual laborers in public works other than MGNREGA public works; 42: Worked as casual laborers in MGNREGA public works; 51: Worked as casual laborers in other types of works; 61: Did not work owing to sickness though there was work in household enterprises; 62: Did not work owing to other reasons though there was work in household enterprises; 71: Did not work owing to sickness but had regular salaried/wage employment; 72: Did not work owing to other reasons but had regular salaried/wage employment.

Not Working but Seeking/Available for Work (Unemployed)

81: Sought work or did not seek but were available for work (for Usual Status approach);
81: Sought work (for Current Weekly Status approach);
82: Did not seek but were available for work (for Current Weekly Status approach).

Neither Working nor Available for Work (Not in the Labor Force)

91: Attended educational institutions;
92: Attended to domestic duties only;
93: Attended to domestic duties and were also engaged in free collection of goods (vegetables, roots, firewood, cattle feed, etc.), sewing, tailoring, weaving, etc., for household use);
94: Rentiers, pensioners, remittance recipients, etc.;
95: Not able to work owing to disability;
97: Others (including beggars, prostitutes, etc.);
98: Did not work owing to sickness (for casual workers only);
99: Children of age 0–4 years.

Source: National Sample Survey Office (2015).
Note: Activity Status Codes 42, 61, 62, 71, 72, 82, and 98 are used only in the current status (in CWS and CDS).

Indian context, the NSSO has been producing three types of estimates of the employed and the unemployed. These are the Usual Status (US), Current Weekly Status (CWS), and Current Daily Status (CDS). The methodology for assigning the three statuses is different, and therefore, their interpretation also differs.

The estimate of the employed, according to the Usual Principal Status, gives the number of persons who worked for a relatively longer part of the reference period of 365 days preceding the date of the survey. The workforce, considering both the Usual Principal Status and the Subsidiary Status (together referred to as Usual Status), includes the persons who: (a) either worked for a relatively longer part of the 365 days preceding the date of the survey and (b) were among the remaining population that had worked for a shorter time throughout the reference year of 365 days preceding the date of the survey or for a minor period, which is not less than 30 days. The estimate of the workforce, according to the CWS, includes those who worked for at least one hour on any day during the seven days preceding the date of the survey. The workforce measured in terms of the CDS gives the average picture of the number of person-days worked during the survey period. For each person, seven person-days are assigned for the week preceding the date of the survey. Each day of the reference week is seen as comprising either two "half days" or a "full day" for assigning the activity status. For recording the time disposition for activities pursued by a person in a day, an intensity of 1.0 is given against an activity that is done for "full day," and an intensity of 0.5 against the activity which is done for "half day." A person is considered as "working" (employed) for the full day if he/she had worked for four hours or more during the day.

Given the exhaustive and comprehensive nature of its coverage, data from the NSSO's EUS is collected only once every 5–6 years. Another drawback of these surveys is their inability to provide reliable estimates of employment below the state level, that is, the district level. In fact, there are precision issues even for smaller states and UTs. There is also a high margin of errors associated with the UR by gender at the state level in some cases. It is important to mention that NSSO's consumption surveys conducted on an annual basis (i.e., the thin rounds which are undertaken during the intervening period between the quinquennial rounds) had an employment schedule and were conducted until 2003–04. Thereafter, the NSSO conducted several thin rounds of the EUS between the quinquennial rounds of 2004–05 and 2011–12, before the survey was finally discontinued.[4] Realizing the need for regular and frequent labor statistics, the Labour Bureau also began conducting the EUS annually since 2009–10. It has conducted six surveys

---

4. NSSO's annual thin sample is about 40 percent of the sample of households in the quinquennial survey. Although the annual and quinquennial surveys follow identical concepts, schedules of quinquennial surveys provide for detailed probing, which is not available in the annual rounds. There have been some differences in the estimates thrown by the annual and quinquennial data. NSSO does not give any indication of the reliability of its estimates, some of which may be very unreliable due to poor representation in the sample.

since then.[5] However, the results of the last survey for the year 2016–17 have not been released.

Following the recommendations of the 2017 Task Force, both the above-mentioned household surveys have been discontinued and replaced by the PLFS. The report of the first PLFS for the period 2017–18 was released in May 2019. Conducted by the NSSO, the PLFS produces annual estimates of KILM based on the US and CWS approaches. Additionally, in urban areas, a rotational panel sampling design is being used to generate quarterly urban estimates according to the CWS approach. Each selected household in urban areas is visited four times—in the beginning with the first visit schedule and thrice periodically later with the revisit schedule. There is no revisit in the rural samples.

In addition to the introduction of the quarterly module, the PLFS has some other noteworthy features. First, information in the schedule of enquiry has been collected from the sample households using the Computer-assisted Personal Interviewing (CAPI) method. Second, information is collected on the number of hours worked on each day of the reference week. For the persons engaged in economic activity on the days of the reference week, the number of hours worked is recorded and the current weekly activity status for those engaged in economic activity is determined on the basis of time disposition during each day of the reference week (recorded in terms of the number of hours worked). Besides, information is collected on the total number of hours actually worked considering all the work performed during the day. Third, for the persons who are engaged in economic activity on different days of the week, if they are available for additional work on a particular day, information on the number of hours available for work is recorded. Fourth, information on earnings from employment is collected. For RWS employees in CWS, information on earnings for the preceding calendar month is collected. For the self-employed persons in CWS, information on gross earnings from self-employment activity during the last 30 days is collected. For the persons who worked as casual laborers on different days of the reference week, information on wage earnings is collected separately for each of those specific days.

In a departure from NSSO's previous EUS, the recently released report of the PLFS does not provide any estimates using the CDS. The PLFS schedule includes a set of questions on current weekly activity particulars

---

5. The reference period for the Labour Bureau's surveys is as follows: 2009–10 (April 2009–March 2010); 2011–12 (July 2010–June 2011); 2012–13 (October 2012–March 2013); 2013–14 (January 2014–July 2014); and 2015–16 (April 2015–December 2015).

of the household members, which is similar to the questions posed on time disposition during the week in NSSO's EUS questionnaire. While researchers could possibly compute the CDS measures from the unit data, the reason for dropping the CDS measure from the discussion is not clear.[6]

Before concluding the discussion on data compiled from households, it is important to mention that the decennial population Census also collects information on the economic activity of the population. The economic tables of the Census (referred to as the B-Series Tables) provide information on the number of main workers (those who worked for the major part of the reference period, i.e., six months or more); marginal workers (those who did not work for the major part of the reference period, i.e., less than six months), and non-workers (those who did not work at all during the reference period). The main and marginal workers are also classified into four categories based on the economic activity performed by them during the last one year. These are cultivators, agricultural laborers, workers in the household industry, and other workers. Tabulations are also available by religious communities, social groups, and education level. Main workers are also classified by industrial category, education level, age, sex, and religious community. These tabulations are made available at the national, state, district, and city levels. That the economic tables of the Census provide reliable estimates of the number of workers at the district level is noteworthy. Even NSSO's EUS does not provide reliable estimates at the district level as the sample size is not large enough. Despite this advantage of the Census, the above-mentioned tabulations have not attracted much attention in the academic literature. This is probably a consequence of the fact that there is a considerable delay in the release of the series, which makes them dated. For instance, the economic tables for the Census of 2011 were released only in 2017.

3.2. Census and Survey of Establishments

In addition to household surveys, enterprise or establishment surveys, which compile data from the workplace, are an important source of employment data. Data collected from worksites provides a more detailed picture of the industry structure of employment and characteristics of enterprises. In household surveys, where the respondent is the household head or member (who may not be the worker in question), obtaining correct information of the characteristics of the enterprise in which the worker works is challenging (Papola 2014).

---

6. It is also not clear if the methodology for computing the CDS will be the same as before and if the time intensity approach of using 1 or 0.5 will continue in the PLFS now that the actual number of hours being worked on a particular activity are being recorded.

Although agriculture is a sector that employs a significant part of the rural workforce, enterprise surveys typically cover activities other than agriculture. As mentioned earlier, there are two key enterprise surveys in India. The first is the ASI by the Ministry of Statistics and Programme Implementation (MoSPI). It is the main source of industrial statistics in India and provides detailed information annually on the organized manufacturing sector (comprising activities related to manufacturing processes, repair services, gas and water supply, and cold storage). It was launched in 1960 with 1959 as the reference year and has continued for all years since then, except for 1972. The survey gathers information only on "registered" or formal sector firms that are covered under Sections 2m(i) and 2m(ii) of the 1948 Factories Act, that is, those firms that use electricity and hire 10 or more workers, and those that do not use electricity but nevertheless employ 20 or more workers.

The definition of a worker in the ASI includes all persons employed directly or through an agency. It includes those engaged not just in any manufacturing process but also in cleaning any part of the machinery or premises used for the manufacturing process or in any other kind of work connected with the manufacturing process or the subject of the manufacturing process. The total number of persons engaged is defined as production workers (sum of the workers hired directly and contract workers), supervisory and managerial staff, and all working proprietors and their family members who are actively engaged in the work of the factory even without any pay, and unpaid members of the co-operative societies who worked in or for the factory in any direct and productive capacity. Importantly, the number of workers is an average number computed by dividing the total number of man-days worked in the factory by the number of days the factory had worked during the reference year. The total number of man-days worked during a month is, in turn, obtained by summing up the number of workers in each shift over all the shifts worked on all working days during a month. Thus, the number of workers obtained from the ASI would be the actual labor input in the manufacturing process rather than the actual number of individuals who worked in the factory. As such, comparing this number with estimates of the organized sector workforce from administrative sources or the EUS would not be conceptually valid. We will elaborate on the problem in comparing estimates of workers from enterprises and household surveys later.

The second main enterprise survey is the NSSO's Enterprise Survey of Unincorporated Enterprises. The surveys are conducted quinquennially and have typically covered the manufacturing sector. Since 2010–11, they have expanded their coverage to include trade and other service sectors (excluding construction). The NSSO classifies unregistered firms into three categories: (a) own-account manufacturing enterprises, that is, those that operate without any hired worker employed on a fairly regular basis, (b) non-directory manufacturing establishments, that is, those that employ fewer than six workers (household and hired workers taken together), and (c) directory manufacturing establishments, that is, those that employ a total of six or more household members and hired workers. The significance of this survey stems from the fact that it takes into account the self-employed and employment in establishments with less than 10 workers, which the ASI does not take into account.

In this survey, a worker is defined as one who "participates either full time or part time in the activity of the enterprise in any capacity—primary or supervisory—and may or may not receive wages/salaries in return." The average number of persons usually working on a working day during the reference month is recorded. A worker refers to a position rather than a person. It includes working owners, hired workers (full-time and part-time), apprentices (paid/unpaid), and other workers/helpers working without regular salary or wages. In the case of proprietary or partnership enterprises, the owner(s) personally working in the enterprise on a fairly regular basis are treated as working owners.

In addition to the above-mentioned enterprise surveys, the Central Statistics Office under MoSPI conducts the EC. This is a count of all establishments/units engaged in the production of goods and services and is the most comprehensive database of non-agricultural economic establishments in the country. The most recent EC was conducted in 2013–14. Prior to this, it was conducted in 2005–06. While the main purpose of the EC is to provide a frame for other data collection exercises such as the NSS's Unincorporated Non-agricultural Enterprise Surveys, it also provides basic information on the number of establishments/units, their employment location, type of activity, and nature of operation.

PROBLEMS IN COMPARING ESTIMATES OF WORKERS FROM ENTERPRISE AND HOUSEHOLD SURVEYS

Before proceeding, it is important to discuss the issue of comparability of household labor force surveys and enterprise surveys such as the ASI. In the Indian context, given the irregularity of employment patterns, the informal and transitory nature of enterprises, and differences in the concepts and procedures used in the two surveys, we cannot make a direct comparison between them. This can be explained as follows.

First, establishment surveys count the number of positions (jobs) as opposed to the number of employed persons. As explained above, in establishment surveys, the average number of workers is calculated by counting the total number of man-days worked by different workers and dividing this by the total number of working days.[7] As against this, in the EUS, a person is termed as employed (worker) if he or she is engaged in economic activities on the criterion of major time during a pre-specified reference period.

Second, we need to make a distinction between the reference periods of enterprise and household surveys. Many enterprises operate for less than six months and some of them operate for even less than three months. In enterprise surveys, all the persons employed in enterprises are counted as workers, making no allowance for the duration. On the other hand, in the EUS, the reference period for the US criteria is taken as a year. The US criteria for these entrepreneurs will be decided on the basis of the activity pursued by them during the remaining part of the year. They will be considered as employed only in the subsidiary status if they have not followed any other economic activities during the major period.

Third, some workers tend to get excluded from enterprise surveys. For instance, workers who work for households rather than for enterprises (such as domestic servants and drivers) get left out of enterprise surveys.[8] Casual laborers who cannot be assigned to an enterprise also do not get captured in the enterprise survey as these surveys cover those workers (be it part-time or full-time) who participate in the activities of the enterprise on a "fairly regular basis."

Fourth, the treatment of part-time workers poses a problem. According to the NSSO's enterprise survey instructions, full-time workers are those who work for more than half of the normal working hours on a fairly regular basis, while part-time workers are those who work for less than half the normal working hours of the enterprise on a regular basis. In the enterprise survey, two part-time workers will be treated as two and not one full-time worker leading to an overestimation of the number of workers.

3.3. Administrative Data

Following the recommendations of the 2017 Task Force, the government has started reporting administrative data relating to payrolls, social security systems, and provident fund for compiling information about the

---

7. This is then rounded off to a whole number.
8. In enterprise surveys, it is operationally difficult to list all employer households as enterprises.

labor market. The first such series was released in January 2018 pertaining to the time period, April 2017–November 2017. Since then, the series has been released on a monthly basis providing age-wise payroll data for the Employees' Provident Fund Organisation (EPFO), Employees' State Insurance Corporation (ESIC), and National Pension Scheme (NPS). Payroll databases are widely used in advanced economies to gauge the employment situation and provide a count of formal jobs. The introduction of these databases in India is indeed a significant initiative. However, the interpretation and analysis of India's payroll data is not so simple. As outlined in Kapoor (2018), it is an exercise fraught with challenges for multiple reasons.

First, there is significant overlap and duplication across the above-mentioned schemes. We need a common identifier across the multiple datasets to avoid double counting. Attempts are being made to circumvent this problem using the unique *Aadhaar* identity number. While the EPFO and Pension Fund Regulatory and Development Authority datasets have been *Aadhaar* seeded, the ESIC data has not. Second, new entries on these databases do not necessarily reflect new jobs. Given that the EPFO Act applies to all factories in classes of industry specified in Schedule 1 of the Act where 20 or more persons are employed, the addition of even one more worker will result in all the workers of this establishment getting added on the database and being counted as new jobs. Despite the 2017 Task Force pointing to this caveat, these numbers are widely being interpreted as indicative of new formal jobs.

Third, each time the data has been released, the previously released estimates have been revised. This constant volatility begs the question as to whether this data is in fact reliable and accurate in "real time." Conceptually, too, the EPFO database has seen a significant revision. In August 2018, the EPFO started reporting the number of subscribers who ceased their subscriptions and later "rejoined" and "re-subscribed" to the database. This category has now been included in the net additions to databases implying that those who left a formal job and rejoined a formal job are counted as new formal jobs. These revisions not only highlight the fragility of this database, but they also give the sense that this database is still in experimental mode.

Given the above limitations, the excessive focus on the payroll data to understand employment trends serves little purpose. The larger issue, of course, is that it cannot provide a holistic picture of the employment scenario as it focuses simply on the formal sector. Nevertheless, it is important to undertake administrative reforms to strengthen and develop the payroll database such that it can emerge as an important data source in the future.

3.4. Private Data Sources

To fill in the gaps in India's official statistical employment database, the Centre for Monitoring Indian Economy (CMIE), a private agency, has also begun tracking unemployment since January 2016. The CMIE has been compiling an unemployment database that contains detailed information on the employment and unemployment status of the members residing in all households in their Consumer Pyramids sample. The survey, referred to as the Consumer Pyramids Household Survey (CPHS), has a sample size of more than 161,000 households covering about 522,000 people. This makes its sample size larger than that of NSSO's EUS. Employment estimates are based on consecutive waves of the CPHS by tracking a panel of households. Each wave is executed over a period of four months and there are three waves in a year. Complete demographic data of all households in the Consumer Pyramids sample is collected thrice a year. The employment status of the members of the households is recorded as one of the following:

- Employed
- Unemployed, willing to work and actively looking for a job
- Unemployed, willing to work and not actively looking for a job
- Unemployed, not willing to work and not actively looking for a job

Given the high-frequency statistics it generates, the CMIE database has emerged as an important source of employment data. Nevertheless, it cannot be seen as a substitute for the comprehensive household surveys conducted by the NSSO, which provide an in-depth understanding of labor's engagement in economic activities. Conceptually, the surveys are different too. While the NSSO provides employment estimates using three different approaches based on different reference periods, the CMIE survey seeks a response on the employment/unemployment status from every member of the sample household, who is aged 15 years or more on the day of the survey. If the status on the day of the survey is unclear (such as for a daily wage worker), then the status as of the previous day is taken instead. Such an approach helps to ensure that there is no ambiguity regarding status and no problem regarding recall. An important feature of the CMIE survey is the use of technology which enables them to generate estimates at high frequency. Data are captured on a mobile phone on a specially developed software application and validated and uploaded for use by the end of day, every day. This has enabled CMIE to generate estimates on a daily, weekly, and monthly basis. While this is a welcome development, data from private agencies cannot be seen as a substitute for official government data.

4. Issues and Recommendations

The preceding section explains how India's employment data architecture has changed since the original systems were introduced. Despite these changes, significant gaps exist in data collection and analysis. In this section, we examine these gaps and understand how they can be addressed to get a more meaningful picture of India's dualistic labor markets. We provide feasible solutions where possible. Significantly, these recommendations (summarized in Table 5) do not entail conducting new surveys but making more effective use of the data being currently generated.

4.1. The Relevance of Measuring Indicators using Three Approaches

The move from NSSO's quinquennial EUS to the annual PLFS requires us to revisit the issue of the approach to adopt in measuring employment. India's household surveys have produced employment measures using three approaches—Usual Status, Current Weekly Status, Currrent Daily Status. The policy debate thus far has been anchored around US measures.

TABLE 5. Summary of Key Suggestions

1. Continue with the NSS quinquennial EUS round while concomitantly holding the annual PLFS.
2. In addition to the UR, create three new measures of labor underutilization in line with the recommendations of the 19th ICLS: combined rate of underemployment and unemployment; combined rate of unemployment and potential labor force, and composite measure of labor underutilization. These three measures should be included amongst the KILM reported in all the survey results.
3. Re-introduce the CDS measure in the PLFS to understand the extent of underemployment and daily changes in activities.
4. Incorporate additional questions on worker classification to understand and categorize different work arrangements such as contract workers, fixed-term employees, gig-economy workers, and homeworkers.
5. Create a headline rate of informal employment which combines the enterprise-based definition of informal sector with the job-based definition of informal employment to provide a more holistic picture of the extent of informality in the economy. This measure should also be included in the list of KILM provided in the PLFS reports.
6. Supplement the quarterly module in urban areas with a quarterly module in rural areas and expand the sample size.
7. Implement a National Business Register and ensure that states complete their State Business Register.
8. Present results in a more user-friendly and accessible manner.
9. Leverage technology to reduce the time lag in the collection and dissemination of data.

Source: Author's summary.

As it pertains to the activity status of a person during the reference period of 365 days preceding the date of the survey, its interpretation is fairly uncomplicated.

However, as the PLFS moves towards providing annual estimates of KILM at the national and rural levels, and quarterly estimates in urban areas, it may no longer be appropriate to base policy discussions on US measures. Given the predominance of self-employment and large-scale employment in the agricultural sector, the US measures are not expected to fluctuate over short periods. Being inherently smoother, they are unlikely to capture changes in activity patterns caused by seasonal fluctuations and witness much variation over short periods. Given this shortcoming of the US approach, the PLFS estimates employment and unemployment using the CWS concept as well. For the urban quarterly estimates, it reports only the CWS measures. The increased importance of CWS in the PLFS is indeed a positive development, as this is the most widely used approach across various national labor force surveys.

However, it is important to mention that there is a challenge in interpreting the CWS. In all NSS surveys, the reference period is fixed in relation to the date of the survey. For the US, an entire year is referenced, though the year may be different for different persons in the sample. To obtain the rate of unemployed or the workforce participation, we consider the total number of persons getting classified as unemployed or employed in the numerator, while the denominator is the estimated total number of persons in the labor force or the relevant population cohort. There is no problem in understanding such a measure as an average rate for the persons in the population. However, the CWS cannot be interpreted in a similar manner (Mohanan 2019a). In the CWS, for each person, we consider a particular week out of the 52 weeks in the year. Different weeks are considered for different persons. Based on the criteria outlined in the concept of CWS, a week is classified as an "employed" week, "unemployed week," or "out of labor force week." Thus, we have a large number of weeks classified according to these three criteria, though they pertain to different persons.

The question that then arises is whether the status of a single week of a person can be added to that of another person for another week and divided by the number of persons to obtain any meaningful average. Given the diversity of employment situations in India and the fact that the status of persons changes during the year frequently for a very large segment of the population, it would not be correct to equate the status obtained on the basis of a single week in the year/quarter to the status of the person during the survey period. Therefore, the rate cannot be called a rate for persons. Instead, it can be referred to as the unemployed (employed) person-weeks (Mohanan 2009). A similar problem arises in the interpretation of the CDS as it gives ratios in terms of person-days. Thus, these two measures are conceptually not suited to building up estimates of either employed or unemployed persons. However, this does not mean that we should not use these measures. On the contrary, they are particularly important in the Indian context.

In fact, the CDS approach, which has been dropped in the PLFS, provides the most comprehensive and detailed picture of the employment situation by reporting a day-to-day account of the available labor time during the week. Understanding these day-to-day changes of the week is particularly useful for workers engaged in informal employment as their activity pattern is not expected to be the same every day. Typically, the appropriate choice is between the week or the day as the reference period depends on national conditions, particularly on the extent of weekly and daily fluctuations of activity status. Where the dominant form of employment is regular full-time employment, the "week" should be the preferred reference period. In such employment conditions, a reference week or a reference day (of the same week) will generally give similar average results, but the advantage of choosing the week is that it will lead to results with lower variances. Where a week of employment does not generally represent a whole week of full-time employment, that is, where casual and intermittent work and part-time and temporary jobs and other types of short-term employment are widespread, then the one-day reference period may be preferable, since it would give a sharper snapshot of the employment and unemployment situation of the country than a weekly measure. The International Labour Office (Hussmanns, Mehran, and Verma 1990) notes that in economies such as India, where casual and intermittent work are widespread, the daily measure would give a clearer snapshot of the employment scenario. Further, the Report of the Special Group on Targeting Ten Million Employment Opportunities per Year (Planning Commission of India 2002) has also noted that CDS is a better measure than the US, as the latter includes the underemployed workforce and gives a misleading picture to policymakers about the extent of labor underutilization.

Having discussed the pros and cons of all three measures, the question of which actually works best arises. Given the preponderance of informality, wherein a major section of the workforce works in the household sector, while a small proportion are engaged in highly formal employment, NSSO surveys have devised multiple reference periods and multiple concepts of employment and unemployment. These have served their purpose well and it is pertinent to continue with all three approaches going forward. It is also important to bring back the CDS measure in the discourse and clarify that CDS and CWS measures need to be interpreted in terms of person-days and person-weeks, respectively.

4.2. Measuring Labor Underutilization

Labor underutilization refers to mismatches between labor supply and demand, leading to an unmet need for employment among the population. While unemployment is at the core of the concept of labor underutilization, the UR by itself provides only a partial view of the labor underutilization in an economy such as India where the latter often takes the form of underemployment. According to the 1996 resolution of the 11th International Conference of Labour Statisticians (ICLS), underemployment "exists when a person's employment is inadequate, in relation to specified norms or alternative employment, account being taken of his occupational skill (training and working experience)."

There are two principal forms of underemployment: visible and invisible. The former reflects an insufficiency in the volume of employment and according to the 13th ICLS (1982), it is defined as comprising "persons in paid or self-employment, whether at work or not at work, involuntarily working less than the normal duration of work determined for the activity, who were seeking or available for additional work during the reference period."[9] On the other hand, invisible underemployment is characterized by low income, underutilization of skills, and low productivity. Compared to visible underemployment, which is a statistical concept directly measurable in the labor force, invisible underemployment "is primarily an analytical concept reflecting a misallocation of labor resources or a fundamental imbalance as between labor and other factors of production" (ICLS 1982). The NSSO has also been attempting to compute measures of visible and invisible underemployment in its quinquennial household surveys. We will briefly outline how this has been done in the NSS 68th Round (2011–12), as follows.

1. *Visible Underemployment:* Some of the persons categorized as usually employed may not have work throughout the year due to seasonality in work or other reasons. Their labor time is not fully utilized and they are, therefore, underemployed. In the same way, persons categorized

---

9. For the purpose of classifying persons as visibly underemployed, the normal duration of work for an activity should be determined in the light of national circumstances as reflected in national legislation to the extent it is applicable, and usual practices in other cases, or in terms of a uniform conventional norm.

as employed in current weekly status may not have work for all the days of the reference week. Underemployment of such employed persons is termed as visible underemployment if they report themselves to be not employed with respect to a shorter reference period. Three measures of visible underemployment are derived by NSSO by classifying: (a) usually employed persons by their current weekly status, (b) usually employed persons by their current daily status, and (c) persons employed in current weekly status by their current daily status. This classification generates the following rates of visible underemployment:

i. Proportion of usually employed persons who did not have work during the reference week
ii. Proportion of person-days of usually employed persons that were not used for work
iii. Proportion of person-days of persons employed in current weekly status that were not used for work

A cross-examination of the activity status of the population with respect to each of the three approaches can throw light on the extent of visible underemployment and provide a nuanced understanding of labor market underutilization. In fact, the need to capture visible underemployment reinforces the need to incorporate the CDS measures in the PLFS reports.

2. *Invisible Underemployment:* Some persons categorized as employed according to the framework adopted in NSSO's EUS may not have enough work or may feel that their labor potential is not fully utilized or that the work they pursue may not fully fulfill their requirements. Therefore, they may want additional and/or alternative work. Such underemployment is termed as invisible underemployment and is not directly measurable. To estimate invisible underemployment, NSSO's EUS questionnaire posed a set of probing questions to the usually employed (Table 6 reports these questions which appeared in Block 6 of the NSS Schedule of Enquiry). The questions pertained to whether the usually employed were available for additional/alternative work and the reason for seeking such additional/alternative work (Columns 10–13 of Block 6 of the NSS Schedule). More specifically, those seeking additional work were asked whether they did so to supplement their incomes and/or they did not have enough work or there were some other reasons (Column 11). Similarly, those seeking alternative work were asked if they did so because their present work was not remunerative enough, provided no job satisfaction, lacked job security,

TABLE 6. Block 6 of the NSSO Schedule of Enquiry for the Employment Unemployment Survey (2011–12): Follow-up Questions on Availability for Work, Existence of Union/Association and Nature of Employment for Persons Working in the Usual Principal or Subsidiary Status (i.e., those with codes 11–51 in Column 3 of Block 5.1 or Block 5.2)

(1)	(2)	(3)	(4)	(5)	(6)	(7)	(8)	(9)	(10)	(11)	(12)	(13)	(14)	(15)	(16)
srl. no. as in col.1, Block 5.1	age (yrs.) as in col.2, Block 5.1	Usual Activity Status Code		Whether Engaged Mostly in Full Time or Part Time Work during Last 365 Days (Full time -1, Part time -2)	Whether Worked More or Less Regularly during Last 365 Days (Yes-1, No-2)	Approximate No. of Months without Work (Months)	If Entry >= 1 in Col. 7, Whether Sought/Available for Work during Those Months (Code)	For Codes 1 & 2 in Col. 8, Whether Made Any Efforts to Get Work (Code)	Whether Sought/Available for Additional Work during the Days He/She Had Work (Code)	For Codes 1 & 2 in Col. 10, Reason (Code)	Whether Sought/Available for Alternative Work during the Days He/She Had Work (Code)	For Codes 1 & 2 in Col. 12, Reason (Code)	Is There Any Union/Association in Your Activity? (Yes -1, No -2, Not Known -9)	For Code 1 in Col. 14, Whether a Member of Union/Association (Yes-1, No-2)	Nature of Employment (Permanent-1, Temporary-2)
		Principal (as in col. 3, Block 5.1)	Subsidiary (as in col. 3, Block 5.2)												

Source: National Sample Survey Office (2015).

Notes: *Codes for Block 6*

col. (8): whether sought/available for work during those months: yes: on most days -1, on some days -2; no -3.

col. (9): whether made any efforts to get work: yes: registered only in government employment exchanges-1, registered only in private placement agencies-2, registered in both government employment exchanges and private placement agencies-3, other efforts -4; no effort-5.

col. (10): whether sought/available for additional work during the days he/she had work: yes: on most days -1, on some days -2; no -3.

col. (11): reason for seeking/available for additional work: to supplement income -1, not enough work -2, both -3, others -9.

col. (12): whether sought/available for alternative work during the days he/she had work: yes: on most days -1, on some days -2; no -3.

col. (13): reason for seeking/available for alternative work: present work not remunerative enough -1, no job satisfaction -2, lack of job security -3, workplace too far -4, wants wage/salary job -5, others -9.

the workplace was too far, they desired a wage/salary job instead, or there were other reasons[10] (Column 13). The proportion of the usually employed who reported their availability for additional/alternative work gives an overall share of the employed who did not have enough work, or at least felt the need for additional/alternative work, and, in that sense, were underemployed. Two other important follow-up questions posed to the usually employed, which helped estimate invisible underemployment, were: (a) whether they worked more or less regularly during last 365 days (Column 6), and (b) whether they were engaged mostly in full-time or part-time work during the reference period of 365 days (Column 5). The EUS also asked the usually employed the approximate number of months they spent without work[11] (Column 7). Mohanan (2009) has undertaken a detailed analysis using these questions to understand the nature of underemployment amongst the usually employed for NSSO's EUS 61st Round (2004–05).

Although the above-mentioned questions offer important insights into the nature of usual status employment and reasons for the usually employed seeking additional/alternative work, the PLFS has dropped them from the questionnaire. Instead, it only asks workers if they were available for additional work and how many hours they were available for such work during the day. The PLFS Report provides details on the percentage of workers in the CWS who were available for additional work. It provides this distribution by the employment status of the worker (i.e., self-employed, RWS employees, and casual laborers) on a quarterly basis. While this information can potentially give us a sense of time-related underemployment, simply providing the number of hours for which they sought additional work without understanding the reason for doing so offers little insight into the nature of the underemployment.

In order to get an estimate of visible and invisible underemployment, we propose re-introducing the detailed questions in Table 5 to the PLFS questionnaire. While we understand that incorporating elaborate follow-up questions

---

10. For instance, in the NSS 68th Round (2011–12), of those who sought additional work, 59.6 percent in rural areas and 62.2 percent in urban areas said they did so to supplement their income. Approximately 15 percent in rural areas and 11.5 percent in urban areas said they sought additional work as they did not have enough work at present. The report also finds that of those who sought alternative work, 57.8 percent in rural areas and 59.5 percent in urban areas said their present work was not remunerative enough. Close to 15 percent sought alternative work as they had no job satisfaction in their current work.

11. These months were to be counted after deep probing and identifying all months without work even if they were isolated months and the days were rounded off to the nearest month.

in the PLFS, which is an annual survey, is difficult and cumbersome, the exclusion of these questions hinders our understanding of the nature of usual status employment in India. The continuation of NSSO's quinquennial EUS, which has an exhaustive and comprehensive questionnaire, is imperative to gain more detailed insights into the nature of employment, in particular, underemployment. It is worth noting that the PLFS was never meant to replace the thick quinquennial rounds, which had a more extensive coverage of issues. The latter were meant to be held every 4–5 years, while the PLFS was conducted concomitantly at an annual frequency in rural areas and at a quarterly frequency in urban areas.

We propose exploiting the information on invisible and visible underemployment, compiled by NSSO's EUS (through questions asked in Block 6) to create new measures of labor underutilization in line with the 19th ICLS's (Work Statistics Committee 2013) resolution on statistics of work, employment, and labor underutilization. Recognizing the limitations of the UR as a measure of labor underutilization, the resolution laid out the following four measures of labor underutilization:

1. LU1: Unemployment Rate = (Unemployment × 100) / Labor Force
2. LU2: Combined Rate of Time-related Underemployment and Unemployment = (Time-related Underemployment + Unemployment) × 100 / Labor Force

where time-related underemployment is defined as persons in employment whose working time is insufficient in relation to alternative employment situations in which they are willing and available to engage.

3. LU3: Combined Rate of Unemployment and Potential Labor Force = (Unemployment + Potential Labor Force) × 100 / (Labor Force + Potential Labor Force)

where potential labor force is defined as persons not in employment who express an interest in it but for whom existing conditions limit their active job search and/or their availability.

4. LU4: Composite Measure of Labor Underutilization = (Time-related Underemployment + Unemployment + Potential Labor Force) × 100 / (Labor Force + Potential Labor Force)

The ICLS framework can be applied to that of the NSSO in the following manner. While LU1 would continue to be the definition of the UR as used by the NSSO thus far, the LU2 measure would need to be adapted to NSSO's

FIGURE 1. New Measures of Labor Underutilization to Complement the Unemployment Rate

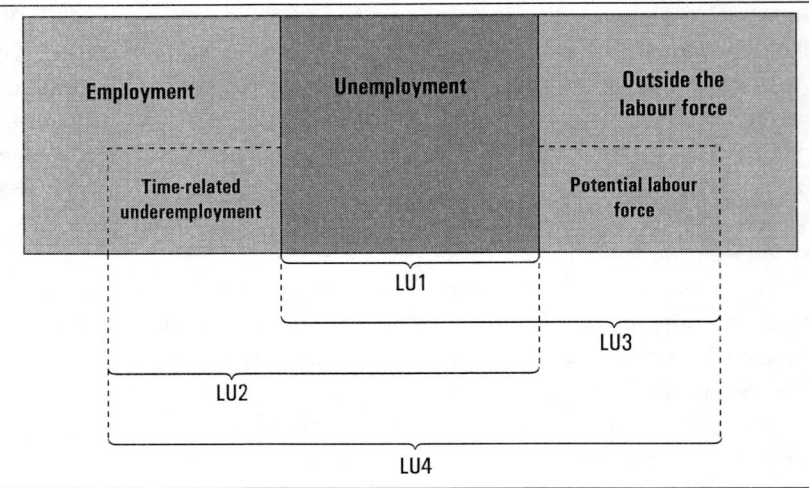

Source: International Labour Organization (2018).

concepts. We propose creating a modified measure of underemployment for India, which includes visible underemployment as defined by the NSSO above. Ideally, we would like to incorporate a measure of invisible underemployment in this framework but given that there is no single metric of this measure, including it in the definition of LU2 is tricky. Nevertheless, it is important that we continue to separately report the three measures of invisible underemployment that the NSSO has reported in the 68th Round, that is, the usual Principal Status workers who did not work regularly throughout the year; the ratio of persons who sought or were available for additional work in the US; and the ratio of persons who sought or were available for alternative work.

To construct LU3, we would need to have a measure of the potential labor force, a concept that has not been explicitly laid out in household surveys in India thus far. The Resolution adopted at the 19th ICLS defined the potential labor force as all persons of working age who, during the short reference period, were neither in employment nor in unemployment, and:

(a) Carried out activities to "seek employment," were not "currently available," but would become available within a short subsequent period established in the light of national circumstances (i.e., unavailable job seekers); or

(b) Did not carry out activities to "seek employment," but wanted employment and were "currently available" (i.e., available potential job seekers).

The potential labor force can be computed from the information in Block 6 of the NSS schedule (Table 5). The workers defined in Category (b) above can be computed from the information in Columns 7–9 of Block 6. In order to estimate those in Category (a) above, we would need to modify the question in Column 9, that is, "whether made any effort to get work" to not just those who reported codes 1 (i.e., sought/available work on most days) and 2 (i.e., sought/available work on some days) in Column 8, but also those who reported code 3 (i.e., who were not available). Additionally, the difference between seeking/not seeking work and being available/not available for work needs to be spelt out explicitly to capture the potential labor force.

The idea of measuring the potential labor force is relevant in the Indian context. With a rise in education levels and income levels, the aspirations of the educated youth have risen. They may no longer be willing to join the labor force if they feel that they will be unable to find a suitable job commensurate with their qualifications or desires. In this context, it would be useful to separately identify a category of discouraged job seekers in line with the recommendations of the 19th ICLS. This category comprises those workers who did not "seek employment" for labor market related reasons such as their past failure to find a suitable job, lack of experience, qualifications or jobs matching the person's skills, lack of jobs in the area, and being considered too young or too old by prospective employers.

Creating the above-mentioned four headline labor underutilization indicators will enable us to have a wider picture of the extent of labor underutilization. In order to understand where the challenges lie from a policy perspective, it would also be useful to look at the composition of labor underutilization. This can be done by calculating the shares of unemployment, underemployment (both visible and invisible), and the potential labor force in overall labor underutilization.

4.3. Including Additional Activity Status Classifications

Household surveys report various activity status classifications for the employed—self-employed, casual labor, and regular wage salaried employees. However, over time, the heterogeneity of employment types has increased, and new forms of standard and non-standard employment have emerged. Thus, there is a need to rethink the existing classification and incorporate additional categories of employment. Although we are not proposing doing away with the existing status classification as that would introduce problems of comparability over time, it would be useful to add additional sets of questions in the survey to understand changes in the nature of employment and the relationship between employers and employees.

This can best be explained through the example of homeworkers who are defined as those who carry out work for remuneration in premises of their choice, other than the workplace of the employer, resulting in a product or service as specified by the employer, irrespective of who provided the equipment, material, or inputs used (ILO Home Work Convention, 1996). Homeworkers constitute a subcategory of home-based workers (i.e., those who carry out remunerative work within their homes). Traditionally, NSSO has considered the homeworker or outworkers as self-employed in its surveys. However, in the NSS 55th Round, they categorized these workers separately by posing a set of additional questions about the location of their workplace, whether they worked under given specifications, whether they were provided equipment, raw material, or inputs by the employer, and if they received remuneration on a piece rate basis. These questions have, however, been discontinued after the NSS 61st Round, and do not find mention in the PLFS. The identification of homeworkers or outworkers from among the self-employed is crucial given that this category accounts for half the workforce, and we need a better understanding of the nature and quality of self-employment.

The category of RWS employment also merits inclusion of different types of contracts. In addition to permanent jobs, the RWS classification includes several temporary jobs. The nature of contracts is changing as short-term and temporary jobs are becoming more prevalent. For instance, in 2018, the government introduced the provision of fixed-term employment to provide enterprises flexibility to adjust their workforce. Thus, there is scope for suitably restructuring the codes for types of job contracts for RWS workers. Additionally, the last two decades have seen a surge in contract worker usage. While the enterprise surveys make a distinction between workers directly hired by enterprises and those hired via contractors, the classification used in household surveys does not allow us to distinguish contract workers from others. Typically, these workers are subsumed in the category of RWS workers. Even in the enterprise surveys, there is very limited information about contract workers. The ASI schedule does not even collect information on the gender breakdown of contract workers.

Finally, another classification of workers, which is attracting attention globally, is that of gig economy workers. Typically gig workers have non-traditional contracts and work as independent contractors or freelancers. They are included in the count of the self-employed. However, as the gig economy emerges as an important avenue of employment generation, it would be useful to measure and understand trends in the growth of such non-traditional working arrangements. As there is no internationally accepted definition of gig economy workers, it would be difficult to create a separate category or code for them in the existing activity status classification. However, given that a key feature of the gig economy is the use of digital labor platforms, it might be useful to design and incorporate structured questions around defining features of the gig-economy work to identify workers. As mentioned above, it could be challenging to incorporate such detailed questions in the annual PLFS. They could instead be posed in the quinquennial EUS.

4.4. Estimating Informal Employment and Understanding Conditions of Employment of Workers

As described in Section 2, India's labor markets are characterized by informality. Given the significance of the informal workforce and the need to understand the quality of employment, it would be relevant to include the "rate of informal employment" as a KILM and report this measure in all official reports when survey data is released. However, computing such a statistic is fraught with challenges unless we have a clear definition of what constitutes informal employment.

The 15th ICLS in 1993 defined the informal sector as consisting of all private unincorporated enterprises (excluding quasi-corporations), that is, enterprises owned by individuals or households that are not constituted as separate legal entities independently of their owners, and for which no complete accounts are available that would permit a financial separation of the production activities of the enterprise from the other activities of its owner(s).

However, this definition was criticized as it captured only work that took place in unincorporated enterprises. The notion of informal employment is much wider as it includes several additional types of employment outside informal enterprises, in particular, persons working in formal enterprises who are not covered by social protection through their work. Consequently, in the 17th ICLS in 2003, a broader concept of informal employment comprising the total number of informal jobs, whether carried out in formal sector enterprises, informal sector enterprises, or households during a given reference period, was laid out.

The two-dimensional matrix in Figure 2 provides a conceptual framework for estimating formal and informal employment as per the 17th ICLS. The framework uses a building block approach which disaggregates total

FIGURE 2. Conceptual Framework for Estimating Informal Employment

Production Units by Type	Jobs by Status in Employment									
	Own-account Workers		Employers		Contributing Family Workers	Employees		Members of Producers' Cooperatives		
	Informal	Formal	Informal	Formal	Informal	Informal	Formal	Informal	Formal	
Formal Sector Enterprises	■	░	■	░	1	2	░	■	░	
Informal Sector Enterprises (a)	3	■	4	■	5	6	7	8	■	
Households (b)	9	■	■	■	■	10	■	■	■	

☐ Informal jobs　　░ Formal jobs　　■ No jobs by definition

Source: Adapted from Bhalla (2009), citing Hussmanns (2004).
Notes: (a) As defined by the 15th ICLS (excluding households employing paid domestic workers).
(b) Households producing goods exclusively for their own final use and households employing paid domestic workers.
Cells in dark gray refer to jobs, which by definition do not exist in that type of production unit. Cells shaded in light gray refer to formal jobs (including cell 7 in informal sector enterprises). Unshaded cells refer to different types of informal jobs. Thus, *Informal Employment* is comprised of Cells 1–6 and 8–10. *Employment in the informal sector* is represented by Cells 3–8. *Informal employment outside the informal sector* is represented by Cells 1, 2, 9, and 10.

employment according to two dimensions: type of production unit and type of job. The type of production unit is defined in terms of legal organization and other enterprise-related characteristics, while the type of job is defined in terms of status in employment and other job-related characteristics.

In the Indian context, it would be useful to construct a measure of "informal employment" as defined in the above matrix, which combines the enterprise-based and jobs-based definitions of informality. This is particularly pertinent in the light of the increasing informalization of the formal sector. Reporting such a combined measure along with the UR would enable us to understand the overall changes in the quality of employment.

It is worth pointing out that the ICLS has not endorsed the term "employment in the informal economy," which has been used by the ILO to refer to the sum of employment in the informal sector and informal employment outside the informal sector. The 17th ICLS noted that for statistical purposes, it would be better to keep the concepts of informal sector and informal employment separate. This was perhaps a result of the fact that different operational criteria were being used for defining informal jobs in different countries and a combined metric would not be comparable across countries. However, for the purpose of getting a comprehensive measure of informality in India and understanding what is happening to the quality of employment over time, this would be a useful exercise.

4.5. Extending the Quarterly Module to Rural Areas

A significant feature of the PLFS has been the introduction of a quarterly module in urban areas which will allow us to generate KILM at quarterly frequency. However, often the workforce that resides in rural areas commutes to urban areas to work, and vice versa. For instance, Chandrashekhar (2011) estimates that a total of 12.42 million non-agricultural workers commuted across the rural–urban boundary, in one direction or the other, for work in 2009–10. Labor force surveys estimate the size of the workforce by place of residence and not by workforce. Typically, the size of the rural (urban) workforce is set equal to the number of workers living in rural (urban) areas. Given the significant movement across rural and urban areas, there is a need to make adjustments in estimates of the rural and urban workforce accounting for the fact that several rural residents work in urban areas, and vice versa (Mohanan 2008).

The challenge of addressing the commuting worker becomes a serious cause of concern now that the rural and urban modules will be held at a different frequency. It would be appropriate to extend the quarterly module to rural areas as well and make the necessary adjustments for commuting workers. This will also enable us to understand the size of the rural–urban linkage. However, it needs to be noted that the exercise of extending the quarterly module to rural areas will be meaningful and worthwhile only if the sample size is large enough that the quarterly changes can be measured with precision. In fact, at this point, it is unclear if the sample size in the urban quarterly module is also large enough to accurately measure changes in urban labor market parameters.

4.6. The Need for a Business Register

While we have two separate establishment surveys for the organized and unorganized sectors, in practice, the distinction between the two is not so neat and clean. In principle, the unorganized manufacturing sector should not include units that use electricity and hire more than 10 workers, and those that do not use electricity but nevertheless employ 20 or more workers.

Nevertheless, it is often noted that many big units with a sufficiently large number of workers are included in the NSS Unincorporated Enterprise Survey. For instance, in 2015–16, over 12,000 of the surveyed enterprises in the NSS 73rd Round hired 10 or more workers. In the 2010–11 survey, there were close to 10,000 surveyed units having 10 or more workers (Kapoor 2017). These units should have, in fact, been in the ASI frame. Just as there are several larger units included in the NSS frame, it has been observed that there are several units hiring less than 10 workers which have been reported in the ASI database. The chief inspector of factories in each state maintains the live register of factories that form the frame for conducting the ASI. However, it is often observed that the live register includes several factories which have been closed for years. Additionally, there is large-scale evasion of registration under the Factories Act (Nagaraj 2002). The above-mentioned exclusions and inclusions have serious implications for estimating not just employment but also GVA and GVA per worker in both the organized and unorganized sectors.

Given the above problems, there is an undisputed need to get the ASI frame right. With this objective, the National Statistical Commission (NSC; 2001) recommended the creation of a "Business Register," a list which would cover all enterprises with at least 10 workers, including those covered under ASI and public sector enterprises. It was suggested that the creation of the Business Register would be associated with the development of a unique coding system (or a Business Identification Number) identifying all enterprises included in the list. The use of the unique code by the units would be made mandatory for purposes like paying sales tax, electricity bill, telephone bill, or in getting facilities like bank loans.

Despite this recommendation, the idea of the Business Register has hardly taken off. According to NSSO's recently released Technical Report on the Services Sector (2019), only 11 states have implemented it.[12] And here, too, their coverage is skewed and limited.[13] While the Department of Company Affairs has initiated a computerized 21-digit code for registered companies, called the Corporate Identity Number, this alone is not enough. The idea needs to be extended to a unique business numbering system that is mandatory for all factories/companies, and for use in all official transactions (Nagaraj 2002). Such a numbering would be like a social security number system used in the developed countries for their citizens. MoSPI has

---

12. This includes Andhra Pradesh, Arunachal Pradesh, Himachal Pradesh, Manipur, Nagaland, Punjab, Rajasthan, Tamil Nadu, Telangana, Uttar Pradesh, and Uttarakhand.

13. In the Business Register, 7.1 percent of all sample enterprises were non-traceable/closed and 13.5 percent were misclassified/out of coverage.

indicated that it plans to compile a national business register of all business enterprises in the country that would be updated periodically, but there has not been much progress on this front.

An additional problem vis-à-vis enterprise surveys is the under-listing of enterprises in the EC. The above-mentioned enterprise surveys are, in fact, follow-up surveys of the EC and the inability to get an accurate count of enterprises in the EC creates problems in the follow-up surveys, too. It has been observed that the number of enterprises and the number of workers reported in the EC is, in fact, lower than the Unincorporated Enterprise Survey estimates. Manna (2010) explains that one of the limitations of the EC is that the number of own-account manufacturing enterprises (OAMEs) estimated from it are significantly lower than those reported by the NSS Enterprise Survey. He finds that the total number of establishments in the EC (2005–06) is about 22 percent lower than NSS's Survey of Unorganized Manufacturing Enterprises conducted during the same year. For the most recently conducted EC and NSS Survey of Unincorporated Non-agricultural Enterprises (2015–16), we once again find this discrepancy. In the manufacturing sector specifically, the EC reports that the total number of enterprises without hired workers is 7.21 million. For the NSS Enterprise Survey, however, we find the number of OAMEs to be 16.8 million. But this figure should, in fact, be lower than the EC's figure given that the latter must have universal coverage. Manna and Bhattacharjee (2004) have noted that the under-listing is largely confined to smaller or invisible units or to those units carrying out their activities without fixed premises.

The importance of ensuring universal coverage in the EC cannot be emphasized enough. This is essential to have a single accurate frame that captures non-agricultural enterprises. This requires additional resources to be spent on the survey and the use of modern technology. In fact, it is largely because of the absence of an appropriate frame for enterprises that household surveys have been more widely used for data collection on employment statistics. There is an acute need to strengthen sources of enterprise and establishment level data. This requires wider coverage across enterprises of different sizes and sectors. It also requires enterprise surveys, in particular the unincorporated enterprise survey, to be carried out at a greater frequency. The EC should also be conducted at regular intervals.

4.7. The Role of States

A key feature of the process of data collection undertaken by the NSSO is that for each round, two types of samples known as "Central samples" and "state samples" are allotted for conducting these surveys. The surveys of

Central samples are conducted by the Government of India, while those of state samples are conducted by state agencies. The sizes of Central and state samples are equal for most of the states/UTs (equal matching sample). In some states, the number of sample units surveyed by state statistical agencies is double that of the size of the Central sample. One of the objectives of the states' participation in the NSS program is to provide a mechanism by which the sample size would increase and the pooling of the two sets of data would enable better estimates at the lower sub-state level, particularly at the district level. At the state level, this will increase the precision of the results.

Given the importance of pooling the Central and state sample data, the 13th Finance Commission made a special provision for additional funds in each district to carry out this exercise. Despite this, little progress was made in terms of evolving a uniform methodology of pooling and testing for poolability of the two sets of data. Only a few states pooled the results of the Central and state samples for the NSS Employment–Unemployment rounds. And here too, there was often a lack of uniformity in their approach. This resulted in a loss of comparability of pooled data. It was against this backdrop that the NSC appointed a professional committee under the chairmanship of Dr R. Radhakrishna, former Chairman, NSC, to examine the above-mentioned issues. The Committee in its report gave a detailed methodology for pooling and suggested tests for poolability.[14] Following the recommendations of the Committee, the Data Processing Division of the NSSO took initiatives to provide technical guidance and support to the states in pooling the data collected in the NSS 66th Round.

However, despite all these efforts, only a few states have made attempts to process and tabulate the state samples such that they could be merged with the Central samples to generate more reliable state-level estimates and, more importantly, district-level estimates. The absence of any district-level employment data barring the economic tables provided in the Population Census described in Section 2 is a problem and points to the importance of pooling the state and Central samples. In fact, in the PLFS, standard errors at the state level are relatively large, making these results less reliable. Involving state agencies in data collection is indeed imperative. This necessitates greater initiative on the part of the states to invest in data collection

---

14. It suggested that the poolability test of two sets of data must be exercised before pooling the two independent estimates derived at a particular domain using weights as an inverse of estimated variances of the estimates or using weights as a matching ratio of the States' participation in the NSS program. Thus, in contrast to earlier methodologies of pooling the data by merging two datasets and recomputing weights based on merged data, the new methodology suggested the pooling of estimates using weights as stated above.

and establish a mechanism of rigorous data quality checking through inspection, scrutiny checks, training, and managing the field operations in a time-bound manner.

4.8. Presentation of Survey Results in a User-friendly Manner

It is often noted by data users that the results of the surveys, in particular, household surveys, are not presented in a readily usable form. This can be elucidated through the following example. If one wanted to know from the survey report the size of the labor force and workforce at the national level, this would not be a simple calculation. First, the report lays out the labor force participation and worker population rates separately for rural male, rural female, urban male, and urban female, for the three different concepts (US, CWS, and CDS). Second, these rates would need to be multiplied with the population figures obtained from the Census and not the population estimates obtained from the household survey. This is because it has been observed that the population estimates derived from the NSSO are, in general, on the lower side as compared to the Census population. This difference arises mainly due to the differences in coverage and methods adopted in NSS in comparison with the Census operation. While a note of caution is always sounded in the report on this issue, it often creates considerable confusion among users. To avoid such confusion, it would be useful if the NSSO provides an additional summary publication giving the estimates of KILM (as well as informal employment and the extent of labor underutilization) using the Census population. Also, to make these estimates internationally comparable, it would be appropriate to report results based on the reference period of a week as is done in most other national labor force surveys.

4.9. Leveraging Technology to Conduct Surveys

Given the vastness of the country and the varied sources from which data are to be compiled, transmitted, tabulated, and analyzed, a manual system of data compilation and transmission is hardly viable in India. There is a need for massive computerization of labor statistics with computer networking so that online data are available at specified points, the delay in transmitting data from the field is minimized, and dissemination of data is speedier. All this is easily possible given the current state of information technology in the country.

The PLFS has taken a major leap forward in this context by collecting information from sample households using the CAPI method. Prior to the PLFS, data under the socio-economic surveys of NSSO were collected from the field by using paper schedules. After the completion of data collection, it took about a year to make available the results of the survey. Given this delay, the NSS adopted the World Bank-CAPI solution platform for the PLFS. Data for the PLFS were collected in the field using tablets and the CAPI solution with an in-built data validation process. This not only proved useful in the collection of primary data from the households but also helped reduce the time involved in data transfer and processing of the survey results. CMIE's experience also shows how data collected on a specially loaded application on mobile phones can be validated and uploaded for use by the end of day, every day, thereby enabling generation of high-frequency estimates. The forthcoming EC (2019) also proposes to include geo-tagging data of business enterprises to ensure that no bogus enterprises are included in the official statistics. This will help clean the data organically as field officials will enter the live location of enterprises via mobile phones. Thus, there is considerable scope for using modern technology to improve the accuracy and reliability of data and reduce the time spent in data collection, verification, processing, and dissemination by leveraging technology. To exploit these potential gains, a concerted effort is required not just to increase investments in technology but also to train investigators in the use of these tools.

5. Conclusion

As countries the world over are pressed to produce labor market statistics at quarterly or monthly frequency, the desire to produce high-frequency employment data in India is understandable. However, simply aggregating the number of unemployed and employed at a macro level periodically serves little purpose in the Indian context. Employment statistics are not very meaningful unless they are able to convey information about the quality of jobs being created and how the conditions of employment are evolving.

Following the recommendations of the 2017 Task Force set up to revamp the employment data architecture, India's employment statistics are undergoing significant revision. Impatience with the absence of high-frequency data has led to a frantic quest for such data. This search has culminated in the recent release of monthly estimates of administrative data obtained from the EPFO, ESIC, and NPS. Despite several caveats, it is disconcerting that the EPFO database, which has never been made available in the public domain, is being viewed as a substitute for NSSO's household surveys. The EPFO databases are still at a very nascent stage and need to be cleaned up and processed to produce estimates that can be of any significant use. In the best of circumstances, administrative data can only give us a partial estimate of formal employment, let alone be a replacement for household surveys.

NSSO's EUS, which is a very elaborate and comprehensive survey, has done a remarkable job of capturing the complex realities of India's labor market and provides a rich source of data for decades. The importance of conducting NSSO's EUS, which asks in-depth comprehensive questions, cannot be emphasized enough. Of course, given its level of detail and costly operations, it cannot be conducted annually. Therefore, it should be conducted quinquennially and supplemented with the PLFS.

While many have argued that India is in need of a fresh employment data architecture, we believe that the focus should not be on conducting new surveys. India's statistical data collection machinery, in particular, household surveys, have been lauded globally. Instead of dispensing with the current structure, it is worth trying to understand how the existing machinery can be strengthened to produce more relevant and comprehensive labor market data. In the foregoing discussion, we have tried to illustrate relatively better ways of understanding changes in the employment landscape. To address the information gaps, we propose asking more probing questions about the nature of the employment arrangement and contracts, extending the quarterly module of the PLFS in rural areas, and putting in place a National Business Register, which provides a complete frame for follow-up enterprise surveys. Given that it is the unemployment rate that invariably attracts the most attention in the policy discourse each time survey results are released, we propose creating estimates of informal employment and labor underutilization and reporting these with NSSO's other Key Indicators of the Labour Market. This will be particularly important for understanding the gravity and enormity of India's employment challenge.

The discussion in this paper in no way claims to be an exhaustive coverage of employment data issues in India. In addition to the issues described here, significant challenges loom. Some key concerns deserve mention here. The first is the absence of a good dataset on the services sector. The second is the lack of understanding about the activity pattern of those who are outside the labor force. This is particularly important in a young economy where the youth inactivity rate (i.e., the share of youth who are not in employment, education, or training) stands at over 20 percent. Third, qualification and skill mismatches are becoming a critical issue of policy concern as the world of work is being transformed by the forces of technology, demographics, globalization, migration, and climate change. The absence of data on workers' skills and the task content of occupations poses a serious challenge in designing skilling policies in India. In fact, establishment surveys in India collect no information on the education or skill qualification of their workers.

Implementing any of the suggestions laid out in this paper requires strengthening the capacity of the national statistics systems. This entails not only greater investments in the data collection machinery but also addressing the shortage of regular field investigators faced by the NSSO and training them to ensure that they can correctly implement the concepts and definitions applied in the survey. However, against the backdrop of the controversy surrounding the results of the PLFS (2017–18) Report, what is even more significant is to restore faith in India's statistics and re-establish the credibility and independence of the institutions that produce them. Unless we recognize official data as a "public good" (Mohanan 2019b) and provide researchers access to data to enable informed debates and discussions, any effort to improve the employment data architecture would serve little purpose.

References

Bhalla, S. 2009. "Definitional and Statistical Issues Relating to Workers in Informal Employment." *Working Paper No. 3*. New Delhi: National Commission for Enterprises in the Unorganized Sector, January.

Chandrasekhar, S. 2011. *Estimates of Workers Commuting from Rural to Urban and Urban to Rural India: A Note*. Mumbai: Indira Gandhi Institute of Development Research.

Dantwala Committee. 1970. "Report of the Committee of Experts on Unemployment Statistics." New Delhi: Planning Commission of India, Government of India.

Ghose, A.K. 2016. *India Employment Report 2016: Challenges and the Imperative of Manufacturing-Led Growth*. New Delhi: Institute for Human Development.

Hussmanns, Ralf, Farhad Mehran, and Vijay Verma. 1990. *Surveys of Economically Active Population, Employment, Unemployment and Underemployment: An ILO Manual on Concepts and Methods*. Geneva: International Labour Office.

Hussmanns, Ralf. 2004. "Measuring the Informal Economy: From Employment in the Informal Sector to Informal Employment," *Working Paper No. 53*, Policy Integration Department, Bureau of Statistics. Geneva: International Labour Office.

International Labour Organization. 2018. *Avoiding Unemployment Is Not Enough: An Analysis of Other Forms of Labour Underutilization*. Geneva: International Labour Organization.

Kapoor, R. 2017, "Waiting for Jobs." *Working Paper No. 348*. New Delhi: Indian Council for Research on International Economic Relations, November.

———. 2018. "Rethinking India's Employment Data Architecture." *Economic & Political Weekly,* 53(40): 14–16.

Manna, G.C. 2010. "Current Status of Industrial Statistics in India: Strengths and Weaknesses." *Economic & Political Weekly,* 45(46): 67–76.

Manna, G.C. and J.P. Bhattacharjee. 2004. "Enlarging the Scope of Annual Survey of Industries." *Economic & Political Weekly,* 39(48): 5163–5166.

Ministry of Statistics and Programme Implementation. 2019. *PLFS Annual Report 2017–18.* New Delhi: Ministry of Statistics and Programme Implementation, Government of India.

Mohanan, P.C. 2008. "Differentials in the Rural-Urban Movement of Workers." *The Journal of Income and Wealth,* 30(1): 59–67.

———. 2009. "Background Paper for the Workshop on Conceptual Issues in Measurement of Employment–Unemployment." Available at http://mospi.nic.in/sites/default/files/workshop/nsc_background_paper_12jan09.pdf (accessed May 28, 2021).

———. 2019a. "Data on Employment–Unemployment: An Appraisal", Unpublished Paper.

———. 2019b, February 12. "Because Data Is a Public Good." *The Indian Express.* Available at https://indianexpress.com/article/opinion/columns/because-data-is-a-public-good-nsc-p-c-mohanan-employment-survey-5578946/ (accessed 28 June 2019).

Nagaraj, R. 2002. "How to Improve India's Industrial Statistics." *Economic & Political Weekly,* 37(10): 966–970.

National Sample Survey Office. 2015. *Employment & Unemployment Situation in India, NSS Report No. 563, 68th Round, July 2011–June 2012.* New Delhi: Ministry of Statistics and Programme Implementation, Government of India.

National Statistical Commission. 2001. *Report of Dr Rangarajan Commission.* New Delhi: Ministry of Statistics and Programme Implementation, Government of India.

NITI Aayog. 2017. *Report of the Task Force on Improving Employment Data.* New Delhi: NITI Aayog, Government of India.

Papola, T.S. 2014. *An Assessment of the Labour Statistics System in India.* New Delhi: International Labour Organization Country Office for India.

Planning Commission of India. 2002. *Report of the Special Group on Targeting Ten Million Employment Opportunities per Year over the Tenth Plan Period.* New Delhi: Government of India.

Work Statistics Committee. 2013. "Report II: Draft Resolution Concerning Work Statistics." Paper presented at International Conference of Labour Statisticians (ICLS), October 2–11. Geneva: International Labour Office.

To view the entire video of this IPF session and the General Discussion that ended the session, please scan this QR code or use the following URL:
https://www.youtube.com/watch?v=4dZTQd6fvMA

Comments and Discussion*

Chair: **Pravin Srivastava**
Secretary, Ministry of Statistics and Programme Implementation
Government of India

G. C. Manna
NCAER and Former Director General, NSSO and CSO

The author gives a clear description of various data sources for employment (and unemployment) statistics in India, along with coverage of the respective data sources, and strengths as well as weaknesses of the datasets emanating from them. As suggested by the author, India's labor market has a dualistic structure, which is characterized by the presence of an organized sector that co-exists with a large unorganized sector. This fact is substantiated in the paper by citing the related estimates (Table 3 of the paper) of the number of workers by organized–unorganized enterprises and formal–informal employment based on the NSS 61st Round (2004–05) and NSS 68th Round (2011–12). As regards the estimates of the aggregate number of workers presented in this table, the author needs to clarify how the aggregates have been derived and for doing so, whether the NSS employment rates have been multiplied with the projected population based on the Census, and if so, the reference date considered for the projected population. It would also be useful to clearly spell out the methods followed in categorizing the workers under the organized–unorganized and formal–informal break-ups. Further, the sector-wise classification of workers in which services is shown as a separate sector beyond non-manufacturing needs modification because the services sector comes within the ambit of the non-manufacturing sector as per the standard concept.

Under "Issues and Recommendations" (Section 4), the paper describes the challenges and difficulties in interpreting the CWS-based estimates of employment, as per the existing definition, by also narrating the views of some other authors in this regard. The author finally advocates the need

---

* To preserve the sense of the discussions at the India Policy Forum, these discussants' comments reflect the views expressed at the IPF and do not necessarily take into account revisions to the conference version of the paper in response to these and other comments in preparing the final, revised version published in this volume. The original conference version of the paper is available on www.ncaer.org.

for continuation of all the three approaches of measurement of labor force parameters, viz., Usual Status, Current Weekly Status, and Current Daily Status. Given the complexities of India's labor market situation with a huge percentage of workers employed in the informal sector and in short-term employment, this recommendation seems to be a reasonable one. As regards the suggestion of some authors to change the definition that has been cited in the paper, it may be useful if the author also highlights the effect of such a change in the cross-country comparison of CWS-based estimates, since many countries may be following the same definition as adopted in the NSS.

Based on the existing approach of data collection, the problem of estimating the total number of jobs has been discussed in Section 4.3, citing, for example, the difficulty in capturing multiple activities based on the CDS approach given the provision to record at the most two activities on a single day. In this context, it may be useful for the author to highlight the extent of the prevalence of more than two activities by analyzing the information on day-wise total hours actually worked, while considering all the work vis-à-vis the time spent in maximum two activities performed during the day that is being collected in the ongoing PLFS. The difference between the two times as stated above is likely to throw some light on the prevalence of multiple activities.

Regarding the suggestion (Section 4.4) to incorporate additional categories of status classification to capture new forms of standard and non-standard employment and restructure the codes for types of contract, one needs to be a little careful because the modification of the existing code structure might lead to data comparability issues. Instead, it may be more appropriate to include a supplementary set of questions to meet the proposed additional data requirements, without disturbing the existing classification.

In Section 4.6, the author recommends extension of the quarterly module of the PLFS to rural areas as well. Before such a step is taken, it would be useful to study the sample size requirements since my limited data analysis and study in this regard suggest the need for a drastic increase in the sample size if one has to detect changes in the quarterly labor force parameters at the state level through the PLFS.

After highlighting the limitations of the EC database and the inadequacies of the ASI frame in terms of erroneous exclusions (of units with 10 or more workers) and inclusions (units with less than 10 workers), the paper underlines the need to implement a National Business Register (Section 4.7) that could serve as a frame for various establishment surveys. The cited problem of imperfect frames is a genuine one and concerted efforts are undoubtedly warranted for developing a proper sampling frame. Similar to the evidence given of a number of larger manufacturing units that got covered in the NSS 73rd Round, though they were supposed to be covered in the ASI frame instead, a similar study based on the NSS 73rd Round could also be carried out for the services sector (including trade) to throw some light on the weakness, if any, of the EC frame of services sector establishments with 10 or more workers.

Finally, the recommendation to continue the traditional NSS quinquennial round along with the annual PLFS appears to be a reasonable one, given the importance of additional items of information, relevant in the context of measurement of labor underutilization, included in the quinquennial round but dropped from the PLFS module.

Rinku Murgai
World Bank

My task is easier because we have seen a very clear presentation and excellent comments as well from Dr Manna. I won't use up time summarizing what has been said. I agree with many of the things that Radhicka says in her paper. I would only suggest that for anybody who is going to work on employment data in India, this is going to become a must-see reference manual. It is very comprehensive, clearly done, and excellent.

Let me focus on the big picture questions here. The first question I was asking while reading the paper was: Is India's employment data architecture in good shape, and where have we come? I think there has been a lot of concern. The last comprehensive round until very recently was 2011–12, and there were various sporadic efforts, which were hard to interpret—data being released, data not being released—and therefore lots of reasons for concern. The fact that the PLFS is now in place is a major advancement. I think we have taken a big step there. There are reduced time delays in processing due to the adoption of CAPI, which is a big step. There is a new dissemination policy issued by the MoSPI. If adhered to, that is a major step in the right direction. There is adoption of the International Household Survey Network approach for the systematic production of metadata. We are seeing some important steps that are relevant not just for the employment data architecture but for other data as well.

But there is obviously much more to be done. Anybody who has not been living in a bunker knows that there is a lot of noise around India's statistics. So the question is: What are the priorities and how should the priorities be set? Let me talk about four broad areas. One of them concerns the set of priorities in improving the employment data that comes from household surveys. There I was going to endorse the suggestion of a quarterly PLFS in rural areas as well, but I agree with Dr Manna's point that it has to be done carefully in relation to the resources that are available and can be mobilized by the Ministry to expand sample sizes. Clearly, it seems that we also need to potentially expand sample sizes in urban areas if we are going to detect changes, but I think the quarterly addition to the annual survey is an important step that needs to be taken.

Second, I also endorse the idea of supplemental modules, not necessarily reviving the EUS quinquennially but concurrently every few years with the PLFS. In the areas where PLFS is being done, supplemental modules may be added. Many countries do this on questions that do not require annual or quarterly monitoring. Those suggestions made a lot of sense to me.

The third question, which I think is in the paper but to my mind is not done sufficiently and systematically, is experimentation. There are questions, for example, when you look at what has been happening to India's female labor force participation. When you compare that with the population Census, and with the NCAER India Human Development Survey, in some cases you get different trends. So the question is, why that is so. Is it something about the questionnaire design, is it something about the way the surveys are being fielded? We need to get a much better understanding of these issues, and this is something that the Ministry must do. It could be in partnership with think tanks, such as MoSPI's partnership through its MoU with NCAER, it could be with other agencies. MoSPI and NSSO have been used to doing experiments. The 55th Round created a lot of noise, but it came at the end of a lot of experiments that were very useful. It is important to do those experiments more often, more systematically.

In this context, the suggestion to extend to the gig economy by adding a set of questions has to be done in experimental mode so that we can understand what works and what does not. There is a time-use survey that MoSPI is going to do. If properly designed as an experiment and analyzed, it will provide insights into how you might improve the measurement of women's work.

Here, I have a model in mind that Statistics Canada follows—they have what they call "pathfinder projects." When there is an issue that is clearly of relevance to citizens, to the public, to policymakers, they mobilize teams and resources to specifically look for solutions on how they can strengthen both the data collection mechanisms and analysis. The advantage of signaling that these are pathfinder projects is that it avoids the confusion that happened when the analysis of the payroll data was released in India. As Radhicka says, what is being done is somewhat experimental. But I think it must be done. We need to move in that direction not as a substitute for household surveys but for supplementing our understanding of what is going on in the economy. However, it is important to put them in the right context, that these are experimental, so that they are not misquoted and misunderstood by both the users and policymakers. It is the job of the statistics agency to signal that they are in experimental mode in some things before a decision is taken to adopt and scale up.

The fourth area that I would suggest on the household survey side is the need for conceptual clarity. There are many examples in Radhicka's paper where she has already clarified several concepts. With the PLFS becoming a major source of employment data, going forward, there has to be conceptual clarity on comparability of the PLFS with previous surveys. I am not a statistician, but my understanding of the stratification design is that the headline numbers at the all-India level and at the state level are indeed comparable to the EUS. That is not what the official position of the government is, but I think this is the kind of debate that is needed so that clarity may emerge.

There are other reasons why the PLFS may or may not be comparable to previous rounds. It is a panel survey. We need to understand attrition. There are issues related to non-compliance rates that seem to be different from previous rounds. The PLFS was fielded using CAPI, not paper. Again, it is important to get the research in place that allows you to assess whether or not using the CAPI approach versus the paper-based schedule has changed the responses. It has to be a routine exercise but should provide clarity, and it requires both the statistics agencies and the research community to work on these questions.

The final point I would make on the household survey side, which I think will add to the data architecture, is to have an announced advance release calendar. Just the way it exists for parts of the national accounts in compliance with the Special Data Dissemination Standard (SDDS), an advance release calendar will help add trust and credibility to the system. This is already stated as a proposal in the new dissemination policy.

On the enterprise survey side, let me just make one comment. I think there the priority must be to build an integrated statistical business register. It will help not only with the frame but also with moving towards getting much more real-time data on economic demography, not on the informal sector which is where the vast numbers of people are employed, but on the formal sector. The opportunities now are tremendous. With the Economic Census (EC) going into the field very shortly, the availability of the Goods and Services Tax Network (GSTN) and the Ministry of Corporate Affairs (MCA), it is very important to launch a research program that starts looking at the differences between these different sources, the opportunities for linking the EC with the GSTN and MCA. It means working very differently for MoSPI. It means signing memorandums of understanding to access the GSTN and MCA data. The kind of careful work that was done for the 74th Round is what is needed, in addition to other building blocks, for developing a business register.

I am less pessimistic on the use of administrative data for starting to track real-time measures of changes in firms, and to my mind there are three issues. One is that we have to get the foundational statistical infrastructure in place. Currently, data is extremely siloed and the classifications, issues of consistency over time, and many other such issues make it very difficult to actually use administrative data. There needs to be a strong data quality assurance framework. There is a framework that has been notified, not yet operationalized—that has to be a big priority. There are questions about whether or not there is a need for a chief data officer in India, and how to handle that in a decentralized statistical system.

My last point pertaining to the employment data strategy for India, to stronger national accounts, and to strengthening any arm of the national statistical system, is that we have to ask the question whether our institutions are strong enough, whether we have a legal framework that permits data aggregation and sharing of databases, and whether rules are in place that enable data flows under confidentiality guarantees. I would also say it is time to think about whether the right roles are currently assigned between the Chief Statistician of India and the NSC. Is there too much overlap? Are both entities sufficiently empowered? My own feeling is that it is time to do a white paper around these questions and then figure out whether we should go for legislative backing. For instance, as regards the NSC, currently it is not a statutory body, but it was meant to become a body that had legislative backing through the NSC Bill. I know this is a little far removed from the issues that Radhicka talks about in her paper, but they are fundamental to having any data architecture that is strong enough to deliver what users need, that is, a system that is credible, and is seen to be credible.

General Discussion

Sudipto Mundle concurred with the paper that conceptually household surveys and employment and enterprise surveys would not be comparable, but at an aggregate level, they should be and should move in the same direction. He asked what might explain the huge difference seen in the paper.

Kaushik Basu asked about labor force participation rates, a major concern in India, and whether it was possible to say anything about what "unavailable" means. The paper touched upon ILO's concept of decent work but without clarifying further about what discouraged dropouts and other dropouts mean.

Dilip Mookerjee asked whether the data could show if unemployment was voluntary or involuntary. One way of determining this would be to ask if the unemployed person had quit their last job or if they were laid off. He also asked if the data measured the duration of unemployment—short-term, chronic, or long-term.

Indira Rajaraman asked for Dr Manna's views as a discussant for this paper on using point estimates from sample surveys, something that Dr Mahalanobis, who designed the NSS surveys, had warned against doing. She also asked the extent to which the shift from permanent NSS field survey staff to contract employees had resulted in poor training and contributed to poor data quality.

Sonalde Desai agreed that interviewer quality and training were a major issue in comparing NSS 2004–05 and 2011–12 data on the subsidiary employment status of women, which dropped significantly, and this was responsible for a large chunk of the apparent decline in female labor force participation. This drop did not affect men as much as women. The data suggests that in about a quarter of marginal farms, nobody from the household was working, which seemed unbelievable.

Pranab Bardhan raised several issues. First, the 1970 Dantwala Committee Report had recommended the use of current daily status instead of usual daily status, which is what Bardhan had used even in his 1984 book *Land, Labour, and Rural Poverty*. The problem is that the daily status data, which are better for capturing India's unemployment and underemployment rates, are collected in terms of days rather than people. The PLFS collects current daily status but does not estimate any measures from it. The public thinks of employment and unemployment in terms of people, but both the numerator and denominator for the current daily status are in days. The better concept is actually in terms of days rather than people, but perhaps we should call it a labor utilization rate rather than an underemployment rate. He wondered if other countries, particularly Mexico, which has a large informal sector, faced the same problem, and if so, whether they used the concept of a labor utilization rate in terms of days. Related to public perceptions, Bardhan also pointed out that in comparing two rounds, the media often talks about job losses between two rounds, but that is, of course, not something that such a comparison can possibly capture.

Second, on potential underemployment, particularly for women, Bardhan pointed out that many rural women go in and out of the labor force through the year, and NSS sub-rounds should capture this seasonality. In the busy farming season, women come into the labor force, and exit in the lean season. It is important then to ask women, who report that they are not seeking work, if they would be available for work, such as tailoring and animal husbandry, if such work were available at home. It would be useful to add this question to the NSS because women's participation is extremely important for the economy. Some NSS Rounds may have added this question, but more recently, he thought, it had been dropped.

Third, Bardhan spoke about multiple subsidiary activities. He thought that the usual daily status data captured only two subsidiary activities and the current daily status captured more than two. The problem with the current daily status data was that it was captured only at the two-digit industrial code level and therefore was not easily comparable to other data. This was particularly important for subsidiary activities for women.

Fourth, Bardhan referred to the discrepancy between NSS population estimates and those from the Census. He thought that one reason for the discrepancy might be that a single household in the 2011 Census might have split into two households with a lower family size in each, and the population estimate from this household sampled say in the NSS 2017–18 would probably show a lower overall population count.

Bishwanath Goldar noted that enterprise-based employment data are not taken as seriously as household-based employment estimates and a good question to ask would be how to improve the enterprise survey-based data, especially on the quality of jobs, to make them more reliable so that they could complement each other in providing good estimates of the quality and number of jobs being created. Second, on business registers, he noted that only if such a register could be maintained accurately over time, then the employment estimates from the enterprise surveys could be used to compute an average employment per establishment and multiplied by the number of establishments in the business register to estimate overall employment in that sector.

R. Nagaraj observed that the ASI data has a separate labor schedule that is given to the Labour Bureau for processing. This schedule is probably the weakest part of ASI, but it has immensely rich data on factory workers and their earnings, which can help address the question of labor market rigidity in India. Second, there is currently a lot of emphasis on formal sector employment, and the most widely available formal sector information is the one-page data on unemployment in the *Economic Survey*. Another source of employment data is the Labour Bureau, which processes data on all labor laws in India, which, in turn, is compiled into its annual reports, and some of it is summarized in the *Indian Labour Year Book*. However, the *Year Book* often contains obsolete and repeated data, especially on labor welfare or labor laws. This database needs to be reviewed and updated urgently.

Santanu Pramanik thought that greater use should be made of other administrative data sources in a statistical modeling framework along with survey data to come up with predictors of employment/unemployment and to produce shrinkage type estimates, which are basically weighted combinations of estimates from the NSS surveys and regression synthetic estimates from the model. This may be a better option than increasing the sample size and overburdening the survey, especially to get to disaggregated estimates at the state and district levels.

The discussion ended with the Chair, Secretary, MoSPI, Praveen Srivastava, thanking the panelists and the audience. He suggested that the Ministry of Labor and Employment should be included in discussions on employment since they are a key stakeholder. He said that a recent positive development has been that people are taking data more seriously now, and the government is also looking at data as a public good, which is why MoSPI has made data available free of charge in recent months. That is the Ministry's contribution to research. Citing an off-hand figure, he said that the Ministry earlier used to get about 200 paying users in a year and about ₹1 crore in revenue. But this has gone up to more than 2,000 users spread across the world, and if monetized, this would be a revenue of more than ₹3 crores just over the preceding two months.

He also said that a huge cost is attached to data generation in terms of manpower, resources, training, and capacity building. He noted that the Ministry is improving its training programs and revamping its systems. It has created a Division on Data Quality Assurance to improve data collection right from the capturing stage. This would help resolve a lot of issues over the next few years. While people criticize the EPFO data, they need to know that the data being captured from September 2017 onwards is uniquely identifiable to one particular person which prevents any duplication. The Ministry of Labour has undertaken a massive exercise to de-duplicate the EPFO database. He requested the research community to look at various administrative datasets available, the survey data available, and different elements in the large matrix of the time-use survey and the EC, which would be updated every three years. The Ministry also plans to integrate elements from the GSTN, the EPFO, the ESIC, and the database of the Ministry of Corporate Affairs.

The Ministry also held a session with several research organizations to discuss the UN's Sustainable Development Goals. It has come out with a framework of 300 indicators, but this covers only 80 of the 230-odd indicators assessed globally, thereby leading to a huge data gap. He finally noted the establishment of a new NSC, among other measures for strengthening institutions in the data ecosystem.

Shekhar Shah asked about the implications of the merger of the NSSO and the Central Statistics Office (CSO) and whether that raised the issue of the independence of the statistical establishment in India, which has been taken for granted for the last 70-odd years.

Praveen Srivastava noted that there was no dilution of any institution's autonomy and said that the merger of the NSSO and CSO was a logical step that should have happened a long time back. This is because there are a lot of commonalities in the work of the two institutions. The data produced by NSSO is used by CSO, and some of the results of the CSO are used to corroborate the data of NSS, and bringing them to a common entity was global best practice. The merger will bring synergies within the existing resources, including both survey data and administrative data. This would also ensure that all stakeholders work in the right direction for making data available as a public good.

The session video, the paper, and all presentations for this IPF session are hyperlinked on the IPF program available on the NCAER website by scanning this QR code or going to the following URL:
https://www.ncaer.org/IPF2019/Agenda/Agenda_IPF_2019.pdf

SUDIPTA GHOSH[*]
University of British Columbia

VIKTORIA HNATKOVSKA[†]
University of British Columbia

AMARTYA LAHIRI[‡]
University of British Columbia

Rural–Urban Disparities in India in the Time of Growth[§]

ABSTRACT   The period since the 1990s has seen an aggregate growth takeoff in India during which the rural agricultural sector has gradually ceded space in both employment and output share to non-agricultural sectors. How have agriculture-dependent rural workers and households fared during this episode relative to their urban counterparts? Using household-level survey data, we find that rural–urban education gaps have declined significantly between 1983 and 2012. Moreover, occupation choices in the two sectors have become more aligned with an expansion of non-farm occupations in rural India. Consumption gaps between rural and urban households also declined between 1983 and 2005 for the bottom 45th percentile of the distribution. The period since 2005 has, however, witnessed a rise in consumption gaps. Using state-level data, we show that per capita income levels and growth rates are positive correlates of rural–urban consumption gaps, while the education gap is a negative correlate.

Keywords: Rural–Urban Disparity, Consumption Gaps, Education

JEL Classification: E2, O1, R2

1. Introduction

Periods, when macroeconomic growth takes off in countries, are often accompanied by an underlying microeconomic churn. Such periods are typically characterized by a shrinking of the rural agricultural sector and

[*] *gsudipta01@gmail.com*
[†] *hnatkovs@gmail.com*
[‡] *amartyalahiri@gmail.com*
[§] The authors would like to thank, without implicating, the discussants Rohini Somanathan and Jeff Hammer, the editor Karthik Muralidharan, and participants at the IPF 2019 Conference at NCAER, New Delhi, for their comments and suggestions.

an expansion of the urban non-agricultural sectors. How do these episodes impact the fortunes of rural and urban households? The question is often also at the heart of discussions regarding the evolution of inequality in developing economies. Not surprisingly, in a recent cross-country study on a sample of 65 countries, Young (2013) finds that around 40 percent of the average inequality in consumption is due to urban–rural gaps.

In this paper, we examine the fortunes of rural and urban workers in India between 1983 and 2012. We provide a comprehensive empirical documentation of the trends in rural and urban disparities in India since 1983 in education, occupation distributions, and consumption. In addition, the paper examines state-level evidence to both corroborate the aggregate evidence and uncover potential driving forces for the evolving pattern of rural–urban disparity.

Using seven thick rounds of the National Sample Survey (NSS) of households in India between 1983 and 2012, we analyze the evolution over time of education attainment, occupation choices, and consumption levels of rural and urban workers. Our analysis yields several results.

First, while the educational attainment rates of both rural and urban individuals have been rising, the gap between them has been shrinking dramatically over time in terms of both the years of schooling and the relative distribution of workers in different education categories. Second, the shares of non-farm jobs (both white- and blue-collar) have expanded dramatically in rural areas, leading to a reduction in the dissimilarity between the occupation choices of rural and urban households.

Third, mean per capita consumption differences between urban and rural households have narrowed up to the bottom 15 percentile of the consumption distribution. For higher percentiles, however, the consumption gaps have widened between 1983 and 2012. We find that this widening of rural–urban consumption gaps is a relatively recent phenomenon that has set in after 2004–05 with a sharp widening of the gap post 2009–10.

Fourth, we examine the disaggregated state-level data to find the key determinants of the evolving rural–urban gaps in consumption using the panel structure of the state-level data for identification. We find that the rural–urban consumption gaps, both in mean and quantiles, are significantly greater in states with higher levels and growth rates of per capita Net State Domestic Product (NSDP). In addition, states with lower rural–urban education gaps tend to have significantly lower consumption gaps.

One curious feature of our findings is that consumption gaps between rural and urban households reversed their two-decade-long narrowing trend and began widening after 2004–05. This is particularly puzzling since

India introduced one of the world's largest public works and employment programs in the form of the Mahatma Gandhi National Rural Employment Guarantee Act (MGNREGA) in 2006. MGNREGA guaranteed 100 days of work to all rural workers. This should, in theory, have provided rural households with a consumption boost post-2006.

Our interest in rural–urban gaps is probably closest in spirit to the work of Young (2013), who examined rural–urban consumption expenditure gaps in 65 countries. He found that only a small fraction of the rural–urban inequality can be accounted for by individual characteristics, like education differences. He attributed the remaining gaps to the competitive sorting of workers to rural and urban areas based on their unobserved skills.

Our work is also related to empirical literature studying rural–urban gaps in different countries (see, for instance, Nguyen et al. [2007] for Vietnam; Qu and Zhao [2008] and Wu and Perloff [2005] for China). These papers generally employ household survey data and relate changes in rural–urban inequality to individual and household characteristics. Our study is the first to conduct a similar analysis for India for multiple years, as well as to extend the analysis to the state level.

The rest of the paper is organized as follows: Section 2 presents the data and some motivating statistics. Section 3 delineates the main results on the evolution of the rural–urban gaps as well as the analysis of the extent to which these changes occurred due to changes in the individual characteristics of workers. Section 4 presents the results of urban–rural gaps across states in India. Section 5 investigates the possible factors driving the dynamics of rural–urban consumption gaps. Section 6 contains concluding thoughts.

2. Data

Our data comes from successive rounds of the NSS of households in India for employment and consumption. The survey rounds that we include in the study are 1983 (Round 38), 1987–88 (Round 43), 1993–94 (Round 50), 1999–00 (Round 55), 2004–05 (Round 61), 2009–10 (Round 66), and 2011–12 (Round 68). Since our focus is on determining the trends in outcomes of the workforce in rural and urban India, we restrict the sample to individuals in the working age group of 16–65 years, who are not enrolled in any educational institution, and for whom we have educational information as well as information on their weekly activity status (unemployed, regular salaried worker, casual worker, or self-employed). This restriction excludes individuals who report home production as their primary weekly

FIGURE 1. Ratio of Urban to Rural Labor Force Participation and Employment Rates

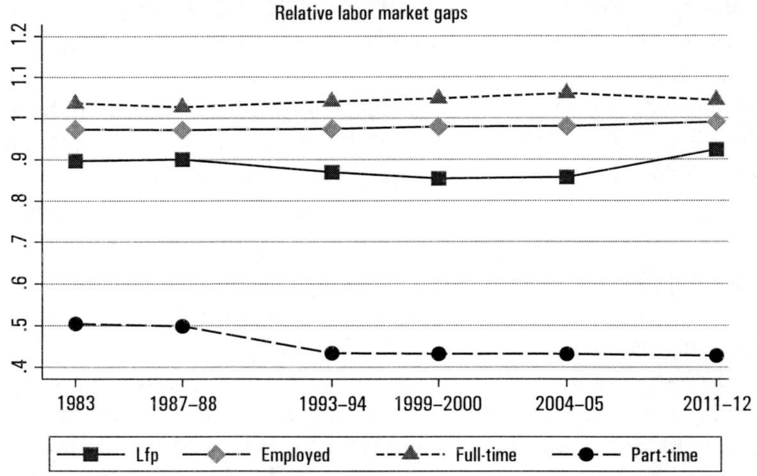

Source: Authors' calculations from NSS data (see text for details).
Notes: "Lfp" = ratio of urban to rural labor force participation rates; "employed" = ratio of urban to rural employment rates; "full-time" = ratio of urban to rural full-time employment rate, and "part-time" = ratio of urban to rural part-time employment rates.

activity. We further restrict the sample to individuals who belong to male-led households.[1] These restrictions leave us with a sample size that varies between 159,000 and 221,000 individuals per survey round.

Figure 1 plots the urban to rural ratios in labor force participation rates, overall employment rates, as well as full-time and part-time employment rates. As can be seen from the figure, there was some increase in the relative rural part-time work incidence between 1987 and 2012. Apart from this, all other trends were basically flat. Details on our data are provided in Appendix A.1.

We summarize demographic characteristics in our sample across the rounds in Table 1. The table breaks down the overall patterns by individuals and households and by rural and urban locations. Clearly, the sample is overwhelmingly rural with about 75 percent of households, on average, being residents in rural areas. Rural residents are less likely to be male, slightly more likely to be married, and belong to marginally larger households than their urban counterparts. Lastly, rural areas have more members

---

1. Male-led households are the norm in India.

of backward castes as measured by the proportion of Scheduled Castes (SCs) and Scheduled Tribes (STs).

The panel labeled "Urban–Rural Difference" in Table 1 reports the differences in individual and household characteristics between urban and rural areas for all our survey rounds. Clearly, the share of the rural labor force has declined over time. The average age of individuals in both urban and rural areas has increased over time. Families have also become smaller in both locations, but the decline has been more rapid in urban areas, leading to a

TABLE 1. Summary Statistics for NSS Data from 1983 to 2011–12 for Individuals in the Working Age Group 16–65 used in this Paper

	(a) Individuals			(b) Households		
		Proportion		Proportion		Household
Urban	Age	Male	Married	Urban	SC/ST	Size
1983	35.57	0.83	0.73	0.25	0.16	6.36
	(0.07)	(0.00)	(0.00)	(0.00)	(0.00)	(0.03)
1987–88	35.70	0.83	0.73	0.24	0.16	6.15
	(0.06)	(0.00)	(0.00)	(0.00)	(0.00)	(0.03)
1993–94	36.16	0.81	0.75	0.26	0.16	5.70
	(0.06)	(0.00)	(0.00)	(0.00)	(0.00)	(0.02)
1999–00	36.52	0.82	0.74	0.27	0.19	5.79
	(0.07)	(0.00)	(0.00)	(0.00)	(0.00)	(0.03)
2004–05	36.69	0.81	0.74	0.27	0.18	5.57
	(0.08)	(0.00)	(0.00)	(0.00)	(0.00)	(0.03)
2011–12	37.94	0.82	0.77	0.31	0.18	5.14
	(0.09)	(0.00)	(0.00)	(0.00)	(0.00)	(0.03)
Rural	Age	Male	Married	Rural	SC/ST	HH Size
1983	35.86	0.71	0.79	0.75	0.29	6.52
	(0.04)	(0.00)	(0.00)	(0.00)	(0.00)	(0.02)
1987–88	35.79	0.72	0.79	0.76	0.30	6.42
	(0.04)	(0.00)	(0.00)	(0.00)	(0.00)	(0.02)
1993–94	35.99	0.69	0.80	0.74	0.31	6.08
	(0.04)	(0.00)	(0.00)	(0.00)	(0.00)	(0.02)
1999–00	36.28	0.69	0.80	0.73	0.33	6.23
	(0.05)	(0.00)	(0.00)	(0.00)	(0.00)	(0.02)
2004–05	36.71	0.68	0.80	0.73	0.32	6.03
	(0.05)	(0.00)	(0.00)	(0.00)	(0.00)	(0.02)
2011–12	38.21	0.74	0.81	0.69	0.32	5.52
	(0.08)	(0.00)	(0.00)	(0.00)	(0.00)	(0.03)

(Table 1 Contd.)

(Table 1 Contd.)

Urban–Rural Difference	Age	Male	Married	Rural	SC/ST	HH Size
1983	−0.29***	0.12***	−0.06***	−0.50***	−0.13***	−0.16***
	(0.08)	(0.00)	(0.00)	(0.03)	(0.00)	(0.03)
1987–88	−0.09	0.11***	−0.06***	−0 52***	−0.14***	−0.27***
	(0.08)	(0.00)	(0.00)	(0.03)	(0.00)	(0.03)
1993–94	0.17	0.12***	−0.05***	−0.48***	−0.15***	−0.38***
	(0.08)	(0.00)	(0.00)	(0.03)	(0.00)	(0.02)
1999–00	0.27*	0.13***	−0.06***	−0.46***	−0.14***	−0.44***
	(0.08)	(0.00)	(0.00)	(0.03)	(0.00)	(0.03)
2004–05	−0.02***	0.13***	−0.06***	−0.46***	−0.14***	−0.46***
	(0.10)	(0.00)	(0.00)	(0.04)	(0.00)	(0.03)
2011–12	−0.27***	0.08***	−0.04***	−0.38***	−0.14***	−0.38***
	(0.12)	(0.00)	(0.00)	(0.04)	(0.00)	(0.03)

Source: Authors' calculations. See text for details of data being used of 16–65-year-old working age individuals.
Notes: Columns (a) give statistics at the individual level, while Columns (b) give statistics at the household level. The section labeled "urban–rural difference" reports the difference in characteristics between urban individuals/households and rural individuals/households. Standard errors are reported in parentheses: *p value ≤ 0.10, **p value ≤ 0.05, ***p value ≤ 0.01.

large differential in this characteristic between the two areas. The shares of male workers remained stable in urban areas but showed a sharp increase in rural areas in the last survey round.

Education in the NSS data is presented as a category variable with the survey listing the highest education-attainment level in terms of categories such as primary and middle. In order to ease the presentation, we proceed in two ways. First, we construct a variable for the years of education. We do so by assigning the years of education to each category based on a simple mapping: not literate = 0 years; literate but below primary = 2 years; primary = 5 years; middle = 8 years; secondary and higher secondary = 10 years; graduate = 15 years, and post-graduate = 17 years. Diplomas are treated similarly, depending on the specifics of the attainment level.[2] Second, we use the reported education categories but aggregate them into five broad groups as follows: 1 for illiterate, 2 for some education but below primary school, 3 for primary school, 4 for middle, and 5 for secondary and above. The results from the two approaches are similar. While we use the second

---

2. We are forced to combine secondary and higher secondary into a combined group of 10 years because the higher-secondary classification is missing in the 38th and 43rd Rounds. The only way to retain comparability across rounds, then, is to combine the two categories.

method for our econometric specifications as these are the actual reported data (as opposed to the years series that was constructed by us), we also show results from the first approach below.

For our analysis of occupation choices, we aggregate the reported three-digit occupation categories in the survey into three broad occupation categories: *white-collar* occupations such as administrators, executives, managers, professionals, technical, and clerical workers; *blue-collar* occupations, like sales workers, service workers, and production workers, and *agrarian* occupations including farmers, fishermen, loggers, hunters.

We obtain consumption as the monthly per capita expenditure (MPCE) of rural and urban households. We convert nominal MPCE into real terms using state-level poverty lines that differ for the rural and urban sectors. We express all consumption figures in the 1983 rural Maharashtra poverty lines.[3]

3. Empirical Findings

How did urban and rural workers fare during our sample period? We characterize differences in education attainments, occupations, labor income, and consumption of the rural and urban workforce to answer this question.

3.1. Education

Table 2 shows the average number of years of education of the urban and rural workforce across the six rounds in our sample. The two features that emerge from the table are: (a) education attainment rates as measured by the number of years of education were rising in both urban and rural sectors during this period, and (b) the rural–urban education gap shrank monotonically over this period.

The average number of years of education for the urban worker was 170 percent higher than that for the typical rural worker in 1983 (5.56 years to 2.06 years). This advantage declined to 78 percent by 2011–12 (8.34 years

---

3. In 2004–05, the Planning Commission of India changed the methodology for estimation of poverty lines. Among other changes, it switched from anchoring the poverty lines to a calorie intake norm towards consumer expenditures more generally. This led to a change in the consumption basket underlying poverty lines calculations. To retain comparability across rounds, we convert the 2011–12 poverty lines obtained from the Planning Commission under the new methodology to the old basket using the 2004–05 adjustment factor. That factor was obtained from the poverty lines under the old and new methodologies available for the 2004–05 survey year. As a test, we used the same adjustment factor to obtain the implied "old" poverty lines for the 1993–94 survey round, for which the two sets of poverty lines are also available from the Planning Commission. We find that the actual old poverty lines and the implied "old" poverty lines are very similar, giving us confidence that our adjustment is valid.

TABLE 2. Education Gap: Average Years of Schooling

	Average Years of Education			Relative Education Gap
NSS Rounds	Overall	Rural	Urban	Ratio of Urban/Rural
1983	2.90	2.06	5.56	2.70***
	(0.01)	(0.01)	(0.03)	(0.02)
1987–88	3.14	2.29	5.89	2.57***
	(0.01)	(0.01)	(0.03)	(0.02)
1993–94	3.71	2.81	6.63	2.36***
	(0.01)	(0.01)	(0.03)	(0.03)
1999–00	4.27	3.30	7.21	2.18***
	(0.02)	(0.02)	(0.03)	(0.02)
2004–05	4.66	3.75	7.49	2.00***
	(0.02)	(0.02)	(0.04)	(0.01)
2011–12	5.77	4.69	8.34	1.78***
	(0.02)	(0.03)	(0.04)	(0.01)

Source: Authors' calculations. See text for details.
Notes: This table presents the average number of years of education for the overall sample and for urban and rural populations. The reported statistics are obtained for each NSS Round, which is shown in the first column. Standard errors are in parentheses. *p-value $\leq$ 0.10, **p-value $\leq$ 0.05, ***p-value $\leq$ 0.01.

to 4.69 years). To put these numbers in perspective, in 1983, the average urban worker had slightly more than primary education while the typical rural worker was literate but below primary level. By 2011–12, the average urban worker had about a middle school education, while the typical rural worker had almost attained primary education. While the overall numbers indicate the still dire state of literacy of the workforce in the country, the movements underneath do indicate improvements over time, with the rural workers improving faster.

Table 2, while revealing an improving trend for the average worker, nevertheless, masks potentially important underlying heterogeneity in education attainment by cohort, that is, variation by the age of the respondent. Panel (a) of Figure 2 shows the relative gap in the number of years of education between the typical urban and rural worker by age group. There are two key results to note here: (a) the gaps have been getting smaller over time for all age groups, and (b) the gaps are smaller for the younger age groups.

Is the education convergence taking place uniformly across all birth cohorts, or are the changes mainly being driven by aging effects? To disentangle the two, we compute relative education gaps for different birth cohorts for every survey year. These are plotted in Panel (b) of Figure 2. Clearly, almost all of the convergence in education attainments takes place through cross-cohort improvements, with the younger cohorts showing the smallest gaps. Aging effects are symmetric across all cohorts, except the eldest. Most strikingly, the

FIGURE 2. Education Gaps by (a) Age Groups and (b) Birth Cohorts: Ratio of Urban to Rural Average Years of Education

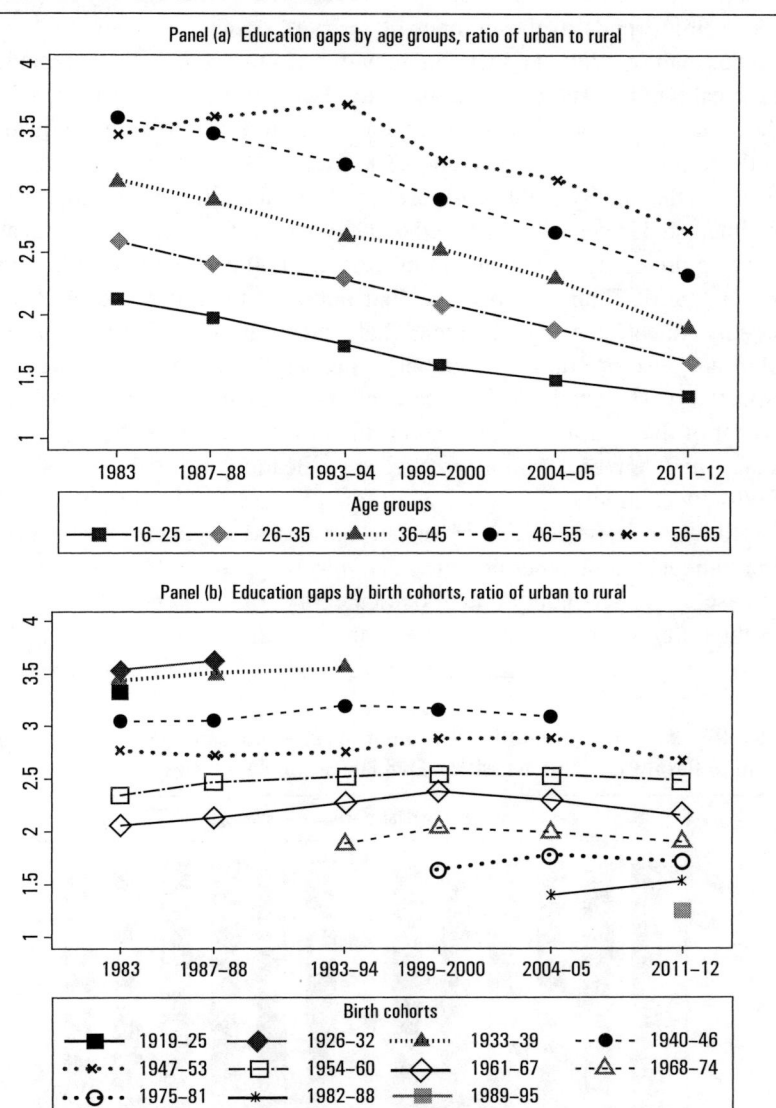

Source: Authors' calculations.
Notes: The panels in this figure show the ratio of the average number of years of education between the urban and rural workforces over time for different age groups and birth cohorts.

average gap in 2011–12 between urban and rural workers from the youngest birth cohort (born between 1989 and 1995) has almost disappeared, while the corresponding gap for those born between 1954 and 1960 stood at 150 percent. Clearly, the declining rural–urban gaps are being driven by declining education gaps amongst the younger workers in the two sectors.

The time trends in the number of years of education potentially mask changes in the quality of education. In particular, they fail to reveal what kind of education is causing the rise in years: Is it people moving from middle school to secondary, or is it movement from illiteracy to some education? While both movements would add a similar number of years to the total, the impact on the quality of the workforce may be quite different. Further, we are also interested in determining whether the movements in urban and rural areas are being driven by very different movements in the category of education.

Panel (a) of Figure 3 shows the distribution of the urban and rural workforce by education category. Recall that education categories 1, 2, and 3 are "illiterate", "some education but below primary", and "primary education", respectively. Hence, in 1983, 55 percent of the urban labor force and over 85 percent of the rural labor force had primary or below education, reflecting the abysmal delivery of public services in education during the first 35 years of post-Independence India. By 2012, the primary and below category had come down to 30 percent for urban workers and 50 percent for rural workers. Simultaneously, the other notable trend during this period is the perceptible increase in the secondary and above category for workers in both sectors. For the urban sector, this category expanded from about 30 percent in 1983 to over 50 percent in 2012. Correspondingly, the share of secondary and

FIGURE 3. Education Distribution of Rural and Urban Samples and Ratio of Urban to Rural Distributions within Five Education Categories

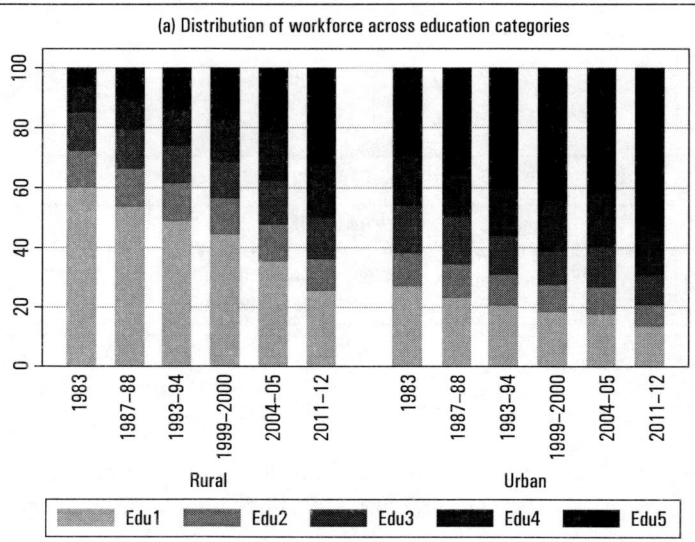

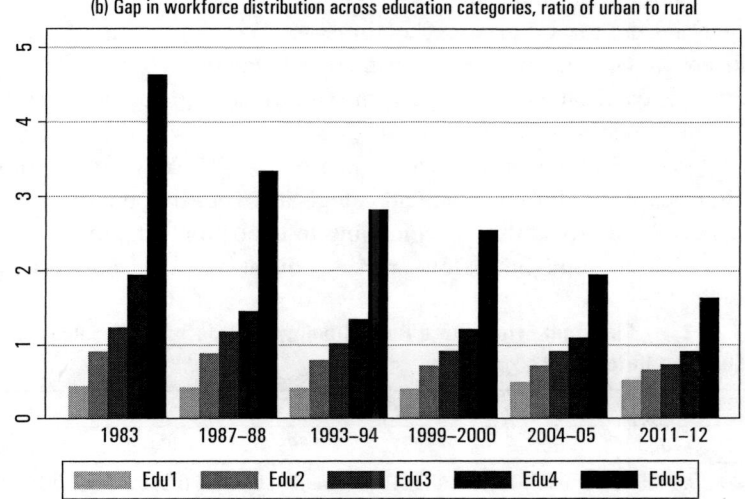

(b) Gap in workforce distribution across education categories, ratio of urban to rural

Source: Authors' calculations.

Notes: The definition of our education categories is: Edu1 illiterate; Edu2 some education but below primary school; Edu3 primary school; Edu4 middle school; and Edu5 secondary and above. For more details see Section 2 of this paper. Panel (a) presents the distribution of the workforce across five education categories for different NSS rounds. Panel (b) presents relative gaps (ratio of urban to rural) in the distribution of urban relative to rural workers across the five education categories.

higher educated rural workers rose from just around 5 percent of the rural workforce in 1983 to about 30 percent in 2012. This, along with the decline in the proportion of rural illiterate workers from 60 percent to around 25 percent, represents the sharpest and most promising change since 1983.

Panel (b) of Figure 3 shows the changes in the relative education distributions of the urban and rural workforce. For each survey year, the figure shows the fraction of urban workers in each education category relative to the fraction of rural workers in that category. Thus, in 1983, urban workers were over-represented in the secondary and above category by a factor close to 5. Similarly, rural workers were over-represented in the education category 1 (illiterates) by a factor of 2. Clearly, the closer the height of the bars is to one, the more symmetric is the distribution of the two groups in that category, while the further away from one they are, the more skewed is the distribution. As the figure indicates, the biggest convergence in the education distribution between 1983 and 2012 was in categories 4 and 5 (middle, and secondary and above) where the bars shrank rapidly. The trends in the other three categories were more muted as compared to the convergence in categories 4 and 5.

While the visual impressions suggest convergence in education, are these trends statistically significant? We turn to this issue next by estimating ordered multinomial probit regressions of education categories 1 to 5 on a constant and the rural dummy. The aim is to ascertain the significance of the difference between rural and urban areas in the probability of a worker belonging to each category as well as the significance of changes over time in these differences. Table 3 shows the results.

Panel (a) of Table 3 shows that the marginal effect of the rural dummy was significant for all rounds and all categories. The rural dummy significantly raised the probability of belonging to education categories 1 and 2 ("illiterate" and "some but below primary education", respectively) while

TABLE 3. Marginal Effects of a Rural Dummy in Ordered Probit Regressions for Education Categories

	Panel (a): Marginal Effects, Unconditional					
	1983	1987–88	1993–94	1999–00	2004–05	2011–12
Edu1	0.3489***	0.3391***	0.3215***	0.3026***	0.2757***	0.2242
	(0.0026)	(0.0022)	(0.0023)	(0.0025)	(0.0025)	(0.0031)
Edu2	−0.0021***	0.0051***	0.0151***	0.0231***	0.0319***	0.0421***
	(0.0004)	(0.0004)	(0.0004)	(0.0005)	(0.0006)	(0.0010)
Edu3	−0.0496***	−0.0393***	−0.0197***	−0.0037***	0.0072***	0.0245***
	(0.0006)	(0.0005)	(0.0004)	(0.0004)	(0.0005)	(0.0008)
Edu4	−0.0889***	−0.0762***	−0.0656***	−0.0538***	−0.0480***	−0.0169***
	(0.0010)	(0.0008)	(0.0007)	(0.0007)	(0.0006)	(0.0007)
Edu5	−0.2082***	−0.2287***	−0.2514***	−0.2681***	−0.2668***	−0.2738***
	(0.0022)	(0.0020)	(0.0023)	(0.0028)	(0.0031)	(0.0040)
N	203,456	221,228	199,579	210,209	220,786	159,193
	Panel (b): Changes over Time					
	1983 to 1993–94		1993 to 2004–05		2004 to 2011–12	1983 to 2011–12
Edu1	−0.0274***		−0.0458***		−0.0515***	−0.1247***
	(0.0035)		(0.0034)		(0.0040)	(0.0040)
Edu2	0.0172***		0.0168***		0.0102***	0.0442***
	(0.0006)		(0.0007)		(0.0012)	(0.0011)
Edu3	0.0299***		0.0269***		0.0173***	0.0741***
	(0.0007)		(0.0006)		(0.0009)	(0.0010)
Edu4	0.0233***		0.0176***		0.0311***	0.0720***
	(0.0012)		(0.0009)		(0.0009)	(0.0012)
Edu5	−0.0432***		−0.0154***		−0.0070***	−0.0656***
	(0.0032)		(0.0039)		(0.0051)	(0.0046)

Source: Authors' calculations. See text for details.
Notes: Panel (a) of this table reports the marginal effects of the rural dummy in an ordered probit regression of Education Categories 1–5 on a constant and a rural dummy for each survey Round. Panel (b) of the table reports the change in the marginal effects over successive decades and the entire sample period. N refers to the number of observations. Standard errors are in parentheses. * p-value ≤ 0.10, ** p-value ≤ 0.05, *** p-value ≤ 0.01.

it significantly reduced the probability of belonging to categories 4–5. In category 3, the sign on the rural dummy had switched from negative to positive in 2004–05 and stayed that way in 2011–12.

Panel (b) of Table 3 shows that the changes over time in these marginal effects were also significant for all rounds and all categories. There are clearly significant convergent trends for education categories 1, 3, and 4. Category 1, where rural workers were over-represented in 1983, saw a declining marginal effect of the rural dummy. Categories 3 and 4 (primary and middle school, respectively), where rural workers were under-represented in 1983, saw a significant increase in the marginal effect of the rural status. Hence, the rural under-representation in these categories declined significantly. Categories 2 and 5 were, however, marked by a divergence in the distribution. Category 2, where rural workers were over-represented, saw an increase in the marginal effect of the rural dummy, while in category 5, where they were under-represented, the marginal effect of the rural dummy became even more negative. However, this divergence is not inconsistent with Figure 3. The figure shows trends in the relative gaps while the probit regressions show trends in the absolute gaps.

In summary, the overwhelming feature of the data on education attainment gaps suggests a strong and significant trend towards education convergence between the urban and rural workforce. This is evident in the comparison of the average number of years of education, the relative gaps by education category as well as the absolute gaps between the groups in most categories.

The convergence results on education come with the obvious caveat that education attainment rates, even when the education categories are examined, may not necessarily reflect the quality of education. Thus, a middle school education from rural areas might not imply the same degree of proficiency as a middle school education from urban areas. This is unfortunately a natural limitation of the data that we are using.

3.2. Occupational Choices

We now turn to occupational choices being made by the workforce in urban and rural areas. Figure 4 shows the distribution of agrarian, blue-collar, and white-collar occupations in urban and rural India across the survey rounds (Panel (a)) as well as the gap in these distributions between the sectors (Panel (b)).

The urban and rural occupational distributions have the obvious feature that urban areas have a much smaller fraction of the workforce in agrarian occupations, while rural areas have a minuscule share of people working in white-collar jobs. The crucial aspect, though, is the share of the workforce in

FIGURE 4. Occupational Distribution of Rural and Urban Samples and Ratio of Urban to Rural Distributions within Three Occupational Categories

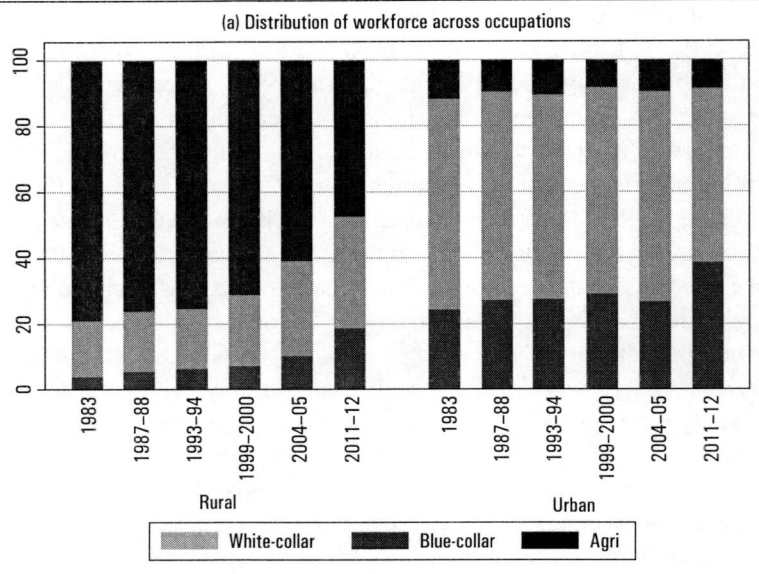

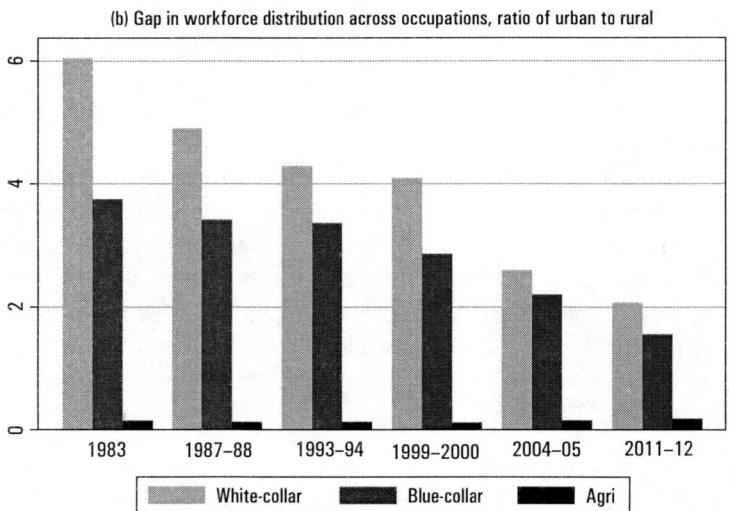

Source: Authors' calculations.
Notes: Panel (a) presents the distribution of the workforce across three occupational categories, white-collar, blue-collar, and agriculture for different NSS rounds. Panel (b) presents relative gaps in the distribution of urban relative to rural workers across the three occupational categories. We construct the three occupation categories by combining the three-digit occupation categories in the surveys into three broad groups: *white-collar* occupations such as administrators, executives, managers, professionals, technical, and clerical workers; *blue-collar* occupations, such as sales workers, service workers, and production workers, and *agrarian* occupations including farmers, fishermen, loggers, and hunters. See Section 2 of this paper.

blue-collar jobs that pertain to both services and manufacturing. The urban sector clearly has dominance in these occupations. Importantly, however, the share of blue-collar jobs has been rising in rural areas. In fact, as Panel (b) of Figure 4 shows, the shares of both white-collar and blue-collar jobs in rural areas are rising faster than their corresponding shares in urban areas.

What are the non-farm occupations that are driving the convergence between rural and urban areas? We answer this question by considering disaggregated occupation categories within the white-collar and blue-collar categories. We start with the blue-collar jobs that have shown the most pronounced increase in rural areas.

Panel (a) of Figure 5 presents the breakdown of all blue-collar jobs into three types of occupations. The first group comprises *sales workers*, which include manufacturer's agents, retail and wholesale merchants and shopkeepers, salesmen working in trade, insurance, real estate, and securities, as well as various types of moneylenders. The second group comprises *service workers*, including hotel and restaurant staff, maintenance workers, barbers, policemen, firefighters. The third group consists of *production and transportation workers and laborers*. This group includes, among others, miners, quarry workers and various manufacturing workers.

The main result that emerges from Panel (a) of Figure 5 is the rapid expansion of blue-collar jobs in the rural sector. The share of rural workers employed

FIGURE 5. Occupational Distribution of Rural and Urban Samples within Blue-collar Jobs

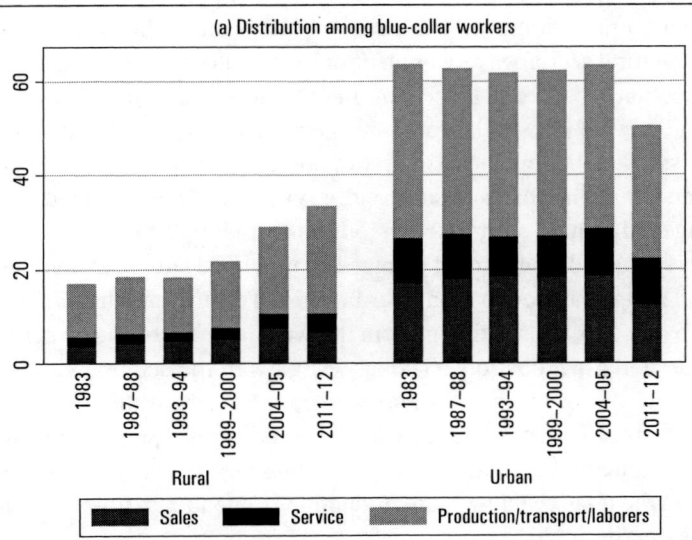

(Figure 5 Contd.)

(Figure 5 Contd.)

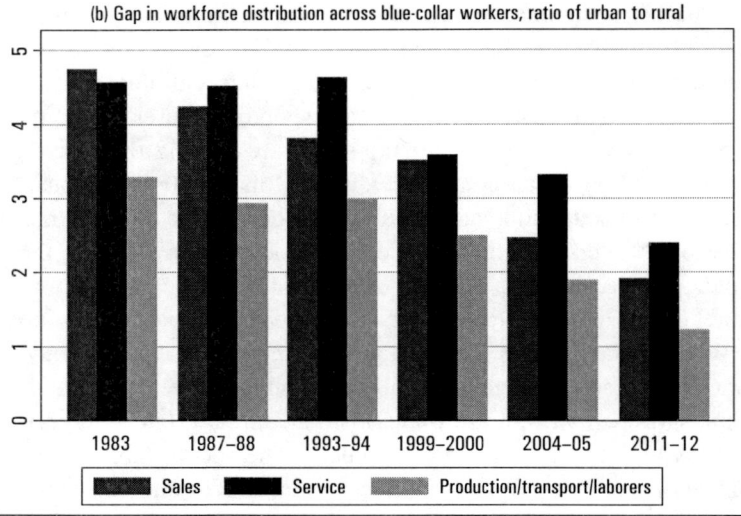

(b) Gap in workforce distribution across blue-collar workers, ratio of urban to rural

Source: Authors' calculations. See text for details.
Notes: Panel (a) of this figure presents the distribution of the workforce within blue-collar jobs for different NSS rounds. Panel (b) presents relative gaps in the distribution of urban relative to rural workers across different occupation categories among blue-collar workers.

in blue-collar jobs increased from under 18 percent to 37 percent between 1983 and 2012. This increase in the rural sector is in sharp contrast with the urban sector, where the share of blue-collar jobs remained roughly unchanged at around 60 percent during this period. Most of the increase in blue-collar jobs in the rural sector was accounted for by a twofold expansion in the share of production jobs (from 11 percent in 1983 to 27 percent in 2012). While sales and service jobs in the rural areas expanded as well, the increase was much less dramatic. In the urban sector, however, the trends have been quite different: While the shares of sales and service jobs have remained relatively unchanged, the share of production jobs has actually declined.

Clearly, such distributional changes should have led to a convergence in the rural and urban occupation distributions. To illustrate this, Panel (b) of Figure 5 presents the relative gaps in the workforce distribution across various blue-collar occupations. The largest gaps in the sectoral employment shares were observed in sales and service jobs, where the gap was more than four times in 1983. The distributional changes discussed above have led to a decline in the urban–rural gaps in these jobs. The more pronounced decline in the relative gap was in production occupations: from 3.25 in 1983 to almost parity in 2012.

Next, we turn to white-collar jobs. Panel (a) of Figure 6 presents the distribution of all white-collar jobs in each sector into three types of occupations. The first is *professional, technical, and related workers*. This group includes, for instance, chemists, engineers, agronomists, doctors and veterinarians, accountants, lawyers, and teachers. The second types of occupations comprise *administrative, executive, and managerial workers*, which include, for example, officials at various levels of the government, as well as proprietors, directors, and managers in various business and financial institutions. The third type of occupation consists of *clerical and related workers*. These include, for instance, village officials, bookkeepers, cashiers, various clerks, transport conductors and supervisors, mail distributors, and communications personnel.

Panel (a) of figure 6 shows that administrative jobs signify the fastest-growing occupation within the white-collar group in both rural and urban areas. It was the smallest category among all white-collar jobs in both sectors in 1983 but has expanded dramatically ever since to overtake clerical jobs as the second most popular occupation among white-collar jobs after professional occupations. Lastly, the share of professional jobs has also increased while the share of clerical and related jobs has shrunk in both the rural and urban sectors during the same time.

Have the expansions and contractions in various jobs been symmetric across rural and urban sectors? Panel (b) of Figure 6 presents relative gaps

FIGURE 6. Occupational Distribution of Rural and Urban Samples within White-collar Jobs

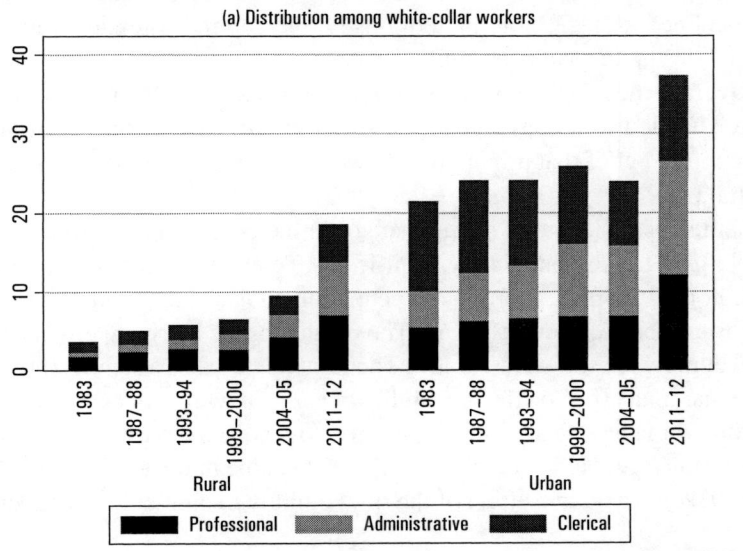

(Figure 6 Contd.)

(Figure 6 Contd.)

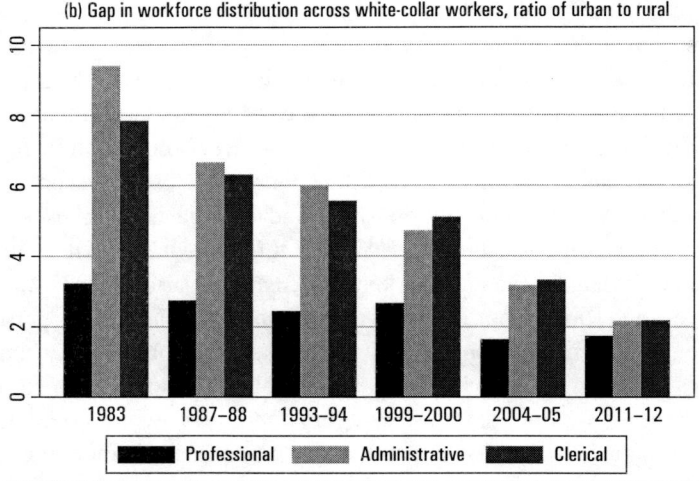

(b) Gap in workforce distribution across white-collar workers, ratio of urban to rural

Source: Authors' calculations. See text for details.
Notes: Panel (a) of this figure presents the distribution of the workforce within white-collar jobs for different NSS rounds. Panel (b) presents relative gaps in the distribution of urban relative to rural workers across different occupational categories.

in the workforce distribution across various white-collar occupations. The biggest difference in occupation distribution between urban and rural sectors was in administrative jobs, but the gap has declined very sharply between 1983 and 2012. Similarly, the relative gap in clerical jobs has fallen, though the decline has been more muted. Lastly, the gap in professional jobs has halved during the same period.

Overall, these results suggest that the expansion of the rural non-farm sector has led to a convergence of rural–urban occupations, contrary to the popular belief that urban growth was deepening the rural–urban divide in India.

Is this visual image of sharp changes in the occupation distribution and convergent trends statistically significant? To examine this, we estimate a multinomial probit regression of occupation choices on a rural dummy and a constant for each survey round. The results for the marginal effects of the rural dummy are shown in Table 4. The rural dummy has a significantly negative marginal effect on the probability of being in white-collar and blue-collar jobs while having significant positive effects on the probability of being in agrarian jobs. However, as Panel (b) of the table indicates, between 1983 and 2012, the negative effect of the rural dummy in blue-collar occupations declined (the marginal effect became less negative), while the positive effect on being in agrarian occupations became smaller, with both changes being highly significant. Since there was an initial under-representation of blue-collar occupations and over-representation of agrarian occupations in the rural sector, these results indicate an ongoing process of convergence across rural and urban areas in these two occupations.

At the same time, the gap in the shares of the workforce in white-collar jobs between urban and rural areas has widened. Note that this result is not inconsistent with Figure 4, which indicates convergence in the workforce distribution in white-collar jobs. The key difference is that Table 4 reports *absolute differences* in workforce distribution between the rural and urban workforce, whereas Figure 4 reports *relative differences* in that distribution. Crucially, blue-collar and agrarian jobs have shown convergence over time in both absolute and relative terms.

TABLE 4. Marginal Effect of Rural/Urban Dummy in Multinomial Probit Regressions for Occupations

	Panel (a): Marginal Effects, Unconditional					
	1983	1987–88	1993–94	1999–00	2004–05	2011–12
White-Collar	−0.1900***	−0.2028***	−0.2042***	−0.2187***	−0.2153***	−0.2904***
	(0.0026)	(0.0024)	(0.0026)	(0.0031)	(0.0033)	(0.0044)
Blue-Collar	−0.4834***	−0.4568***	−0.4580***	−0.4381***	−0.4084***	−0.2692***
	(0.0031)	(0.0029)	(0.0030)	(0.0035)	(0.0038)	(0.0049)
Agrarian	0.6734***	0.6596***	0.6622***	0.6568***	0.6236***	0.5596***
	(0.0023)	(0.0021)	(0.0022)	(0.0023)	(0.0025)	(0.0034)
N	179,646	193,585	172,005	178,803	189,195	132,360

	Panel (b): Changes			
	1983 to 1993–94	1993 to 2004–05	2004 to 2011–12	1983 to 2011–12
White-Collar	−0.0142***	−0.0111***	−0.0751***	−0.1004***
	(0.0052)	(0.0059)	(0.0055)	(0.0051)
Blue-Collar	0.0254***	0.0496***	0.1392***	0.2124***
	(0.0043)	(0.0048)	(0.0062)	(0.0058)
Agrarian	−0.0112***	−0.0386***	−0.064***	−0.1138***
	(0.0032)	(0.0033)	(0.0042)	(0.0041)

Source: Authors' calculations.
Notes: Panel (a) of this table reports the marginal effects of the rural/urban dummy from a multinomial probit regression of occupational choices on a constant and a rural dummy for each survey round. Panel (b) reports the change in the marginal effects of the rural dummy over successive decades and over the entire sample period. N refers to the number of observations. Agrarian jobs are the reference group in the regression. Standard errors are in parentheses: *p-value ≤ 0.10, **p-value ≤ 0.05, ***p-value ≤ 0.01.

3.3. Household Consumption

In studying urban–rural real consumption convergence, we are interested not just in the mean or median consumption gaps but rather in the behavior of the real consumption gap across the entire consumption distribution.

We start by taking a look at the distribution of log real MPCE for rural and urban households in our sample. In order to present the results, we break up our sample into two sub-periods: 1983 to 2004–05 and 2004–05 to 2011–12. We do this to distinguish long-run trends since 1983 from the potential effects of the Mahatma Gandhi National Rural Employment Guarantee Act (MGNREGA) that was introduced in 2005. MGNREGA provides a government guarantee of 100 days of wage employment in a financial year to all rural households whose adult members volunteer to do unskilled manual work. This Act could clearly have affected rural and urban wages. To control for the effects of this policy on real wages, we split our sample period into the pre- and post-MGNREGA periods.

We begin with the pre-MGNREGA period of 1983 to 2004–05. Panel (a) of Figure 7 plots the kernel densities of log MPCE for rural and urban households for the 1983 and 2004–05 survey rounds. The plot shows a very clear rightward shift of the consumption density function during this period for both rural and urban households. Panel (b) of Figure 7 presents the percentile (log) MPCE gaps between urban and rural workers for 1983 and 2004–05 household consumption densities functions in those two survey rounds. An upward sloping gap schedule indicates that consumption gaps are higher for higher consumption groups. A rightward shift in the schedule over time implies that the consumption gap has shrunk. The plot for 2004–05 lies to the right of that for 1983 till the 45th percentile, indicating that the gap between poorer urban and rural household consumption declined over this period. Interestingly, in 2004–05, rural consumption was actually higher than urban consumption for the bottom 30th percentile of the consumption distribution. This was in stark contrast to 1983 when urban consumption was higher than rural consumption for all the percentiles.

We now turn to an analysis of the post-MGNREGA consumption distributions. Panel (a) of Figure 8 shows the percentile consumption gaps between rural and urban households in 2004–05 and 2011–12. The figure shows that the urban–rural consumption convergence between the relatively poorer households that we uncovered for the 1983–2005 period reversed itself in the post-reform period. Panel (b) shows that as a result of the widening urban–rural consumption gaps between 2004 and 2012, the percentile consumption gaps in 2011–12 are higher than the corresponding gaps for 1983 for all except the bottom 15 percentiles. In fact, the median consumption premium of urban households increased from under 10 percent

FIGURE 7. Log Consumption Distributions of Urban and Rural Households for 1983 to 2004–05 and Consumption Gaps

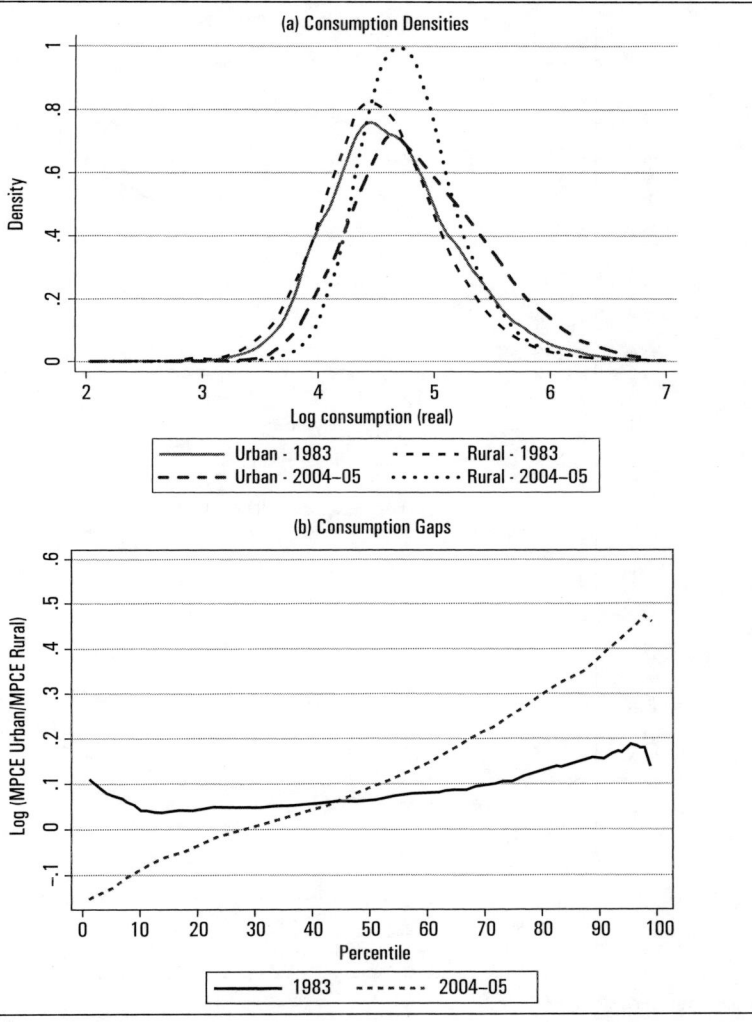

Source: Authors' calculations.
Notes: Panel (a) of this figure shows the estimated kernel densities of log real MPCE for urban and rural households, while Panel (b) shows the difference in percentiles of log MPCE between urban and rural households plotted against the percentile. The plots are for the 1983 and 2004–05 NSS rounds.

to close to 20 percent between 1983 and 2012 as a result of the widening rural–urban consumption dispersion since 2004–05.

To examine whether changes in the urban and rural consumption gaps are statistically significant, we estimate Recentered Influence Function (RIF) regressions developed by Firpo, Fortin, and Lemieux (2009) of the log real

FIGURE 8. Consumption Gaps between Urban and Rural Households, 2004–05 and 2011–12 and 1983 and 2011–12

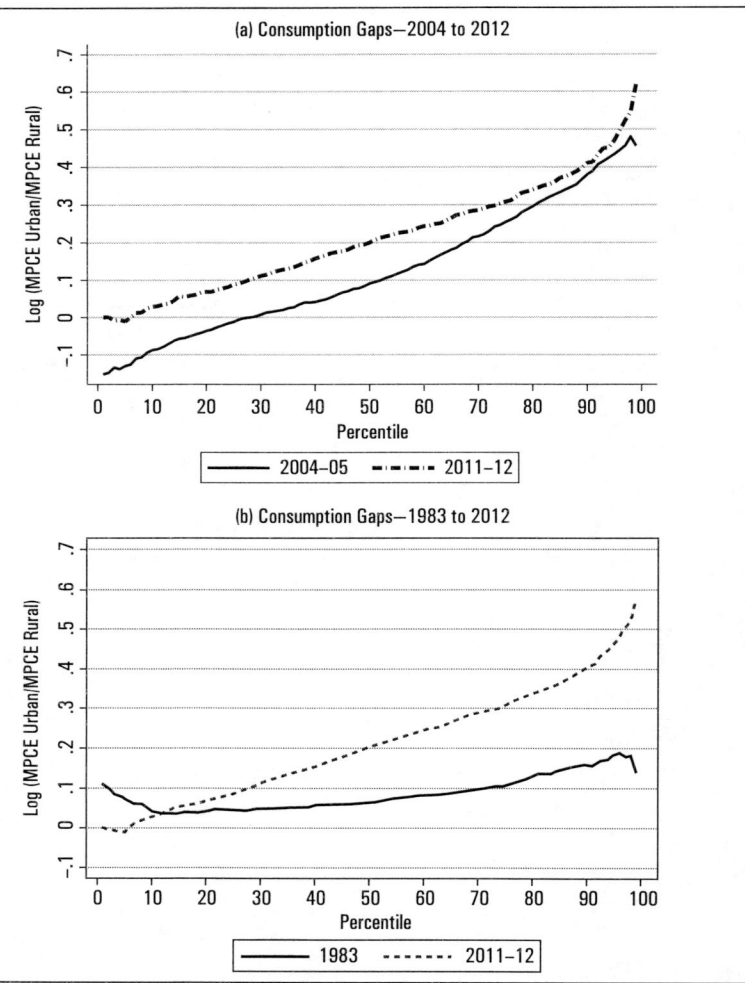

Source: Authors' calculations.
Notes: Panel (a) of this figure shows the percentile gaps in log real consumption differences between urban and rural households in 2004–05 and 2011–12, while Panel (b) shows the corresponding percentile consumption gaps in 1983 and 2011–12.

consumption in our sample on a constant and a rural dummy for each survey Round. Our interest is in the coefficient on the rural dummy. We perform the analysis for different unconditional quantiles as well as the mean of the wage distribution.[4]

4. We use the RIF approach (developed by Firpo, Fortin, and Lemieux 2009) because we are interested in estimating the effect of the rural dummy for different points of the distribution, not

Panel (a) of Table 5 reports the estimated coefficient on the rural dummy for the 10th, 50th, and 90th percentiles as well as the mean for different survey rounds. The rural status significantly reduced household consumption for all percentiles of the distribution in 1983. Panel (b) of Table 5 shows that the size of the negative rural effect became significantly smaller over time for the 10th percentile between 1983 and 2012 but widened for all other quantiles during this period. These results corroborate the visual impression from Figure 7.

TABLE 5. Are Changes in Urban–Rural Consumption Gaps Significant?

	Panel (a): Rural Dummy Coefficient					
	1983	1987–88	1993–94	1999–00	2004–05	2011–12
10th Percentile	−0.0491*** (0.0084)	0.0563*** (0.0073)	0.0118*** (0.0067)	0.0240*** (0.0080)	0.0833*** (0.0084)	−0.0279*** (0.0096)
50th Percentile	−0.0637*** (0.0062)	−0.0332*** (0.0053)	−0.0871*** (0.0053)	−0.0970*** (0.0060)	−0.0731*** (0.0066)	−0.1781*** (0.0082)
90th Percentile	−0.1641*** (0.0107)	−0.1802*** (0.0098)	−0.2862*** (0.0107)	−0.3533*** (0.0117)	−0.4245*** (0.0144)	−0.4753*** (0.0164)
Mean	−0.0842*** (0.0056)	−0.0514*** (0.0056)	−0.1120*** (0.0049)	−0.1397*** (0.0057)	−0.1209*** (0.0064)	−0.2088*** (0.0071)
N	97,844	103,079	94,236	98,256	100,229	81,420

	Panel (b): Changes			
	1983 to 1993–94	1993 to 2004–05	2004 to 2011–12	1983 to 2011–12
10th Percentile	0.0609*** (0.0107)	0.0715*** (0.0107)	−0.1112*** (0.0128)	0.0212*** (0.0128)
50th Percentile	−0.0234*** (0.0082)	−0.0399*** (0.0085)	−0.1050*** (0.0105)	−0.1144*** (0.0103)
90th Percentile	−0.1221 (0.0151)	−0.2443*** (0.0179)	−0.0508*** (0.0196)	−0.3112*** (0.0196)
Mean	−0.0278*** (0.0074)	−0.0089*** (0.0080)	−0.0879*** (0.0096)	−0.1246*** (0.0090)

Source: Authors' calculations. See text for details.
Note: Panel (a) of this table reports the estimates of coefficients on rural dummy from RIF regressions of log MPCE on a rural dummy, age, age squared, and a constant. Results are reported for the 10th, 50th, and 90th percentiles. The row labeled "mean" reports the rural coefficient from the conditional mean regression. Panel (b) of this table reports the changes in the estimated coefficients over successive decades and the entire sample period. N refers to the number of observations. Standard errors are in parentheses. *p-value ≤ 0.10, **p-value ≤ 0.05, ***p-value ≤ 0.01.

---

just the mean. However, since the law of iterated expectations does not go through for quantiles, we cannot use standard mean regression methods to determine the unconditional effect of rural status on wages for different quantiles. The RIF methodology gets around this problem for quantiles. Details regarding this method can be found in Firpo, Fortin, and Lemieux (2009).

A couple of caveats regarding the consumption results are in order. First, the data does not allow us to distinguish between durable and non-durable expenditures of households. While durable expenditures are included in the household MPCE measure, we are unable to compute the flow of services from these durable purchases due to data limitations. Consequently, any systematic differences in durable expenditures between rural and urban households which impact the flow of consumption services over many years are not accounted for in our analysis.

Second, there may be heterogeneity in publicly provided consumption goods between rural and urban areas, which would impact the overall consumption differences between the locations. Since these are not accounted for in the MPCE measure, our analysis does not account for this. While this is an important issue, a careful accounting of this would take us well beyond the remit of this paper.

4. Rural–Urban Gaps in States

The aggregate patterns in rural–urban gaps in education, occupation, and consumption gaps suggest that there has been a trend towards the narrowing of the gaps since 1983. These patterns raise two important questions. First, do the aggregate trends signify a general phenomenon throughout the country or have they been driven mostly by changing trends in a few, possibly populous states? Second, what are the main factors driving these trends? Answering the first question naturally requires an examination of the trends in individual states. Answering the second question using only the aggregate time-series data is problematic due to the relatively limited length of time since 1983. Analyzing trends in a panel of individual states facilitates more robust identification.

4.1. State Education Gaps

We start with the state-level evidence on rural–urban education gaps. In order to examine the pattern of convergence in individual states over any given time interval, we plot the ratio of the average number of years of education of urban and rural workers in 1983 (the initial year of our sample) against the corresponding gap in the terminal year of our sample. A number greater than one indicates that urban workers enjoy an education premium, that is, they have more years of education than their rural counterparts. Panel (a) of Figure 9 shows the relative gap in the number of years of education of urban and rural workers in 1983 against 2004–05. Panel (b) of the figure shows the relative education gaps in 1983 against 2011–12.

The main takeaway from Figure 9 is that the urban–rural education gaps in 1983 were higher than the corresponding gaps in both 2004–05 (Panel (a) of the figure) and 2011–12 (Panel (b) of Figure 9). The solid diagonal lines in the figure are the 45-degree lines which indicate points of no change in the gaps. In both panels of the figure, most of the observations lie below the 45-degree line, indicating that the gaps in the terminal year were lower

FIGURE 9. Cross-State Educational Convergence, Ratio of Urban to Rural, 1983 compared to 2004–05 and 2011–12

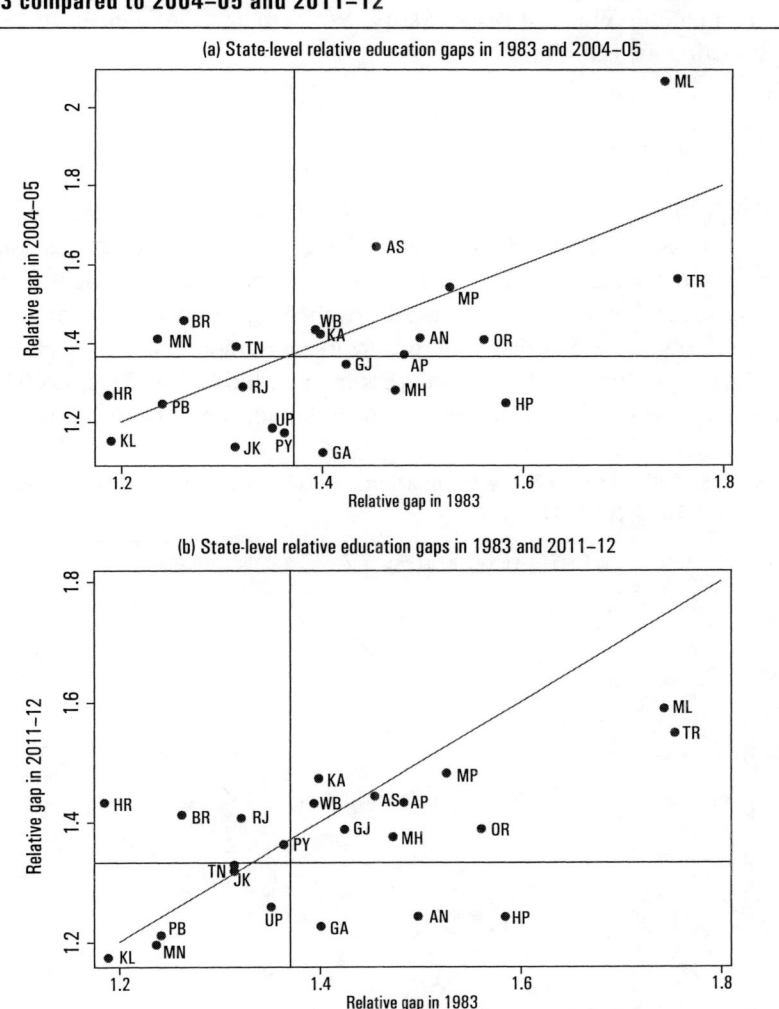

Source: Authors' calculations. See text for details.
Notes: Panel (a) of this figure shows the relative urban–rural gaps in the number of years of education for each state in 1983 and 2004–05, while Panel (b) shows the corresponding education gaps in 1983 and 2011–12. The solid diagonal lines are 45-degree lines.

than in 1983. Importantly, there has been no change in the convergent trend after the introduction of MGNREGA in 2006.

4.2. State Occupation Gaps

Our second variable of interest is the occupation distribution of rural and urban workers. Our specific interest lies in the evolution of the occupation distribution of rural and urban workers since 1983 in each state: Have they become more similar or dissimilar over time? To examine this issue, we compute an index of dissimilarity. We compute the Duncan Index of Occupational Dissimilarity:

$$D = \frac{1}{2} \sum_j \left| \frac{N_j^U}{N^U} - \frac{N_j^R}{N^R} \right|$$

where N_j^k, $k = U, R$ indicates number of Type k workers in occupation j and N^k, $k = U, R$ is the total number of workers of Type k. The Duncan Index is bounded between 0, which is no dispersion, and 1, which indicates maximum dispersion as per this measure. Higher values of D indicate greater dissimilarity between urban and rural workers in their occupation choices.

Panel (a) of Figure 10 shows the Dissimilarity Index in 1983 and 2004–05 for each state, while Panel (b) shows the index for 1983 and 2011–12. Both

FIGURE 10. Cross-State Occupational Dissimilarity Index, 1983 compared to 2004–05 and 2011–12

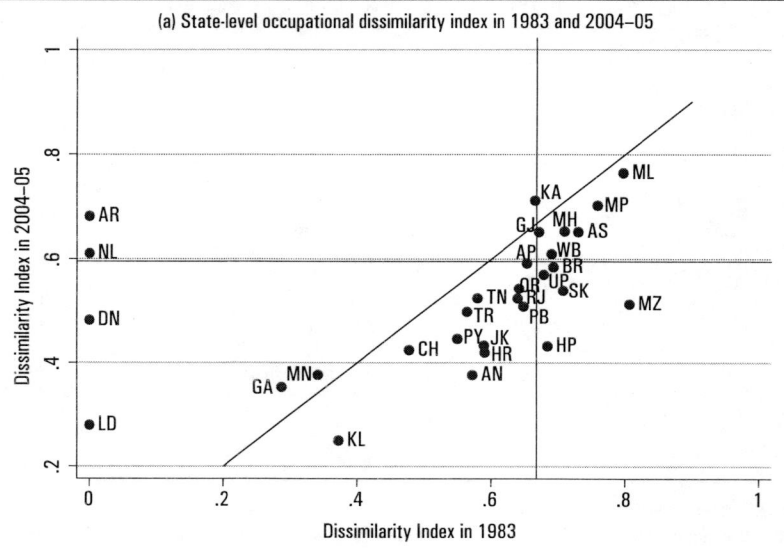

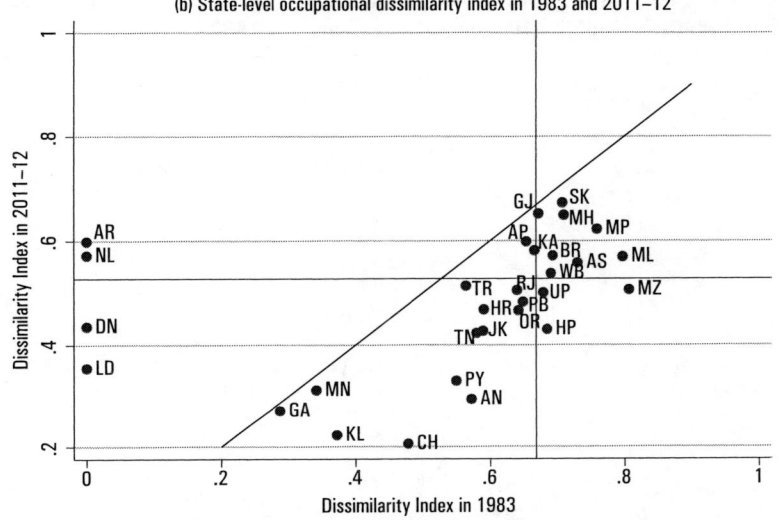

(b) State-level occupational dissimilarity index in 1983 and 2011–12

Source: Authors' calculations. See text for details.
Notes: Panel (a) of this figure shows the Occupation Dissimilarity Index for each state in 1983 and 2004–05, while Panel (b) shows the corresponding Dissimilarity Index in 1983 and 2011–12. The solid diagonal lines are 45-degree lines.

panels reveal the same pattern: The occupational dissimilarity between urban and rural workers has declined since 1983 for almost all states since most points on the scatter lie below the 45-degree line.

Panels (a) and (b) of Figure 10 also indicate that there was no reversal in the occupational dissimilarity trends till 2004–05 after the introduction of MGNREGA in 2006: The occupation distribution of urban and rural workers has continued to become similar over time.

4.3. State Consumption Gaps

We now examine the trends in gaps in monthly per capita consumption expenditures of urban and rural households. Recall that our analysis of the aggregate NSS data showed that the urban–rural consumption gaps had contracted between 1983 and 2004–05 but widened between 2004–05 and 2011–12. Consequently, we examine the trends in the state-wise disaggregated data by breaking up the sample into the pre- and post-2005 trends.

Panel (a) of Figure 11 shows the relative gap in the mean consumption expenditure of urban and rural households in 1983 against the corresponding gap in 2004–05. Panel (b) of the figure shows the mean urban–rural relative consumption gap in 1983 against the gap in 2009–10, while Panel (c) of

FIGURE 11. State-Level Urban–Rural Consumptions Gaps, Ratio of Urban to Rural MPCE in 2005, 2010, and 2012 compared to 1983

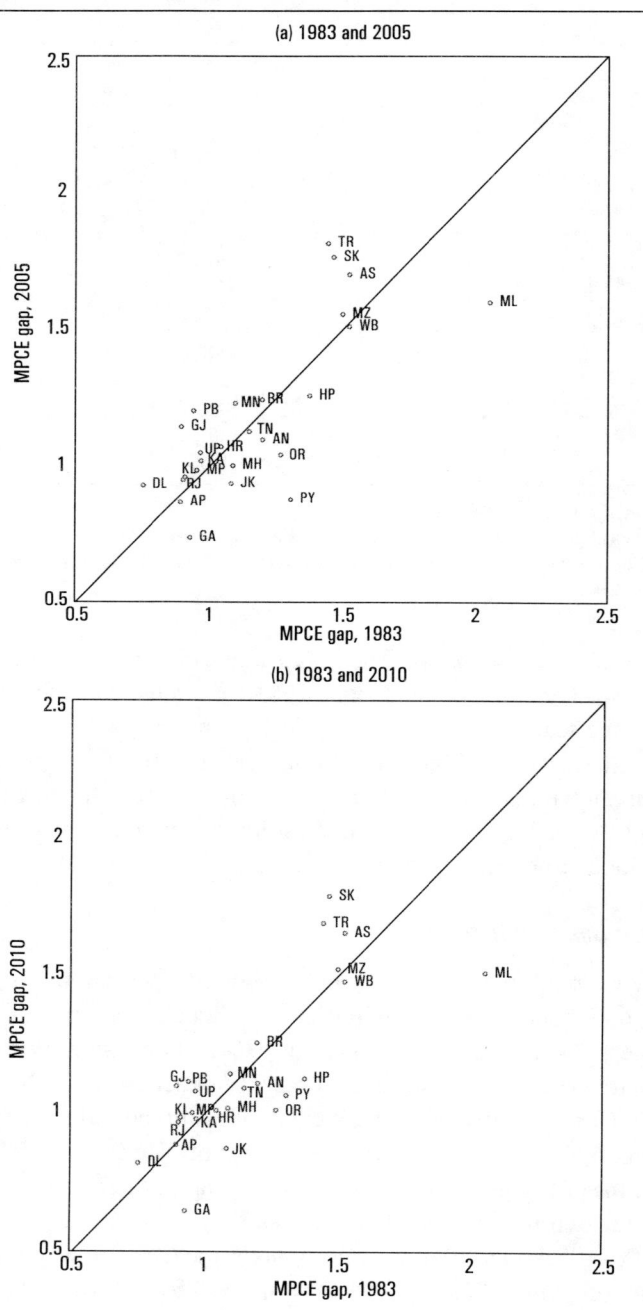

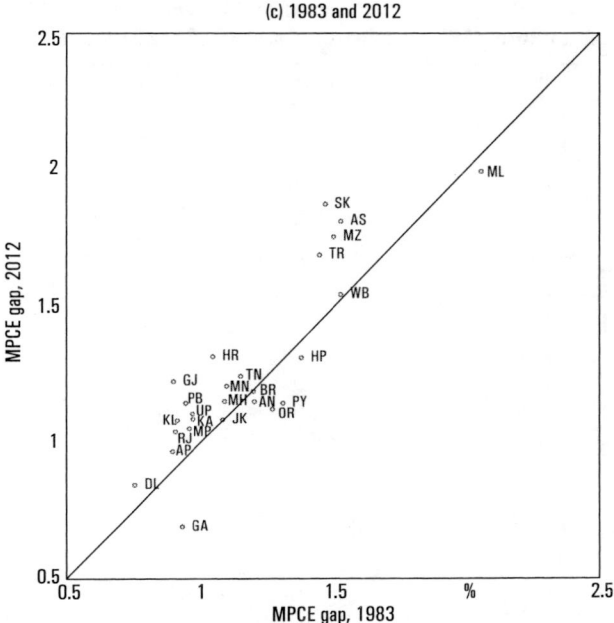

(c) 1983 and 2012

Source: Authors' calculations. See text for details.
Notes: Panel (a) of this figure shows the urban–rural mean consumption gap for each state in 1983 and 2004–05; Panel (b) shows the gap in 1983 and 2009–10; Panel (c) shows the gap in 1983 and 2011–12. The solid diagonal lines are 45-degree lines.

the figure shows the mean urban–rural relative consumption gap in 1983 against the gap in 2011–12.

Consistent with the aggregate pattern we saw in Figure 7, the urban–rural consumption gap declined in most states between 1983 and 2005 since the majority of the scatter points are below the 45-degree line. This pattern of convergence actually continued till the 2009–10 NSS round as indicated by the scatter of points below the 45-degree line in Panel (b) of the figure. The scatter of points, however, shifts up in Panel (c) of the figure, indicating that there has been a widening of the consumption gaps between urban and rural households since 2009–10.

The preceding figures showed the patterns in the urban–rural gaps in mean consumption expenditure. Do these patterns apply to the entire consumption distribution? The question is important from a distributional perspective. As we saw in the aggregate picture in Figure 7, the convergence trend was not uniform across the consumption distribution. We examine this in the state-level data in Figure 12, which shows the consumption gaps

FIGURE 12. State-Level Urban–Rural 25th Percentile Consumptions Gaps, Ratio of Urban to Rural MPCE, comparing across 1983, 2010, and 2012

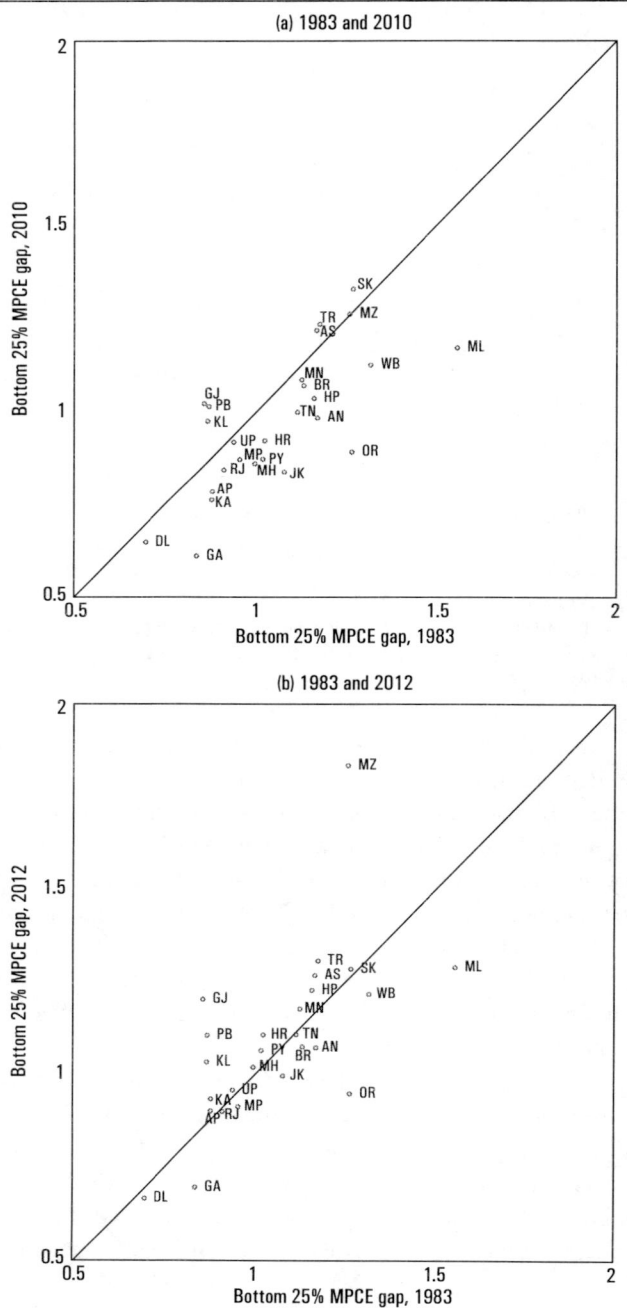

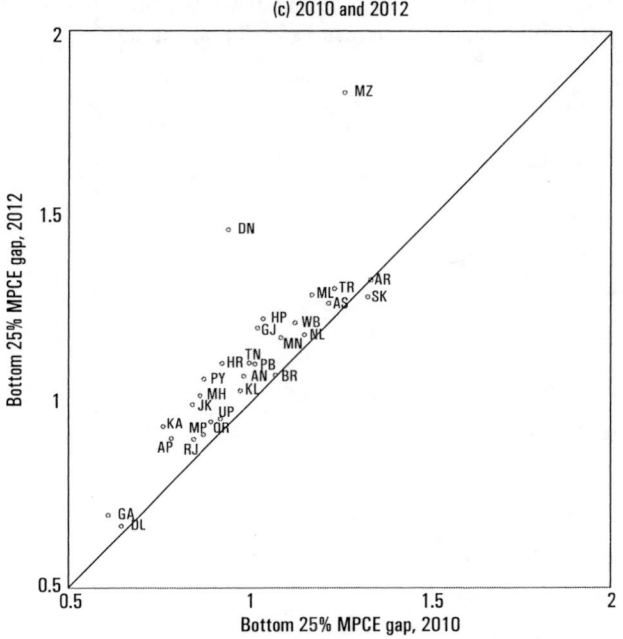

(c) 2010 and 2012

Source: Authors' calculations.
Notes: Panel (a) of this figure shows the urban–rural 25th percentile consumption gap for each state in 1983 and 2009–10; Panel (b) shows the gap in 1983 and 2011–12; Panel (c) shows the gap in 2009–10 and 2011–12. The solid diagonal lines are 45-degree lines.

for the 25th percentile of the distribution, and Figure 13, which shows the evolution of the median consumption gaps.

Both figures reveal a similar trend: narrowing consumption gaps across the consumption distribution from 1983 till 2004–05 and widening of the gap between 2009–10 and 2011–12. Between 2004–05 and 2009–10, the consumption gaps either stayed constant or marginally declined. These findings corroborate the patterns in the aggregate data that we saw previously.

5. Explaining the Trends

What can explain the differences in state-level gaps in consumption expenditures? One hypothesis is that these gaps are influenced by differences in income levels across states and their different growth rates.

To investigate this hypothesis, we construct a panel of state-year observations on urban–rural consumption expenditures gaps and various state characteristics. The years correspond to the NSSO survey rounds. We then

FIGURE 13. State-Level Urban–Rural Median Consumptions Gaps, Ratio of Urban to Rural MPCE, comparing across 1983, 2010, and 2012

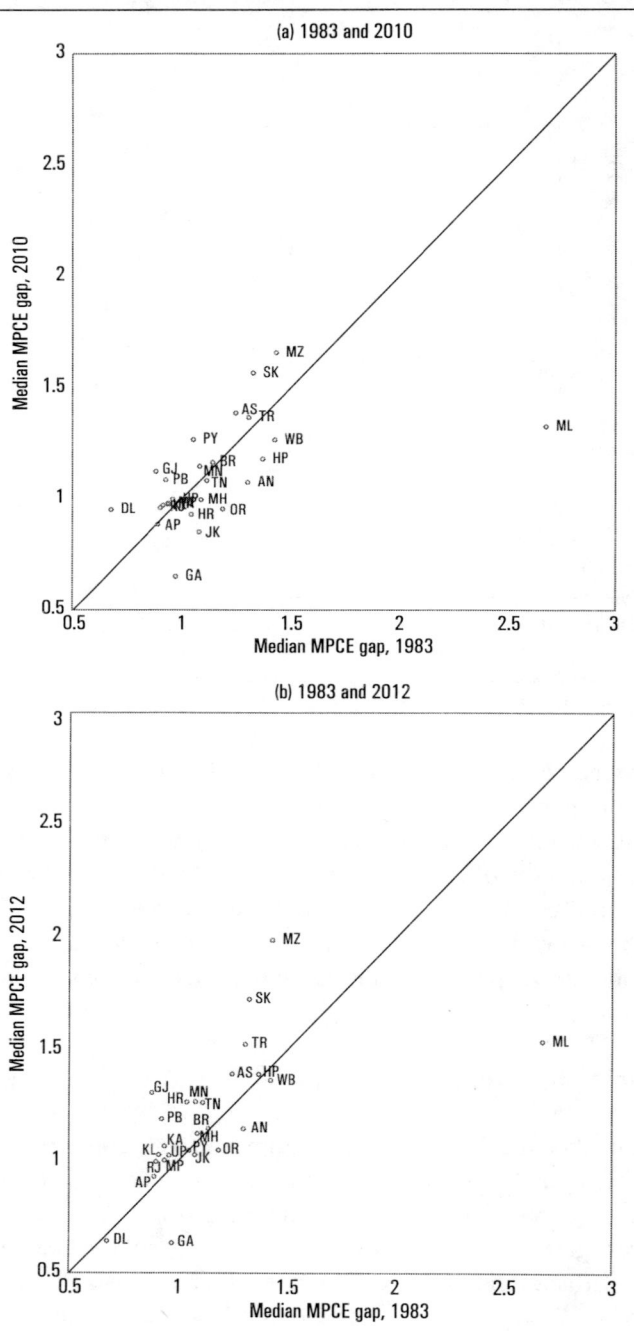

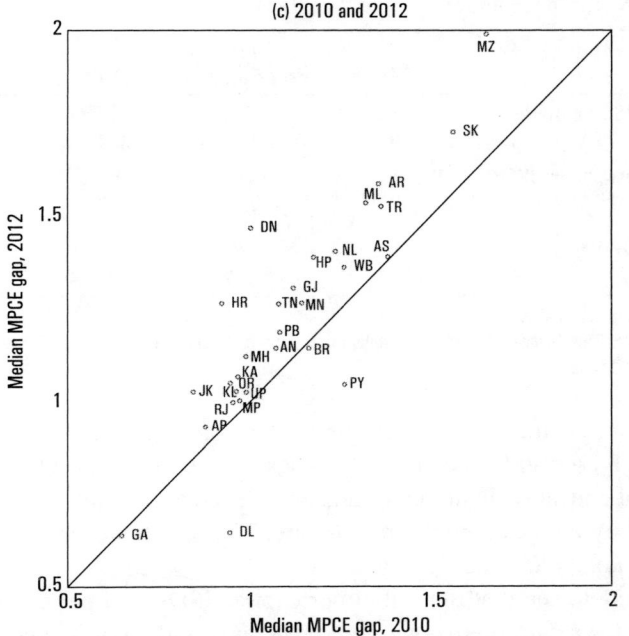

Source: Authors' calculations. See text for details.
Notes: Panel (a) of this figure shows the urban–rural median consumption gap for each state in 1983 and 2009–10; Panel (b) shows the gap in 1983 and 2011–12; Panel (c) shows the gap in 2009–10 and 2011–12. The solid lines are 45-degree lines.

estimate a panel regression of urban–rural consumption expenditure gaps on the initial level of per capita income, measured by the (log) per capita NSDP, and the growth rate of per capita NSDP in the period preceding the measured gap. To account for unobserved state-level characteristics, we include state fixed effects. In addition, since we showed that consumption gaps exhibit common trends across states, we also included survey round time fixed effects in the regressions. This specification is estimated for the mean gaps, median gaps, and gaps in the 25th and the 75th percentiles. The results are presented in Table 6.

We found that initial per capita income has a positive and significant effect on consumption expenditure gaps at different points of the distribution, that is, higher initial income is associated with higher gaps. Our results also imply that high per capita NSDP growth led to higher consumption expenditure gaps. While this may seem somewhat surprising, it suggests that high income and faster growth benefited urban areas more relative to rural areas. These results are confirmed for the median and percentile gaps.

TABLE 6. Consumption Expenditure Gaps

	(1) MPCE Mean	(2) MPCE Median	(3) MPCE 25th	(4) MPCE 75th
Per capita NSDP growth	1.127***	1.010**	1.572***	2.029**
	(0.409)	(0.446)	(0.420)	(0.814)
Log (initial per capita NSDP)	0.141**	0.161**	0.167**	0.126
	(0.069)	(0.075)	(0.070)	(0.137)
N	162	162	162	162
R-square	0.203	0.119	0.174	0.13

Source: Authors' calculations.
Note: The regressions include state and time (round) fixed effects. Standard errors in parentheses. *$p \leq 0.10$, **$p \leq 0.05$, ***$p \leq 0.01$.

Next, we include additional controls in our regression specification. Specifically, we add education gaps (measured by the ratio of the number of years of education in urban to rural areas), and a measure of urbanization measured by the rural employment share. The results of these regressions are summarized in Table 7.

It is easy to see that the initial per capita NSDP and per capita NSDP growth rates retain their positive coefficients and significance. In addition, urban–rural education gaps exhibit a positive and significant effect on consumption gaps. Specifically, a one-unit increase in the number of years of the education gap leads to about 0.3–0.4 unit increase in the consumption expenditure gap. Lastly, an increase in the rural employment

TABLE 7. Consumption Expenditure Gaps, Extended Regressions

	(1) MPCE Mean	(2) MPCE Median	(3) MPCE 25th	(4) MPCE 75th
Per capita NSDP growth	0.818**	0.750*	1.246***	1.977**
	(0.379)	(0.432)	(0.398)	(0.794)
Log (initial NSDP)	0.105*	0.131*	0.127*	0.130
	(0.063)	(0.072)	(0.066)	(0.132)
Edu Gap	0.404***	0.340***	0.390***	0.223
	(0.080)	(0.092)	(0.084)	(0.168)
Initial mean rural employment share	0.175*	0.152	0.046	0.643***
	(0.089)	(0.101)	(0.093)	(0.186)
N	162	162	162	162
R-square	0.351	0.218	0.296	0.215

Source: Authors' calculations.
Note: The regressions include state and time (survey round) fixed effects. Standard errors in parentheses. *$p \leq 0.10$, **$p \leq 0.05$, ***$p \leq 0.01$.

TABLE 8. Changes in Consumption Expenditure Gaps

	(1) ΔMPCE Mean	(2) ΔMPCE Median	(3) ΔMPCE 25th	(4) ΔMPCE 75th
Per capita NSDP growth	0.313	0.413	0.285	1.249
	(0.401)	(0.433)	(0.344)	(0.981)
ΔEdu gap	0.325***	0.175*	0.107	0.362*
	(0.084)	(0.091)	(0.072)	(0.205)
ΔMean rural employment share	−0.519*	−0.866***	−0.093	−1.266*
	(0.283)	(0.306)	(0.243)	(0.693)
N	159	159	159	159
R-square	0.131	0.098	0.026	0.068

Source: Authors' calculations.
Note: The regressions include state fixed effects. Standard errors in parentheses. *p ≤ 0.10, **p ≤ 0.05, ***p ≤ 0.01.

share is associated with an increase in the consumption gap, and this effect is significant for the mean and the top 25 percent of the consumption expenditure distribution.

Next, we turn to the changes in the consumption expenditure gaps over time (across rounds). We relate those changes to per capita NSDP growth, changes in the education gap between urban and rural areas, and changes in rural employment shares. The results of these regressions are presented in Table 8. We found that changes in the education gap map in a significant way into changes in the consumption gap, with the relationship between the two being positive. Changes in urbanization (measured by the change in the rural employment share) contribute to the reduction in the gap, with the effects being particularly pronounced for the mean and median gaps, as well as the 75th percentile of consumption distribution.

Overall, our results emphasize the importance of education in explaining both levels and changes in consumption gaps. Urbanization also plays a role, with greater urbanization reducing the levels of gaps but increasing them in changes.

6. Conclusion

The evolution of inequality in times of economic growth is a continuing area of applied interest to academics and policymakers. In this paper, we have examined the evolution of disparities between rural and urban workers in India between 1983 and 2012, a period that saw a sharp takeoff in growth in the country.

Our results suggest that rural–urban gaps in education and occupation choices have contracted sharply and significantly during this period. The evidence on consumption gaps between rural and urban households is more nuanced. There was a decline in the rural–urban consumption gaps for the bottom 45th percentile of households between 1983 and 2004–05. Some of this narrowing inequality has, however, reversed itself between 2004–05 and 2011–12. As a result, for the entire period 1983–2012, rural–urban consumption gaps have declined for only the bottom 15 percent of households. This widening of rural–urban consumption gaps since 2004–05 is a puzzle, particularly since the employment guarantee scheme for rural workers, MGNREGA, was introduced in 2006.

Our analysis of the data at the state level found that the aggregate patterns were general: The trends in rural–urban gaps in education, occupation, and consumption in most states were similar to the aggregate trends in India between 1983 and 2012. The state-level analysis, however, allowed us to identify the proximate determinants of rural–urban consumption gaps. We find that states with higher per capita income and higher per capita income growth are associated with higher consumption gaps, while states with lower education gaps tend to have smaller consumption gaps. Explaining changes in consumption gaps is more difficult, though changes in the education gap and changes in the rural labor force share do have significant explanatory power.

The results of rural–urban inequality also extend to the wage differences between rural and urban workers. In Hnatkovska and Lahiri (2016), we have shown that rural–urban wage disparities in India declined very sharply between 1983 and 2010. In fact, the size of the decline in the rural-urban wage gaps in India is a bit of a puzzle since it cannot be explained by standard worker covariates, such as education and demographics. Indeed, in Hnatkovska and Lahiri (2016), we show that the rural–urban wage gap dynamics in India stand in sharp contrast to China, where they have actually worsened since 1988.

These results on rural–urban inequality corroborate our findings of declining inequality across castes, falling inequality across genders, and the robustness of these patterns across states since 1983 that we have previously documented in Hnatkovska, Lahiri, and Paul (2012), Hnatkovska and Lahiri (2012), Hnatkovska, Lahiri, and Paul (2013), and Bhattacharjee, Hnatkovska, and Lahiri (2015). Clearly, the past three decades have seen a widespread decline in inter-group inequality for a large set of groups and across different socio-economic markers.

A couple of concerns regarding our results are worth clarifying. First, any discussion of rural–urban disparities is subject to issues surrounding the re-classification of rural areas into urban areas over time. India's urban population growth was concentrated in large cities with populations exceeding one million. In 1981, there were just 12 cities in India with populations exceeding a million; they accounted for 26 percent of the urban population. By 2011, the number of million plus cities rose to 53, which collectively accounted for 43 percent of the urban population. Crucially, the average population density of the million-plus cities declined from 39,000/sq. km to 26,000/sq. km.[5] In effect, a number of rural areas adjoining large urban areas got absorbed into their proximate cities.

The effect of this form of re-classification on the rural–urban gaps is uncertain. It depends on the economic positions of the groups being re-classified, both with respect to the typical rural households and the typical urban households. As an example, if the re-classified rural area was amongst the higher economic groups in rural areas and amongst the lower economic groups in urban areas, then such a re-classification would reduce both rural and urban averages, leaving their effect on the relative gaps unclear. Consequently, we do not believe our results are trivially induced by such re-classifications.

A second issue is with respect to migrants. Our data does not have information on migrants across all rounds. A logical question that could be asked is whether rural consumption levels are being boosted by remittances from rural migrants to urban areas. This is certainly possible. However, this channel would imply that household consumption gaps between rural and urban areas should have declined faster than wage gaps between rural and urban workers. Our results on wage gaps in Hnatkovska and Lahiri (2016) suggest the opposite: Rural–urban wage gaps have shrunk much more sharply than consumption gaps.

Overall, our results suggest that periods of rapid economic growth are periods of declining inter-group inequality. In effect, growth tends to lift all boats.

Appendix on the Data

The National Sample Survey Office (NSSO), set up by the Government of India, conducts rounds of sample surveys to collect socio-economic data. Each round is earmarked for particular subject coverage. We use the latest six large or thick quinquennial Rounds—38 (January–December 1983), 43 (July 1987–June 1988), 50 (July 1993–June 1994), 55 (July 1999–June 2000), 61 (July 2004–June 2005), and 68 (July 2011–June 2012) on employment

---

5. Data on population and urban trends are derived from the Census of India (various rounds) and IIHS (2011).

and unemployment (Schedule 10). Rounds 38 and 55 also contain migration particulars of individuals.

The survey covers the whole country except for a few remote and inaccessible pockets. The NSS follows multi-stage stratified sampling with villages or urban blocks as first-stage units (FSUs) and households as ultimate stage units. The fieldwork in each round is conducted in several sub-rounds throughout the year so that seasonality is minimized. The sampling frame for the FSU is the list of villages (rural sector) or the NSS Urban Frame Survey blocks (urban sector) from the latest available census. The NSSO supplies household-level multipliers with the unit record data for each round to help minimize estimation errors on the part of researchers. The coding of the data changes from round to round. We recoded all changes to make the variables uniform and consistent over time.

In our data work, we only consider individuals that report their three-digit occupation code and education-attainment level. Occupation codes are drawn from the National Classification of Occupation (NCO) 1968. We use the "usual" occupation code reported by an individual for the usual principal activity over the previous year (relative to the survey year). The dataset does not contain information on the number of years of schooling for the individuals. Instead, it includes information on general education categories given as: (a) not literate-01, literate without formal schooling: EGS/NFEC/AEC-02, TLC-03,[6] others-04; (b) literate: below primary-05, primary-06, middle-07, secondary-08, higher secondary-10, diploma/certificate course-11, graduate-12, post-graduate, and above-13. We aggregate these into five similarly sized groups as discussed in the main text. We also convert these categories into the number of years of education. The mapping we have used has been discussed in the main text.

The NSS only reports activities undertaken by an individual over the previous week (relative to the survey week). Household members can undertake more than one activity in the reference week. For each activity, we know the "weekly" occupation code, number of days spent working in that activity, and the wage received from it. We identify the main activity for the individual as the one in which he/she spends the maximum number of days in a week. If there is more than one activity with an equal number of days worked, we consider the one with paid employment (wage is not zero or missing). Workers sometimes change their occupation due to seasonality or for other reasons. Lastly, we drop observations if the total number of days worked in the reference week is more than seven.

---

6. EGS is Education Guarantee Scheme, NFEC is Non-formal Education Courses, AEC is Adult Education Centres, and TLC is Total Literacy Campaign.

References

Bhattacharjee, S., V. Hnatkovska, and A. Lahiri. 2015. "The Evolution of Gender Gaps in India." *India Policy Forum 2014–15*, 11: 119–149. New Delhi: National Council of Applied Economic Research.

Firpo, S., N. M. Fortin, and T. Lemieux. 2009. "Unconditional Quantile Regressions." *Econometrica,* 77(3): 953–973.

Hnatkovska, V. and A. Lahiri. 2012. "The Post-Reform Narrowing of Inequality across Castes: Evidence from the States." In J.N. Bhagwati and A. Panagariya (eds.), *Reforms and Economic Transformation in India*, pp. 229–252. Oxford: Oxford University Press.

———. 2016. "Urbanization, Structural Transformation and Rural-Urban Disparities." *Working Paper*. Vancouver: University of British Columbia.

Hnatkovska, V., A. Lahiri, and S. Paul. 2012. "Castes and Labor Mobility." *American Economic Journal: Applied Economics,* 4(2): 274–307.

———. 2013. "Breaking the Caste Barrier: Intergenerational Mobility in India." *Journal of Human Resources,* 48(2): 435–473.

IIHS. 2011. "Urban India 2011: Evidence Report." Bengaluru: Indian Institute for Human Settlements.

Nguyen, B.T., J.W. Albrecht, S.B. Vroman, and M.D. Westbrook. 2007. "A Quantile Regression Decomposition of Urban–Rural Inequality in Vietnam." *Journal of Development Economics,* 83(2): 466–490.

Qu, Z.F., and Z. Zhao. 2008. "Urban–Rural Consumption Inequality in China from 1988 to 2002: Evidence from Quantile Regression Decomposition." *IZA Discussion Papers 3659*. Bonn: Institute for the Study of Labor (IZA).

Wu, X., and J.M. Perloff. 2005. "China's Income Distribution, 1985–2001." *The Review of Economics and Statistics,* 87(4): 763–775.

Young, A. 2013. "Inequality, the Urban–Rural Gap and Migration." *The Quarterly Journal of Economics,* 128(4): 1727–1785.

To view the entire video of this IPF session and the General Discussion that ended the session, please scan this QR code or use the following URL:
https://www.youtube.com/watch?v=vZOh93diE3c

Comments and Discussion[*]

Chair: **Kaushik Basu**
Cornell University

Rohini Somanathan
Delhi School of Economics

I think this is the perfect IPF paper because it provides us with the numbers and perspective we need for sensible discussions about policy. The paper uses seven thick rounds of the NSS between 1983 and 2012 and tracks rural–urban disparities in education, non-farm employment, and consumption. The analysis is done both at the national and at the state levels and the authors look beyond averages to the performance of particular quantiles in the distribution. They ask how growth is related to structural transformation in rural India—an enormously important policy question. Without these types of figures at hand, we are often discussing policy in a vacuum.

The following patterns emerge from the analysis: (a) average rural–urban education gaps are shrinking; (b) non-farm employment is rising; (c) rural–urban consumption gaps narrowed for the bottom 15 percent in the consumption distribution but widened for higher quantiles; and (d) at the state level, education gaps explained consumption gaps with consumption inequality being most prevalent in the richest and fastest-growing states.

My first set of comments relates to measurement issues. I then go on to alternative ways of decomposing the data to understand the mechanisms underlying the patterns in education and consumption that you observe.

My first comment on measurement relates to sample selection. I was a bit puzzled by what the authors kept out of the sample. They excluded female-headed households and also those not between the ages of 16 and 65 years. This may be a problem for measuring educational convergence because those above 16 years might still be enrolled in educational institutions. So if, for example, secondary and higher education is much higher in urban areas, then convergence is going to be over-estimated because these

---

[*] To preserve the sense of the discussions at the India Policy Forum, these discussants' comments reflect the views expressed at the IPF and do not necessarily take into account revisions to the conference version of the paper in response to these and other comments in preparing the final, revised version published in this volume. The original conference version of the paper is available on www.ncaer.org.

people are not kept in the sample. So the authors might want to think of doing this with completed education, maybe look at 24–65-year olds.

Another measurement issue relates to the classification of employment. In periods of structural transformation in other Asian countries (China is a good, recent example), agricultural work was combined with other work and the non-farm sector was growing while agriculture remained the main activity for many people. The authors may, therefore, want to examine contributions to the non-farm sector for those who are primarily in agriculture by looking more closely at secondary activities. Another small point on occupation: The authors use "agrarian," "white-collar," and "blue-collar" as categories. What do we mean when thinking about white-collar? If someone opens a little kiosk for cellphone repair, are they white-collar or not? We see these small enterprises, selling a little bit in little shops dotted all over the country. Where do you place them?

A bigger question relates to the spatial distribution of urban growth. If one looks at the map of India for the Census years 2001 and 2011, the majority of urbanization is actually taking place in the West and the South. There is no growth in the rural population of Andhra Pradesh, Karnataka, and Kerala, while there is rapid rural population growth in the northern heartland. If we look at rural–urban gaps at a macro level, we are disproportionately capturing the West and the South for urban India and the North for rural India. Thus, the authors may want to look at state-wide differences, keeping this in mind.

Turning now to rural–urban gaps, we see the maximum movement from below primary to primary level in rural India and from primary to middle school level in urban India. One can think about decomposing this gap in terms of what households are doing differently given the facilities they have, and what is happening to the facility locations. There was a big expansion in primary schooling in the 1970s and 1980s, so now there is a primary school within easy access of most villages and within the village for 80 percent of villages. If this expansion in facilities was responsible for the closing of education gaps, then for the convergence to continue in future, we would need to expand rural facilities at higher levels. We still have high schools in only about one-fifth of Indian villages.

The authors might also want to exploit the NSS participation and expenditure survey in 2007–08 for more detailed information on household investments in education. These would allow for the mapping of quantiles in education with those of consumption expenditure. Broadly, it is observed that the bottom quintile went mainly to public schools for primary schooling, while 30 percent of the top quintile attended private schools. However, when one goes from primary schools to high schools, things seem to change. So in the bottom quintile, 50 percent of the 12–18-year olds are enrolled in a public school and 5 percent are enrolled in a private school. For the top quintile, we have 58 percent enrolled in a public school and 20 percent in a private school. Public school expansion is, therefore, going to have quite different effects on educational inequality depending on the types of schools that are built.

Every time someone discusses this paper, they will see it through the lens of their own work. Because mine has been mainly on public goods, when I look at consumption convergence, I think about systematic measurement errors caused by the fact that public good access is not accounted for in income. If a household goes to a public school or hospital, it is not going to show up in their consumption expenditure, whereas if they go to a private hospital, it will. So households that don't have adequate public schooling and healthcare look richer in NSS consumption data than they really are because they are forced to go to private providers. How does this affect the convergence results in this paper?

The above comments suggest a few avenues for the authors to explore with their data. Overall, this is a very nice paper that has direct implications for policy and also opens up a number of interesting research questions on the spatial correlates of macroeconomic trends in education, consumption, and employment. I look forward to more of the authors' work in this area.

Jeff Hammer
NCAER

This paper is a straightforward comparison of the changes in consumption, education, and occupation between urban and rural India over the past few decades using repeated rounds of NSS. It finds that not only have all three changed (for the better, if we judge farm work to not be so great) but that differences between urban and rural areas have declined as well. I am sure it is true that there has been an overall improvement, but it is not possible to say honestly if the disparities between urban and rural areas have changed, and if so, in which direction. The reasons, unfortunately, lead us deep into the weeds of how these three variables are measured in the NSS surveys.

First off, on occupation, of course, there has been convergence. There has clearly been a big increase since the mid-1980s in off-farm employment in rural areas, which is found in the NSS surveys and many other sources. Whatever people do off-farm is likely to look much more like categories appearing in urban areas, so the two regions will look more similar over time. It is nice to see this documented. A hypothesis that needs to be looked at is whether the liberalization of 1991 had anything to do with that trend and why.

In education, things are a bit more obscure. Yes, averages over years of schooling might be closer together between urban and rural areas. But two characteristics of "years of schooling" make the interpretation harder than it seems. As has been noted in the IPF Roundtable on the New Education Policy at this IPF, there is no clear connection between grades completed and any meaningful definition of education such as the ability to read, write, and do arithmetic at typical, age-appropriate levels. It is easy to get children into school and pass them from grade to grade, and that is apparently what has happened in both rural and urban areas. Since the rural areas in the 1980s were way behind the urban areas, simple measurements are going to favor increases starting from such a low base. Whether there was convergence in the real learning of reading, among other things, is anyone's guess.

The quantile regressions that the paper presents confirm this point. There seems to be a reasonable amount of explanatory power of education on consumption (say) at lower levels of both. At higher levels, the connection is much looser. At higher levels of education, the appropriate jobs actually require that knowledge has been gained in school. At lower levels, having been through school at all will lead to somewhat better jobs, making the connection between education and consumption clearer. This disappears at the higher end.

The second aspect of the education story is an artifact of the nature of its measurement. "Progress" or "development" or "consumption"—all concepts of a higher standards of living—are continuous and unbounded. But education is tightly bounded at 12+ years, and well before that, years tend to bunch up at the 5th, 8th, 10th, and 12th standards. So if there is general overall improvement, there will naturally be "convergence" since there is a limit to how high people tend to go through schooling, getting stuck at those specific cutoffs.

As for consumption itself, here is where the nature of the data raises most problems. The underlying theme of this IPF is the need to collect better data and handle it with care. While a workhorse of empirical research, "consumption per capita" is not exactly the same as the underlying concept of the standard of living. In the Indian case, the operational definition of consumption per capita is the particular module of the NSS, not necessarily a perfect match with that underlying concept. The intention is not to criticize the methods used in the NSS, since fixing at least some of its problems is very hard. However, there are at least four problems with its measurement that could very well differentially affect measurements in urban and rural areas, causing even more problems in making conclusions about convergence between them.

Specifically, the NSS consumption module does not include: (a) housing (mostly, however, this has been corrected in the most recent NSS Round that has not been released), (b) consumer durables older than one year, (c) adult equivalent weights when making per capita calculations, and (d) the true market value of goods that are subsidized by the government. Each of these four differentially affects urban and rural sectors, so the gaps in true consumption may vary over time due to what is captured or not in the surveys.

If the economy were static, these left-out items would not vary much over time or between sectors. But we are in a period of rapid growth and there may be major discrepancies between changes in the true versus the measured concepts of well-being.

On durables, we have spending on new televisions but not the amortized value of ownership over the whole life of the appliance. Since there has been more rapid electrification in rural than urban areas, the former increasing from 20 percent to over 80 percent since the 1980s, we are likely to have many more new purchasers of things that use electricity in rural areas relative to urban areas. The NSS captures the flow of money for expenditure, but we do not get the flow value of consumption derived from the stock of durables. In a growing sector, the ratio of new purchases to the stock will be higher and the bias of measured consumption will be lower. If rural areas are getting electricity faster than urban areas, we will be overstating the improvement in consumption in rural areas. The true gap will be larger.

On adult equivalents, the problem is that all calculations are in pure per capita terms, that is, a household consisting of three adult brothers and a household of a couple and their infant daughter have the same denominator of three. Obviously, the baby does not eat as much as an adult nor does she demand as much furniture, living space, clothing, or anything as much as an adult. The couple did not actually get 33 percent worse off by having the baby. Some might argue they are better off. But in straight per-capita terms, no adjustment for household composition (or anything else related to scale economies at the household level) is made. This probably affects the comparison of urban and rural areas.

Table 1 of the paper has summary statistics showing family sizes getting smaller faster in cities. The questions are: How does the composition of the family change? What is the relative mismeasurement of the underlying concept? If the difference was all the number of children, then ignoring correction for adult equivalents will tend to push up our measure of the relative improvement of urban areas, that is, overstating urban improvement. The denominator has fewer children in it (who should have been discounted in the first place).

As regards the market value of subsidized goods, this varies substantially between states and has changed over time. Also, if the relative incidence of subsidies differs between urban and rural areas, changes in the unmeasured subsidy will underestimate the value of consumption more in one than the other. In Tamil Nadu, there are free rice, free pots and pans, and free cooking fuel. The subsidies have increased substantially and differentially affect urban and rural areas. Other states are less generous, and the relative value of the subsidized goods has varied over time, meaning that state effects will not correct for such differences. Measures of consumption evaluated at PDS prices, say, will understate the growth of "real" consumption at market prices in rural areas relative to urban areas.

Housing is really complicated. If everybody paid rent, this would not be a problem. But formal rent payments are not that common, particularly in rural areas. And in urban areas, home ownership with no mortgage payments is missed entirely. Tenants could look much richer than their landlords because we measure the rent but not the quality of housing services for owners even if they have identical floors of a multi-family structure. So we capture some people's housing services and not others. In recent fieldwork, I have noticed that one way of saving or smoothing consumption over time is to add on to your house, in which case the adding on to your house looks like a consumer durable. If you did it this past year, we got you, but if you put in a *pucca* floor a year and a half ago, we miss you entirely. This is really a big problem. In the National Family Health Surveys between 1992 and 2006, households with *pucca* floors went from 15 percent to 85 percent in rural areas. Nothing like that happened in urban areas. It is possible that NSS consumption understates the growth in the true value of housing and, therefore, understates rural/urban convergence.

On the other hand, there has been substantial urbanization over the period. If that is accompanied by a big increase in the number of renters, this will make urban areas look like (i.e., in terms of measured consumption by NSS) they are getting richer faster than they really are in terms of changes in housing services. If there is a big increase in owners, then the bias goes the other way, and the increase in consumption in urban areas will be measured as being slower than it is. So for a large proportion of people's overall budget, we have arguments going in either direction. Correcting this measurement issue could lead to either more or less convergence between the sectors over time.

In any case, this is a good and clear paper. I just wonder how our view of things might be biased by the nature of the surveys used.

General Discussion

Initiating the discussion, Kaushik Basu, the chair, pointed out that there could be a natural explanation for the increase in the urban–rural gap in India after 2004, as highlighted in the paper. He urged the authors to examine the data to assess if poorer segments in urban areas were staying back or returning to their rural homes to participate in MGNREGA, or whether the rural workers who could have migrated to urban areas were not doing so for the same reason. The results could explain if the rural areas were becoming better off financially, or if the urban averages were improving. Both outcomes are entirely possible, and it would be very interesting to dig into the data to explore the reasons for the seemingly paradoxical findings of urban versus rural growth in the paper.

Another broad issue he raised was that conventionally one thinks of urbanization as people moving into urban areas or even new cities coming up, whereas the data used in the paper hints at a novel conceptual category, that is, almost as if rural areas are morphing into urban areas. It would be interesting to study this concept in a broader framework if the data throws up a hint of such a development.

Dilip Mookherjee said that the findings in the paper were not very surprising, and that the authors should, perhaps, have asked a different set of questions. It is well known that the returns to education are much higher in urban than in rural areas for obvious reasons. Skilled labor is more complementary to capital, and there is more capital in urban sector jobs than in rural sector jobs. Irrespective of the factors contributing to endogenous growth, agglomeration and technical change is happening much more in urban areas. Hence, the results derived by the authors in the paper are to be expected. These results are a natural part of the development process. Instead, the question that needed greater focus in the paper is: Why is there so little structural transformation in India?

Devesh Kapur said that the authors should look more carefully at the Indian definition of "urban" since it is not the same as the standard UN definition. For instance, Census towns do not show up in the Indian categorization of urban areas. Hence, a very significant fraction of the so-called rural population could exhibit very urban-like characteristics, if it were not measured by the very peculiar Indian definition of what is urban and if India were to adopt the international definition of urban. Many parts of what we call peri-urban areas or areas that are actually legally rural have completely urban characteristics in many more ways, such as in terms of occupation.

He asked the authors to think much more about this definition since it could shape many of their results.

Sudipto Mundle suggested an explanation for the conundrum that consumption had not converged between urban and rural India. Convergence can be a very positive story or not so positive depending on the growth context. In the case of a situation of dynamic employment growth, convergence leads to a positive story or a classic Lewis-type model. However, in a situation where employment is not growing or, at least, quality jobs are not growing, which has been occurring in India in recent times, the convergence may actually point to simply a survival strategy.

Sonalde Desai noted that occupation codes had changed between 2004–05 and 2009–10, so that the big jump in the number of white-collar workers may have something to do with the way in which the codes had changed. She also noted that the occupation trends being examined by the authors, who were probably combining both male and female workers, did not take into account the recent significant transformation in women's work. There has been a substantial expansion of government-created white-collar jobs for women in rural areas, such as those for *Anganwadi* and health workers, and simultaneously, there has been a big decline in self-employment and agricultural work. The authors should consider producing separate employment figures for men and women.

Rinku Murgai asked the authors to speculate on why consumption was diverging when wages were converging. She also noted that using the NSS data, it is possible to create a series separating the small towns from the big cities. There is a big difference between the million-plus cities and rural areas but much less difference with the smaller towns: The small towns and villages are beginning to resemble each other.

The session video, the paper, and all presentations for this IPF session are hyperlinked on the IPF program available on the NCAER website by scanning this QR code or going to the following URL:
https://www.ncaer.org/IPF2019/Agenda/Agenda_IPF_2019.pdf